The Me 262 Stormbird

The Me 262 Stormbird

From the Pilots Who Flew, Fought, and Survived It

Colin D. Heaton and Anne-Marie Lewis

Forewords by
Jorg Czypionka and Barrett Tillman

ZENITH PRESS

First published in 2012 by Zenith Press, an imprint of MBI Publishing Company, 400 First Avenue North, Suite 300, Minneapolis, MN 55401 USA

© 2012 Zenith Press

Text © 2012 by Colin D. Heaton

Zenith Press titles are also available at discounts in bulk quantity for industrial or sales-promotional use. For details write to Special Sales Manager at MBI Publishing Company, 400 First Avenue North, Suite 300, Minneapolis, MN 55401 USA.

To find out more about our books, join us online at www.zenithpress.com.

ISBN-13: 978-0-7603-4263-3

Library of Congress Cataloging-in-Publication Data

Heaton, Colin D.
 The ME 262 Stormbird : from the pilots who flew, fought, and survived it / Colin D. Heaton. -- 1st ed.
    p. cm.
 Includes bibliographical references.
 ISBN 978-0-7603-4263-3 (hbk.)
  1. Messerschmitt 262 (Jet fighter plane) 2. Germany. Luftwaffe. Jagdgeschwader 7--History. 3. Fighter pilots--Germany--Biography. 4. World War, 1939-1945--Aerial operations. I. Title. II. Title: Messerchmidt 262 Stormbird.
 UG1242.F5.H43 2012
 940.54'4943--dc23
                         2011044702

Credits:
All photographs are from the author's collection unless noted otherwise.
Front cover: Me 262 photos *Jim Larsen*; Bomber photo *U.S. Air Force*
Back cover: *Ray Toliver*
Me 262 schematics by Igor Mikhelevich courtesy of Onno Van Braam

Printed in the United States of America
10 9 8 7 6 5 4 3 2 1

*This book is dedicated to all the airmen from all nations
who flew in World War II and never came home.*

*Certain proceeds from the sale of this book will support the Wounded
Warrior Project and the Volksbund Deutsche Kriegsgräberfürsorge e.V.*

Contents

Tables

Foreword

Jorg Czypionka, 10./NJG-11

There are only a very few of us left of the generation who actually flew the fighters like the Bf 109, the Fw 190, and especially the Me 262 during the war under combat conditions. Our generation has been dying out progressively and with it the knowledge of how things really were—all those aspects that go beyond the metal bits and pieces that are called airplanes.

Many of these fighters are still in great condition in museums or even flying. And there are many curators, mechanics, and young pilots who know a great deal about the mechanics of how they function. There are many historians who research how they came to be designed and built and have learned some of the intrigues that surround them. Performance data and statistics and stories of their actions in the war can also help future generations understand these great war machines. But much of this is only about metal, armaments, fabric, wood, and paint. It is not about the planes' souls—which are the pilots and their memories.

This book represents an effort to preserve what can still be preserved of the human dimension—a less tangible but equally important element in black and white. A written record can only inadequately reflect the stories those old pilots who are still around will tell over a glass of wine. But this book, which contains many personal stories, will go some way toward preserving their memories, the human feelings and experiences that make our planes that now stand in museums come alive for the generations following ours.

This can obviously only go so far, but the author has tried very hard to blend history and technical aspects with the human element, and I commend him for that.

Barrett Tillman

I was fortunate to get acquainted with some of the Me 262 pilots you will meet in this book. I dealt with Adolf Galland when Champlin Museum Press republished two of his volumes in the 1980s, and through him I met the enormously entertaining Walter Krupinski. Talking to Johannes Steinhoff left me almost awestruck: Behind that ruined face remained an active, penetrating mind who expressed heartfelt emotions in flawless English. Franz Stigler became a flying buddy of sorts, as my father and I sometimes shared ramp space with him at Northwest airshows. I'll always remember how his wife, Haya, swept the hangar floor with any pilot ambitious enough to polka with her.

In reflecting on the conversations with those *Luftwaffe* veterans, I was reminded of Brian Keith's line in the John Milius film *The Wind and the Lion*. As Teddy Roosevelt, he tells his daughter, "Sometimes your enemies are a lot more admirable than your friends."

Here's why:

Galland, Steinhoff, Lutzow, and others faced a chilling atmosphere in 1944–1945. Yet they went nose to beak with Göring *and* Hitler in defense of their aircrews who were excoriated as slackers and cowards while suffering 25 percent personnel losses *per month*.

Fast-forward to 1991 when the first Bush administration launched the Tailhook witch-hunt against thousands of innocent naval aviators. A handful of verified cases of sexual harassment at a professional symposium ignited a political firestorm that set back naval aviation morale and retention for nearly a decade. That was because most of a generation of admirals and marine generals failed to match the standards of senior German airmen nearly five decades before.

Why the *Luftwaffe* produced such a depth of leadership is a subject still ripe for examination. But in these pages you will meet professional officers who, while born into a nation eventually ruled by an evil regime, never broke faith with their comrades. Having gotten to know a few of them, I believe that the reason was twofold: Long-suffering subordinates expected it of their leaders, and the leaders expected it of themselves. Protecting their retirement benefits did not enter their minds.

Putting a new technology into service is difficult enough, let alone at the height of a global war. The industry and determination of *Jagdwaffe* personnel in delivering "Turbo" to combat sets another yardstick. To place that accomplishment in context, Germany and Britain had simultaneously developed jet engines in 1937 and the *Luftwaffe* flew a test aircraft in 1939. The Me 262 reached operational status five years later. In comparison, today's sophisticated military aircraft can spend fifteen years or more from inception to squadron delivery—and sometimes they trap pilots in their cockpits, lose navigation systems upon crossing the international date line, and unexpectedly run out of oxygen. One theory holds that the reason is not so much technical as motivational: Today's stealth aircraft have no genuine war to fight, with none on the horizon.

Whatever the relative technical advances and glitches between the 262 and today's crop, the most obvious distinction is combat use. Large-scale aerial combat has been extinct on planet Earth since 1982, but the *Sturmvogel* was hatched in war and faced an immediate, pressing need. As Colin Heaton describes in this volume, the political machinations that delayed the 262's introduction as an air-superiority fighter were immensely frustrating to the *Jagdwaffe*. Since 1945, the question has often been asked whether an earlier commitment to jets could have benefited Nazi Germany. At most, it might have delayed the inevitable, but a prolonged air war would have meant greater casualties on the ground. Therefore, everyone can be thankful for Hitler and Göring's mismanagement.

Strategic bombing took over three years to achieve the strength and consistency required to affect the war's outcome. But from early 1944 onward, U.S. and RAF bombers crippled enemy oil production and transport, leading to a descending spiral from which Germany could not recover. But it's intriguing to postulate an alternate scenario: What if the Reich's diminishing petroleum production had concentrated on the simpler task of refining kerosene rather than the labor-intensive high-octane fuel for piston aircraft? Combined with greater emphasis on building jets, the air war might have taken a significant change of direction. That presumes, of course, that German industry could have produced enough aircraft and engines, especially since the 262's Jumo engines typically lasted eight to twelve hours.

The other part of the 262 story, of course, is the Allied perspective. The author not only presents detailed tables for reference, but allows U.S. and British airmen to speak for themselves. How they coped with the sudden appearance of enemy aircraft that outstripped their fighters by 100 miles per hour is well worth studying.

Fighter pilots being what they are (let's face it: they're supreme egotists), it's instructive to note the prestige attached to downing a jet. Then Lt. Col. Gabby Gabreski, the leading American ace in Europe, is quoted as saying he would have traded half his total victories for one confirmed jet kill.

Those of us privileged to have known "the greatest generation" of aviators recognize that the biggest difference among combat airmen is the paint on their airframes. The World War II generation not only fought a unique war but flew a fabulous variety of aircraft that can never be matched. Consider this: The men who learned to fly in biplanes during the early 1940s finished their careers in jets capable of Mach 2. That kind of progress can never occur again. Meanwhile, the ghastly prices for twenty-first-century aircraft ensure that there will never be another air war on the scale of Korea, let alone World War II.

So sit down, strap in, and turn up the oxygen regulator to 100 percent with the gun sight set for 30 mils. You're in for a rare ride.

Acknowledgments

The people involved in making this book come to life are far too numerous to list. Suffice to say that the primary contributors are mentioned and quoted within these pages. Those who must be noted here are historians Barrett Tillman and Jon Guttman, both of them outstanding and unselfish in their assistance. I continue to learn much from them. Many years ago, Arno Abendroth provided Me 262 data on production numbers, unit losses, work numbers, and other materials that proved critical for this project. Without his information, this would be an incomplete work.

Without Norman Melton and his assistance over many years, I would not be writing this so easily. I would certainly never have received my education and become an author. Thanks to my agent, Gayle Wurst of Princeton International Agency for the Arts, who, in conjunction with my wife and previous coauthor of other books, Anne-Marie Lewis, has indulged and educated me on many of the pitfalls within my profession, therefore keeping me focused on the target.

Special thanks to Kurt Schulze for allowing me to make copies of the massive collection of reports and interviews from the Ray Toliver collection, and special thanks to the late Ray Toliver for his many years of support, access to his records and photographs, and also Trevor Constable for being part of the process that sparked my interest so long ago.

I would also like to thank Lt. Col. Robert Schmidt, USAF, and Kurt Schulze for their great friendship and assistance, and for introducing me to Jorg Czypionka. As Robert and I attended the German Fighter Pilot reunions over the years and became better acquainted with the men mentioned in this book, I reflect upon those days with great fondness. Kurt gave me many contacts over the last twenty years who provided additional assistance.

I also wish to thank Steven Daubenspeck at Zenith Press for suggesting the Me 262 book concept and senior editor Richard Kane at Zenith for supporting the concept. I want to mention Scott Pearson, editor at Zenith, who is really the best editor to work with. This book was their idea, and I hope that I have done their suggestion justice. Thanks to my best friend from our army days, Greg Kopatch, who always supported me in all of my wildest endeavors. I would like to jokingly remind him that I "finally got that plaque." Only he will understand what that means.

A very special thanks to Albert Wunsch III, Esquire. Without his assistance on many levels, this project's completion would not have been possible. And thanks to the late Jeffrey L. Ethell, who worked with Ray Toliver and me collecting the data that made this book and many others past, present, and future come to life.

I should also thank the following American air warriors who have since left us, who over the course of many years provided me with invaluable information, granted interviews, responded to letters, submitted photographs, and opened up contacts for me from both sides of the war: Gen. James H. Doolittle, Gen. Curtis E. LeMay, Col. Hubert Zemke, Brig. Gen. James M. Stewart, Col. Donald Blakeslee, and Gen. Benjamin O. Davis, just to name a few.

Finally, I need to thank all of the German Me 262 jet pilots of the *Luftwaffe*, who over the years provided interviews and letters and detailed their experiences. I also wish to thank the American and British aviators who gave me their perspectives. These men made the history, and fellows like us are just very lucky to have recorded it.

Introduction

Aviation history has always fascinated me since I was a boy, and as the years passed, I was fortunate to have met and gotten to know dozens of combat pilots from many conflicts. Combat pilots from the World War II generation were the most abundant and most willing to discuss their experiences. Luckily, I would be able to meet the vast majority of these aces, who came from several nations, and decades later start a career teaching and writing on the subject.

I was twelve years old when I first read Ray Toliver and Trevor Constable's *Horrido! Fighter Aces of the Luftwaffe*. I was captivated by the stories of men such as Adolf Galland, Erich Hartmann, Hans-Joachim Marseille, Johannes Steinhoff, Dietrich Hrabak, Wolfgang Falck, Hajo Herrmann, Günther Rall, and many others. Having the good fortune to later know and interview some of these men and the many others mentioned in this book and becoming their friend before they passed away was quite an experience.

This book focuses upon those men who flew the Messerschmitt Me 262, whether in transition training or in operational combat, as well as comments from some of the Allied airmen who fought against them. These German pilots were the first to fly jet-powered aircraft in combat, and the aircraft they flew was plagued with a very tenuous and unpredictable array of technical problems, political intrigue, growing shortages of fuel and munitions, losses of pilots and other critical assets, a growing, technologically proficient and dedicated enemy, and, perhaps most importantly, the fact that nearly every pilot who climbed into the cockpit of his jet knew that he was fighting a losing war.

Yet, to a man, they still flew and fought for their country, risking their lives in a cause that was already lost. They were still soldiers. They still did their duty. I have known and interviewed dozens of these men, and to their credit, they never held any postwar grudges against their American or Western European counterparts. The same may be said of the American fighter pilots. It is, after all, a brotherhood.

It is my hope that all readers of aviation history will find the comments of these pilots, detailing the war in the first jets as they fought it, of great interest. Some of the comments reproduced here were extracted from previously published works and are so cited. Many publications have focused on the Me 262 and *Luftwaffe* pilots. Many of the comments are first-person extracts of more detailed interviews conducted over the years.

However, the wealth of previously unpublished material from the men themselves related to their war in the air is eye opening, and much is quite new to the field, as few publications used detailed interviews. Throughout their testimonies, the intensity of gripping aerial combat as seen from the cockpit counterbalances the reality of a nation bombed into submission and a national leadership tottering on the brink of self-destruction. The relevant parts of their interviews as related to this subject are included.

The legacy of the Me 262 lives on today in modern jets, and just as the men who flew it pioneered the first jet tactics, the men who flew against them had to devise counter-tactics, and the result of their efforts during the war created what was the fastest revolution in aviation technology the world has ever seen. This book is their story, in their own words. I am simply fortunate enough to be able to write it with their blessings.

Colin D. Heaton
August 1, 2011

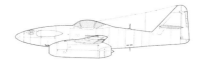

CHAPTER 1

Too Little, Too Late

Great ideas come from having time on your hands.
Failure comes from not using those ideas wisely.

Adm. Otto Kretschmer

By June 1941, Adolf Hitler had perhaps come to the realization that he was not going to win the war in the west, and by May 1943, he must have known that the war in the east was lost as well, as he had recently lost North Africa, Sicily and Italy were under threat, and the setback at Stalingrad had secured the second major German defeat of World War II in February 1943 on the heels of the stalemate at Moscow in the winter of 1941. In his many meetings with the members of his staff within the High Command, Hitler often spoke of these new "wonder weapons" that German science and technology were developing.

With these new tools, Hitler tried to convince his followers *en masse* that Germany could turn things around as the war progressed. Among these many revelations was a series of revolutionary new aircraft, one of which would become the first operational jet fighter in history to see active regular combat service, the Messerschmitt Me 262. Propaganda had always been the most successful weapon employed by the National Socialists, reinforcing the hopes of the true believers, while attempting to convince through coercion and enervation those who opposed them; so the continuance of false prophecies and wishful thinking was given new life with every new idea, concept, and development, realistic or not.

Just as with other nations, where institutions of political authority made the determinations on the viability of projects, the Germans were no exception. Reorganization for the procurement and assessment of technological innovations was undertaken in September 1933. The result was the creation of the *Reichsluftfahrtministerium* (RLM). Following Adolf Hitler's successful appointment as chancellor and with Hermann Göring relinquishing his control of the *Geheime Staatspolizei (Gestapo)* to *Reichsführer-SS* Heinrich Himmler, German aircraft designers, builders, and scientists—solely focused upon *Luftwaffe* concerns—could, in essence, simply perform "one-stop shopping" to sell the ideas. The maze of independent departments that had often delayed decisions for years and that had been fraught with interdepartmental and political infighting was now reduced.

The purpose of this restructuring was to increase effectiveness and reliability and combine the efforts among the various military and technical departments. The result was the creation of six independent subdepartments: *Luftkommandoamt* (LA), *Allgemeines Luftamt* (LB), *Technisches Amt* (LC, but more often referred to as the *C-amt*) in charge of all research and development, *Luftwaffenverwaltungsamt* (LD) for construction, *Luftwaffenpersonalamt* (LP) for training and staffing, and the *Zentralabteilung* (ZA), central command. In 1934, just as Hitler was building up German military power in secret, there was the creation of the *Luftzeugmeister* (LZM), which controlled all logistics concerns.

The major aircraft designers were not working completely in their own personal vacuums. The technology for jet propulsion was not new; all were aware of the patent filed by Frank Whittle years earlier. Rocketry already had been firmly established when Robert Goddard took the ancient Chinese technology to the next level, and the Germans began applying a liquid fuel component to increase the life span and range of their rockets at *Peenemünde* on the Baltic. Hitler had given the German people many promises, and he kept all of them. However, he also gave them many prophecies, many of which would fail to emerge—although many would, thus increasing the "Hitler Myth" as stated by eminent historian Ian Kershaw.

The Messerschmitt Me 262 was one such prophecy that was to prove factual, lethal, yet far too little and much too late. Along with other fantastic creations such as the V-1 Buzz Bomb, V-2 rocket, Me 163 *Komet* rocket fighter, Arado Ar 234 jet bomber, and the HeinkelHe 178 single jet engine and He 280 twin-jet fighter, the Me 262 was eventually accepted and produced as the world's first operational jet-powered fighter/bomber aircraft. It was perhaps the most revolutionary fighter aircraft of World War II.

With over a dozen major design options, the fighter version bristled with the firepower of up to four 30mm nose-mounted cannons, as well as the ability to carry twenty-four R4M air-to-air rockets, and it was capable of flying 120 miles per hour faster than the North American P-51 Mustang. It was also the only mass-produced German fighter that could contend with the speed of the vaunted de Havilland Mosquito. When a skilled Me 262 pilot had an advantage, anything non-German was a potential victory. German aeronautical engineering and science had created a formidable weapon.

Despite the great promise of being an air superiority fighter, given the heavy hitting power of the weapons array, it was soon to be proven to be a far more effective heavy bomber killer as opposed to a dogfighter. Senior German pilots who were aware of the aircraft, especially those flying on the Western Front, wanted it immediately just for this reason. Adolf Hitler ranted to *Reichsmarschall* and *Luftwaffe* Commander in Chief Hermann Göring incessantly for his fighter pilots to earn their pay and decorations by eliminating the Allied bomber threat.

The British Royal Air Force had been bombing German cities since December 1939 and later adopted night bombing; starting in the late spring of 1943, the United States Army Air Corps, primarily the Eighth Air Force heavy bomber squadrons based in the United Kingdom, after a few months of familiarization missions to French targets, started pounding German cities and industry by day.

By 1943, most of the *Luftwaffe*'s fighter strength had been spread throughout the Third Reich. The vast majority of fighter units were positioned on the Eastern Front, from the Arctic Ocean to the Black Sea, with almost a quarter of these forces spread throughout the Mediterranean from Libya to the Balkans. Only three primary day fighter units were permanently stationed in Western Europe on the English Channel coast: *Jagdgeschwader* 2 (JG-2) *"Richthofen"* and JG-26 *"Schlageter"* were both in France. JG-5 *"Eismeer"* was spread throughout Norway and Finland, while the growing night fighter units under Wolfgang Falck were scattered all over Europe by the end of 1943.[1]

The Germans were continuously developing new and enhancing existing aircraft designs (as were the Allies). The first major development post-1937 was the introduction of the radial engine Focke-Wulf Fw 190, which was designed by Prof. Kurt Tank and was a great departure from the inline Daimler-Benz–powered, liquid-cooled Messerschmitt Me 109 that had been the tip of the spear during the latter part of the Spanish Civil War and had led Germany to rapid victory during the *blitzkrieg* by providing air support and establishing air superiority from the first day of the war on September 1, 1939. Hermann Buchner commented on his comparison between the Me 109 and the Fw 190, as well as the Me 262:

"I really felt comfortable in the Me 109, and this was the mainstay fighter. But the Fw 190 was truly a much better fighter. It was more powerful, stronger, built better, and was in its structure able to withstand more damage than a 109. The weapons platform was incredible, and you had a lot more firepower, especially when the A-6, A-8 and F models were built. Later the Dora was built, which was also faster, just as strong, but now had a liquid cooled engine, instead of the radial air-cooled engine.

"I did in fact like the Focke-Wulf better than the Messerschmitt 109 or even the Me 262, as far as reliability. The only real advantage the 262 had was its speed, and the 30mm cannons were very powerful. Other than that, if the Fw 190 had had the speed of a 262 I would have stayed with the Focke-Wulf."[2]

By the time World War II began, piston-powered fighters had greatly increased in their sturdiness with all-metal construction, survivability, and engine power, and they had almost quadrupled their airspeed since World War I, as technology and science allowed for greater experimentation. World War II became the shortest period in human history that actually produced the most revolutionary technological and scientific developments through absolute necessity.

Germany's greatest pilots who flew in World War II all started their training in gliders and then graduated into World War I—or recent postwar–era biplane trainers. Ironically, when Adolf Hitler sent *Generaloberst* Hugo Sperrle and the Condor Legion into Spain to support Francisco Franco, the frontline fighter was in fact the Heinkel He 51 biplane. This was one of the primary training aircraft used during the 1930s. It was not until later that the Me 109C and D models were produced, with the first of these fighters being flown by such future luminaries as Werner Mölders and Günther Lützow. Some of these men who started their careers in biplanes would end their careers— and sometimes their lives—in jets during the most remarkable period in aviation history. Several famous German airmen cross-trained in the jet though did not fly it in combat, but their perspectives are of interest.

Generalmajor Hannes Trautloft, a Spanish Civil War veteran, group leader, Inspector of Day Fighters under Adolf Galland, and fifty-four-victory ace with the Knight's Cross in World War II, explained what it was like to be a pilot during this period of technological transition, from fabric-covered biplanes to all-metal mono-wing designs:

"It was a very interesting period. I recall that when I started flight school, I had never even seen a mono-wing all-metal aircraft. It was not until the mid-1930s that I first flew in the air races, and I was able to fly in several models. Once I flew the Me 109 D, I knew that I was in the best fighter aircraft in the world at that time, and then the Emil came and the later versions. I also flew the Fw 190 models, which I feel were better, more rugged, wider landing platform, and carried more firepower. This transition from the early biplanes to fast all-metal single-wing fighters was almost like going from riding the bus to driving a fast race car. But, when I flew the Me 262, this was an entirely new universe, absolutely the best experience I ever had in an airplane during the war."[3]

Major (later *Generalleutnant*) Günther Rall, a 275-victory ace with the Knight's Cross and Oak Leaves and Swords, test flew the Me 262, although never in combat. He had his comments on the new technology: "It was certainly a new dimension. The first time I sat in it, I was most surprised about the silence. If you are sitting in a standard piston-powered aircraft, you have a hell of a lot of noise and static and such, which I did not experience in the Me 262. It was absolutely clear. With radio from the ground they controlled the flight. They gave me my orders, such as 'Now accelerate your engines, build your rpm.' It was very clear. Totally clear.

"One other thing was you had to advance the throttles very slowly. If you went too far forward too fast, you might overheat and set the engines on fire. Also, if you were up to 8,000 rpm, or whatever it was, you released the brakes and you were taxiing. Unlike the Bf 109, which had no front wheel and was a tail dragger, the Me 262 had a tricycle landing gear. It was a new sensation, beautiful visibility. You could go down the runway and see straight forward.

"This was, however, also a weak moment for the Me 262. The aircraft at this point was a little bit stiff and slow during landing and takeoff, but fine when coming up to speed gradually. It was absolutely superior to the old aircraft. You know, I never did get to shoot the weapons, because when I had about fifteen to twenty hours I became commander of JG-300, which was equipped with Bf 109s. I only made some training flights, but never flew the jet in combat."[4]

The highest scoring fighter ace in history, *Major* (later *Oberst*) Erich Alfred Hartmann, with 352 confirmed victories and the Diamonds to his Knight's Cross, had this to say about the Me 262: "It was really a lovely aircraft, and many advanced features, great power, and a wonderful visibility forward and all around with the canopy. I really was impressed by the speed and performance, but not so enthusiastic about the inability to turn tightly, or dogfight, as in the 109, which I flew through the entire war and loved very much. I was invited to transfer to the defense of Germany and fly it, but I felt a responsibility to my comrades in JG-52."[5]

Between the wars, the United States, Soviet Union, Italy, Great Britain, and National Socialist Germany had been neck and neck against each other wanting to lead the world in their aircraft designs and developments—with Imperial Japan following close behind the Europeans. Each nation had its stable of engineers and designers, but the global depression meant that nations did not have the liquidity to spend massive amounts of money unless a project was seen to be a good investment with a reasonably rapid return.

Germany was able to take the lead simply because with Germany a dictatorship, Adolf Hitler did not have to worry about congressional or parliamentary restrictions on military expenditures. Although the Soviet Union and Japan were also unencumbered by those political limitations, the political issues in those nations, combined with the great purges initiated by Josef Stalin in the USSR and the limited natural resources of Japan, prevented them from exploiting their potential until much later in the war.

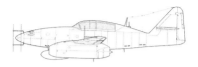

CHAPTER 2

On the Drawing Board

*It was a very revolutionary
design, far beyond its time.*

James H. Doolittle

When World War II began in Europe, the Me 262 jet was already in the process of being developed as *Geheim Projekt* P.1065. The design was presented in April 1939 before the start of World War II. Funding for the jet program continuously suffered for many reasons—the required assets were allocated to other manufacturing areas and many high-ranking officials believed that there was no need for an expensive new aircraft. Many of the "old guard" believed that the war could easily be won with the existing conventional aircraft. It was the new generation of pilots and engineers who looked to the future.

Ernst Heinkel had been working on the concept of a gas turbine engine design since the early 1930s, and when Dr. Hans-Joachim Pabst von Ohain joined his team, following a career at University of Gottingen, he conducted the first successful static operation of his S2 design, powered by hydrogen. Simultaneously, *Bayerische Motor Werke* (BMW) in Munich was also working on a jet engine program, at first using a centrifugal engine design, but then changing to the axial flow design created by the Bramo works at Spandau.[1]

In 1937, Ohain, along with Adolf Max Müller, had a working prototype, seven years after Sir Frank Whittle patented his own jet engine design. Ohain had won the race to produce the first working jet, mainly because he worked for a government that spared no expense in developing technology, while Whittle was mired in the political squabbling and financial restrictions that Hitler's Germany did not share.

The company deeply involved in the production of jet fighters was that founded by Dr. Hugo Junkers, an engineer whose firm was building internal combustion aircraft engines before World War I. Junkers also expanded his company to include many aircraft designs, the most famous being the Ju 52, and later the Ju 87 Stuka dive bomber and Ju 88 and Ju 188 series of medium bombers. His company's great contribution to the jet program would be the first mass-produced jet turbine engines—the Jumos.

In 1938, two engineers named Hans Mauch and Helmut Schelp were working in the *Reichsluftfahrtministerium* (RLM) on the plans for the establishment of an official jet engine propulsion and production research and development team. This was in conjunction with Hans Antz, who was working on various airframe designs. This group of designers also worked with Dr. Alexander Lippisch as well as Prof. Dr. Willi Messerschmitt developing the Me 163 *Komet* airframe and the Me 262. However, with regard to the proposed Me 262 power-to-weight ratio, and despite all the advanced mathematics and engineering wizardry, the final test would be a flying machine with the combined weight of fuel and a pilot in the cockpit.

Unlike the Me 262, Ar 234, He 280, and other jet designs, the Me 163 used a motor built by the inventor Professor Hellmuth Walter, which burned a hydrogen peroxide, hydrazine, and water mixture as the fuel. Lippisch, a brilliant aeronautical designer, constructed its shape. The *Komet* reached an average of 623 miles per hour (1,003 kilometers per hour) in a test in 1941, but it had a very limited operational life, although it did have some successes. The fuel would burn out within five to six minutes, although in that time the small "power egg" would have reached its operational altitude of 25,000 to 30,000 feet in two and a half to three minutes and been in the midst of the enemy bombers. The most unique feature of the Me 163 was that more pilots were killed in accidental explosions and leaks due to the volatile fuel than were actually lost in combat.

Messerschmitt GmbH was interested in securing the jet program production contracts, and the appointment of Robert Lusser, the chief of Messerschmitt production, into the program increased the rapid rate of design development. Lusser then had to coordinate the efforts of many companies and design engineers, organizing a workforce that would eventually include a dozen major companies and hundreds of subcontractors.

Messerschmitt's original design as proposed in April and then submitted in June 1939 had two engines, both comfortably located in each wing root with a traditional tail-wheel landing configuration. The theoretical speed of the new aircraft was anticipated to be approximately 600 miles per hour (900 kilometers per hour), and the company received the order for three of the prototypes. This included the static test airframe, which was the design schematic being developed by Dr. Rudolf Seitz.

Other members of the design team were Waldemar Voigt (with the firm since 1933), Karl Althoff, Walter Eisenmann, Wolfgang Degel, and Richlef Somerus, who was also the chief of the aerodynamic research and testing branch.[2] The initial tests were promising, and the firm had envisioned a multi-roled aircraft, one that could be built to certain specifications as a generic template, while being modified as required in subsequent versions for additional roles that may be required. Messerschmitt knew that it was easier to modify an existing aircraft design for future requirements than it was to design a new aircraft to fit the new role.

Messerschmitt was awarded the initial probationary contract to design a strong and functional airframe around the axial-flow turbojets being developed by BMW. The engines were expected to produce 1,323 pounds (600 kilograms) of thrust and be tested, proven, and ready for production by December 1939. The upgraded version would produce around 1,984 to 2,000 pounds of thrust, and with two Jumos mounted, the Me 262 showed great promise. In proper German fashion, the design and development process was not conducted with tunnel vision, as the research conducted by Waldemar Voigt examined the concepts of using both single-engine and twin-engine jet designs.

By May 1940, the inaugural static tests were completed with the recommendation for further strengthening the airframe and wing spars to better support the powerplants, which was soon implemented. Following these modifications and a slight redesign of the mounts, the Me 262 was a cleaner and better aerodynamic design according to wind tunnel tests, exceeding the expectations of all involved.

The design of the fuselage had not undergone too many drastic changes from the original concept. The Me 262 was always a "swept wing" design, although the degree of sweep was established at 18.5 degrees following wind tunnel tests. This was decided after the proposed engines proved to be somewhat heavier than originally planned, so weight distribution and aerodynamic integrity were the primary considerations. The design also addressed the aerodynamic considerations relative to the position of the center of lift due to thrust relative to the center of mass, thereby increasing the aircraft's speed.

The swept wing design had been presented in 1935 by Adolf Busemann, while Prof. Herbert Wagner's airframe design work at Junkers was not unknown (as well as the internal fighting between Wagner and Otto Mader working on the Jumo engines), and upon further collaboration Willi Messerschmitt had advanced the concept within his design in 1940. In April 1941, it was proposed that the Me 262 design incorporate a 35-degree swept wing (*Pfeilflügel II*, or "arrow wing II"). Ironically, it would be this same wing sweep angle that would be used later on both the North American F-86 Sabre and Soviet MiG-15 fighters, the two primary jets that would duel in the skies over Korea. Although aerodynamically sound on paper, and feasible in a production application, this wing design concept was not used in the final design. Messerschmitt continued with the projected HG II and HG III (*Hochgeschwindigkeit*, "high speed") designs, producing test versions in 1944, which were designed with both a 35-degree and 45-degree wing sweep in test models.

Messerschmitt's test pilots conducted a series of flight tests with the production series of the Me 262. In dive tests, it was determined that the Me 262 went out of control in a dive at Mach 0.86 and that higher speeds led to a nose-down attitude, resulting in a freezing of the stabilizers that could not be corrected, as mentioned later in this project by pilots who experienced this phenomenon. The resulting uncontrolled steepening angle of the dive would in turn lead to even a higher speed, airframe stress, and structural compromise and possible disintegration of the airframe due to the increased negative g stress.

The stress of g forces could prove deadly in any aircraft, but in the Me 262, it was often fatal. Unless the pilot was prepared, any quick movement could be his last, as experienced by *Oberfeldwebel* Hermann Buchner during a mission on April 8, 1945, as cited in Foreman and Harvey:

"I flew a *rotte* operation (two aircraft) in the Hamburg area. At about 8,000 meters over the city I spotted a Spitfire, 1,000 meters lower, flying north. I looked for bombers, and awaited instructions from ground control. A few minutes later, this aircraft, which appeared to be a reconnaissance aircraft, returned, heading northwest towards the Elbe. Since I was in a good tactical position, I was able to close very fast on the Spitfire from behind without being seen.

"It was going very fast, and in the final moment I believe that the Tommy was able to turn his aircraft to come at me head-on. Then I made a mistake; instead of opening fire, I broke to the left, so hard that my aircraft flicked over and went down out of control. I was momentarily terrified and then had my hands full trying to get the aircraft back to normal flight. By this maneuver, I lost my wingman, and thus we returned to Parchim separately. I was richer from the experience, although no success was granted to me. I believe also that our nerves were unduly stressed."[3]

In an interview with author Colin Heaton, Buchner had this to say about the electronic trimming issues he faced: "The jet was an absolute wonderful thing to fly when all was well. But when things were not well, you were in a nightmare. If the aircraft rolled and lost engine compressibility, you had better get out; you were not going to recover, especially if a flat spin was the result. Another thing was the negative g forces that could be experienced, if inverted, especially at high speed could very easily, and in my case did on occasion, render the electric trimming capabilities useless. You were not getting out of a dive if that happened either. I know that many pilots were lost because of this fact."[4] (Jorg Czypionka, however, stated that these problems were not conclusive.)

The HG test series of Me 262 prototypes was estimated to be capable of breaking Mach 1 numbers in level flight, if operating at higher altitudes. Naturally, this depended upon the reliability of the proposed engine powerplants, and the durability of the airframe. What was unknown at that time was the effect of breaking the sound barrier, that mystical wall that was more of a theory at this time than a reality, since it had never been breached. It seems ironic that, given the desires for faster fighters, and the known capabilities of the V-2 rockets that emerged as a regular weapon of choice in 1944, Willi Messerschmitt never pursued a program to surpass the estimated Mach 0.86 limit for the Me 262 in the streamlined fighter mode.

The first pilot to break 1,000 kilometers per hour in level flight was *Feldwebel* Heinz Herlitzius, in work number 130007, marked as VI+AG, on June 25, 1944. Hans-Guido Mutke (later interned in Switzerland) may have been the first pilot to exceed Mach 1 in a vertical 90-degree dive on April 9, 1945. Mutke did not have the required on-board instruments to record the actual speed, and all pilots knew that the pitot tube used to measure airspeed can give improper readings as the pressure inside the tube increases at high speeds. Finally, the Me 262 wing had only a slight sweep incorporated for trim reasons and likely would have suffered structural failure due to divergence at high transonic speeds. It is possible that an Me 262 (HG1 V9, work number 130004) with the identifier of VI+AD was built with the low-profile *Rennkabine* racing canopy to reduce drag, and this jet may have achieved an airspeed of 606 miles per hour.[5]

After the war, the British tested the Me 262, trying to exceed Mach 1. They did achieve speeds of Mach 0.84, and during this process they also confirmed the results of the German dive tests, where British pilots discovered what the Germans already knew: Steep dives and high speed meant death at a certain point. Captured jets were also tested by the Americans and Soviets. Everyone was impressed with the design and its capabilities.

The Messerschmitt name had already been synonymous with excellence in aircraft designs and production. The single engine, single-seat Bf 109 series (also known as the Me 109 by the Allies and is so designated throughout the rest of this book) was the most widely produced combat aircraft in history, with some 35,000 units being produced. The additional inclusion of the twin engine Bf 110 *Zerstörer* (Destroyer), as well as the later Me 210 and 410 models for reconnaissance and night fighting, had cemented Willi Messerschmitt as a designer favored by Hitler and the hierarchy.

The company also built an experimental four-engine bomber, the Me 264, which was named the "New York Bomber" because they hoped it would have the range to attack New York City and other major locations on the east coast of the United States. However, the *Luftwaffe* actually chose to use a rival bomber, the Heinkel He 177, which was farther along in its development. The engines of the He 177 displayed a major design flaw, an unpleasant tendency to catch fire in flight, a similar situation facing the British with their Avro Manchester heavy bomber. The He 177 was never produced in large numbers and was rarely flown in combat operations, but it was used as a transport on occasion.

The Messerschmitt company also built the first large transport plane, the six-engine *"Gigant,"* which was originally designed as a glider, then upscaled to a powered configuration, a behemoth that weighed a massive fifty tons when fully loaded and was capable of mounting up to fifteen MG-36 or MG-42 machine guns. It was able to carry twenty-two tons of cargo, or one heavy tank, or two light tanks, or up to 120 fully equipped infantrymen. Its wingspan was 180 feet (55 meters). Few were built and it was rarely used.

Messerschmitt made aeronautical history, yet after the war a price would be paid. Willi Messerschmitt was arrested, tried, and imprisoned after the war for using slave labor. However, this was not unique to the Messerschmitt company, due to the fact that all of Germany's manufacturing centers were required to use whatever manpower was provided, without question. He finally regained his freedom in 1947 and went back into business, initially making sewing machines, drill machines, and even prefabricated housing. In 1958, he was able to return to the production of aircraft, a legacy that would continue long after World War II, and his firm later produced an advanced American fighter under license, the Lockheed F-104 Starfighter.

After 1960, the West German aviation industry consolidated into fewer but economically stronger companies that could compete effectively in the international market. In 1969, it became a large combined corporation, Messerschmitt-Bolkow-Blohm, and Willi Messerschmitt was named as the honorary chairman for life until his death in 1978. Yet all of this was far in the future. Messerschmitt had made a name for himself that would last for all time, just as Ernst Heinkel, Alexander Lippisch, Hugo Junkers, and Kurt Tank had also carved their names into aviation design history.

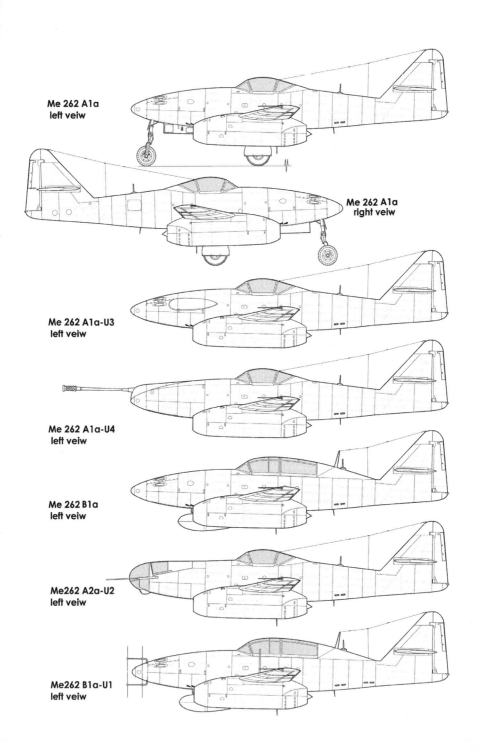

Me 262 A1a
left veiw

Me 262 A1a
right veiw

Me 262 A1a-U3
left veiw

Me 262 A1a-U4
left veiw

Me 262 B1a
left veiw

Me262 A2a-U2
left veiw

Me262 B1a-U1
left veiw

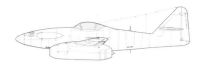

CHAPTER 3

Test Flights

When I took my first test flight in the jet, I thought
"we are invincible," and then I lost an engine, crash
landed, and realized that nothing was perfect.

Wolfgang Schenck

Regarding German early aircraft development, there was no shortage of young men eager to climb into the cockpits of new and experimental aircraft. As early as 1939, test pilot Fritz Wendel flew a specially built Messerschmitt prototype aircraft and set a speed record of 469 miles per hour (755 kilometers per hour), a record for propeller-driven planes that stood firm for the next thirty years. Wendel would also be one of the first men in history to strap into a jet aircraft and experience what would become an aviation standard for the next century and beyond. When the Me 262 test flights began on March 25, 1942, Fritz Wendel achieved a top-level flight speed of 541 miles per hour (871 kilometers per hour).

Wendel was the first pilot to consistently fly the first Me 262 V1, coded PC+UA, work number 000001, from Augsburg. (See Table 1 for dates and duration of each flight test.)

In his own words, Wendel described his perceptions of the Me 262: "I knew that I was sitting in the most important aircraft since the Wright brothers had built theirs. This aircraft was as critical to aviation as was the first flight, as both made history. The aircraft still had a conventional piston engine in the nose in case the jet engine failed so that we would not risk losing the aircraft. As it turned out, I needed that other engine, because I lost both jet engines, they were BMW [003] first one, and then the other.

TABLE 1: ME 262 V1 FLIGHT TESTS

Flight No.	Date of Flight	Flight Duration (minutes)
1	April 18, 1941	18
2	April 21, 1941	31
3	May 5, 1941	11
4	May 6, 1941	25
5	May 13, 1941	21
6	May 16, 1941	31
7	May 22, 1941	27
8	May 22, 1941	30
9	June 7, 1941	28
10	June 10, 1941	42
11	June 17, 1941	30
12	June 19, 1941	4
13	June 20, 1941	45
14	June 23, 1941	31
15	June 26, 1941	41
16	July 4, 1941	17
17	July 7, 1941	38
18	July 7, 1941	45
19	July 9, 1941	45
20	July 9, 1941	24
21	July 18, 1941	40
22	July 31, 1941	45
23	August 5, 1941	53
24	March 25, 1942	5
25	July 29, 1942	15
26	August 4, 1942	19
27	September 3, 1942	7
28	September 4, 1942	17
29	no record	
30	September 8, 1942	22
31	September 23, 1942	18
32	September 28, 1952	19
33	September 29, 1942	30
34	October 4, 1942	12
35	October 23, 1942	20
36	October 27, 1942	26[1]

TABLE 2: ME 262 V3 FLIGHT TESTS

Flight No.	Date of Flight	Flight Duration (minutes)	Airfield
1	July 18, 1942	12	Leipheim
2	July 18, 1942	13	Leipheim
3	July 28, 1942	14	Leipheim
4	August 1, 1942	18	Leipheim
5	August 7, 1942	20	Augsburg
6	August 11, 1942	20	Augsburg
7	August 11, 1942	20	Augsburg
8	March 21, 1943	25	Lechfeld
9	March 21, 1943	29	Lechfeld
10	March 22, 1943	27	Lechfeld
11	March 24, 1943	25	Lechfeld
12	March 25, 1943	31	Lechfeld
13	April 12, 1943	25	Augsburg
14	May 14, 1943	27	Lechfeld
15	May 17, 1943	32	Lechfeld
16	May 18, 1943	30	Lechfeld
17	May 20, 1943	23	Lechfeld
18	May 22, 1943	9	Lechfeld
19	May 22, 1943	18	Lechfeld
20	August 6, 1943	19	Lechfeld[4]

"They just flamed out. These engines were very slow, and the takeoff distance was incredible. Later it also was learned that had the piston engine not been in the aircraft, thereby reducing airflow, there might not have been the overheating that cracked the fan blades. The jet needed free flowing air coming through the intake, and this was restricted. Well, we learned something, saved the aircraft. I was just very lucky to have been a part of all of this." [2]

The second full test flight version with both Jumo 004 engines in conjunction with the conventional backup engine was Me 262 V2, PC+UB, work number 000002, and it flew on October 2, 1942, at Lechfeld, with the first flight lasting twenty minutes. This aircraft flew forty-eight times until the crash that killed Wilhelm Ostertag on April 18, 1943, while in a high-speed dive. This incident could have been the result of the high-speed loss of the control surfaces, experienced by a few pilots, such as the incident described by Hermann Buchner.

The first jet to fly on jet power alone was Me 262 V3, PC+UC, work number 000003. This aircraft flew from Leipheim, and on July 18, 1942, Wendel took off and flew at a conservative 600 kilometers per hour at an altitude of 2,000 meters. After twelve minutes, he landed and was very enthusiastic about the experience. This was when he reported that the rudder was ineffective for the first 600 meters of takeoff, but after liftoff all was well, even though the ailerons required attention due to high forces until airborne and the jet was trimmed out.

As stated in Morgan, Wendel wrote: "My engines ran like clockwork, it was a pure pleasure to fly this new aircraft. I have rarely been so enthusiastic about a test flight in a new aircraft as I was by the Me 262."[3] Wendel flew most of the mission in this version, with Heinrich Beauvais flying this model on August 11, 1942, the second flight of that day after Wendel. Beauvais ground looped the jet by not having enough takeoff speed, causing a long delay between tests while the aircraft was repaired. (See Table 2. As posted in Morgan, the flight record for this Me 262 is incomplete, but interesting nonetheless.)

Wendel was the chief test pilot of Germany's aircraft manufacturers, flying every aircraft Germany created. Only the bravest and most experienced pilots in the Third Reich would join him, including the famed aviatrix Hanna Reitsch.[5] Wendel would also fly the machine a year later, on March 2, 1943, with the new Jumo 004 engines and without a conventional engine backup.

Me 262V4, PC+UD, work number 000004, first flew on May 15, 1943, by Wendel. This aircraft was flown for a review by Göring at Rechlin airfield on July 25, 1943. The next day test pilot Gerd Lindner crashed on takeoff from Schkeuditz. This was ironically the first Me 262 that Adolf Galland flew. His report to *Generalfeldmarschall* Erhard Milch follows:

Der Oberbefehlshaber der Luftwaffe
General der jagdflieger
Berlin
    25 May 1943
    Dear Field Marshal,
    On Saturday, 22nd of this month, I flight tested in Augsburg the Me 262 in the presence of several gentlemen of the Air Ministry. With regard to the Me 262 aircraft, I would like to state the following:
    1-The aircraft is a big blow, which will guarantee us an unbelievable advantage during operations, presuming the enemy continue flying with piston engined aircraft.
    2-From the pilot's viewpoint, the flight performance of the aircraft produced quite an impression.
    3-The engines convince the pilot, except in take offs and landings.
    4-The aircraft will give us revolutionary new tactical opportunities.

I kindly ask that you consider the following suggestions.

We do have the Fw 190D under development, which can be considered nearly equal to the Me 209 with regard to all performances. Both aircraft types, however, will not be able to considerably surpass hostile aircraft, above in all altitudes.

It can only be taken for granted that with regard to the armament and speed, progress can be achieved.

Therefore I do suggest;

to stop Me 209 production

to concentrate the total production capacity on Fw 190s with BMW 801, DB 603 or Jumo 213 engines

to have those development and production capacities that will become available then immediately transferred to the Me 262 program.

After my return I will inform you immediately.

Signed

A. Galland

Galland's enthusiasm was understandable. Like Wendel, everyone who flew the Me 262 had nothing but praise for the experience, although reservations remained about the reliability of the Jumo engines. Galland's praise for the aircraft in his memorandum to Milch should have been the final say on the project going forward. However, there were still concerns, many of which Galland could debate from a position of authority and experience. Other factors, which are discussed later, were far beyond his control. Galland was a warrior and a soldier of the sky, and the world of political intrigue was not his world. He was never comfortable in it, and he would eventually become a victim of it.

The next version to be tested was Me 262V4, PC+UE, work number 000005, which first flew on June 6, 1943. It used the Jumo 004A-O engines and the new tricycle undercarriage configuration, although the nose wheel was nonretractable. The only additional adjustment was the use of two Borsig RI-502 rockets mounted on the fuselage. This "RATO" (rocket-assisted takeoff) unit provided 2,220 pounds of thrust for six seconds. After the initial flight, the rockets were repositioned farther down the underside of the fuselage, and the takeoff distance was reduced by around 300 yards. The results were moderately positive, although this aircraft would later crash with a nose gear collapse at the hands of *Hauptmann* Werner Thierfelder on August 4, 1943, never to fly again.[6]

The pilot in the cockpit on this test flight was Karl Baur, who also test flew the Ar 234 and other revolutionary aircraft. Baur would later become just one of many German experts rounded up in Operation Paperclip, along with engineers, rocket scientists, and military intelligence experts. He would fly these aircraft in the United States after the war, assisting that government and military in the emerging Cold War.

Me 262V6, call sign VI+AA, work number 130001, was the first true preproduction model of the Me 262, and the first flight took place on October 17, 1943, with the Jumo 004B-O turbojet engines. This jet was also the first to incorporate a retractable hydraulically operated tricycle landing gear configuration, thus allowing for high-speed horizontal takeoffs and test flights with reduced drag.

As would be expected with a preproduction model, the airframe, right down to the gun ports in the nose housing for the 30mm cannons, were in place. This aircraft was tested and approved by Gerd Lindner, who would be the pilot to fly this same aircraft at the demonstration flight for Hitler and at Insterburg on November 26, 1943. Galland was also present at this famous flight, and Hitler, being duly impressed with the event, made his decision on the jet bomber program for the Me 262. This aircraft perished along with test pilot Kurt Schmidt on March 9, 1944, after twenty-seven additional test flights.[7]

Despite all the deserved praise heaped upon the Me 262, there were still "bugs" in the system. Even as late as November 5, 1943, Dr. Anselm Franz, working with the Jumo design, communicated with both Erhard Milch and Hermann Göring as they visited the plant at Dessau:

"The difficulties we still have involve individual components of the engine, and I would like to select only two from this group. One is the turbine. Recently we have had certain difficulties with the turbine wheel, with unexpected failures in the turbine blades due to vibration. The second component is the control system, and here I will touch on the problem of opening and closing the throttles, which was raised by the *Reichsmarschall*.

"I mentioned in Regensburg that we had things under control up to 8,000 meters. Beyond that we are still somewhat unsure. But we have already flown to over 11,000 meters. However, it cannot be guaranteed with certainty that we will have the problem at upper altitudes rectified by the time series production begins, so that the pilot will be able to open and close the throttles without worrying about a flame-out."[8]

Oberfeldwebel Hermann Buchner, who flew the Me 262 with *Kommando Nowotny* and later JG-7, had his opinion on the Jumo engines and jet flying in the war: "I had success in the jet, no doubt. I shot down twelve confirmed victories with this aircraft, fighters and bombers. [But] many times I had to land a jet without engine power, due to a malfunction in the engines or even the throttle mechanism. The problems had not been worked out all the way. There was not any real thorough, peacetime research and development. They had this engine, it worked well enough, and they rushed it into production. Otherwise, the 262 would have been the perfect fighter."[9]

Initially, the combustion chambers were made of mild (not tempered) steel and coated with a baked-on aluminum glaze to prevent them from oxidizing. However, when the engine was running, these combustion chambers slowly buckled out of shape. The turbine blades were made of a steel-based alloy that contained some nickel and chromium. That material was insufficiently resilient, however; when the engine was running, the centrifugal forces caused the blades to elongate, or "creep." What was needed was much harder material that could withstand the intense heat and pressure.

The running life of preproduction Jumo 004s rarely reached more than ten hours. Throughout a flight, the pilot had to be very careful when advancing the throttle, which was vital to avoid an engine flameout or excessive overheating. At altitudes of above 13,000 feet, the engine became increasingly temperamental, where throttle movement was not advised. If a flameout occurred, the pilot had to shut off the fuel to the engine, since flooding could easily cause an engine fire, then descend to thicker, more oxygenated air before attempting a reignition. If the conditions were excellent, the engines could be restarted below 13,000 feet and at speeds between 250 and 300 miles per hour. Any higher altitude or faster speed made it virtually impossible, but flying below 250 miles per hour with a dead engine brought on new dangers—the pilot had better be on approach for a landing or prepared to jettison his canopy for a bailout under those circumstances. There are numerous examples in the loss records of German jets of all designs meeting their end in such ways. Due to these issues, the early version of the Jumo 004 had too many problems to allow mass production.

Ar 234 pilots found the aircraft a pleasure to fly overall, despite engine flameouts being a worrisome problem, the difficulty in escaping a damaged jet, and a variety of issues caused by inconsistent quality and grades of fuel, exacerbated by increasing fuel shortages. Pilots new to flying the jets often had great difficulty understanding the long takeoffs and high landing speeds, leading to a higher than normal accident rate. However, 8/ZG-76 managed to obtain a two-seat Me 262 jet trainer to familiarize new Ar 234 pilots, and following this adaptation, training accidents were greatly reduced. Interestingly, bomber pilots, as opposed to fighter pilots, had a much easier transition period with all jet versions.

The Jumo 004B-1 engines were ready for testing, and Me 262V7, coded as VI+AB, work number 130002, first flew with these engines on December 20, 1943, with Gerd Lindner behind the stick. This model was again different from its predecessors, since it incorporated an adjusted cockpit control mechanism to adjust the tail plane control, the very failure that had killed Wilhelm Ostertag. In addition, the new variant had a pressurized cockpit, a new and radical departure from existing versions of the Me 262, and a feature only incorporated in 1944 as standard equipment on the later Me 109K, Focke-Wulf 190D, and Ta 152 designs.[10]

This aircraft was finally destroyed on May 19, 1944, with the twenty-four-year-old test pilot *Unteroffizier* Hans Flachs killed in the process. As cited by Morgan, the official Messerschmitt flight record has the following comments about Flachs:

"*Uffz* Flachs, born on 3 November 1919, was initially a pilot in a destroyer squadron, and had several victories to his credit. He had been awarded the Iron Cross First Class, and was a member of the Evaluation Command (Ekdo) 262. He did his conversion training on the Me 262 and was considered as trained. He was then transferred to the Messerschmitt AG. The Flight Section held the hope that Flachs was on the way to becoming a first class test pilot, and both in and out of the cockpit, he had created an excellent impression." This report was posted on May 26, 1944. (See Table 3 for the flight test record of this aircraft.)

On March 18, 1943, Me 262V8, VI+AC, flew using the same Jumo 004B-1 engines, and it was the first test-flown variant to be equipped with the complete *Rheinmetall-Borsig* 30mm quad-mounted cannons in the nose. This was to allow the test pilots to fly the aircraft under fully operational weight conditions. This became the first Me 262 to be delivered to *Kommando Thierfelder* on April 19, 1944; however, this aircraft was destroyed in a landing incident in October 1944.[11] (This aircraft is not reflected in the loss records located in Appendix 3: Recorded Me 262 Losses. Losses of training and research and development aircraft were not recorded within the same department and method as losses from operational units.)

Testing of the Me 262 was not conducted only to examine flight characteristics and weaponry. Me 262V9, VI+AD, work number 130004, was a test platform for both communications gear and electrically operated acoustic homing and detection devices. This was the version that would examine the aircraft's capabilities of possibly being used in the role of the radar-guided night fighter variant. On October 1, 1944, this model was fitted with the new lower-profile streamlined "racing" canopy. The tail fin and rudder were also larger to provide greater control surface response, and the elevators were wider.

The test pilot was Karl Baur during January 1945, with both Baur and Lindner flying the machine at various times. The new improvements

TABLE 3: ME 262V7 FLIGHT TESTS

Flight No.	Date of Flight	Flight Duration (minutes)	Pilot	Airfield
1	Dec. 16, 1943	Static	N/A	Augsburg
2	Dec. 20, 1943	5	Lindner	Lechfeld
3	Dec. 21, 1943	19	Lindner	Factory field
4	Jan. 3, 1945	Static	N/A	Factory field
5	Jan. 4, 1945	13	Lindner	Factory field
6	Jan. 5, 1945	18	Lindner	Factory field
7	Jan. 5, 1944	24 (night)	Beauvais	Factory field
8	Jan. 9, 1945	24	Lindner	Factory field
9	Jan. 13, 1944	8 (night)	Behrens	Factory field
10	Jan. 13, 1944	7	Lindner	Factory field
11	Jan. 28, 1944	12	Lindner	Factory field
12	Jan. 29, 1944	46	Schmidt	Factory field
13	Jan. 30, 1944	51	Schmidt	Factory field
14	Jan. 31, 1944	48	Schmidt	Factory field
15	Jan. 31, 1944	17 (night)	Behrens	Factory field
16	Feb. 1, 1944	52	Schmidt	Factory field
17	Feb. 1, 1944	46	Schmidt	Factory field
18	Feb. 2, 1944	8	Schmidt	Factory field
19	Apr. 2, 1944	Static	N/A	Factory field
20	Apr. 11, 1945	18	Tesch	Factory field
21	Apr. 12, 1944	32	Tesch	Factory field
22	Apr. 16, 1944	36	Tesch	Factory field
23	Apr. 18, 1944	26	Ruther	Factory field
24	Apr. 19, 1944	25	Ruther	Factory field
25	Apr. 20, 1944	47	Ruther	Factory field
26	Apr. 21, 1944	20	Ruther	Factory field
27	Apr. 23, 1944	39	Tesch	Factory field
28	Apr. 29, 1944	32	Tesch	Factory field
29	May 6, 1945	Static	N/A	Factory field
30	May 8, 1944	25	Tesch	Factory field
31	May 9, 1944	11	Tesch	Factory field
32	May 9, 1944	37	Tesch	Factory field
33	May 13, 1944	Static	N/A	Factory field
34	May 14, 1944	27	Tesch	Factory field
35 (last flight)	May 19, 1944	15	Flachs	Factory field

that had been incorporated paid dividends, as the high-dive-speed control issues had been resolved. The airflow over the canopy was reduced, thus allowing the pilot to maintain greater elevator and rudder control without the surfaces "freezing" and possibly causing a crash. These advances came far too late to make a great difference in the production of future jets, however, let alone alter the course of the air war.

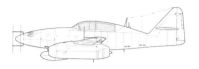

CHAPTER 4

In the Field

Maintaining fighters in the field was tough, even before we had the jet. Luckily field maintenance on the 262 was an easy task compared to other types, when we had the parts.

Georg-Peter Eder

By this time in the Me 262 story, the reports from the combat units had been coming in, and the reports and complaints from the pilots themselves were received and reviewed. Willi Messerschmitt is believed to have read every single one of them, which would seem true to his nature. Each design change or alteration incorporated into the next variant was always due to the comments of test pilots and, even more important, combat pilots. Several pilots stated that they wrote their reports following their various individual incidents while flying the jet, such as the previous control freeze experienced by Hermann Buchner. According to Buchner:

"I wrote my report after this happened, and I actually received a letter from Prof. Messerschmitt himself, signed. He thanked me for my detailed report, and asked that, should there be anything else I could examine and put forth as a constructive criticism, he would be very welcomed to read it. I thought that was very professional and friendly of him to send that."[1]

Wolfgang Schenck also stated that his men were filing reports based upon their experience flying the Me 262 in the ground attack fighter-bomber role: "My pilots and I wanted to let the designers know that we found a way to modify the catch release for the bombs. I personally found that when attacking in a high-speed dive, as I did in my first few test flights, as this was the preferred method of attack, they would not always fall away. In order to drop the bombs and then pull out and up to evade ground fire, the bomb release often had to be pulled more than once, or you had to kick the rudder left and right, creating an agitation to disrupt the air flow, and sometimes they would still not disengage from the jet, probably due to the drag of the bombs and the pressure against the bomb against the aircraft.

"If we tried to release the bombs in level flight it actually worked perfectly most of the time; however, this gave ground gunners plenty of time to track you, and lead your aircraft, as evasive maneuvers on a bomb run did not produce great results. I wrote this up, I think in August of '44. Soon we were using electrically operated bomb releases, but this still did not resolve the issue of high-speed dive release failure.

"The problem was finally solved when one of our mechanics, a young boy from Austria, said that we should try welding a small rounded air deflector, placed about ten centimeters or so in front of the bomb. This would perhaps shield the bomb from the heavy buffeting of the wind, allowing the bomb to fall away. You know, it worked, and I wrote this up and sent it to Berlin. I received a letter from Messerschmitt, stating that he understood the situation, and they would test this out. I wrote back and basically said 'don't bother' we already have and it worked. We modified our bombers at the airfield, it took perhaps two to three hours, but we could have a jet so altered. This was never done in production, and I think that was because the Ar 234 was being built and released as a bomber, so that the 262s could be sent to Galland's pilots as fighters."[2]

Despite all of its revolutionary technological innovations, the Ar 234 was a failure as a bomber. It was unable to carry a bomb load capable of inflicting as much comparative damage as the heavy bombers that were smashing the Reich. However, as a reconnaissance aircraft it proved extremely effective; the airframe was solid, and in the photographic reconnaissance role it was unsurpassed and was even better in that role than the Me 262. Yet, the Ar 234 would pale in comparison to its main competitor. Only a few pilots' reports reflected negatively upon the aircraft.

The Me 262 was a different matter, given its premier role as a fighter and its alternate role as a bomber. Many of these pilots' reports regarding the Me 262 had nothing to do with the airframe design issues, but rather the weapons systems. One such problem several Me 262 pilots experienced was the failure of the R4M rockets. Johannes Steinhoff was one such pilot, who, given his prestige as an *oberstleutnant* and highly successful ace and respected leader, tended to make an impression. Steinhoff had been foiled more than once when his rockets failed to fire:

"I was angry as hell about these damned rockets. When they worked, they worked beautifully, but when they did not, then I was carrying a few hundred pounds of rubbish, increasing my drag and reducing my speed and aerodynamic capabilities. I spoke with Galland about this, and he completely agreed, as did many others in JG-7 and JV-44. Once we let the rockets go, we picked up the extra eighty to one hundred miles per hour, which was our life insurance against the American fighter escorts. However, if these damned things did not fire, you could not just jettison them as you would a bomb, and they would just hang up from time to time.

"So, here I am, going into a perfect three-quarter flank attack, lined up wonderfully, knowing that I have Mustangs and whatever else coming down on me. I know that when I fire I will hit, or maybe even destroy something, and I can then pick up my airspeed and climb away from the attack on my six o'clock. But then nothing happens, and I am going too fast to switch to guns at that time. This requires me to come around for another attack. This is really bad, because now they not only know I am there, they know my intentions, and they know from where I will arrive. I return to the attack and brace myself for the impact of fifty-caliber bullets hitting my aircraft from the gunners on the bombers.

"Then I must also prepare to be hit by the escort fighters, because they are not stupid. They follow me into the attack, and the smartest enemy pilots will anticipate where my approach will come from and ambush me from higher altitude. I fire the cannons and get good strikes, but then I have to dive away. The only time that these damned rockets stuck to my jet are a positive thing is in a dive. Then I have to make sure that I can pull out of a dive without hitting the ground, once I know that my pursuers are far enough behind me. In essence, this was bullshit, and I said so!

"I drafted a report and gave it to Galland, and all of us shared the same opinion. We should either have reliable weapons or just leave the damned things off the jets. This was in March of 1945. I knew that it was too late in the war to make a difference at the production side of things, but I damned sure wanted the problem discovered and resolved so that if necessary we could make modifications in the field.

"One of our enlisted guys, an electrician who worked magic, once even wiring up a complete jet on a couple of occasions [Krupinski's aircraft was one example], decided to take one of the units apart and examine them. What he found, from what I understood, was that the wiring, while being rubber coated and electrically triggered from the cockpit, was connected by a small flat copper flange. This was what connected the rocket motor wire to the cockpit. During take-off the wing vibration where the rockets were mounted sometimes shook these small connections loose. When that happened, there was no firing, but the connection in the cockpit was never affected.

"So, we recommended that rather than use the very soft copper connector, despite its great ability to conduct electricity, that a more sturdy metal, such as silver or even nickel, or a combination be used. Galland came back to me and said that when they read that report in Berlin, if it got that far, we would be hearing the laughter all the way to Munich-Riem. Due to the shortages of all materials, both metals were in rare supply, as Galland pointed out.

"Then I thought about it, as I looked at his Knight's Cross, and then I felt my own. 'You know, there is enough silver in one Knight's Cross to probably fix three or four jets.' Galland looked at me, and smiled. He was very funny and said, "All right, I will call Berlin and tell Milch that we should stop making the medals and use that for the rockets, and also while I am at it, have them melt down anything already made for the production line.' I liked the idea, but Galland said no, as it would be a waste of time. Well, we knew what to look for on the rocket pods, and we had the chiefs use solder to reinforce the connections on every aircraft with what silver or nickel we could find. They worked well after that, being more reliable."[3]

Messerschmitt and the other various companies that brought the Me 262 to life all read the reports that reached them, and in most cases, they took corrective action, such as with the enlarged vertical and horizontal stabilizers and tail assembly, and solving landing gear problems. The one test jet that finally incorporated all of these drastic changes was Me 262V10, coded as VI+AE with work number 130005.

This aircraft was the one design that was a response to Wolfgang Schenck's issues while using the jet as a fighter-bomber. Part of the problem was the issue of pilot control at high speeds while at low altitude, where drag was increased due to thicker and warmer air, thus increasing the pressure as experienced by *Kommando Schenck* pilots, as well as those in KG-51 "*Edelweiss*," which was formed in July 1944 and commanded by *Oberstleutnant* Wolf-Dietrich Meister until he was succeeded by *Major* Wolfgang Schenck on December 5, 1944; pilots in KG-54, originally a Ju-88 bomber unit commanded by *Oberstleutnant* Baron Volprecht Riedesel *Freiherr* von zu Eisenbach until he was killed in action on February 9, 1945, and replaced by *Major* Hans-Georg Bättcher, and even the training unit of EJG-2 experienced these issues.[4] The secret was in the joystick.

The traditional joystick that frequently became sluggish or even nonresponsive in previous Me 262 versions was modified. Along with the increased control surfaces and streamlined canopy, the new joystick was built with the sealed ball bearing gearbox encased in lubricant fluid, which was a combination of ethylene glycol and petroleum distillate. This design provided lubrication and reduced friction while preventing the mixture from congealing at low temperatures while operating at subfreezing altitudes.

The design and corrective action of the airframe was a much easier process than solving the engine issues. The swept wing design of the Me 262 was actually too shallow to achieve any significant aerodynamic advantage without an accompanying powerplant to compensate for the weight. What made the difference was the actual angle of the wing surface reducing drag while achieving lift. The lift-to-weight ratio was critical with jet power, as the Germans quickly learned. This was especially true once bombs and rockets were attached. Therefore, to achieve universal harmony and aerodynamic stability, the wing was repositioned slightly aft of the original design.

Following Schenck's recommendations further, this variant was also tested for an increased bomb load and expanded fuel capacity during trials in May 1944. The hope was to fulfill Hitler's demand to have a "blitz bomber" with enough punch and range to be effective, as stated by *Generalmajor* Dietrich Pelz:

"The Me 262 bomber idea was, of course, all Hitler's idea. I supported it, until I examined the Ar 234. But, I also knew that it would take more time to modify existing 262s to fit this role than it would be to simply build them at the various factories and roll them out already configured for this work. It was a matter of time and money, but mostly it was just simple logic. I was interested to see what they would come up with."[5]

Gerd Lindner flew the new test version of the jet bomber, using the new bomb release mechanism—the bombs on each wing were mounted to a trolley that would be released when he detonated a small charge. The high-speed dive resulted in one bomb falling away while the other was still attached under the wing. Schenck had made a valid argument.

Lindner also tested the later variants to emerge from the Messerschmitt works, such as the Me 262, V167, work number 130167, which was to test the newer rudder assembly and flight stability. Baur, Wendel, Hans Herlitzius, and others flew newer and renovated designs. (For more on this subject, Morgan's book is highly recommended.) All of their efforts were to prove valuable in the field, yet too late to really make any difference for the *Luftwaffe*.

After thousands of man-hours and trial and error, the airframe issues had been largely resolved, but the powerplants still had issues; by late June 1944, the Jumo 00484 emerged with an average estimated operational life span of approximately twenty-five hours. However, these estimates were conducted on static tests and controlled test flights—not conducted under combat conditions. According to Johannes Steinhoff: "I was the technical officer for a while with JG-7 and then *kommandeur*, and in that unit if we managed to squeeze ten to fifteen hours out of an engine, we were very lucky. As a safety precaution, it was suggested that engine checks be conducted after every four hours, fan blade checks before and after every mission, and fuel line checks every day.

"Usually when an aircraft is in production, lessons are learned, corrections are made, and the aircraft gets better. This was true in many areas with the Me 262, but the Jumos was not one of them. As the war went on it seemed as if the quality control went right out the window, where mass production seemed to be more important than delivering a quality product. There we were, strapping our asses into a flying coffin, and hoping that our own engines would not fail us, causing us to die. Given that reality, I cannot even imagine how those poor *Komet* pilots did their job. At least we had a fighting chance if things went wrong.

"When I joined JV-44, the engines on the jets, even new ones, that had been rated for twenty-five hours at the laboratory, and had lasted about fifteen hours in the early production models, now lasted perhaps ten hours. We needed more replacement engines just to keep up the same ratio of sorties to aircraft. This was intolerable, but we had to work with what we had. I spoke with Dolfo about this, and he made an inquiry to Messerschmitt, who was in charge of design and production. I recall Galland saying that Prof. Messerschmitt had no control over what Junkers was sending him. He could only put them together.

"This was also an unacceptable condition, so Galland paid a visit to Milch at some point, right before our first large-scale operational mission as an official unit. I am not aware of the details of that meeting, but I do know that Galland said that we were pretty much screwed, and had to work with whatever they sent us. This was not the most comforting thing to have in the back of your head when climbing into the cockpit. I know that every pilot was watching the clock when it came to how many hours his engines had been used. [Eduard] Schallmoser once said that he was better off ramming his jets into enemy aircraft, because it was easier to get a new complete jet than it was to get a complete replacement engine that lasted long enough. His logic may have been twisted, but it made sense. You sort of had to be there in order to appreciate the irony."[6]

Wolfgang Späte also commented on the dangers of losing an engine in combat, as stated in his own book, *Top Secret Bird*, when referring to the Me 262 and the Jumo 004 engines: "Frequently, after an Me 262 hit an enemy aircraft and flew through the wreckage, an engine would flame out because of damage to the compressor. In that situation, there was nothing else for the Me 262 pilot to do except to break off the engagement and head home. Then the pilot had to make sure that he didn't meet up with a Mustang or Thunderbolt.

"Under those conditions, they were faster and more maneuverable than the 262 and were definitely not going to let such a fat target get away from them. Not even Nowotny was able to make it out of a similar situation. He had an engine flameout after he shot down another airplane. Because he was no longer fast enough and maneuverable enough, he was shot down by one of the escort fighters."[7]

Galland stated his opinions on this issue regarding the engines, as related in Morgan: "A disadvantage of the powerplants was that they were not reliable. My JV-44 jets accumulated only twelve hours and twenty minutes between engine changes. This was a very short time when one considers that engines of today last up to 40,000 hours. Often we took a new engine out of its packing case, fitted it onto the wing and in the test run it suffered a massive mechanical failure of some sort. [Authors' note: These were engines produced after April 5, 1945, and the reason was the loss of available metals for alloy use, such as nickel and chromium, among other factors.]

"The powerplant needed much more development and testing time, which we didn't have, and we were also very short of high grade steel, crucial for their manufacture. The engines were very sensitive to acceleration and power settings, and by the end of the war, there had been a device developed and fitted for automatic acceleration.

"This meant that we could handle the throttle as we wanted—a device, therefore, that made progressive power setting by itself, rather than the pilot having to do it. There was no question that the engines stalled quite often, and needed considerably more thrust. We also had another advantage that is not commonly known. In the control stick, we had two gears. One gear for takeoff and general movements and another gear, which was very sensitive for flying at high speed. Naturally we didn't have 'fly-by-wire' at this time, and everything had to be done mechanically."[8]

Despite these advances in speed and firepower regarding the engines and the previous comments, certain reliability problems remained—but the *Luftwaffe* needed the jets immediately. During September 1944, engine production allowed the *Luftwaffe* to receive ninety Me 262s. These were divided among the newly established *Kommando Nowotny*, *Ekdo 262*, *Kommando Schenck*, *Kommando Stamp*, KG-51, and KG-54. Active combat testing was the litmus test required to ensure the quality of the product.

This activity, while not fully endorsed or even looked upon favorably by the *Reichsluftfahrtministerium* (RLM), did pique the interest of other noteworthy people, not the least of which was Adolf Hitler. While Messerschmitt and Heinkel had both worked on their designs, Hans A. Mauch became head of rocket development at the RLM on April 15, 1938. He quickly increased his responsibilities to emphasize turbojet development, working with an experimental department under Helmut Schelp of the RLM research branch. By mid-1938, they had established a functional, comprehensive program of jet engine development that incorporated turbojet and turboprop projects.

One would think that they had plenty of time to produce a largely error-free powerplant ready for mass production with spare parts and trained personnel long before 1944. A plausible argument is that if the politics had been kept out of the science, Germany would have fielded the Me 262 easily by 1943, if not even in 1942, during the halcyon days of victory when materials were abundant, the leadership of the Third Reich was more compliant, and Hitler was in a much better mood and less affected by his drug use.

With Hitler's quiet support, seconded by the ever-compliant Deputy *Führer* Rudolf Hess (until his defection to Britain in May 1941) and also supported by *Reichsmarschall* Hermann Göring, who took over the position as de facto second in command from 1941 forward, to their credit, the jet program silenced most of the critics in the *Luftwaffe* hierarchy, including *Generaloberst* Hans Jeschonnek.

According to Adolf Galland: "Jeschonnek's opposition was only due to the costs involved at the expense of building more conventional aircraft for the war. Unlike many others, he was not opposed to new technology, just the opposite; he just wanted to make sure other areas of critical interest did not suffer as a result. I think that this was just one of many reasons he decided to commit suicide later, as he and Göring were constantly at odds. Erhard Milch, on the other hand, was a fanatical supporter of the new aviation sciences, as he was not so entrenched in the old ways. Ernst Udet was also a great supporter, although he and Milch had a parting of the ways shortly after the war started, much of this having to do with the development of jet aircraft."[9]

Another reason for the halfhearted support for the "new sciences," as mentioned by Galland, was the long period of delays from design to production to delivery. Laymen like Hitler could not comprehend the groundbreaking and revolutionary scientific barriers that had to be overcome. It had taken two decades for piston-powered aircraft to reach 400 miles per hour from only 120 miles per hour in World War I due to better engine technology and airframe designs. German scientists (and also the British working on the Gloster Meteor jet at the same time) were on the verge of breaking the speed of sound in level flight. They still had not even addressed the human factors, however, such as increased g forces upon pilots and pressurization of cockpits.

The lifesaving g suits so common today were over a decade away at this time. This was completely virgin territory. In fact, when the Allies collected all of the data captured from the Germans at the end of the war, it took them another five years to work out the issues of swept wing designs and an axial flow turbo jet that would be reliable and operational based upon the German research and development, which was years ahead of the Americans and British.

The first preproduction series was the Jumo 004A-0 (actually the 109-004A-015), which was the engine for the initial powered flight tests. The design team deciding against using the BMW engine, despite a successful test flight of the He 178 on August 27, 1939, using a von Ohain–designed single BMW engine centrally mounted within the fuselage. The end result was a successful five-minute flight, but in the final analysis it was determined that the airframe was not stable enough for the heavy engine. Heinkel would then design the more rugged H-280.

This early Jumo engine consistently failed due to overheating and cracking of the turbine's fan blades, giving the Ohain BMW design a chance at being awarded the contract. German engineers tried to overcome the technical problems and worked on developing metals that were strong, light, and able to handle the extreme heat generated by the fuel. It was by all measures a frustrating process, as there were no previous benchmarks from which to review previous experiments. The engine development continued under the direction of Anselm Franz at the *Otto-Mader-Werke*, which had been involved with the project from the first days in 1939.

The reconstruction of the Jumo 004A for online production (with material upgrades) began in the summer of 1941. The first engines were completed and ready for production in early 1942. The engines for the Me 262 V1 eventually arrived from Spandau in November 1941, being the backup BMW 003 that produced 1,213 pounds of thrust. Fritz Wendel described his first flight at the controls with the BMW 003:

"I took off in this thing, which was the early tail-dragging model, and the original engines were underpowered for the weight, but this would later be corrected with using Jumos. I was moving the throttles forward to increase my takeoff speed, and I was perhaps only fifty meters off the deck when both engines just blew out. There was no strange sound, just a 'whoosh' sound and then a sudden silence; and I found myself in a very heavy glider. I managed to set the aircraft down on the nacelles, sliding across down the airstrip. The damage to the aircraft was minimal, and I was impressed with how survivable the airframe was in such an emergency landing."[10]

These engines were finally abandoned in favor of the Jumo design, and this engine later underwent intensive tests through early 1943. The results proved worthwhile, as the Jumo 004B was given an upgraded and more reliable compressor, and the improved blades that were designed for the compressor proved to be more heat tolerant. The previous hollow blades, designed for lighter weight, had consistently failed after cracking, so the solid blade was introduced, proving to be satisfactory.

The next phase was to determine how many hours the blades and compressors would last before repair or replacement were required. Full production began in the summer of 1943 at both the Junkers facility in Leipzig and at the Opelwerke at Russelsheim. These two locations alone were to prove problematic, as Allied bombing plans targeted those cities with devastating effect. Allied intelligence did not choose their targets at random; they knew what the Germans were working on to a large degree. They simply did not know how far the Germans had come in their research and development.

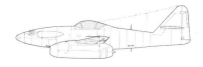

CHAPTER 5

Competition and Innovation

I think it was the correct decision, as future jet bomber development was taken over by Arado, and that proved successful.

Dietrich Pelz

Since 1939, the Allies had an Enigma code machine, and later in 1941, they had a complete unit with the code books, captured on U-110. The wizards at Bletchley Park broke the code, the Ultra Project, and kept it secret. In July 1944, when the U-505 was captured with an updated Enigma machine, the British were reading everything as soon as the Germans sent it. However, electronic code breaking, as valuable as it was, was only as good as the hard data to support the traffic received. Aerial photoreconnaissance was a valuable tool, but hands-on intelligence was even better.

Top-secret plans on many German designs, including the Me 262, Me 163, He 178, He 280, Ar 234, and the V-1 project, were in British hands courtesy of a Swiss agent passing them on to the British RAF Air Attaché in Bern in 1943. Also received were the German developments in the creation of new and synthetic fuels, production facility locations, numbers of workers, and information of that nature. Perhaps of even greater interest were the projected dates of these weapons being operational and deployed to forward units. Even during the early days, the British received information that kept them concerned. However, this was not the first collection of valuable intelligence gathered by the British on German aviation developments.

In 1939, Ernst Heinkel had the first successful flight of the He 178 when Erich Warsitz lifted off in the aircraft, which was powered by the turbojet engine designed by Hans von Ohain. Little support was initially forthcoming from the RLM from either *Generalfeldmarschall* Erhard Milch or Hermann Göring. Both were open to new ideas, but both also had to answer to Adolf Hitler, who watched every mark and pfennig in a financial micromanagerial method that would cripple many ingenious designs and concepts.

One of the great "what-ifs" in history is the possible development and mass production of other jets; the He 280 could have become the first operational jet aircraft, if not a fighter, instead of the Me 262. The Heinkel company began the development on the He 280 project after the He 178 had been met without enthusiasm from the *Reichsluftfahrtministerium* (RLM). The chief designer, Robert Lusser, began the project under the initial designation He 180 in late 1939. The design had a typical Heinkel fighter-styled fuselage, elliptically shaped wings, and a dihedral tail plane with twin fins and rudders. The landing gear was the retractable tricycle configuration with very little ground clearance. One major design innovation was the inclusion of the compressed air–powered ejection seat, the first aircraft to ever be so equipped.

The first He 180 (280) prototype was completed in June 1940, but the He S8 turbojet engine intended to be the powerplant had mechanical difficulties. On September 22, 1940, while work on the engine problems continued, the first prototype started glider tests with adjusted ballast replacing the missing engines to provide an accurate aerodynamic test. It would be another six months before *Flugkapitän* Fritz Schäfer would be able to take the second prototype into the air under its own power on March 30, 1941. The self-propelled prototype was then demonstrated to *Generalfeldmarschall* Ernst Udet, then head of RLM's development wing on April 5. However, Udet, a *Pour le Mérite* sixty-four-victory ace from World War I and stunt pilot and barnstormer between the wars, was less than impressed.

This is where history took a strange course. Had Udet been impressed enough to approve continued development, Heinkel would have received the extra funding they needed. This infusion of capital and political support would likely have led to the firm solving all of the problems they were having with the engines. This situation was true concerning all jet engine development in Germany. If there was no government funding, ideas tended to die on the vine.

A contest flight to demonstrate the new design was organized in 1941, comparing the He 280 with the Fw 190A to determine if the cost of continued research, development, and production was worth the effort. The Fw 190 had effectively replaced the Me 109 series in the West as the mainstay fighter with the intentions of being the premier anti-bomber fighter, given its armament, armor plating, and radial air-cooled engine. Ernst Heinkel designed a smaller jet fighter airframe for the He 280 that was well matched to the lower-thrust jet engines available in 1941.

During the demonstration, the He 280 completed four laps on the oval circuit course before the Fw 190 could complete three. The maximum weight displacement of the He 280 was 4,296 kilograms (9,470 pounds) compared with 7,130 kilograms (15,720 pounds) for the Me 262. The He 280 could have gone into production by late 1941 and maintained the air superiority, which the Fw 190 had been designed and built for. The initial teething problems experienced with the He S8 engine would have had plenty of time to be ironed out just as production of the fighter airframe had begun.

The major factor that Heinkel pushed was the fact that the He 280 jet engines could burn kerosene, which was much cheaper, more readily available, and much safer with a higher flash point than the high-octane fuel used by piston-engine aircraft. This argument was not inconsiderable, although Messerschmitt had the same argument.

The He 280 may have had a better chance at a contract—and thus a more important entry in the aviation history books—had the company pushed the aircraft as an anti-shipping fighter-bomber. This would have then allowed the *Kriegsmarine* to join the *Luftwaffe* in supporting the design, as it would complement the Fw 200 *Condor* anti-shipping aircraft, working with the U-boat force against the Allied trans-Atlantic convoys. It was not a highly maneuverable jet, but it had the speed and the power to lift ratio to carry a respectable bomb load for such work.

While the R4M rockets that would prove so devastating to the Allied bomber formations later in the war (as these were not available until 1944) would have also been highly effective against shipping, the Germans did develop the airborne version of the highly effective *Nebelwerfer* in 1941, which was a 150mm (5.9-inch) artillery rocket launcher. These tubes could have been mounted under the wings of a jet. Had the German government given its complete support to the He 280 project, this aircraft could have gone into production in late 1941 or early 1942 and been delivered to the anti-maritime units of the *Luftwaffe*, placing it into active operations a full two years earlier than the Me 262. In a sense of heightened irony, Udet's opposition on that April day changed the course of history.

Earlier during the war, when the British were minimally aware of German developments in technology, the future was still uncertain;

there was still the serious competition for the jet contracts. Heinkel had also been developing a twin-engine fighter with their jet fighter. This design was designated the Heinkel He 280 V2, and the British were well aware of when the first prototype flew from Rostock on March 30, 1941, with test pilot Fritz Schäfer at the controls. The engine was a six-stage axial-flow BMW P 3302 and was actually Germany's first jet aircraft—months ahead of the Me 262 in development and years ahead of the Arado Ar 234 bomber.

The report from Fritz Schäfer was promising, despite the engines being underpowered and unreliable, and the final report landed on the desk of Ernst Udet. The Heinkel He 280 proved to be a serious competitor to the Me 262 early on, and the comparisons between the two aircraft are quite revealing. (See Tables 4 through 7 for a comparison between the He 280, Ar 234, and Me 262 production specifications.)

TABLE 4:
ARADO AR 234B PRODUCTION SPECFICATIONS

Crew	1
Wingspan	14.1 meters/46 feet 4 inches
Wing area	26.4 square meters/284.16 square feet
Length	12.6 meters/41 feet 6 inches
Height	4.30 meters/14 feet 1 inch
Empty weight	5,200 kilograms/11,464 pounds
Max loaded weight	9,850 kilograms/21,715 pounds
Maximum speed	740 kph/460 mph
Service ceiling	10,000 meters/32,810 feet
Operational radius	800 kilometers/500 miles (435 nautical miles)

TABLE 5:
ARADO AR 234C PRODUCTION SPECFICATIONS

Crew	1
Wingspan	14.1 meters/46 feet 4 inches
Wing area	26.4 square meters/284.16 square feet
Length	12.6 meters/41 feet 6 inches
Height	4.30 meters/14 feet 1 inch
Empty weight	5,990 kilograms/13,200 pounds
Max loaded weight	9,890 kilograms/21,800 pounds
Maximum speed	873 kph/542 mph
Service ceiling	12,000 meters/39,370 feet
Operational radius	660 kilometers/410 miles

TABLE 6:
HE 280 PRODUCTION SPECFICATIONS

Crew	1
Wingspan	12.20 meters/40 feet
Wing area	21.5 square meters /233 square feet
Length	10.40 meters/34 feet 1 inch
Height	3.06 meters/10 feet
Empty weight	3,215 kilograms/7,073 pounds
Loaded weight	4,280 kilograms/9,416 pounds
Max takeoff weight	4,300 kilograms/9,470 pounds
Maximum speed	820 kmh/512 mph
Service ceiling	10,000 meters/32,000 feet
Operational radius	370 kilometers/230 miles
Rate of climb	1,145 meters per minute/3,756 feet per minute
Powerplant	2 × Heinkel He S.8 turbojet, 5.9 kN (1,320 pounds) each
Armament	3 × 20mm MG 151/20 cannons

There were several reasons for the Me 262 being awarded the final production contract, supplanting the He 280 as a fighter design. Perhaps the most prevalent reason was that the airframe design allowed for many different aerodynamically feasible configurations. This ability to adapt the airframe to multiple roles would be both a blessing and a curse. The flexibility of the design intrigued Göring, who wanted aircraft that could perform many roles without having to resort to the expense of new designs. The negative effect of having this multiple role capability would provide Hitler with the opportunity to become just one of many problems that would delay fighter production.

Of all the proposed jet designs, the Me 262 was provided with the greatest array of options. (See Table 8 for operational variants.) This was probably due to the great interest and belief in the design, not only as a multi-role aircraft, but also because, despite its revolutionary airframe design, the fuselage was cheaper to produce than any other German aircraft made during the war. The airframe was not a multi-faceted riveted cross-section of various components, unlike the Me 109 and Fw 190. In addition, unlike the Ar 234 and He 280, it required less armored glass and the design allowed for the hydraulic, electrical, and fuel lines to be laid out without the circuitous bending and binding to fit into small spaces, thus reducing building time in man-hours as well as using fewer materials.

The first full production model Me 262A-1a flew on June 7, 1944, with the first delivery of the A-0 version previously delivered at Rechlin in May 1944; the first experimental combat unit (EK-262/*Thierfelder*) received theirs on June 30, 1944. The first regular squadron (8/ZG-26) received their jets in September 1944, while *Kommando Nowotny* also received limited numbers by late August.

The Ar 234 was given great consideration by the RLM, hence it later becoming Hitler's "Blitz Bomber" to release Me 262s for fighter service. The success of the Ar 234 was due to many factors. In many ways, the Ar 234 was a far more advanced jet aircraft than the Me 262. However, there were also a few drawbacks that allowed the Me 262 to take the premier fighter role.

TABLE 7:
ME 262 PRODUCTION SPECFICATIONS

Crew	1
Wingspan	12.48 meters/40 feet 11 ½ inches
Wing area	21.70 square meters/233.58 square feet
Length	10.60 meters/34 f 9 ½ inches
Height	3.84 meters/12 feet 7 inches
Empty weight	3,800 kilograms/8,378 pounds
Max takeoff weight	6,400 kilograms/14,110 pounds
Maximum speed	870 kmh/540 mph at 6,000 meters/19,685 feet
Service ceiling	11,450 meters/37,565 feet
Operational radius	1,050 kilometers/652 miles without auxiliary fuel tanks on standard cruise speed at 300 mph
Powerplant	Two Junkers GmbH 900 kw/1,984 horsepower thrust *Jumo* 004B turbojet engines
Armament	Four 30mm MK 108 cannons in the nose, two guns with 100 rounds each and two with 80 rounds each; (262A-1a/U1) two 30mm MK 103 cannons, two MK 108 cannons and two 20 mm MG 151/20 cannons; (A-1b) as A-1a plus twenty-four fin stabilized R4M 50mm rockets; (B-2a) A-1a plus two inclined MK 108 cannons behind the cockpit in *Schräge Musik* installation; (D) SG 500 *Jagdfaust* with twelve rifled mortar barrels in nose; (E) 50mm MK 114 gun or 48 R4M rockets; (A-2a bomber) one 1,102-pound (500-kilogram) bomb or two 551-pound (250-kilogram) bombs in the Me 262A-2a fighter-bomber version.

TABLE 8:
ME 262 OPERATIONAL VARIANTS

Me 262A-0	Preproduction test model.
Me 262A-1a	Me 262A-1a/U1: With two 30mm MK 103, two MK 108, two 20mm MG 151/20 cannons.
262A-1a/U2	All-weather fighter, with the standard radio replaced with the FuG 125.
262A-1a/U3	Unarmed reconnaissance aircraft with two RB 50/30 focal length cameras.
Me 262A-1b	The same as A-1a, but including twenty-four spin-stabilized R4/M 55mm rockets.
Me 262A-2a	Fighter-bomber, identical to the 1a variant but with the addition of bomb racks.
Me 262A-3a	Had increased armor protection around the cockpit.
262A-5a	Armed reconnaissance aircraft with two MK 108 cannons and a pair of drop tanks for extended range of up to 950–1,000 miles at cruising speed of 300 mph.
262B-1a	Two-seat trainer for transition flight instruction.
262B-1a/U1	Converted to night fighter two-seater version prior to dedicated night fighter construction.
262B-2a	Dedicated night fighter, which was the same as A-1a but included two-inclined MK 108 behind the cockpit in *Schräge Musik* installation, as well as some models carrying the SG 500 *Jagdfaust* with twelve rifled mortar barrels inclined in nose. Other carried the 50mm MK 114 gun or forty-eight R4M rockets.
Me 262C	Experimental model flown in February 1945 using auxiliary rocket boosting, what is today called RATO (rocket assisted takeoff), but only three models were ever produced.
Avionics	Me 262B-1a night fighter, SN2 *Lichtenstein* radar. All other variants were standardized for simplicity of production and maintenance.
History	First flight for the Me 262V-1 on the Jumo 210 piston engine was April 4, 1941, with subsequent flights, including the April 18 flight. Me 262V-3 first flew on two Jumo 004-0 turbojets flew on July 18, 1942.[1]

The Ar 234 had a high landing speed and was the first mass production aircraft to provide a drag chute for deceleration as standard equipment. The rounded nose of the aircraft was covered with Plexiglas, which provided the pilot an excellent view to the front, which was especially valuable to reconnaissance pilots, although the design did not provide a view to the rear, except through a periscope, which was not standard equipment on the prototypes. It was in fact this very Plexiglas nose design that made Kurt Welter decide not to employ the Ar 234 as a night fighter.

Welter's observations are interesting, when considering the fact that a few Ar 234B night fighters were fitted with FuG 218 *Neptun* long-wave radar, featuring nose-mounted aerials, much like the Ju 88 and Me 410 night fighters, and an under-fuselage twin 20mm MG-151/20 cannons. The second crewman, a radar operator, sat behind the wing. There is no evidence within the existing records that any Ar 234B night fighters ever scored a kill. None of the Ar 234 night fighters were equipped with ejection seats.

Although an experimental ejection seat had been introduced in a few jet prototypes, the Ar 234B was not so configured. The pilot entered and exited the aircraft through a transparent hatch above the cockpit. This configuration made bailing out of a damaged Ar 234 a difficult process to say the least. The Ar 234 handled very well at all speeds, even at both low and high altitudes, and was capable of tight turns, loops, and other aerobatics. The same problem plagued the Ar 234 that haunted the Me 262: the unreliability of the early Jumo 004 engines, even the 004B version, which still required a complete overhaul or replacement after as little as ten hours of operation. The brakes also tended to wear out rather rapidly after three landings, requiring the pads and often the hydraulically operated calipers to be replaced frequently.

The fuel consumption of the Jumo engines varied widely with the aircraft they were installed in, the type of mission, and the operational altitude. As with piston-powered aircraft, operations at 33,000 feet required a third less fuel consumption than at sea level. The jet engine was a much better performer in thin, colder air. Therefore, low-altitude bombing missions limited the operational radius of the aircraft only about 120 miles, while in the high-altitude reconnaissance role, the range increased to approximately 450 miles when fitted with external drop tanks.

In addition to these variables, by the time the Ar 234 was production ready, it was not very difficult to find enemy targets within the 120-mile bombing radius of the Ar 234, and these targets were usually protected by fighter cover and antiaircraft batteries. This also meant that their operational bases were within the range of any Allied fighter-bomber in the inventory, requiring extreme vigilance when taking off and landing, just as with the Me 262 pilots.

When operated as a bomber, the Ar 234 was far more versatile than the Me 262 and was quite at home in shallow dive attacks, low-level horizontal attacks, or high-altitude horizontal bombing. In the shallow dive missions, the pilot would drop to under 4,920 feet, aiming the bombs through the periscope sight mounted just above the cockpit. In the low-level horizontal bombing mission, the pilot simply flew level and, much like the Me 262 pilots, dropped the bombs by calculation.

The first bomber missions did not take place until December 24, 1944, when nine Ar 234Bs were dispatched to attack Liege in Belgium, dropping 1,100-pound bombs in support of the Ardennes ground offensive. These missions continued until early January; when the weather broke, Allied fighters swarming the area made such flights suicide missions.

As expected, Allied fighters made daylight operations quite dangerous, as exemplified in early January 1945 when eighteen Ar 234s were bounced by Spitfires, shooting down three jets and damaging two others, killing two jet pilots as they came in to land. Despite these dangers when the weather improved, the Ar 234s performed as many bombing missions as possible, attacking targets throughout Belgium, Holland, and Luxembourg. The Ar 234s attacked in force February 21, 1945, as the American forces were fighting to take Aachen.

The last great mission for the Ar 234 occurred on March 7, 1945, when the Americans seized the Ludendorff Bridge spanning the Rhine River at Remagen. While German demolition specialists had badly damaged the bridge, it remained intact. A furious Göring ordered it destroyed at all costs. Over the course of the next ten days, Ar 234Bs flew several sorties in attempts to take it down. This was a failure, and the jets fell prey to antiaircraft fire. By the time the bridge finally collapsed on March 17, the Americans had occupied the east bank of the Rhine and had built pontoon bridges to transport men and supplies.

The Germans had started conducting reconnaissance operations with the Ar 234Bs in September and October 1944, including missions to southern and eastern England to determine if the Allies were preparing any additional amphibious landings following Operation Overlord, with the most likely targets being Belgium and Holland with their easily accessible ports. The Ar 234 was such a worthwhile reconnaissance aircraft, it remained undetected until P-51s on a bomber escort mission over Holland observed one of the jets on November 21,

1944. The Mustang pilots tried to pursue, but the German immediately opened the throttle up and disappeared.

Likewise, the Me 262 reconnaissance version was also a very successful aircraft, especially those that were clean jets, lacking any armament, which reduced the weight of the aircraft by over 300 pounds. While fast when armed with cameras, the pilot of the Me 262 did not have the advantages afforded to the Ar 234 pilot, such as forward, downward, or even lateral visibility.

The comparative analysis between the jets is interesting, especially so because all these aircraft could be eventually produced using the same Jumo 004 engine following the reports that the BMW and Heinkel engines were less reliable and had shorter operational longevity. The use of the same engine also simplified and accelerated aircraft production and created a universal system of parts and training for ground crews.

The Jumo engines were in fact much larger and heavier than the other models due to the more solid construction of the internal components, and they were in fact too large for the He 280's airframe design. Udet and even Erhard Milch considered the best way to utilize all of their resources, reduce cost, and meet the anticipated delivery schedules. According to Fritz Wendel: "The He 280 aircraft was slower and generally less fuel-efficient than the Me 262, with a slower roll and climb rate, but a steady bird in flight aircraft nonetheless. It would have been adequate as a level bomber, but in my opinion, not so great as a fighter."[2]

Udet was well aware of the developments within the scientific and aviation communities. He was also one of Messerschmitt's greatest supporters, along with Milch, and this interest on their part was no small contribution when it came to influence within the political minefield that was the RLM. With all the technical data, flight reports and suggestions in hand, Heinkel was ordered to abandon the He 280 fighter project and focus their attention solely upon bomber development and construction. Messerschmitt had won the fighter war, and history was made.

Generalmajor Dietrich Pelz, a bomber pilot and holder of the Knight's Cross with Oak Leaves and Swords, was also well informed of these developments, but only after the decision had been made. He provided his comments: "The Heinkel 280 had great promise. It would have still been superior to anything the Allies had, although in the end pragmatism had won the day. I think it was the correct decision, as future jet bomber development was taken over by Arado, and that proved successful."[3]

The Me 262 V3 third prototype airframe design, with the production code PC+UC, became the first fully powered jet when flown on July 18, 1942, in Leipheim near Günzburg, Germany, piloted again by Fritz Wendel. The rear tail wheel configuration created a conventional tail-down static and takeoff profile on the ground, which caused the jet exhaust to deflect off the runway, with the turbulence created disturbing the air flow for the elevators, thus creating turbulence on takeoff. According to Wendel: "It was something of a wild ride."[4]

Wendel aborted the first takeoff attempt due to the great shaking he experienced, but on the second attempt, he managed to solve the problem by tapping the aircraft's brakes at takeoff speed, lifting the horizontal stabilizer above the airflow and reducing the turbulence upon the wings and running surfaces. As Wendel stated:

"Once I was able to adjust the sway and trim, compensating for the lack of balance in the tail section, it was a smooth flight. However, I could see that there had to be some changes made, and I wrote my report and recommendations. Karl Baur also had the same issues, as he was also one of the test pilots. Between the two of us, there could be no doubt that the modifications would be made, and I looked forward to flying the aircraft again when this was done."[5]

The first four prototypes of the Me 262 V1-V4 were built with this "tail-dragging" configuration. Willi Messerschmitt then decided (at Wendel's insistence) that a fixed nose wheel should replace the tail wheel. This was completed with the fifth prototype, or the V5. Although this gear was a fixed configuration, the retractable tricycle landing gear was mounted on the "V6" with the code VI+AA. As noted by Hugh Morgan, Voigt addressed the landing gear issue pragmatically:

"At the expense of a fairly long intake duct, we reduced the fuselage cross-section and total wetted area to a minimum. The fuselage, which translated to a small cross-section tail-boom aft and above the engine, and which permitted the use of an extremely short efflux duct, was contoured to cockpit, powerplant, armament, and equipment, like a close-fitting glove, but the undercarriage was a nightmare. Its attachment to the fuselage, and the accommodation that it demanded, interfered seriously with both engine installation and the fuselage/wing structure, while the tail wheel was obviously slap in the way of the engine exhaust during takeoff and landing."[6]

Despite the great concepts that the Messerschmitt company had placed into the design, the fight for contract supremacy was not over. Heinkel had also submitted the design for the He 280, a revolutionary design that was the first production aircraft to have a reliable, working compressed-air ejection seat with a pressurized cockpit. In addition, when the first Me 262 airframe was flown, it did so with a conventional piston engine, while the He 280 also flew, but with von Ohain's early version of the BMW, reaching 485 miles per hour.[7]

The Me 262 airframe, which was almost twice the size and weight of the Me 109, actually flew faster than the lighter fighter when the first powered flight was undertaken using the Junkers Jumo 210G, a twelve-cylinder, liquid-cooled piston engine. The aerodynamic design and reduced coefficient drag allowed the designers to anticipate the much faster speeds, given that the test engine only developed 750 horsepower.[8]

In comparison to the early tail-dragger design of the Me 262, the He 280 used a nose wheel landing gear configuration, which was a major problem solver where the jet engine method was concerned. This factor, in conjunction with Wendel's report (along with other pilots) and Voigt's observations, brought about the change in the Me 262.

The landing gear was an easy design change, as the four heavy 30mm cannons in the nose allowed for the weight to be properly distributed to support the tricycle landing gear posture. The retractable landing gear was to be built into a triangular cross-section design into the fuselage, which when viewed from the front resembled an actual "triangle" design. The added benefit was the reduction of aerodynamic drag in flight, while the approved wing sweep further increased the performance characteristics, the marriage of the wing and fuselage adapted well to a perfect left and right wing wheelwell retraction system. This design method was then used on all succeeding production aircraft, and this final version was also flown by Wendel. Following this flight and other subsequent recommendations, this was the last of the major changes that were made. In essence, the final product was born.[9] Wendel stated his pleasure at the final product:

"Once I flew the finished design, it was really perfection in flight. It took some time to start and get the aircraft up to speed, but the visibility was perfect, the stability was really good, and once takeoff speed was reached, just a gentle pulling back on the stick allowed for a smooth takeoff. Once the electric powered landing gear bumped into the wells, the speed picked up quickly, since the drag was reduced. Yes, it was a dream to fly. I wish I could have bought one for myself."[10]

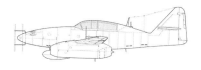

CHAPTER 6

The Stormbird Takes Wing

*Flying the jet in combat was much less draining
than the logistics in keeping them operational.*

Johannes Steinhoff

Mass production was seriously affected by Allied air attacks
upon the Messerschmitt Regensburg factory, which was building the
airframes and electrical components. Aircraft industries were a high-
priority target, along with U-boat shipyards and petroleum facilities,
following the Casablanca Conference and the subsequent directive of
1943. Engine deliveries finally began in earnest in June 1944, permitting
the steady deliveries of the Me 262A, as the *Luftwaffe* had accepted
513 by the end of the year. By war's end, 1,433 had been delivered as
completed operational units.[1]

However, less than 40 percent of the planned numbers were
available by the start of 1944 due to transport and materiel problems.
The production Me 262 that finally saw assignments to combat units
in June 1944 was equipped with the later 004B engine, with a total
of 7,916 Jumo 004B engines having been built by Junkers alone. The
004C engine was designed as a replacement, although none were built
since the war ended before this powerplant could be introduced. Hitler
received all the reports, and he was apparently impressed. However,
obtaining the required materials and having the fuel to train replacement pilots properly were still major issues, as stated by Galland:

"One of Speer's best arguments was the dire need for copper,
manganese, aluminum, cobalt, iron ore, among other metals for war
materiel. This was especially needed for aircraft and anything with
engine generators. I explained to Hitler that if we sent these new
fighters with young pilots against the Americans we would lose them

rapidly. I also explained that each American bomber shot down cost us at least one fighter, and half the time the pilot was lost as well."[2]

Speer was to be the secret behind the "quiet" production of Me 262s as fighters, and he worked closely with Willi Messerschmitt to see that these were completed. Hitler wanted regular reports on all production figures, including aircraft and engines as well as costs. Perhaps Speer's greatest ally was his direct subordinate, Karl Otto Saur, who handled all of the necessary number-crunching minutia that Hitler always longed for, or basically "cooking the books" for the *Führer*, as cited by Morgan, relating Göring's information during his postwar interrogation:

"He [Saur] was Speer's man, but practically he was responsible to the *Führer* and had a lot of influence with him. I never had the slightest influence on these matters. The *Führer* had appointed him personally. Saur was completely sold on figures, and lived only for his numbers, numbers, numbers."[3]

The compressor issue for the Jumo engine—which had proved to be the first great challenge as later stalls were common and dangerous while in takeoff or landing mode—was resolved, while blade fractures that were common after only a few hours of operation were also corrected. AVA Göttingen built the prototypes of these early compressors and the turbine blades were developed by AEG GmbH. Eighty of the experimental Jumo 004A engines (V-series) were built, with the first controlled static test run of the Jumo engine conducted on October 11, 1940.

By 1943, the problems with Junkers Jumo 004 jet engines still remained. Despite being the most reliable engines made in Germany during the war, they would not be produced in any quantity until the spring of 1944. This lack of engine building had slowed production of the aircraft considerably, as airframes sat waiting for powerplants, primarily due to the inability to achieve certain limited availability metals required for engine construction, such as cobalt, nickel, chromium, bauxite, and aluminum. Another reason was the continuous night and day Allied bombing campaign, which damaged or destroyed subsidiary manufacturing companies supplying everything from electrical wiring to rubber for gaskets and tires.

The other issue raised by field commanders was the need for the jet to be easily serviced in the field, thereby reducing turnaround time for repairs and engine changes. Changing a Jumo 004 engine should have required three hours under ideal conditions, but this sometimes took three times as long due to poorly made parts that were not always interchangeable, the inadequate training of ground crews, or weather conditions, unless in a sheltered environment.

Another problem was the availability of all the necessary components, including ammunition, wiring, and instruments for replacement. For example, *Major* Walter Nowotny, who was in command of his *Kommando Nowotny*, even mentioned this problem to Galland, and the General of the Fighters decided to create a special school for the mechanics at Achmer.[4]

Nowotny's problems were actually nightmares with which he had no familiarity. He was a very successful fighter with 255 confirmed and 32 unconfirmed kills on the Eastern Front before his appointment by Galland; he had been a very effective section and even a very competent squadron leader with JG-54 under his commanding officer, *Oberst* (later *Generalmajor*) Hannes Trautloft. However, he had never been in the position of handling acquisitions, maintenance reports, and other such encumbrances, such things that were the nuts-and-bolts headaches of commanding a large unit as a *geschwader*. On top of this new assignment, he was also dealing with a brand-new and relatively unproven weapon system, where research and development was effectively completed as trial by combat.[5]

In a report he filed to Galland, Nowotny outlined his deficiencies and his inability to overcome so many issues. He was not always able to coordinate fuel deliveries and replacement parts, mainly due to the effective Allied interdiction of rail lines and roads. Transportation sometimes ground to a halt. Factories making the various components were bombed and in some cases suffered internal sabotage.

Nowotny described the shortages he experienced toward the end of the war: "In these final weeks of the war our supply system had, to all intents and purposes, collapsed. As we were receiving hardly any replacement parts for our jet fighters, the mechanics cannibalized damaged machines for usable spare parts in order to keep the others flying. Due to engine damage to his Me 262, one of my pilots had been sitting on the ground for three days."[6]

Nowotny had also loudly complained about the lack of qualified mechanics to service the jets. It was estimated that three qualified mechanics—one main engine technician, one avionics specialist, and one hydraulics and airframe inspector—be assigned to each aircraft. Most jet units were lucky if they had three such men to service twenty or more aircraft, and the fledgling *Kommando Nowotny* was no exception. Armorers were usually not in such high demand. One of the facts often left out of the history of the jet units was that unlike the conventional German units (and the Allied units for that matter), Me 262 pilots often had to work as mechanics on their own aircraft when shorthanded.

Walter Nowotny's older brother, infantry officer *Oberleutnant* Rudolf Nowotny, stated that his brother complained about the conditions, but that he was still quite excited about his new command: "Walter was absolutely overjoyed at the prospect of commanding the jet unit. He had been in command of a fighter-training unit in France, and he absolutely hated it. He felt as if it was a form of punishment, but we all knew that it had been a quiet word from Hitler or Göring that had put him there. They had a way of taking the Diamond holders out of combat, hoping to keep them alive as national heroes to maintain morale for the war effort.

"I know that Walter was excited; he called me once when I was on leave at our parent's home. He finally managed to get away and I was able to see him for the first time in two years. The last time I saw him he looked haggard, drained, completely exhausted. I thought he was on the verge of a breakdown, to be honest. He had flown repeated missions without a break for a year. Now, this time he looked like the old Walter of his youth. This was the last time I would see and speak with him. He told me of the problems with operations and not having everything he needed. He felt like a beggar at a poor man's banquet; there was just not enough materiel to go around. But, I told him, knowing him as I did, that he would find a way to make things work."[7] (Rudolf was captured by the Soviets at the end of the war and survived the gulags in Siberia.)

Georg-Peter Eder related his experience in the unit and compared his experience in his conventional fighter wings: "It is true that we often had to do a lot of work on our fighters. Most of us were not trained in these matters. I was no engineer or mechanic, but I did learn a lot by working with my mechanics on Me 109s and Fw 190s. However, none of us knew anything about the Jumo engines. We had technical manuals that might as well have been written in Sanskrit for all the good it did us, or at least me. I was a pilot, not an aeronautical engineer"[8]

Knight's Cross with Oak Leaves recipient Walter Krupinski, who scored 196 victories, with two kills in the jet, experienced this shortage while assigned to *Jagdverband* (JV-44) under Galland's command: "Our problem was that not all the jets were ready for flights. We were short on parts, fuel, even ammunition, or sometimes small technical problems happened. I flew one 262 that did not have a working fuel gauge or altimeter. Another one I flew actually had the complete instrument panel, but none of the wires were hooked up! One of our mechanics was also an electrician, and he managed to get a wiring diagram for the jet and repaired it."[9]

With the airfields always under threat, and the limited availability of jets in general, having idle machines was unacceptable. Yet, despite these issues, field maintenance was still faster than working on an Me 109 or Fw 190 in the field. *Luftwaffe* ace and Knight's Cross with Oak Leaves holder Georg-Peter Eder, who assumed command of the unit on the day of Nowotny's death, had this to say about maintenance:

"The engines were very easily removed and replaced, with only a few long bolts mounting them to the aircraft wings, but only if you had the parts. Once the cowls were opened, the engines could be dropped onto a carriage, a new engine mounted, and the old one taken in for maintenance. I once clocked the men, and it required only four men, and they dismounted both engines, and replaced them in less than two hours. Repairs took longer, but as long as we had replacement [engines] this was not a great problem for us. We were able to maintain operational status much more easily than with 109s and 190s. This made a great difference."[10]

Major Wolfgang Schenck, whose *Kommando Schenck* used the Me 262 as bombers, was not immune to the difficulties of procuring all the required materiel for operational sustenance: "It was a problem to be sure, not having engine parts, for example. It was much easier to just replace an engine than to repair one, but once the bad engine was off, then the mechanics would have to go to work. We even had a master machinist working in his own building trying to make metal parts for anything we needed, but were having a hard time receiving.

"We were even able to get replacement fan blades made—of inferior quality to be sure, but they gave us an additional few hours of flying time until we managed to get the actual quality replacement parts. The bad part about this was that when we inspected the fan blades for cracks and replaced them, if we replaced them in time, it was fine. However, if a crack went unnoticed, the cracked blade would often snap and tumble around, destroying the engine, causing a fire more often than not. It was a dice game. We also patched up our birds when they took hits, and we repaired quite a few nose gears. We played with what we had."[11]

The other factor that played into the favor of the jet's supporters was the issue of fuel. The piston-powered fighters required high-octane aviation fuel and oil as engine lubricant, with both of those commodities becoming difficult to obtain by 1944. However, the Jumo engines burned a much simpler, cheaper, and available fuel source, since the jet fuel being requisitioned was a kerosene-based product. Not only was it cheaper and easier to produce, it was less volatile and flammable than high octane, and it was also readily available in large amounts.

Starr Smith in the book *Jimmy Stewart: Bomber Pilot* recounts Göring's comments to his interrogators regarding the Me 262 and the fuel issue: "If I had to design the *Luftwaffe* again, the first plane I would develop would be the jet fighter, then the jet bomber. The jet fighter takes too much."[12] Every German jet pilot interviewed with regard to this project experienced such shortages on a regular basis.

By the time the Me 262 was in steady production, there would be three main operational variants and one training version. The A1-a (*Schwalbe*) fighter, the A-2 (*Sturmvogel*) fighter, and the B-1a (*Jabo*). The later two-seat night fighter version was built but in far fewer numbers. All of these day fighter and fighter-bomber variants were single-seat aircraft powered by the two Junkers Jumo 004B turbojets developing 900 kilograms (1,980 pounds) of thrust each. The maximum speeds were the following: Me 262A-1a, 540 miles per hour (870 kilometers per hour); Me 262A-2a, 470 miles per hour (755 kilometers per hour); Me 262B-1a, 497 miles per hour (800 kilometers per hour).

When not encumbered with additional external ordinance, such as bombs or rockets, the Me 262 could climb at 1,200 meters per minute (or 3,700 feet per minute) to a ceiling of approximately 11,500 meters, or almost 38,000 feet. The operational range at cruising speed on internal fuel was 1,050 kilometers (650 miles), and this was greatly reduced in combat. The fighter variants were finally armed with four 30mm Rheinmetall-Borsig cannons in the nose, with the bottom two carrying one hundred rounds each and the top two carrying eighty rounds each.

It was decided that the high-explosive contact ammunition that had proven so effective with the night fighters was to be used, with every fifth round being a tracer that allowed the pilot to adjust his fire. This would prove critical when attacking aircraft at the higher speeds, where the Me 262 pilot had perhaps two to three seconds to acquire, lead, and fire for effect, as stated by Georg-Peter Eder:

"When attacking the heavy bombers, using adjustment in the firing pattern was much less an issue than when attacking a faster moving enemy fighter. We were able to attack from the six o'clock position, even attacking in a shallow climb to attack them from below, which was impossible on the 109 or 190. Our rapid closure rate in the 262 reduced the time the enemy gunners could lock onto us. We had no speed brakes, none at all, and if we did then we would have lost our speed advantage, and then we would have had to throttle back up, and this meant risking an engine flame out."[13]

Galland also commented on the speed brake issue: "It is often reported that our jets suffered due to a lack of speed brakes. Of this requirement, I cannot agree. On the contrary. I'd have done everything to not develop engine stall, because if we had not flown at one hundred fifty knots higher speed than any Allied aircraft, then we would have lost our advantage. To re-accelerate the Me 262 after having slowed down took a long, long time because of the relatively low thrust. So, if we had speed brakes, and our pilots when attacking bombers had used them in order to reduce the speed, they would have lost all their superiority."[14]

Steinhoff gave his opinion as well: "I can tell you, from my limited experience, that if we had speed breaks, I would have only used them in an emergency landing if necessary. If I had a gaggle of Mustangs on me and I needed to get down quickly, I could see them being useful and then deploying full flaps and gear down. However, if you had to get down quickly, most pilots said to hell with the landing gear, which took almost a full minute to deploy and sometimes longer to retract. They just slid the jet in on the engines so they could jump out before the damned thing was strafed. No, speed brakes in combat for the Me 262 would not have been a good idea, unlike the piston fighters; but then again, in those, you could just chop the power and you lost airspeed rapidly anyway."[15]

Wolfgang Späte had his own comments on the lack of air brakes: "I once went into an attack, and I was closing fast, but I had hit a Liberator, but could not confirm the kill. However, I came back around, and to another, but the bombers had turned, and I was headed right at them head on. I had been in a shallow dive, but the aircraft began to shudder as I hit above the maximum airspeed indicator, so I pulled the nose up to bleed of speed. I was just then thinking that speed brakes would have been a good idea, but then thought twice, knowing that at that speed I would have ripped a wing off."[16]

The necessity of having full speed to attack heavy bomber formations was well known to those *Luftwaffe experten* who had mastered the techniques in piston-powered fighters. According to Georg-Peter Eder: "The way to attack the bombers, whether you were in a head-on attack, flank or rear attack, the principal was the same. You had to come in fast, hit it accurately with everything you had, and then get away quickly. Even if the bombers did not have fighter escorts, the defensive fire could kill you, or force you down.

"When I was with *Kommando Nowotny*, I once climbed into a B-17 formation at full throttle, led the bomber slightly and fired a short burst. The rounds exploded in the left wing and bomb bay, as this was before they had dropped their payloads. I saw a quick flash of fire, and then, when I was still more than five hundred meters away when it just exploded. I hit the left rudder hard as hell, pulled up vertical and then rolled away. I could feel the concussion of the blast throw my fighter all the way over. I could see the enemy tracers going past me, as I lost control of the jet for a few seconds, but the sudden attack had caught them by complete surprise. The only damage to my jet was shrapnel from the B-17's fuselage and the fragments of the five-hundred-pound bombs that had detonated."[17]

Eder's comments are not unique. The 30mm cannon was extremely lethal, being capable of cutting any Allied fighter in half with a single 330-gram (11-ounce) explosive round, which had an impact blast radius of almost two feet. They were also capable of carrying twenty-four 55mm R4M rockets, with twelve rockets mounted in racks under each wing. These weapons gave the German pilots the ability to fire into a formation without selecting individual targets, much like firing a shotgun into a flock of geese. However, if they did not fire, the excess drag made the jet quite vulnerable to enemy fighters. Regarding this fact, Johannes Steinhoff's comments are noteworthy:

"Once we received the R4M rockets, this was an entirely new development. We were able to score more hits on the enemy bombers, and these weapons probably accounted for half the victories I scored in the jet. The one thing we all agreed upon was that we wanted to fire those rockets as soon as possible, since they increased drag and reduced our airspeed. This was a real problem if you found yourself in a fight with enemy fighters. Sometimes they would not fire at all, and I often bruised my fist pounding the dashboard in absolute frustration.

"I remember one mission we flew into a large formation of B-17 bombers; we were mixed up with some JG-7 aircraft. During this time Theo Weissenberger and perhaps Buchner, or another pilot, I think, were in the area at that time. I was on [Leutnant Gottfried] Fährmann's right wing, [Oberstleutnant Heinrich] Bär was on mine. We reached altitude, and were perhaps three thousand meters above the bombers when we gained visual contact. We all rolled over on my command, and I led the way. Fährmann fired his rockets, and they spread out and he hit four bombers, I think, but no kills. Galland had one, and the Rammer also hit one, but I do not know if it went down. Krupinski also hit a bomber, but again, I do not know if it was a kill shot.

"Bär also fired his rockets, and a blinding flash prevented me from seeing anything, but I fried my rockets anyway. I was unable to see anything until I was in the middle of this American hornet's nest. I flew through this debris, and felt dozens of bullets and shrapnel striking my aircraft. I think that I must have ingested some debris into my right engine, or enemy bullets had killed it, as it flamed out and I was losing airspeed. I then took a quick look around and saw Bär pulling way up followed by three others. I was the only guy unable to climb, so I decided to break off and head back home. I made it back with a smoking jet and wrote my after action report.

"When I fired I had downed one and damaged another. Usually, by the time the rockets impacted, we were already pulling away to avoid a collision. The rockets gave us that extra reach and increased our margin of safety. This was when we would bank around and then come back in for a stern attack, which was the best for most pilots. It also reduced the bomber's defensive fire. However, the flank attack, hitting them from the left or right, allowed for a larger target selection and sight picture, but it also exposed you to the greatest defensive fire. Yes, I would say the rear attack at high speed was the best. Having the rockets also increased our killing ability."[18]

Hermann Buchner also recalled his first experience with the R4M rockets, when he and *Leutnant* Gustav Sturm attacked a B-24 unit: "On the first attack, Sturm shot down one using his R4M rockets. The hits were so good that the Liberator fluttered from the sky."[19] Buchner also had some unflattering things to say about the rockets: "These rockets tended to be affected by wind, so even if you had a good line of sight, the rockets, despite the great range they provided, were not always the most accurate weapons. We still had to get pretty close, and usually firing from distance, we would lead and fire high, so the rockets would land among the bombers. It was random, but it must have really shattered their nerves. That was when we went in with the cannons."[20]

Despite being designed as a fighter, the A-2 could also carry either two 500-pound bombs or a 1,000-pound bomb on the bottom of the fuselage. This payload seriously hindered the flying quality of the jet, which was soon discovered by Allied pilots. As stated in Foreman and Harvey: "Meanwhile, on October 10th [1944], a staff meeting had been held, during which American pilots were called upon to give their conclusions on the initial encounters. They were unanimous that the German aircraft could outclimb both the P-47 and P-51, although the maneuverability was not great. The fighter-bomber versions were easier to engage, since the bomb-load reduced their speed by at least 100 mph (when engaged, however, the bombs were usually jettisoned and the jets escaped). It was concluded that thus far, Me 262s had been brought down by:

    Diving from above
    Fatal tactical errors on the part of German pilots
    When taking off or landing
    Running out of fuel or engine trouble"[21]

Major Wolfgang Späte, a ninety-nine-victory ace and the first commander of JG-400 flying the Me 163B *Komet*, ended the war flying the Me 262; scoring his last five victories in the jet earned the Oak Leaves to the Knights Cross. Späte was very approving of the Me 262, as he wrote in his book *Top Secret Bird: The Luftwaffe's Me-163 Comet* and confirmed during an interview with the author:

"I was transferred under Theo Weissenberger in *Jagdgeschwader* 7 to once again fly the Me 262 . . . After flying several missions from Rusin in the end of April [1945], I developed the definite impression that the Me 262 was just plain invulnerable when attacking American bomber formations if the attack was made directly from the six o'clock at an airspeed of 850 to 900 kilometers per hour.[22] I knew that when I was closing in, as I was one of the last jets to attack, that my arrival was no secret. The tail and waist gunners were waiting for me. My first attack in a 262 was fast, and from the time I saw the formation until I fired my cannons the time was only perhaps ten or eleven seconds. The B-17 sort of crumpled, and fell apart, no fire. It just broke up. I could only think what we could have done with this aircraft in 1942!"[23]

However "invulnerable" in the attack, Späte had previously mentioned the potential for disaster when flying through the debris of a victory, when the compressor could be damaged. In his book, he described how to learn to avoid this hazard: "To have been completely successful on this occasion, I would have had to keep firing for perhaps another two seconds. There were times when an aircraft disintegrated from my first hit while I was still flying in the six o'clock position behind it. If one of my engines caught a little piece of shrapnel from such an explosion, the damage would immediately cause a flameout; then I would be prey for the packs of escort fighters. Therefore, I promptly ceased fire at a very safe minimum distance, just as soon as the pieces started to fly."[24]

Pilots who flew the two-seater night fighter version would also have to worry about the same problems. Generally, the night fighter pilots fired and engaged from much shorter distances, simply due to limited visibility, and the fact that once the radar operator brought the fighter onto the target, the sets were turned off and the pilot completed the target acquisition visually.

The night fighter (B) variants were variously armed with four cannons and two MK 108 20mm cannons inclined to the rear of the cockpit in *Schräge Musik* installation for attacking night bombers, a set of SG 500 *Jagdfaust* with twelve rifled mortar barrels inclined in the nose housing for attacking day bombers (which were not effective, especially since they created considerable drag and instability in the aircraft), or even a

50mm MK 114 gun or forty-eight R4M rockets for attacking bombers. The final dimensions of the Me 262 and its many variants were finally established, and these were to be used as the production models that were expected to begin to be available by 1943.

Another pilot who flew the Me 262 at night had his own opinion on the fighter in that capacity. *Oberst* Hajo Herrmann flew in the Spanish Civil War as a bomber pilot, a role he continued to fulfill throughout World War II until 1943, when he created the *Wilde Sau* (Wild Boar) night fighters, using Fw 190 and Me 109 fighters against the RAF bombers as the cities below were illuminated by the lights below and a glow of the fires created by the bombings.

"I tested out and flew the Me 262 in daytime, and then after a few hours of flight time, I was able to fly the jet at night. This first flight was a single-seat fighter. There were no great problems, and I landed. I was very impressed with the aircraft's performance. I had already created JG-300, and we had proven successful in operating as a night fighter unit using single engine day fighters.

"The next time I flew was in the two-seat night fighter, which was actually a converted trainer. I had a radar operator in the back. Although this was not a combat mission, just night familiarization. Although I loved the jet and saw great promise for it, I felt that it was too easily seen by British gunners, because there was no way you could hide that long bright red and orange flame that trailed behind the fighter. At night, this was like telling the British that you were arriving [and] to be ready."[25]

Likewise, Hitler had no intention of releasing the Me 262 as a night fighter, at least not in large numbers. Even giving them to the fighter arm at all was a difficult maneuver, but there were a few men who decided to do their own examinations and try to select the best new aircraft for their respective spheres of combat. The night fighters were no exception, as stated by former flight instructor–turned–night fighter pilot Jorg Czypionka:

"The famous night fighter Kurt Welter . . . was already two years or so in the *Wilde Sau*, and he was very successful there, and he had even downed some Mosquitoes . . . Kurt talked to some people to get a faster aircraft, and this was the 262 or Arado 234 jet. He told me that he went to Rechlin to try those aircraft out, without any authorization, and he found the Ar 234 unsuitable, because this was a Plexiglas cockpit, and it reflected the searchlights and the lights upon landing.

"He found it irritating. He was perhaps not the most gifted pilot, but he was a good shooter, this is what I think. Then he eventually tried the 262 one night, an armed aircraft, and shot down a couple of

Mosquitoes over Berlin. This had been watched by Göring, who asked him to come to his place the next day, and he was given permission to found a small unit using the 262. This was at the end of 1944."[26]

Night fighter ace *Oberleutnant* Kurt Welter claimed twenty Mosquitoes and two four-engine bombers shot down by night, and another two Mosquitoes by day flying the Me 262. Welter's night kills were achieved in a standard Me 109G, with most of his kills being in the single-seat Me 262 fighter. Even though Welter had tested a prototype Me 262 fitted with FuG 218 *Neptun* radar, he never achieved any kills in that version.

The Me 262 had emerged as a promising weapon. The experts, technicians, and test pilots praised it, and the combat pilots who first pioneered its use also wrote their reports, although most of these came from the bomber units. The fledgling fighter units, beginning with *Kommandos Thierfelder* and later *Nowotny*, were to soon carve their names into history.

Despite the great promise of a new age in technology that allowed Hitler to continue his propaganda crusade, other factors were to interfere with the final production schedule. Hitler, more than others, despite his megalomania and hubris, was truly to become the Me 262's worst enemy, to the frustration of the very men who were being blamed for the bombing of Germany: the fighter pilots.

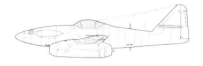

CHAPTER 7

A Questionable
Political Decision

*In 1943 I wondered if Hitler was more concerned
about winning the war than just surviving it.
By 1944 I knew that even Hitler knew
the war was lost.*

Traudl Junge

All of these grand versions of this revolutionary weapon and hopes for a change in Germany's fortunes were still in the future, since the Me 262 project was consistently delayed due to the inability of the *Luftwaffe* and Air Ministry under Erhard Milch to recognize the potential of the jet aircraft. This failure to comprehend the wartime necessity of a supreme potential air superiority weapon when one was so badly needed is incomprehensible, even today, and it was not limited just to Hitler's subjects.

Following his suicide, Udet was succeeded by Erhard Milch, who, despite having an affinity for technology, preferred to concentrate production on existing aircraft of all types, which reduced costs and allowed for the production figures to be uninterrupted—a factor Hitler always examined. In November 1943, *Luftwaffe Oberst* Siegfried Kneymeyer became head of the *Luftwaffe*'s research and development department for technical air armament. He realized that what was necessary was the abandonment of the bomber construction program and the need was to concentrate solely on fighter development; he was especially supportive of the Me 262.

Ironically, Göring even agreed with him, and Milch was brought in to assist with the details. Despite the great developments to date, those who knew nothing of the necessities of the war, such as Martin Bormann, Heinrich Himmler, and Goebbels, persuaded Hitler to maintain the bomber program, as the retaliation raids against Britain were still one of Hitler's top priorities. Göring showed his weakness when he failed to stand against those within the inner circle and defend the fighter project. This silence must have been perceived as tacit acceptance, and therefore Hitler believed that his chief lieutenants were in agreement with him.

However, despite these events unfolding behind the scenes, *Generalleutnant* Adolf Galland, then the young and enigmatic General of the Fighters, was convinced of the need for the aircraft following his test flight. In his own words (which are perhaps some of the most famous in aviation history) he stated:

"On May 22, 1943, before my first flight in the Me 262, I was in Lechfeld for a preview of the jet, which was fantastic, a totally new development. This was 1943, and I was there with Professor Willi Messerschmitt, [*Generalfeldmarschall* Erhard] Milch, Hitler, and other engineers responsible for the development. I spoke with Fritz Wendel and Horst Geyer, and after my first flight I discussed my opinion of the jet, which at that time was a tail-dragging model, in my book *The First and the Last*, and this has become a very well-known story. I knew that this aircraft was not just our last hope in the air war. I could see the future of aviation for the next century right in front of me. I had felt its power, and it was quite intoxicating.

"The fighter was almost ready for mass production even at that time, and Hitler wanted to see a demonstration. Later, in November when the 262 was brought out for his viewing at Insterburg, I was standing there next to Hitler, who was very impressed despite the first fighter having engine flameout on takeoff. The second jet lifted off and performed marvelously. Hitler asked the professor: 'Is this aircraft able to carry bombs?'

"Well, Messerschmitt said: 'Yes, my *Führer*, it can carry for sure a two-hundred-fifty-kilogram bomb, perhaps two of them.' In typical Hitler fashion, he said: 'Well, nobody thought of this! This is the *Blitz* [lightning] bomber I have been requesting for years. No one thought of this. I order that this 262 be used exclusively as a *Blitz* bomber, and you, Messerschmitt, have to make all the necessary preparations to make this feasible.' I felt my heart sink at that moment. "[1]

One of the men also present during this test exhibition flight was *Generalleutnant* Hans Baur, a World War I fighter ace with nine victories, world-record long-distance flying record holder for *Lufthansa* between the wars, and Hitler's chief personal pilot. Baur remembered well Hitler's fascination with new weapons, especially jet and rocket aircraft:

"Hitler was always excited about new things, like a child at Christmas, you could say. If there were any new ideas in tank, U-boat, or aircraft designs, he wanted to see all the blueprints and have them explained to him. His memory was photographic, and he forgot nothing. I remember we were having lunch in Berchtesgaden in March or so, this was 1943. Hitler was discussing this Messerschmitt project with Göring, and Speer, Himmler, and Bormann were there also.

"Hitler asked Göring what he thought about this expenditure in developing the jet. Göring, to his credit, supported the idea and even mentioned the names of a few of our greatest pilots who should oversee the testing and flying. Hitler listened with great interest. Then Speer spoke up, and he mentioned the ongoing issues with the necessary raw materials needed. Then after about ten minutes, Hitler told Speer to wait another day for a letter to be typed and signed by him, giving the authority to obtain whatever he needed to expedite the acquisition of these items. Speer agreed.

"I then remembered that the next day Hitler called his secretary, *Fraulein* Junge, into his study, where he composed the letter. I know because I was discussing the flight plan with him for us to go to the Ukraine for a visit. Later Speer came by, picked it up and gave the party salute and left. The funny thing was that later that day some *gauleiter* from somewhere had called, demanding to speak with the *Führer*. Well, Bormann took the call, and I remember him telling the man on the other end of the line to just 'shut his mouth and give *Herr* Professor Speer whatever the hell he wanted,' and his life would be much easier. 'Bothering the *Führer* with this complaint would not be advised.' And then he hung up the phone.

"Apparently, Speer had gone to some mine or quarry that was providing something he needed for the jet program, and the appointed SS official, I would assume of substantial rank, wanted to complain about it. Speer later told me the man went white when he showed him the letter, on Hitler's letterhead, and signed by him, giving him complete authority. The SS man thought it was a forgery, prompting the phone call that Bormann received. I think that after that event, Speer could have handed a roll of toilet paper with Hitler's name written on it and secured anything he wanted."[2]

The contents of the letter were a mystery until 1998, when Traudl Junge remembered the event in question. She had typed hundreds of official letters for Hitler, and yet this one she remembered, because it was one of the few letters Hitler ever signed giving a person complete authority to invoke his name for a specific purpose. Traudl Junge explained:

"Hitler had called me to come upstairs, and I did. He said to me: 'I have two letters for you to have ready for my signature.' The first was a memorandum to an army group commander in Russia; I do not remember the details. However, I do remember the letter for Speer, because I did so few like this. In fact, I think I wrote only two for Speer like this during the entire time, with the last being in 1945, when Hitler gave the destruction order.

"In this letter, he clearly stated that *Reichsminister* Speer had, by his personal directive, the authority to secure or obtain whatever he needed in order to work on a very secret program. There would be no questioning this authority. Well, then I heard that Bormann had taken a call from someone questioning the letter. I also heard that the caller, whoever he was, was removed from his position not long afterwards."[3]

Hitler's response regarding creating bombers out of the Me 262 program should have been no great surprise. Even before this event in May 1943, Adolf Hitler had envisioned the Me 262 as a very fast offensive ground-attack tactical bomber rather than a defensive interceptor. With the ability to fly through Allied fighters and attack, it could then escape due to its high rate of speed. The aircraft was planned to be used for just that role to penetrate Allied air superiority and attack rear areas during the expected invasion of France. Galland commented on this development:

"This was really the beginning of the misuse of the 262, as five bomber wings were supposed to be equipped with the jet, with Wolfgang Schenck and Werner Baumbach being given the order to oversee this activity. In June 1944, KG-51 was converted to Me 262 training as a jet bomber unit. These bomber pilots had no fighter experience, such as combat flying or shooting, which is why so many of them were shot down. They could only escape by outrunning the fighters in pursuit. This was the greatest mistake surrounding the 262, in my opinion, and I believe the 262 could have been made operational as a fighter at least a year and a half earlier, and built in large enough numbers so that it could have changed the air war."[4]

Regarding Hitler's reflex decision that originally resulted in the concentration upon the bomber variant of the jet, Galland balked and even Speer was concerned. In his memoirs, *Inside the Third Reich*, Minister of Armaments and War Production Albert Speer claimed that Hitler originally blocked mass production of the Me 262 before agreeing to production in early 1944.

Hitler rejected arguments from the fighter leaders, even Galland, that the plane would be more effective as a fighter against Allied bombers then destroying large parts of Germany. He wanted it as a bomber for revenge attacks against the Allies. This is in itself an incredible indictment by Speer, as it was in fact *Reichsmarschall* Hermann Göring (and even Hitler himself) who had been demanding a more visible and effective fighter response to the Allied bombers, pounding Germany night and day.

According to Speer, Hitler believed that the Me 262's superior speed made it perfect for high-altitude straight flying, thereby evading Allied interception. A few historians disagree with this assessment, but Speer is also supported by the German aces who were in their *Führer's* presence. Galland stated:

"Hitler became enraged when he was told by Speer and others that there were continued delays in the delivery of the Me 262 'bombers' he wanted, believing (and not too incorrectly) that Messerschmitt and Speer were delaying to have an excuse to build fighters and not bombers. This was partially true, yet the main reason was the constant air bombardments that destroyed production centers, killed or injured workers, and ruined the railway transportation network. We needed the fighters, and Hitler wanted his bombers. In late August 1943, I spoke with Speer, Dietrich Pelz, and Werner Baumbach about this.

"We knew that there were other jet aircraft being developed. Later, Pelz became the General of the Bombers, and he wanted jets for his arm. After our discussion, it was decided that if Arado could deliver their bombers, he [Pelz] would ease up on wanting the Me 262 as a bomber. We spoke with Speer, who agreed to intervene, and then we shook hands on it. Now, Speer had two jobs; getting Messerschmitt what they needed, and pushing the other bomber into production, so I had the Me 262 for the fighters.

"Ironically, just a few days before our meeting, the Americans had not very successfully bombed Ploesti, the British had bombed Hamburg to terrible effect, and also *Peenemünde*, where our top secret V weapons were being built, killing some top scientists. It was due to these events that Pelz saw the need for more fighters, and he helped me. Later, Hitler agreed to release one Me 262 to us for every other jet bomber delivered."[5]

Because Germany was being bombed intensively, production of the Me 262 was dispersed into hundreds of low-profile small production facilities, sometimes little more than clearings in the forests of Germany proper and in occupied nations. At B8 Bergkristall-Esche II at St. Georgen/Gusen, Austria, Ukrainian and Jewish forced laborers of Concentration

Camp Gusen II produced complete fuselages at a rate of almost 450 units per month on the assembly lines from January to April 1945. Wings for the Me 262 were produced in a well-concealed and covered motorway tunnel at Engelberg, just west of Stuttgart.[6] However, these numbers alone were not enough to replace projected losses, as Galland stated:

"This was discussed in the meeting in August 1944 where Milch decided that Speer's production program should produce four thousand fighters per month. I agreed, but I suggested that one thousand should be jets. Milch was unimpressed with my suggestion, telling me that Hitler did not think we needed the 262 at that time. I was stunned. I could not believe Hitler would throw away the one potential advantage of regaining air superiority, after years of his complaining about the Allied bombing raids.

"I had a talk with Speer behind Milch's back, and he promised me that he would speak with Professor Messerschmitt about getting us some pure jet fighters, while still making a few bomber versions for Hitler. Speer knew the situation. He also knew that the Arado and Heinkel companies were building jets as potential bombers, and this gave me hope."[7]

Under Speer's direct guidance, and being armed with the written word of Hitler behind him, he was able to construct large, heavily protected underground factories to take up production of the Me 262, similar to the facilities building the V-2 rockets, making them relatively safe from bomb attacks, but the war ended before they could be completed. Speer also managed to support Heinkel and Arado with their jet bomber productions, thus releasing the Me 262s for fighter service. However, Allied intelligence was aware of these facilities.

The previous information passed to the British in Bern in July 1943 was supplemented by more critically valuable intelligence over the next year. The Enigma intercepts also clearly told the British that the *Luftwaffe* had been selecting the best-qualified pilots for the jet programs, including all of the information on the creation, staffing, and location of *Kommando Thierfelder* at Lechfeld.

The information regarding the location and exact purpose of the Augsburg factory was smuggled out by French conscripted workers. One French laborer, Lucien Pericaud, had managed to smuggle out the technical data on the jets flown, weight, and power displacement information along with schematics. He was arrested and sent to a concentration camp, probably Dachau, and his fate is, as of yet, undetermined.

In fact, what the British had learned later in the spring and summer of 1944 alarmed them to the point that Air Ministry ordered

120 Gloster Meteors to be delivered as soon as possible. This was an impossible order to fulfill for several reasons, not the least of which was the incomplete assembly of a functional Whittle engine, as stated by Group Captain John Cunningham:

"I had been a test pilot, fighter pilot, and night fighter pilot, and I was very much in the information circles regarding the Meteor. I knew that there would be no possible way that the RAF could field even a dozen operational jets by the end of 1944, let alone an air fleet capable of combating the German jet threat. It was not going to happen."[8]

Like the U-boat pens on the French coast, they were well known, but sometimes hard to hit. Through the end of February to the end of March 1945, approximately sixty Me 262s were destroyed in attacks on the Obertraubling assembly plant, and another thirty jets were damaged at the Leipheim facility, when the Neuberg plant was bombed on March 19, 1945. It should be mentioned that by creating these ad-hoc factories, Speer helped integrate the hundreds of small components and fabrication points into a cohesive assembly and production program.

One of the great tragedies of the modern jet miracle was the fact that hundreds of these workers were forced slave laborers, many from the Ukraine, who were worked to death or killed in the bombings. Yet, by any means, and with Pelz keeping his word, the *Luftwaffe* fighter units began receiving their jets. According to Pelz:

"Once we had several dozen of the Me 262s arriving to KG-54, KG-51, and KG-76, I was informed that the Arado models were coming and already assembled. I had the meeting with Galland and Speer where we agreed to support each other. Besides, erring on the side of pragmatism, the Ar 234 was actually better suited as a bomber for many reasons. It was fast, used the same engines, but was a lighter aircraft and suited for level bombing, which was better than dive-bombing at very high speeds. I received a call from Göring, and he asked me about this. I told him that, as Inspector of Bombers, as long as I had jets, I would use whatever was capable of getting the job done. Hitler finally decided to release the 262s that were still being built to the fighters. All the Ar 234s were to go to my units, and everyone was happy."[9]

British intelligence from the Enigma machines also brought more unwelcomed information in early 1944; data that was corroborated in intercepts deciphered codes that confirmed their worst suspicions a few months later. RAF Bomber Command had already endured almost five years of German radar–controlled and day fighter–operated night fighters, which had cost them nearly 50,000 aircrew killed, captured, or missing. The newest intelligence informed Sir Arthur Harris,

Commander in Chief of Bomber Command, that the new jets were being prepared as night fighters. This information was not openly disseminated throughout Bomber Command due to the fear that it may have affected morale.

The first bomber units were formed in September 1944, at the same time that *Kommando Nowotny* was being created from the remnants of *Kommando Thierfelder*, and per Hitler's order, the first twelve Me 262s with bomb racks were delivered. The first bomber units created were *Kampfgeschwader* (KG-51, transitioning from conventional aircraft), also known as *Kommando Schenck*, commanded by *Major* (later *Oberstleutnant*) Wolfgang "Bombo" Schenck, who wore the Knight's Cross with Oak Leaves and was a well-known and very effective bomber and ground attack pilot. *Kommando Edelweiss* was also created as well as a bomber-training unit designated IV/(*Erg*)/ KG-51, also under Schenck, as he explained:

"In June 1944, I was given responsibility for developing the Me 262 as a fighter-bomber, and so I headed up the unit which became known as *Kommando Schenck*. I soon found myself a *major* at age thirty-one, appointed by Pelz as the *Geschwaderkommodore* of KG-51, which was converting to the Me 262. I maintained this position until I was promoted to *oberstleutnant*, and on the day after I turned thirty-two years of age I became the final Inspector for Jet Fighters from February 1945 up to the end of the war.

"I must say that the controversy over the Me 262 as a fighter or a bomber was far above my level. I was not really involved at all, as all of this occurred in 1943 until early 1944. I was still flying Fw 190F models in a ground attack unit on the Russian Front, where I was wounded again, and then given the new assignment. I will say that I was very much looking forward to flying the jet, as it was perhaps the worst-kept secret in the *Luftwaffe*.

"I was in the meeting with Galland, Pelz, Baumbach, Trautloft, and a few others—even Hajo Herrmann was there, and this was in October 1944. We were discussing the jets, the allocations of replacement parts, supplies, fuel, ammunition, everything, since there were limited supplies to go around. Galland wanted his fighters using the jet to receive priority, given that they were flying against the bomber formations. I understood this, and I even supported his conclusions.

"However, Baumbach was adamant that we needed the 262 as a bomber, since the Soviets were rolling west faster than we could field replacement units. The bomber argument was that we needed to hit the enemy at their supply depots and troop concentrations. Given the coming of the Arado jet bombers for our purposes, this argument did not go much further, but this is an example of how we could not really agree on anything, even as we were losing the war. What I found interesting was the fact that Göring appeared to be playing both sides, fighters against bombers, never really taking a position one way or the other."[10]

Adolf Galland recalled Göring's reaction and his initial position on the jet, a position that would waver with the prevailing winds: "However, as the world knows, Hitler had other ideas. Göring knew the reality, and he was very excited by the 262 and told me personally that he would see to it we received the new fighter. He read the reports on how and why it was a better fighter. It was not just the faster speed and heavier armament, it was also able to operate on much cheaper and readily available fuel and did not require the high-octane fuel that the conventional fighters did. Speer also mentioned that in order to appease Hitler, he would increase construction on the Arado and Heinkel jet models as bombers, allowing us to have the 262 as a fighter.

"Speer and I again met with Hitler, and Speer tried to get him to rescind the order to have the two thousand new fighters just built sent to the Western Front. I agreed, and I explained to Hitler that, given the tactical situation, lack of fuel, few highly qualified and experienced pilots, that the best we could do would be to use these aircraft as a protective force at our critical industries, especially the petroleum and aircraft locations. Speer even gave him the data, which normally Hitler would examine in great detail.

"Speer and I did our best to persuade him. It was like talking to a deaf man. I explained the situation to Hitler, and also gave him proven statistics, but he went mad. He then stated that he would order the halt to all fighter aircraft production, the fighter arm was to be disbanded, and those industries were to be then focused upon building flak guns. He firmly believed that flak guns alone would keep Germany safe. I could not believe it."[11]

Another great problem plaguing the Me 262 production and development as a designated fighter aircraft was the incomprehensible political machinations involving most of the upper echelons within the Third Reich. Propaganda Minister Josef Goebbels, never at a loss to jump on a political opportunity, had joined forces with Heinrich Himmler in proposing that the SS take charge of the jet program. Galland provided his thoughts on this development:

"Himmler did not strike me as being a very intelligent person in any manner. In meetings, he always waited until the end, before saying anything. He seldom had a logical suggestion. Once, he even proposed that the SS take over the Me 262 project, which I said was absolutely insane and did say so in so many words. He also had the ability to make you feel very nervous, as if he were looking for a way to find fault with you.

"Despite all of Göring's faults, I must say that he did support me in the position that the 262 should be specifically built as a fighter. I had his support by the time of my meeting with him in May 1944, after he had come to his senses regarding just how deep American fighters were entering German airspace."[12]

Galland was to later learn just how much grief he was to experience due to his insistence in fighting Goebbels, Göring, and even Himmler in open warfare, which he preferred. Galland was not one to do things behind someone's back. He was an honorable fighter and would take on all comers, as he stated:

"I still had to convince Hitler to continue the flow of jets to JG-7 and other units. The men flying them needed more familiarity before committing them to combat, and the jet never really went through the type of peacetime evolution of refinement through research and development as it should have. The greatest problems were the engines, which were very delicate and often flamed out on takeoff. Even worse, we had reports of flameouts and burned out engines in flight.

"This was not a comforting thought for pilots expecting to go into battle outnumbered fifty to one on a very good day. The unit at Achmer had been doing great things since July 1944 under Werner Thierfelder, proving the value of the jet in combat. This success allowed us to push the issue to Hitler again, building upon that success once we began to get more 262s in the field.

"Before all of this occurred, I had been telling Milch, Göring, and Hitler for a year, since my first flight in an Me 262 in May 1943 at Lechfeld, that only Focke-Wulf Fw 190 fighter production should continue in conventional aircraft, specifically the Dora model and later variants, and to discontinue the Me 109, which was outdated, and to focus on building a massive jet-fighter force.

"Speer was a smart fellow, and he knew that the war was lost, as did I, and much sooner than later unless massive changes were made. Like most clear-headed people late in the war, he also knew that negotiating a peace from a position of strength was preferable to accepting defeat while powerless. Speer even once said that, given the alternative, having Americans and British with our technology was far preferable to the Soviets."

Galland's arguments were sound and his logic undeniable. Everyone knew that fighters were needed, not bombers. Hannes Trautloft recalled the events during his moments within the inner circle: "Milch openly supported him [Galland], but only to a point, and Göring supported him when not in Hitler's presence, and then he would either be silent or side with whatever silliness Hitler was spouting at that time. It was very frustrating, and this one event, perhaps above all others, really led to the forthcoming Fighters Revolt.

"We needed assistance, and quickly, and all we received were accusations and the blame for losing the war. Göring, much like Hitler, could not see the reality of what was happening. I still wonder if it was a matter of false hope or self-delusion. Seeing what kinds of men were leading my nation created a serious dilemma for me, and I spoke to my wife, Marga, about this many times and with Galland and a few trusted men on occasion."[13]

Galland was also unable to comprehend the lack of reality from his superiors: "Not even he [Göring] could dismiss the swarms of Mustangs and Lightnings flying overhead. Having the jet as a fighter was critical, and despite Hitler's bomber order, fighter testing was still allowed. It would most certainly not have changed the final outcome of the war, for we had already lost completely, but it would have probably delayed the end, since the Normandy invasion on June 6, 1944, would probably not have taken place, at least not successfully if the 262 had been operational and in large numbers."

Supporting Galland's description of Göring's response to Allied fighters roaming the Reich at will is Starr Smith's data in the book *Jimmy Stewart: Bomber Pilot*: "I knew first that the *Luftwaffe* was losing control of the air when the American long-range fighters were able to escort the bombers as far as Hanover. It was not long before they were getting to Berlin. We knew then that we must develop the jet planes. Our plan for their early development was unsuccessful only because of your bombing attacks. Allied attacks greatly affected our training program too. For instance, the attacks on oil retarded the training because our pilots couldn't get sufficient training before they were put into combat."[14]

However, Göring also made statements to his American captors that were somewhat contrary to his position in front of Hitler regarding the jet and even in stark contradiction to what he stated to Galland and others in Hitler's absence, as later reported by Galland. According to Göring's postwar interrogation: "I am convinced that the jets would have won the war for us if we had had only four or five months' more time. Our underground installations were all ready. The factory at Kahla had a capacity of one thousand to one thousand two hundred jet airplanes a month. Now with five thousand to six thousand jets, the outcome would have been quite different.

"We would have trained sufficient pilots for the jet planes despite oil shortage, because we would have had the underground factories for oil, producing a sufficient quantity for the jets. The transition to jets was very easy in training. The jet pilot output was always ahead of the jet aircraft production."[15]

Adolf Galland, during his interviews, mentioned these factors, which corroborated Göring's comments to a degree: "This could have been possible, since *Kommando Thierfelder* had been receiving the jets at Achmer since April. I certainly think that just three hundred jets flown daily by the best fighter pilots, even at a ten percent loss with a like replacement ratio, would have had a major impact on the course of the air war. This would have, of course, prolonged the war, so perhaps Hitler's misuse of this aircraft was not such a bad thing after all."[16]

On December 21, 1943, the operational feasibility of the Me 262 had been placed under *Hauptmann* Werner Thierfelder's *Erprobungskommando* 262 at Lechfeld. The *Ekdo* 262 had received several of the early prototype Me 262A-0 aircraft, and these had their teething problems. As with any new weapon system, trial and error had to be part of the research and development.

Although the unit was not an operational success, the lessons learned were to reverberate throughout the jet community. Even after Thierfelder was killed in combat with 15th Air Force Mustangs over Bavaria on July 18 and *Hauptmann* Neumeyer had taken over temporary command, there was a new phase of the Me 262 being discussed. The jet was about to be lifted to new heights, with a new fighter unit soon to be created that would test Galland's theories.

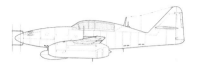

CHAPTER 8

First Encounters

*I remember when I scored my first kill
in the Me 262, it was incredible!*

Georg-Peter Eder

When the first Me 262s were delivered to the field units in April 1944, the primary fighter unit to receive the jets as a dedicated fighter was an ad-hoc group based at Achmer commanded by *Hauptmann* Werner Thierfelder. Officially designated *Erprobungskommando* 262, it was formed in April 1944 at Lechfeld to test the new Me 262. The unit was disbanded not long after Thierfelder was killed on July 18, 1944, reorganized as *Kommando Nowotny*, and relocated to Achmer on September 26, 1944, and given free reign to fly their missions and test their theories. Much was hanging in the balance, both politically and militarily.

The first serious encounter between an Me 262 and an Allied aircraft occurred on July 26, 1944, when an Me 262 from *Ekdo* 262, flown by *Leutnant* Schreiber (work number 130017) shot at a Mosquito.[1] The Allied plane disappeared, trailing smoke, but later safely landed in Italy. In August, Nowotny's band of adventurers began interceptor operations in earnest. It was on August 8, 1944, when the unit scored its first confirmed kill, also a Mosquito.[2]

The Allies had heard of the Me 262 and even had secondhand reports smuggled out of Germany through the OSS (Office of Strategic Services) and underground. Many of these reports came from the forced laborers who were building the aircraft. What the Allies knew was best summed up by Gen. James H. Doolittle, the famed aviator who had been a stellar pre-war racing pilot and innovator and who led the famous Doolittle Raid against Japan from the aircraft carrier

USS *Hornet* on April 18, 1942. His assignment to the Eighth Air Force Bomber Command provided him with access to all the available intelligence. Doolittle was especially interested in German aircraft technology, as he stated:

"We knew of the German rocket base at Peenemünde, and the rumors about these super fast aircraft were taken seriously. There were just too many corroborating reports from many different sources not to take notice, but many of the pilots almost refused to believe the reports coming back about these fast aircraft. What we needed was a visual, and preferably camera confirmation. I would have been ecstatic if we could have captured one, but that would have been high hopes indeed. It was the British who first confirmed what we feared."[3]

Allied pilots were not slowly introduced into the jet fighter, they were rudely awakened, and to the American bomber crews the introduction was heart stopping. General Curtis LeMay, the retired bomber commander and former commander of Strategic Air Command, had this to say:

"In 1944, Hap Arnold called me, as I was stateside already, headed for the Pacific; just a chat I thought, but hell no. I was informed that we had lost some B-24s and B-17s, probably a dozen over the last several days, and the culprits were these new German planes, jets. The discussion was not a long one, but he said that Ira [Eaker] was very upset, more at the potential for bad morale than the actual damage inflicted. After a while, he asked if I had any suggestions. I said, 'Yes, kill the bastards at their airfields. Better yet, bomb their fucking factories; do we know where they are?' He said he thought so, and then I suggested he use an entire air reconnaissance group to get the damned evidence he needed. I called Doolittle, who was still in England and asked him to see what he could do."[4]

General Doolittle remembered that telephone call well: "I already knew about the problem. In fact, I had once spoken to a B-17 crew that had been damaged by a jet attack. It had only lasted for one split second pass, but they had one dead and four wounded, just from the explosive shells. They came in through the bomb bay. Luckily, they were on the return leg of their mission. Otherwise, the bombs on board could have been detonated, and that could have destroyed several aircraft in the box formation. LeMay and I had an animated conversation, and he used language that I will not repeat here. Suffice it to say his language was colorful, part of his charm.

"The pilot was a twenty-two-year-old captain whose name I remember but will not mention here. He was on his sixteenth mission, I think, and remember they only needed twenty-five to get a ticket home. That boy saw his copilot's head come off, and his crew chief bleeding all over the flight deck, and he had been wounded. The rudder was shot up on the way into the target by 190s, and then when leaving the target, a jet hit them in a high-speed pass from underneath.

"This boy was in complete shock. I saw it. I knew it. I knew that he was never going to be an effective leader again. I also knew that we now had a real problem, because if the bomber crews felt that they could not rely on our fighter escorts to protect them, then a curtain of morbidity would fall down on them, just like what had happened with the RAF Bomber Command. I could not let that happen. I then issued the order to have at least one complete recon group, even if a composite of American and British, fly photo missions. I wanted to know where they were being built, how they were being transported, and also where their airfields were."[5]

During one of his many interviews, Adolf Galland mentioned this very situation, as it was during the time he was trying to convince Hitler to provide him with what he needed: "The great problem was that we were losing pilots faster than we could replace them, and this was not an accident. My friend General [James H.] Doolittle had devised the plan to force our fighters into the air to be killed, and we played right into his hands. There was nothing else to do. Our losses were staggering over the next few months [of 1944]. That was when I decided to focus our fighters inside Germany proper, and defend the installations that seemed to be the Allied targets of choice."[6]

Continuing Doolittle's comments: "After the war, Galland and I had a chat about this very subject. He asked me: 'Jimmy, what was your impression of our jets when you first learned of them?' I looked at him, grabbed his arm, and said: "Adolf, I hoped like hell we could bomb your factories, airfields, and kill your pilots before you could force us out of the bombing campaign.'

"I knew that he did not understand what I meant, so I explained it to him. I told him that I understood the political problems he had in getting the jet fighter; our congress was not much different when it came to appropriations. However, he was alarmed when I told him that there were many in our government who wanted to abandon daylight strategic bombing, feeling that it was too costly in aircraft and lives, with little to show for it. This was especially true after Big Week, and even more so after the August through October 1944 losses over Regensburg, Schweinfurt, and other places. And most of those losses came from 190s and 109s, even flak, not even jets. I decided to focus upon swarming the Germans in the air, shooting them down, ambushing them at airfields, everything.

"Galland's response was: 'Well, your bombing of factories was not that significant, but bombing the petroleum and railways was very effective. I would say that what harmed us the most was the killing of our pilots in combat. Planes can be built, but men cannot be made.' I thought that was a perfect vindication for my plan, which I implemented to defeat the *Luftwaffe*. Galland was a great and gallant enemy, but he was an even better friend."[7]

Doolittle had issued the order throughout the Eighth Air Force, and this was mirrored by the Ninth Air Force, which handled the bulk of the tactical bombing roles in Europe. American fighter pilots were to change their habits; no longer would they be chained to the bombers as escorts. They were ordered to go ahead in advance of the strike force, locate the German airfields, strafe and destroy everything they saw, and the next waves of fighters would catch the German fighters rising to engage the bombers. Victory by pilot attrition was Doolittle's plan, and it was in this author's opinion what truly eliminated the *Luftwaffe*.

The response from the fighter units was a resounding applause, as stated by Francis S. Gabreski: "Once we were unleashed, I knew, as did everyone else, that we were going to win the air war. We had the numbers, we had the best pilots, best aircraft, and we were in a sort of blood lust to whack those guys the best and hardest way we could. Ironically, Hub Zemke had started doing just that in 1943, a year before the order was given, and the tactic became doctrine. That was why he was vindicated. Hub made a lot of enemies, because he was a maverick, but he was the most effective fighter leader I ever flew with. He could read the enemy method and think up a method to counter the threat, just like a chess master. He was absolutely brilliant. That is not bullshit either."[8]

USAAF Gen. Carl Spaatz, a bomber officer from the early days, was also involved in this problem-solving scenario. His close working relationship with Doolittle and British intelligence gave him an idea. While the fighter pilots would draw the German fighters into the air and kill them with overwhelming numbers, Spaatz wanted to implement his own revision of the Casablanca Directive. In his opinion, jet production facilities were just as critical to the war effort as the top targets: petroleum refineries and depots.

These targets were easier to hit once the fighter-bombers were established in mainland Europe, although the heavy bombers were still based in England. Given the new relocated forward bases, the bombers had much more fighter protection for longer periods of time. And they also had the time and fuel to strafe targets at will. Jets in the open and their airfields were prime targets, but the fighter-bomber units would be used to supplement the heavy bomber efforts at destroying the jets in the embryonic stage.

However, once forward air bases were established in France and Belgium, the Germans also adopted the "strike first" mentality. One example of this is found in Robert F. Dorr and Thomas D. Jones's book *Hell Hawks: The Untold Story of the American Fliers Who Savaged Hitler's Wehrmacht*, where Brig. Gen. Andrew W. Smoak, at that time a young P-47 Thunderbolt pilot with the 365th Fighter Group Hell Hawks of the Ninth Air Force, was downed by an Me 262 while taking off in early 1945. He never saw the plane that hit him, but the antiaircraft crew told him that he had been hit by a plane "with no propeller," and he only later learned during the debriefing about the jets, as visual confirmations clearly provided the evidence of large numbers of Me 262s in the area.[9]

General of Bombers Dietrich Pelz commented on his doctrine of first strike against the Allied airfields: "Long before Operation Bodenplatte, which was the fighter operation, I had planned a jet bomber strike against all of the Allied fighter fields that we could reach. I was of the impression that if we could destroy at least half of the fighters on the ground, and destroy the airfields, then the fighters would be able to handle the remaining half of the enemy fighters that survived. The plan was a good one, I thought, but we never really had enough jets to put that plan to the test."[10]

The Hell Hawks themselves ended the war in Europe with an impressive air combat record, given that they were a tactical fighter-bomber unit; among their achievements, they shot down 151 enemy aircraft, with five being the vaunted Me 262.[11] They, like most of the Allied fighter units, had managed to adapt to the evolving air war, watching their enemy and learning.

Also, as stated by Starr: "When German jets began to appear in the skies of Europe, no one on the Allied side had a good plan for coping with them . . . Everybody knew the Me 262 was a lot faster than the P-47 Thunderbolt, the portly Jug. Nobody knew much else."[12] That plan was put together by Doolittle, as previously mentioned, and Galland's admission as to the effectiveness proved its worth.

Not long afterward, nearly every American fighter pilot knew of the jets, and probably every one of them wanted to take a crack at shooting one down. S-2 and G-2 (Intelligence) officers collected photos, descriptions of flight characteristics during postmission crew debriefings, underground communications, especially regarding assembly plants, and aerial reconnaissance photos of operational jet airfields. For the most part, Allied pilots (especially Americans) looked for them.

Killing a jet became more prestigious than becoming an ace in some squadrons, according to several American fighter pilots.

For example, Capt. (later Col.) Robert S. Johnson, 56th Fighter Group Zemke's Wolfpack, who became the first American pilot to tie Eddie Rickenbacker's World War I score of twenty-six victories, himself a P-47 pilot, stated: "They took me out of the war before I could rack up any more kills. Pure propaganda crap, and I joined Dick Bong on this war bond tour back home, as he also had equaled my score. He got to go back and become top ace in the Pacific. I really wished they had let me go back to Europe. I began hearing about the jets, and I really wanted to get me one of those damned things."[13]

Also of the famed Zemke's Wolfpack, Col. Francis S. Gabreski, the leading American ace in Europe, commented about his wish to have encountered the jet fighter: "We in the Pack were hot, really hot, knocking things out of the sky left and right after Hub [Zemke] devised our tactics. Everyone wanted a crack at those things. Before I became a POW along with Hub, and even afterward, we always wished that we would have had a chance to shoot more down, he had one. I would have traded half my kills for a jet kill. What a shame really. I did get some jets in Korea later, but that's not the same thing."[14]

Col. Walker "Bud" Mahurin, also of the 56th Fighter Group, stated: "We heard the reports from the other squadrons and groups when they shot down a jet. These were the prizes, every guy in a fighter really wanted to get into the mix. I know for a fact that even guys who were reluctant to go in on these ground attack missions before looked forward to the possibility of nailing one of those suckers. I was one of them, but I was already gone before that could happen."[15]

Doolittle echoed these sentiments: "Many of the fighter pilots, many who often dreaded the ground attack missions that were ordered, due to the expectation that 30–40 percent of the pilots who strafed airfields and other flak-covered targets would not return, were suddenly looking forward to hitting the jet airfields. We knew where they were, and the possibility of catching one in landing or takeoff for an aerial kill really got them going. I would also think, in retrospect, that many of those young fighter pilots probably took even more risks than they normally would have in trying to get those jet kills. The British finally did it and then our fighter pilots decided that they had to ramp up the pressure."[16]

Doolittle's reference was when a de Havilland Mosquito of No. 544 (PR) Squadron, piloted by Flight Lt. A. E. Wall and his navigator Flying Officer A. S. Lobban, was engaged by an Me 262A-2a fighter-bomber of *Einsatzkommando Schenck* (*Major* Wolfgang Schenck) near

Munich on July 25, 1944. Their report was eagerly absorbed by all the S-2 officers in both the RAF and USAAF. The first jet kill over a bomber was a B-17 shot down over Stuttgart on August 15, 1944 (although not claimed as a kill by Georg-Peter Eder of *Ekdo* 262, as there was no confirmation; he claimed a probable). The first confirmed Allied kill over an Me 262 came on August 28, 1944, when Maj. Joseph Myers and his wingman, Lt. M. D. Croy Jr. of the U.S. 78th Fighter Group, managed to jump another *Kommando Schenck* jet, forcing *Oberfeldwebel* Lauer's Me 262 down in a field near Brussels, Belgium.

Kommando Schenck was formed at Lechfeld in July 1944 before posting to the Normandy invasion front. The unit was based at Chateaudun, Etampes, and Creil, before pulling back to Juvincourt, near Reims, in late August. Operations by *Einsatzkommando Schenck* continued in an ad hoc manner until its incorporation into I./ KG-51, which began combat operations from Rheine-Hopsten under *Major* Unrau in October 1944. The Me 262 as an unarmed reconnaissance aircraft was soon recognized, and an unknown number went to the *Einsatzkommando Braunegg*, and less than a dozen to *Nahaufklarungsgruppen* 1 and 6.

The Me 262 for the most part did not have a promising start with the bomber units, as losses mounted with few victories to show for the effort. The bomber units suffered many of these losses. Galland had his own opinion as to why this was the case. "It was true that the Me 262 was difficult to counter, and in fact almost invulnerable if flown by an experienced fighter pilot. Nothing could catch it in flight, but only a fighter pilot really had a chance of fighting and surviving in it."[17]

This was probably the catalyst that allowed Hitler to release a few jets for fighter operations, perhaps seeing that he needed another option. Dietrich Pelz thought so: "I do believe that the mounting losses and few victories, even the lack of real successes in the *schnell* bomber program prompted Hitler to listen to Galland's argument. I still knew that the Ar 234 was available, and it was a much better bomber platform anyway. So, I supported this, and I think that was the final factor in his decision."[18]

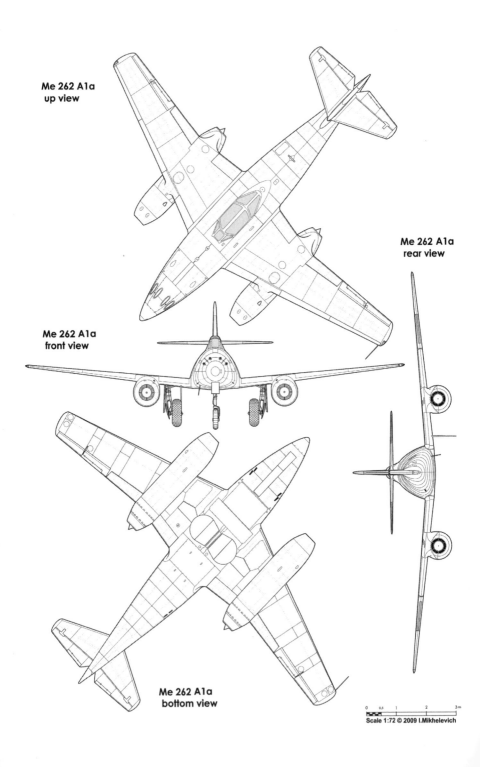

Me 262 A1a
up view

Me 262 A1a
rear view

Me 262 A1a
front view

Me 262 A1a
bottom view

Scale 1:72 © 2009 I.Mikhelevich

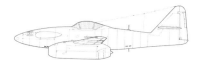

CHAPTER 9

Challenges of the Jet

The 262 was a great beast, when handled correctly. But, if you lost control, especially at low altitude, it was very unforgiving.

Johannes Steinhoff

L ike any other aircraft, the Me 262 did have its shortcomings, although the pilot was protected by a 9mm-thick armored plate behind the seat and a 90mm-thick armored glass shatter-resistant windscreen. The engines were very sensitive to the throttle and did not provide much thrust at low airspeeds, making turns at lower speeds and altitudes dangerous. Finally, by October, the preliminary report was released in the jet's capabilities, and by January 1945, the full intelligence report was disseminated throughout the intelligence sections:

"The outstanding advantages of the Me 262 are its high-level speeds, very high diving speeds, and probably high ceiling. [These] give it good performance at 35,000 feet. Its disadvantages are due chiefly to its high wing loading—namely a high takeoff speed requiring a long takeoff run, a high stalling speed, and poor maneuvering qualities. It will also tend to overshoot its target at high speed, just like any jet-propelled aircraft.

"The Me 262 will have the usual poor performance of a jet at low speed. Thus, it can be attacked most easily by fighters now in service when it is cruising or climbing. In maneuvers, the Me 262 should be forced into tight turns or into a zoom, unless the altitude at which it is encountered is near its ceiling of the attacking aircraft.

"When conventionally-engined aircraft are avoiding the Me 262 they should not dive, since the Me 262's acceleration in a dive will be larger than that of a conventional fighter, enabling it to escape the attack, or to press home an attack on its opponent. If jet-propelled aircraft are used against the Me 262 [something that never happened], diving tactics may of course be employed. In fact, both aircraft can carry the same maneuvers. British jet-propelled fighters now in service [Gloster Meteors] have a lower wing loading than the Me 262, and thus better turning qualities. They should be able to outmaneuver the Me 262."[1]

Georg-Peter Eder explained what it was like to fly the jet from takeoff to landing, including tight maneuvers:

"The throttle response was slow, and if pushed forward too soon resulted in flameouts, so in combat we just set the throttles at full forward and only reduced power gradually as required, such as landing. To bleed off airspeed, we just raised the nose and left the throttles alone. We operated the throttle gently to prevent any quick changes to the engines. Later the automatic throttle regulator was installed on some aircraft, but it did not always solve the problem. The technology was just so new, and we were the guinea pigs, so that was the problem. The one and most important benefit was the great speed we could achieve, that was what made the Me 262 so incredible.

"However, if you go up you must come down. Takeoff was OK, as you had perfect visibility forward, unlike in the tail draggers. One thing that was critical was that once you took off, you had to trim the aircraft immediately upon reaching operational speed. Landing was OK, better than in the Me 109, and coming down ass first was a new feeling from landing front first, where upon reducing power the tail wheel made contact. This was just the opposite; we came down at a fifteen to twenty degree angle, and then reduced power to drop the nose.

"Now—and this was important—landing also placed a great stress on the nose gear. I cannot tell you how many times I witnessed jets coming in and striking the nose gear too hard. It was the one weak point, and it was very unforgiving. The visibility was perfection, with the canopy still opening and closing in the coffin lid method as we had on the Me 109, but the shape and form of the canopy was more along the lines of the Fw 190. We had three-hundred-sixty-degree vision pretty much and that alone will keep a pilot alive in battle.

"In combat, I would want to avoid a turning fight, the 262 just did not have it, and any enemy fighter could turn inside it. That was not so good. In attacking head to head, the four thirty-millimeter cannons meant you always won the fight. I once killed a Mustang in a similar head-on fight. I had just attacked a B-17, in thick clouds, and I emerged below the formation, never knowing if I killed the bomber, and when I pulled up level I had a Mustang coming right at me, about a thousand meters away. This gave me a split second to win or die. If I pulled up or dropped the nose, or banked away, I was dead. I just quickly placed the Revi on him and fired one short burst, perhaps eight cannon rounds, and he just disintegrated. I know, because I flew through the wreckage, and the left turbine ingested some debris and flamed out. I brought the jet back to Achmer and it flew again in a couple of days."[2]

Hermann Buchner mentioned his experience in trying to land the Me 262 when things went wrong: "I learned that when landing you had to be below three hundred kilometers [per hour] before you lowered the flaps, and then less than two hundred [per hour] for the landing gear to land properly and safely. There was none of this using flaps at high speed to tighten your turn in a dogfight, unless you were well below this speed. I did this one time and the result was almost fatal. I lost the left engine once and managed to finally land, and I was not alone. Mustangs had been on a bomber escort mission, and I think they took a real interest in me, because I brought them home, so to speak."[3]

Buchner also wrote about one of his landings where the weak nose gear lived up to its notorious reputation: "We were just about to set down and the snow shower had now reached the middle of the airfield. I slammed my 262 onto the landing strip doing two hundred sixty kilometers per hour and suddenly saw a wheel running in front of me. It had broken off the end of the axle during the hard landing and the wheel had now separated. The aircraft swerved to the left, but, with a great deal of effort and additional help from the left engine, I succeeded in keeping the machine going more or less in the right direction and steered past a fuel truck. After a few frightening seconds I brought my jet to a standstill. All went well, and the machine only needed a new undercarriage."[4]

In Dorr and Jones's book *Hell Hawks*, Eder's comments are vindicated regarding Allied fighters being able to out-turn and score hits on the jets. Citing comments from Charles R. Johnson, regarding Capt. Valmore J. "Val" Beaudrault's encounter with a jet:

"After the unidentified aircraft passed in front of him, the captain bore down on its tail, at which the [German] pilot made a sharp 360 degree turn. Beaudrault had no trouble turning inside of him with his P-47D28. During these maneuvers, Capt. Beaudrault still failed to identify the aircraft, so he held his fire. The plane then rolled out of the turn and applied full throttle and started to pull way away even though the P-47's throttle was to the firewall." Beaudrault took pictures of the jet, and finally identified the Me 262 for what it was. "Nearby, 1st Lt. William F. Peters engaged a second 262 but was soon left behind as the jet outdistanced him in a climb." [5]

Erich Hohagen also gave his impression of taking off, flying and landing in the Me 262: "When you first powered up the left engine, and then the right, in that order, you could feel the aircraft start to vibrate, not like in a 109 where the entire aircraft would shake, but a slight vibration, soft, like something that would put a baby to sleep with the gentle motion. However, and this was important, you had to easily move those throttles forward, I am saying almost by creeping millimeters. This was a very challenging thing to do when taking off under an alarm, or when you knew that enemy fighters were only a few minutes away. One had the tendency of thinking about just jumping out of the aircraft rather than wait for it to power up, to get you rolling down the runway.

"In combat, the climbing maneuver was the chosen method of escape. This allowed you to gain the altitude advantage while leaving the enemy aircraft far below you, only you had to make sure that you were at least five hundred meters away, since the weapons on the American fighters could reach you, and they could arc their rounds into you unless you were out of range. This method also used up a lot of fuel, and our greatest problem was watching that fuel gauge, although we had a reserve tank, and you had to manually switch that thing, otherwise you would starve the Jumos. That would not have been good.

"When landing, reducing power was much easier, especially if you were aligned with the strip and correctly in the glide slope, and like with all aircraft, landing into the wind was the best way, but we did not always have that option. Even if you lost power, the wide landing gear and aerodynamic qualities of the 262 made landing a sheer pleasure, unless someone was behind you firing you up. That tended to become annoying, if you survived it. Most of us did not." [6]

The dangers of takeoff and landing in the Me 262 are highlighted in an article by historian Jon Guttman, providing an American fighter pilot's perspective, when on January 15, 1945, Capt. Robert P. Winks of the 357th Fighter Group engaged and scored a kill over a Me 262:

"'We were on a sweep over southern Germany, in the Munich area,' he recalled. 'The 364th Squadron was over to take pictures of a 262 airfield. Pete Peterson had a camera in his P-51 and we were flying escort. The Eighth Air Force had orders not to strafe those airfields—it had incurred too many losses. I was flying along when I saw a plane doing slow rolls on the deck, over patches of snow—it was an Me 262. I was following what he was doing and called him in to Peterson, who responded with an order to "Go down and get him." At that point the bogey was going back toward the airfield. I dropped my two tanks, cut my engine and went into a straight dive with five degrees of flaps. I was at about a sixty-degree angle when I came at the jet and fired two hundred forty rounds of fifty-caliber into his cockpit and wing root. The German flipped over, caught on fire and banged in. Pete confirmed it.'"

The identity of Winks' quarry has only recently become known. Although Schongau was put under alert because of the Mustangs' presence in its vicinity, *Fähnrich* (cadet trainee) Rudolf Rhode had either just taken off or was already airborne when Winks caught him. "We observed Me 262s taxiing toward protective abutments all over that airfield," Winks recalled. "Whoever was piloting the Me 262 that I shot down must have had a military rank high enough to have been able to countermand the 'alert.' Or so I have always thought."

Killed at age nineteen, Rhode was buried in Schwabstadl, near Lechfeld. In regard to the trainee status of his last victim, Winks remarked: "I denied the *Luftwaffe* an Me 262 aircraft, and a pilot from attacking our bombers. That is what I was hired and trained to do. Speaking, perhaps, for both sides of the conflict . . . what a terrible waste of men, and the world's wealth.'"[7]

Such losses were all too common among the German jet pilots. This was when they were the most vulnerable. As stated, the other major concern was running out of fuel. Dorr and Jones chronicle an event that emphasizes Hohagen's statement regarding the fuel consumption: "[Capt.] Beaudrault's initial adversary, however, was unable to take advantage of his one hundred mile per hour speed advantage over the Thunderbolt. The Me 262 emitted white puffs of smoke from its exhausts. Its engines stopped. In midair, far from any runway, the German jet apparently had run out of fuel.

"Beaudrault pounced on the Me 262 in a three hundred mile per hour dive. He prepared to fire his Thunderbolt's eight .50-caliber machine guns. Before he could squeeze the trigger, however, the 262 veered abruptly, its wing struck the ground, and the German jet disappeared in a tremendous explosion. Johnson wrote that 'there was nothing left but fire and shiny pieces of metal scattered over three acres.'" Beaudrault was awarded the Silver Star for the action. This was the first Ninth Air Force jet kill.[8]

Many of these pilots undoubtedly killed themselves, when perhaps in a moment of panic, or just out of years of training and experience in conventional fighters, they threw the throttles forward to increase their speed rapidly to escape a pursuing enemy fighter. Flaming out an engine was usually the result, either allowing the enemy fighter to close the distance for the kill, or causing the jet to stall and crash. Each fighter or bomber pilot had similar, if not often unique, stories regarding their transition into the jet fight-bomber, such as Hermann Buchner:

"An engineering officer gave lessons about the powerplant, about starting up and switching off; we had to carry out the whole sequence of events blindfolded. After two days of basic instruction we began to practice starting up an Me 262 parked on a field in front of the hall. After a thorough instruction in the cabin, taxiing in the Me 262 began. Taxiing with two engines was somewhat difficult; one first had to have a good grasp of how the engines operated and the revs. A course had been built using pine trees and one had to taxi through these.

"In between a flying instructor explained again and again the starting procedures, the flight and the preparations for landing. On 19 November 1944 I had my first flight in a 262. Everything went like clockwork. It was a magnificent feeling and after twenty minutes an equally exemplary landing followed. The spell was broken—it was easier than expected. I have to say, though, that the instruction and the preparations had been logically and intensively carried out. In truth, nothing could go off the straight and narrow."[9]

Walter Schuck also wrote of his transition period into the jet: "When I am asked today how we transitioned from the Me 109 on to the Me 262, people either find my reply unbelievable or regard all those of us who went through the process as completely crazy. But it was exactly as I describe here. JG-7 didn't have a single Me 262 two-seater trainer on establishment, and every pilot who was to fly the jet on operations began his training by being a spectator!

"No doubt everyone can appreciate that there is a huge difference between being pulled along by a propeller and pushed along by a jet-turbine. Quite apart from the sluggish reactions of the Me 262 during takeoff, when power had to be applied to the two engines carefully and evenly to avoid overheating the turbine blades, a totally different angle and method of approach had to be employed when coming in to land.

"In the air, too, a whole new book of aerodynamics came into play. In the Me 109 you could turn quickly and steeply and if you suddenly needed to slow down at high speed you merely had to pull back on the throttle to produce the desired braking effect in an instant, whereas the jet engine would still continue to produce thrust for a considerable time after the throttles had gently been eased off. Moreover, when flying the Me 262 at low speeds you had to be devilish careful not to stall, or to make any jerky throttle movements that would cause the powerplants simply to flame out altogether."[10]

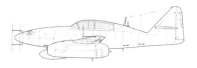

CHAPTER 10

Night and Day

I did not see the 262 as a great night fighter,
as the high speeds made accuracy an issue.

Hajo Herrmann

One pilot who took a unique exception to the flameout problem and sensitivity of the throttles on the jets was *Leutnant* Jorg Czypionka, a former flight instructor who flew with 10.NJG-11 in Me 109G and later with the re-designated *Kommando Welter* in the Me 262, scoring one confirmed night victory in the jet, an RAF Mosquito at night on March 27, 1945, at 2050 hours (8:50 pm). All of his night missions were in day fighter variants, using the old *Wilde Sau* method, even his Me 262 "Red 6." Czypionka discussed the transition he experienced from Me 109 to the Me 262, and he never had a flameout on takeoff. His insights are revealing:

"My principal was concentration. If you fly one hundred percent concentrated and do not think of anything else, concentrate on everything, watch every detail, watch everything that can happen, and treat the aircraft as the aircraft wants to be treated. If you feel that the aircraft does not want to do it easily, then do not do it. This was my principal in flying, and every pilot should think this way."[1]

Czypionka's introduction into the jet fighter as a night fighter was, to say the least, quite unique. When he joined 10.NJG-11, they were using Me 109s, as he explained:

"Early in the war, I spent three years as an instructor pilot, keeping me from the sharp edge of the war until 1944. Only at that stage did I undergo fighter training, including night fighter training. Upon completing my night fighter training, I was assigned as squadron leader of the 5th squadron of NJG-11 in Jüterborg. This unit was equipped with slightly modified Me 109G6 and G14 models, featuring the high-performance DB 605A as turbocharged engines for increased speed and higher cruising altitude. The unit mission was to destroy Mosquito light bombers of the Royal Air Force, which had started to attack northern German cities, particularly Berlin, almost every night. By mid-1944 the RAF had started using their very fast Mosquito bombers in units of around sixty aircraft for night bombing raids, concentrating on the capital city of Berlin. Armed with single two-thousand-pound bombs, they were causing considerable damage. The Me 109 single-seat aircraft were flying, with no radar equipment in a modified *Wilde Sau* system, guided by ground control and supported by target finding searchlights. The *Wilde Sau* tactic essentially required that ground controlled radar officers guided us into a waiting pattern two thousand meters (about six thousand feet) above the incoming bombers.

"Each ground controller had up to six aircraft on his frequency, directing and assisting them with navigation. Our searchlight units would then try to find these bombers, which always flew as single aircraft, and hold them in their beams for as long as possible. Our aircraft were fitted with auxiliary tanks, which extended their endurance by up to one hour, or for three hours if the tank was not jettisoned.

"Because the Me 109's speed did not exceed that of the Mosquito, conventional pursuit as used against conventional, slow bombers was not possible. Indeed, closing in on this much faster enemy aircraft was tricky. To get to the right attack position was very difficult, to the extent that it was mostly a matter of luck still requiring great skill and experience for the attack itself.

"It was one of Germany's night fighter aces, Kurt Welter (over thirty victories in the Me 109 and Fw 190s), who actively worked to replace his unit's Me 109s with a faster aircraft. There were indeed two potential candidates whose speed easily surpassed that of the Mosquito: the Me 262 and the Ar 234 turbojets, which had just become available for operational use for this purpose. Welter tested both at the Laerz/Rechlin (research) air force base for night combat. The Arado Ar 234 was rejected, partly because it had a cockpit with glazing all around, which generated too much glare during landing, and also because the exposed cockpit canopy in the front of the aircraft offered no protection from debris of decomposing aircraft after a hit. By contrast, the Me 262 in single seat and two-seat versions proved to be very well suited to this task.

"In January 1945, *Kommando Welter* was created as a unit of NJG-11. A *Kommando*, or *Kdo*, was a special command or detachment usually named for its commanding officer. It was assigned about ten aircraft. This particular unit operated from Burg bei Magdeburg air force base and, after initial difficulties which caused several fatalities due to pilot error and engine failures, it became quite successful indeed. The small *Kommando Welter* scored almost forty victories in a short period of only three odd months, in the face of equipment and materiel shortages and later, even without an airfield. In March 1945 I was asked to join the *Kommando Welter*.

"I remember my introduction to the Me 262 fondly. I had arrived at Burg Airfield on a March afternoon. 'My' aircraft stood on the start runway, and I was overwhelmed by emotion and admiration when I saw it. It looked as though it had jumped out of future. It was sleek, with a triangular fuselage, nose wheel, and wide stance. The aircraft seemed to have slight forward tilt and two striking nacelles with propellerless engines under its wings. The unit's chief mechanic instructed me how to start and control the engines with regard to temperatures and which engine revolutions had to be maintained, as well as how to master the fuel tank scheme and switches, undercarriage management, flaps, etc. This instruction lasted all of forty-five minutes! After a brief questioning by Welter about aspects of theory, how I would fly the aircraft, handle speed, climb rate, ascent/descent, touch down, and how to handle emergency situations, I was told to go get on with my first flight in this revolutionary aircraft.

"Hajo [regarding Herrmann's ambivalence in using the jet as a night fighter] probably had in mind the [262] fighter against bombers, but we had to have it against the Mosquitoes, to be faster than the Mosquitoes and we were. So, in this short time of *Kommando Welter* and from January to the end of March, or beginning or mid of April [1945] Welter shot down more Mosquitoes than the whole task force had shot down in the year before. [2]

"I approached this task in a very concentrated manner, using all of my previous experience. Everything was a little different from the conventional aircraft of the time. The engine-starting procedure and running the engines was quite different, particularly its whining sound, compared to the roar of a piston engine. Also, I had to stand on the brake with engines revving high. This could be done easily because of the existence of the front wheel. The takeoff run was exceptionally easy, because the aircraft was running in a perfectly straight line, with no torque, and at a high rate of acceleration. The front wheel lifted at one hundred sixty kilometers per hour (about one hundred miles per hour), with a takeoff velocity of some two hundred kilometers per hour (about one hundred twenty-four miles per hour).

"By the yardstick of the day, the climb rate was astonishing. There was literally no noise, the flight being almost glider-like, with the engines running with no vibration behind the cockpit and under the wings. Visibility was unrestricted all around, because of the cockpit's position high on top of the fuselage. The g force in my first turn at speed was significantly higher than I had experienced in traditional propeller aircraft, and this forced concentration. I knew that I had to be careful. Then what followed was a smooth go-around and landing approach.

"One operational fact which had been impressed upon me specifically; 'Never move the accelerator (throttle) fast, or a flameout might be the consequence.' This meant one had to reduce the engines early and judge and adjust the altitude, distance and descent rate early and precisely.

"I was glad that I managed these tasks well on my first flight with the Me 262, but it had been a true challenge. Another lap and the same concentrated procedures resulted in another perfect touchdown and landing. I had fallen in love with this aircraft. After my first two flights of the day at dusk, I flew my first sortie that same night.

"I was returning from this sortie, and was flying home, and my fuel reserve lamp was already on, so I wanted to go home straight. I was about ten or fifteen minutes from our airfield when all of a sudden a Mosquito crossed my way, just in front of my nose, less than ten meters away. He came from the right side in a diagonal angle and passed in front of my aircraft. It was pure coincidence. He was at exactly the same height, at the same time, so I followed him, and so I just decided to fire a burst into him as he came into my Revi. With a very strong armament of four [30mm] cannons, he went down."[3]

Pilots soon learned that the Me 262 was in fact quite maneuverable at high speed, but not a dogfighter, despite its heavy wing loading, lack of low speed thrust, and inability to adjust throttle speed as in the 109 or 190, although it was not designed nor expected to be a dogfighter. It could be out-turned by everything within the Allied inventory. Only its dive and climb rate were insurance policies. However, as Jon Guttman chronicles, even having altitude was not a guarantee of survival:

"On February 15, [1945] he [Dudley A. Amoss] was leading his flight away from strafing a German airfield near Amberg when he spotted a Messerschmitt Me 262 jet at two o'clock at 1,000 feet altitude, on a 175-degree course.

"'It took awhile,' Amoss recalled. 'I was studying him as he was coming at me. He was higher than I was, but as he closed I realized,

'That sonovabitch is a Jerry bastard.' I kept flying lower like I didn't see him. We passed each other and I was below him—I figured he was going to a Kraut field. As soon as I passed underneath him I gave it a little seeing room, then I spun around, got the old drop on him and started checking the guns, kind of got him in the position where he wasn't too happy. I know I drilled the airplane, but I didn't hurt him, because after the war I got a letter from him. That was fine by me—I didn't look to kill 'em, just get the planes.'

"A more formal description of the outcome appeared in Amoss' combat report: 'He was in a shallow turn to port when I came in behind him and started closing. Observing black smoke, I gave full throttle and started firing between 600 and 800 yards. In a six second burst I noticed hits on the blow job's engines, and as he slowed down, I pulled out to the side for a closer look. I pulled in behind again and, at 200 yards, gave him a series of short bursts. This time there were strikes all over the Me 262 and after an explosion he burst into flames. I thought the pilot had been killed and pulled out to the side to watch him crash. The pilot then catapulted ten feet straight out the port side and his chute opened almost immediately at 500 feet. The burning plane turned crazily around about and crashed with another explosion and burned furiously.'"

Amoss' victim on this occasion was Me 262A-1a *Werke Nr.* 110 942, code letters B3+LS of the III *Gruppe (Jagd)* of *Kampfgeschwader* (KG) 54. Its pilot, *Unteroffizier* Hermann Litzinger, described his experience: "I attempted my fifth try at a landing and reported in by radio at the start point and was advised to be aware of enemy planes over Ammersee at six hundred meters. The landing gear would not retract, so I slowed down and went to three hundred meters in the airfield circuit.

"At this time, I heard a groaning noise and suspected it was the landing gear retracting. I suddenly realized it was the first hits from Mustang gunfire. I was completely unaware until now that I was under attack. I looked quickly outside and saw the left turbine had flame coming out of it. I reacted quickly, cabin cover off, seat belt, off, pulled the machine tightly and quickly up, released the stick, and was pulled by air suction immediately out of the seat. After my parachute opened, two Mustangs circled around me and then shot at me. To immediately quicken my descent, I slipped some air from my parachute and quickly landed on a frozen field near the airfield at Neuburg."[4]

The early flights of the Me 262 in 1943-44 were invaluable for the test pilots, but until they were flown operationally in combat, the truest test of all, the unknown factors that would normally prove inconvenient could in fact prove deadly. Conditions that were mentioned by early jet pilots were the sluggish takeoff ability and the very fast landing speeds, even with the flaps extended. Georg-Peter Eder discussed one landing he had that was of particular interest:

"I was coming in after a mission, and I had the entire American air force on my ass. I had to get down. Even though I did not have any damage, my fuel light was on, warning me. I had perhaps a minute of fuel left, and then I would be a slow, heavy glider, and more than likely dead. I saw the field, put the nose down, and dropped the gear. The lock light went on, and I realized I was still doing over eight hundred kilometers per hour. The wheels hit the ground, and I knew that if I applied the brakes at that speed I would rip something off of the undercarriage.

"Well, I lowered the flaps and pulled the throttle all the way back. The engines died, probably from lack of fuel, but I was still going faster than if I were taking off. I ran out of airfield and plowed into the grass at the far end. Ironically enough, I was lucky, because every square foot of ground behind me and where I should have stopped was full of large bullet holes. If I had not overshot the runway I would have been hit and probably killed. Such is war I guess."[5]

The later addition of full-span leading edge slats helped increase the overall lift produced by the wing for faster takeoff and a more controlled landing posture. This improvement also assisted in making tight turns or reducing stall at low speeds, a tactic that some Germans used to great effect when in tight turns while engaged with enemy fighters. The pilots discovered that the Me 262 held its speed in tight turns much better than conventional fighters, and while not as tight, it was more stable at full power, which provided much more energy retention and stabilizing lift in sharp angled and turning maneuvers. Therefore, in effect, as long as a jet pilot was not lured into a low and slow turning fight, or caught landing or taking off, or trying to out-turn an enemy, he had few problems in combat, with exception to pilot error. Walter Krupinski gave his impressions of combat in the jet:

"The only great downside to having the jet was the loss of maneuverability; we could not turn as tight as the other fighters, so speed was our life insurance. The other problem with such a fast attacking and closing speed was that, just as the enemy gunners had little time to lead you for a kill, you had much less time to pick out a target. You had to be right the first time, and if you did not have rockets, you had to adjust your shooting to compensate for the much slower targets. In this case, there was very little deflection shooting. You closed in quickly, fired a quick burst, and then you left."[6]

However, most jet pilots learned that their greatest nemesis was not air combat, it was takeoff and landing, with landing being a very dangerous business after breaking off contact with the enemy. Losses to enemy fighters in this manner would account for the vast majority of combat losses, far exceeding flying accidents, as stated by Krupinski:

"The one method they would use was going to our airfields and shooting them up. They knew where we were; it was no great secret. These guys would hang around and try to catch us landing, hoping for an easy kill. This was why we had Fw 190s or Me 109s that would fly cover for us to protect our landings. The other problem you had was that after you broke contact, and were usually out of ammunition and low on fuel, the enemy fighters would be following a few miles behind you. On a good day, you probably had about ten to fifteen minutes to approach, extend your gear hoping it would work, land, and get out of the cockpit. Many times, we jumped out of our jets to have the shadows of enemy fighters pass overhead as they strafed us.

"We had many such missions, but we also ran into American fighters. Mustangs were a constant problem, and they would always follow us home, hoping for an easy kill. Taking off and landing, as I have said, were the most tense moments for a 262 pilot, as the plane built up speed slowly, and you could stall out easily if you pushed the throttles forward too quickly, which caused a flameout. This happened several times with pilots, and we finally learned how to throttle up slowly without killing ourselves."[7]

Oberleutnant Franz Stigler, who also flew the Me 262, had his personal observations on the dangers of even trying to get into the air when under attack: "When the alert sounded, your heart was really in your mouth. You knew that from a cold start it would take about four to five minutes for the engines to get up to the operating temperature, allowing a takeoff. That is an eternity when you have the worry of an enemy fighter swooping down on you, killing you in the traffic pattern or trying to lift off, or landing. Pray that you do not stall or flame out an engine either."[8]

Galland's comments as related in Morgan substantiate Stigler's observations: "The vulnerability of the jets during takeoff and landing especially was caused by the relatively long time needed for retracting or extending the landing gear, as well as the aircraft's slow acceleration with flaps and undercarriage extended. Therefore we had piston-engined fighters, mostly long-nosed Fw 190Ds, on our jet landing bases to protect the takeoffs and landings of the jets, as the Allied fighters found out very soon that this was the weakest point of the Me 262."[9]

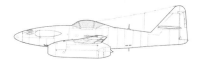

CHAPTER 11

Fighting the Fighters

The first time I encountered a jet fighter,
I thought, "Man, we are so screwed."

Edward R. "Buddy" Haydon

It seems ironic that the first units to receive the jets should be the bomber units, which was part and parcel of Hitler's delusion of striking the enemy behind his own lines with a fast attack. While perhaps making a few Allied personnel nervous and proving an inconvenience, it was not about to turn the tide in the war. The jets did not have great range, they could not carry the heavy payloads of Allied heavy bombers, and their pilots, for the most part, were not trained or experienced in fighting against enemy fighters when engaged. Their losses rose sharply for very little result for their efforts.

The first confirmed Me 262 lost in aerial combat did not belong to a fighter unit, but instead belonged to *Kommando Schenck* and was flown by *Oberfeldwebel* Hieronymus "Ronny" Lauer of I./KG-51. On August 28, 1944, while approaching his airfield, he crash-landed his jet while under attack by Maj. Joseph Myers and 2nd Lt. Manford O. Croy, both flying P-47 Thunderbolts from the 78th Fighter Group. Lauer managed to climb out of the jet as it was finally strafed and destroyed. The first Me 262 lost from 3/KG-51 was flown by H. C. Butmann and shot down by a flight of Spitfire IXs of 401 RCAF on October 5, 1944. This aircraft was designated 9K+BL with work number 170093 and was a total loss as well.[1]

While Schenck and others flew the Me 262 in their bombing missions, they found themselves falling prey to the droves of Allied fighters that always jumped them from higher altitude, a problem well stated by Krupinski and Stigler. Given the types of missions they were flying, and the fact that they seldom operated with fighter cover during their missions and even when they had fighter cover, it was usually limited protection over their airfields, and their longevity was in question. Galland knew that it was a waste of a valuable asset, a stupid decision based upon a layman's lack of understanding. Unfortunately, for Galland and his fighter pilots, that "layman" was the most powerful dictator in the world.

The bomber units were not in the business of devising new tactics, especially fighter tactics, as the majority of these men were not fighter pilots. Air-to-air combat was a learned trade, and the men gained experience through combat. Unless new offensive and defensive tactics were rapidly developed, the new jets in the role of bombers were nothing more than flying targets making Allied aces.

The Germans rapidly realized that although their jets were faster in the climb and they could escape any Allied fighter by pulling the nose up, they were not as fortunate when they tried to dive away from a pursuing enemy fighter. Despite the much higher speed in a dive, several jet pilots soon learned what American P-38 pilots had discovered: the control surfaces had a tendency to freeze at high speed when in a dive. The account by Stigler is noteworthy:

"Once I was flying at around ten thousand meters (over thirty-three thousand feet), and I saw three P-51s above me; they were high. They went into a dive on me, and I know that I was not going to fight them, so I dropped the nose and went into a dive. Within perhaps twenty seconds, they were still five hundred meters above me, diving in, and I was gone. I then tried to pull up, and the joystick just froze. I felt myself grow cold. I thought that I had just killed myself. The plane would not rise, and the airspeed indicator read over one thousand kilometers per hour.

"I was surprised that the aircraft did not rattle, the engines were fine, so I alternated kicking the rudder left and right quickly, and really did some praying. This seemed to break the evil spell, and slowly I regained control. By the time I pulled up, I was looking to my left and saw the shocked faces of a group of farmers in this field. As I banked around, catching my breath, I saw that I had been so low I actually blew all of the hay they had collected off the wagon, some of it was smoking! I learned right then that I would never do that again. I would outrun them straight or climb, but going down steep was taboo. No more of that, and I wrote a report and gave it to Galland. Later the next day we actually had a briefing on my experience. Remember that we were all still learning about these planes. This was a valuable lesson."

Galland and the other leaders knew that the Me 262 was so fast that new tactics had to be devised to attack American bombers and survive Allied fighters. In the head-on attack method, which proved so effective by the few *experten* who could master it in conventional fighters, the closing was very fast, but not so fast as to prevent getting good cannon hits in a diving pass. This method also severely limited the gunners in the bomber formations from getting a solid target acquisition. Walter Schuck explained the best way to knock down a heavy bomber in the Me 262:

"The bombers had to be hit in or near the inboard engines, for it was through this area of the wing that the fuel lines ran. I simply couldn't understand why other pilots would choose to attack a bomber box from the side, from below, or from the front. It was against tactics such as these that the B-17 really lived up to its name as a 'Flying Fortress.'

"Only if one flew with, and not against, the bomber stream, and only if one attacked from above, could one escape the worst of its concentrated firepower. Furthermore, the B-17s' gunners could open fire on us with their heavy machine-guns from an effective range of seven hundred meters, where as our four Mk 108 nose cannons were calibrated for a range of only about three hundred meters."[2]

JG-7 pilots had already learned many of these lessons, which were later passed on to JV- 44, which did not become fully operational until very late in the war in March 1945. Most of that month was spent training and organizing the new unit. During this time the unit scored its first kill, an IL-2 *Sturmovik* shot down by *Oberstleutnant* Johannes Steinhoff, just before the unit was relocated to Munich-Riem.

The purpose of this assignment was twofold: to better protect the railway junctions and jet production plants in southern Germany. By the end of the war, JV-44 had shot down fifty-six aircraft. Johannes Steinhoff recalled his first fighter versus fighter encounter against Soviet aircraft while flying the Me 262 shortly after he joined JG-7, just before taking command replacing Eder, who had in fact been promoted to command the day Walter Nowotny was killed:

"I once engaged about twelve or so Soviet fighters, mostly Yaks, I think, and as I winged over to attack, it looked as if they were standing still, not moving at all. This one guy was above me, and he must have seen me, as he half rolled and pulled tight into a right hand banking maneuver, and then there was another that also banked right, passing right in front of me, just past my nose. I was caught in his propeller wash, the buffeting was intense. He was probably about forty feet off my wing. I never had a chance to shoot either of these guys. But there was another Yak that was turning left, in a shallow bank, and I wanted him. I was below him, also turning left to get in close, and when I sighted him I fired, but missed. I saw the cannon rounds streak behind him. This was when I began to doubt the dogfighting qualities of the Me 262."[3]

The *Luftwaffe* pilots eventually learned how to fight against Allied fighters, developing their tactics and adjusting to the Me 262's higher speed. Once the "ambush" method was perfected (diving in from above or climbing up from below), the Me 262 proved a formidable fighter, with just a couple of hits from the 30mm explosive cannon shells usually being sufficient to bring down any fighter. Georg-Peter Eder explained how the method worked to perfection if performed by two or more experienced jet pilots:

"The great thing about the 262 was that it really did not matter whether you were in the high or the low element. If we were flying, and we were below and behind, one pilot would climb in from behind, achieve the altitude advantage, and then dive in. Once he was noticed, the enemy fighters would usually break left or right . . . knowing they could out-turn us. If that happened, we in the lower element could then just tap the rudder and pull up to lead them.

"If the enemy were above and noticed us, where they had the altitude advantage, we would just climb into them, and if they broke, we could again shift and achieve lead. Either way we could outrun them, that is if everything was working on the jets properly. If the enemy was above and behind us, and they went to bounce us, we could just dive away and then pull up to leave them far behind, and eventually bank around to try and get them.

"If we came at the fighters head-on, we had the firepower advantage; our cannons would just explode them. Once I did this and flew through the debris, which was ingested into the left engine. I limped back to Achmer and landed safely. The plane flew again the next day with a new engine."[4]

However, the Germans also learned that their jets had weaknesses, and if one engine was out due to technical problems or damage, they lost over a hundred miles per hour, making them slower and less maneuverable than their Allied counterparts. When one engine was out, the jet tended to yaw in the opposite direction, forcing the pilot to apply opposite rudder to maintain a proper attitude. When operating perfectly, the jet was a great advantage; when it was not, it could be a deathtrap.

Many of the Germans who scored heavily against Allied fighters used the ambush method, such as *Hauptmann* Franz Schall, who shot down six four-engine bombers, ten of his twelve enemy fighters being P-51 Mustangs. *Oberstleutnant* Heinrich Bär scored sixteen enemy aircraft confirmed while flying the Me 262. Other notable Me

262 aces included Georg-Peter Eder, who shot down twelve enemy aircraft in the jet, with nine being P-51s (one in a collision), while Heinz-Helmut Baudach shot down one Spitfire and two P-51s among his kills. Eder described one of his most interesting fighter kills in the jet:

"I had been pretty good at knocking down the big bombers, where [Egon] Mayer, [Herbert] Rollwage and a few others had been using the head-on attack in Fw 190s, and they were the experts. I thought that this might work when I encountered an enemy fighter. I had great confidence in the four cannons; that was a lot of metal going down range. After shooting down a couple of P-51s with deflection shots before, I came across a group of the Mustangs.

"They were below my flight of five jets, heading at us, perhaps two thousand meters below. I called them out and moved the stick forward; lining up the last guy, as I called out the seven Mustangs, we each took a number, so as to not attack the same aircraft. We went into the dive, picking up speed. My indicator told me that I was at nearly nine hundred kilometers [per hour], and in just perhaps a couple of seconds I led the Mustang, just a quick burst. He flew through the few cannon shells. He just broke apart. There was no explosion, no fire, his wings and tail just dropped off, as if cut by a saw.

"I pulled out of the dive; we had scored three kills, and damaged three others. We were low on fuel so we broke off contact. I was very impressed with the firepower of the cannons. However, although the 262 was not a highly agile fighter, not when compared to the 109 or 190, I found out once that if you extended the flaps, applied opposite rudder to tighten the turn, and maintained your speed above two hundred kilometers [per hour], you could out-turn the P-38 and P-47, but you would also run the very dangerous chance of stalling. This happened once with me, and I lost an engine, but made it back.

"It was November 9, 1944, when I shot down two P-51 Mustangs. This was interesting, because I really had to work for those two kills. [Eder engaged four planes out of several P-47s and P-51s, taking on two of each.] This was when I learned that I could also out-turn the P-51. This was how I scored good hits on one P-47 but did not see it go down.

"The first P-51 kill was the result of my being jumped from higher altitude, so I simply pulled back on the stick and climbed in a sixty or so degree angle. I gained another two thousand meters quickly, and when I leveled and rolled out, I could see the Mustangs could not hold that climb. That was when I just winged over, kept the two Mustangs in sight, and dove down. They saw me, and I saw that I was gaining on one, and he tried to pull up, making me undershoot. This did not happen. Once I saw him raise his nose, I did the same, fired a quick burst, flashed over him, rolled out, looked back and saw he was on fire, going down.

"Then I had to worry, since he had a wingman, and I did not, and the other guys [the P-47s] decided to turn to get me head-on. I thought to myself, 'OK I can do this,' and came out of my roll. Suddenly the P-51 [the original target's wingman] broke right, rolled and then left, and pulled up, firing a lot of bullets into my belly. He did not hit an engine, so I was lucky, but I rolled in the same direction.

"He came out of the turn and leveled, but then he saw me, so he went into a tight turn, trying eventually to turn inside me. This was when I thought 'What the hell' and followed him. I began to lose speed, but the turn got tight when I applied right rudder in the right turn. Then I saw that I was losing sight of him to my left, so I applied left rudder, watched the airspeed, and then I realized that he was going to have to dive, and he did.

"The P-51 and P-47 could out-dive anything we had except the 262, but then again I had to be very careful, since high-speed dives often made the controls freeze due to the stress of the g forces. I figured if the Mustang was going down I would follow, and I dropped from an altitude of about nine hundred meters to almost treetop level in perhaps ten seconds, and my airspeed indicator was all the way to the right, well over one thousand kilometers per hour. [Eder would later learn his ASI was broken.] I gained on him, and I was within a hundred meters when I fired. I saw strikes against him, there was some smoke, and then I saw him try to pull up, but I gave another quick burst into him and he just slammed into the ground."[5]

Johannes Steinhoff explained his learning curve on attacking fighters: "What I had to learn was that, unlike in the Me 109, I could not easily reduce power or flaps to tighten a turn, getting in behind an enemy fighter. It would not work; you could flame out the engines, or go into an unrecoverable stall, usually a flat spin. Bleeding off airspeed by pulling up into the enemy was also not as effective due to the higher speeds, but it would work. The great danger was in diving into the attack. You could rapidly build up so much airspeed the control surfaces could freeze, and bailing out would not be possible due to the external forces.

"We also learned that dogfighting against these fighters was sheer suicide; hit and run, close in fast, fire and get away, and the return for another pass is possible was the only feasible way to successfully engage, especially if the enemy fighters were in large numbers. By late 1944 through the following year, that was pretty much all we had; swarms of American fighters hitting every corner of Europe. I would say that the best attack method was the ambush, but if you could dive in, close fast, sight in and fire a one- to two-second burst accurately, your target went down, often brilliantly."[6]

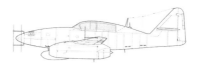

CHAPTER 12

Fighting the Bombers

*I was pretty good at shooting down heavy bombers
in standard fighters, but the jet and its speed and
heavy weapons made me feel sorry for the enemy.*

Georg-Peter Eder

The jet pilots who could shoot down fighters consistently were truly gifted aviators. Shooting down the bombers (the primary targets) required much less flying skill, more nerves of steel, and a lot of luck to survive the ordeal. The jet pilots did not have to worry only about escort fighters, they also had the concern of the bomber formations' defensive fire. This was true of all German fighter pilots, but the jet's higher speed made bailing out more problematic, and if an engine were damaged, 262 pilots had to decide if they would try to land to save the aircraft or bail out. Floating down in a hostile sky was a very unnerving proposition in any case. Further fighting was out of the question. The answer to the attack on bomber formations was the development of the ambush tactic, especially designed for jet combat. All of these men mastered the ambush attack method.

Regarding the Germans attacking bombers, according to Steinhoff: "The closing speed in the Me 262 was too high for accurate shooting in the head-on attack. Even attacking from astern, the closing speed was too great for the short-ranged thirty-millimeter cannons to be used to maximum effect, unless approaching from the five or seven o'clock positions, where the lead was cut down considerably. This was where you would find success."[1] Therefore, the Germans created what was called the "rollercoaster attack."

The Me 262s would approach from astern and about 5,000 to 6,000 feet higher (1,800 meters) than the bombers, and then would go into a shallow dive when three to four miles away from the bombers. This tactic took them through the escort fighters with little risk of interception, as nothing could catch the jet in a dive, not even the vaunted P-47 Thunderbolt. The jets would then pull up, climbing in a shallow angle just below the bombers, and as they pulled up sharply they reduced their airspeed.

The jet pilots would then level out when they were about 1,000 meters away, closing on the bombers and well placed to attack them. The pilots had to get fairly close, placing themselves within the .50-caliber defensive fire of the gunners, since their 30mm cannons were not very accurate beyond 600 meters. The pilots also had to be very cognizant of their speed and distance to the targets, as they had to break off contact at around 200 meters to avoid a collision.

The Me 262 pilots would normally commence firing at around 500 meters, which gave them a three-second burst, which was usually enough. The top turret and ball turret gunners in the formation found their electric gun turrets had problems tracking the jets due to the speed, making target acquisition extremely difficult due to both the closure rate and their breaking contact rapidly after firing.

The other factor was the tactic Nowotny started using, which was to revert to the old *kette* formation of three aircraft, which proved very effective at attacking bombers. This had been the formation before the war, until the Condor Legion fighter pilots under Werner Mölders created the "finger four" formation, called a *schwarm*, that gave two pilots each a wingman to observe and protect the flanks of the center aircraft. The British rapidly adopted this method early in the Battle of Britain, due to the massive successes of the Germans, and the Americans followed.

The plan Nowotny devised was simple: attack rapidly out of the sun if possible, from the stern at between the three, five, seven, and nine o'clock positions; strike quickly with short bursts; inflict heavy damage; and then fly through the formations too fast for the gunner to achieve proper lead. This usually worked the first one or two times. By the third attack, the gunners normally adjusted their lead, and the escort fighters were aware of the problem.

Wolfgang Späte chronicled a mission where he engaged bombers in an on-the-job training attack where he obtained a couple of observations at the end of April 1945: "It was during one of these attacks between Dresden and Chemnitz against four engine bombers that I lost contact with my formation. I got separated because I had pushed my airplane out to nine hundred sixty kilometers per hour. As soon as I tried to maneuver for an intercept so close to the sound barrier, the Mach effect stalled the wings every time I put the slightest amount of positive g on the airplane. With the frightening shudder of a high-speed stall, I had to pull the aircraft up in order to get rid of the excess airspeed (unfortunately, the Me 262 did not have air brakes either).

"The formation of twenty Me 262s that I had been leading had already flown through the bomber formation. The tail gunners had already been forewarned as I came in from behind them utterly alone. Therefore, I directed my attention to the outside wing of the bomber farthest on the outside of the formation. It had separated slightly from the main formation, presumably because it had already been hit. I landed a half-dozen direct hits from a cannon burst, and I immediately whizzed past the target. The rest of the enemy aircraft in the formation slipped past me to the side as though they were flying backwards. And, that quick, I was past them too. A look back confirmed that the Boeing Flying Fortress that I had shot at was descending with a trail of black smoke.

"The next formation was already in front of me, again Flying Fortresses, and again, I took aim at the farthest to the outside. The bomber took a lot of direct hits and, once again, the mass of bombers, machine guns blazing, slid by me flying backwards. I have to confess that this pass, even though it only lasted a few seconds, was frightening. I was likely to break off because I had to assume that every side-firing machine gun was aimed at me.

"And they probably were too. But I never saw any tracers and, after landing, I could not find any hits on my aircraft. It could be that the enemy gunners had never seen such airspeeds before and had never had to aim their gun sights with so much lead. I still think that all of the well-trained American gunners in their turrets simply fired too short."[2]

When the Me 262s attacked in the *kette* formation, the leader would slide in the front and fire, and break away, then the second would attack, following the leader, and the third would finish the job. By the time the last jets made their approaches, the gunners on the bombers had been given enough time to be aware of the threat and prepare accordingly, often with disastrous results for the jet pilots. Georg-Peter Eder mentioned the difficulties of flying as the last man in this attack method:

"The *kette* attack formation worked well with the 262, since we were not expected to engage in twisting and turning dogfights, but mainly attack bombers. The only problem with the method was if you used the one-two-three attack method. This was so that each aircraft would fire, roll away or pull out, followed the next one, and so on. If the targets were destroyed before the last pilot attacked, all was usually well. If it was not destroyed, then by the time the last one came in, the enemy gunners knew what to expect. This was how I was shot down once. It was a very interesting day.

"We were attacking a large B-17 formation, and this was interesting because we also hit a B-24 group, and I was the fifth aircraft to attack. The first four had scored hits on perhaps three bombers, and two were falling out of formation. Another later exploded. As I came in I saw the tracers hitting the front of my fighter, I could feel the impact, but I heard nothing. I sighted quickly, stayed focused, fired, and saw the left wing catch fire, and men started bailing out.

"Unfortunately the gunners hit my right engine, which just stopped, and the canopy shattered. The tail was shot up as I banked right and pulled up, and then I felt many strikes against the underside, just under my armor plated seat. Then I lost power, the left engine blew up internally, and I was then nothing more than a heavy glider and out of control. I decided to try and roll the fighter upside right, stabilize it, and then roll slightly after dumping the canopy. This would then allow me to pull up, bleed off airspeed, and climb out to jump clear of the tail section.

"I was at about twelve thousand feet when I left the jet; my oxygen mask had been blown off, along with my left boot, as the flash of fire that I had felt was in fact the oxygen bottle exploding, which was what blew me out of the jet in the first place, and not the fuel cells. I managed to correct myself as I fell. I just hoped the thing held together. I came in for my landing and I was hit again, the rest of the jet just fell apart, and I hit the ground rolling, then bumping along when the nose wheel collapsed, then the jet slowed to a stop, but I was not in it. I was already out, wounded again."[3]

Eventually, new combat tactics were developed to counter the Allied bombers' defenses. Me 262s that were equipped with R4M rockets would approach from the flanks of a bomber formation, where their silhouettes were widest, and, while still out of range of the .50-caliber guns, fire their rockets, often leading the targets accordingly. The high-explosive warhead of only one or two of these rockets was capable of downing even the famously rugged B-17; a strike on an enemy aircraft meant its total annihilation. This method was effective against bombers, and even without the rockets, the four 30mm cannons could take care of business, as stated by Capt. Eric Brown, CBE, DSC, AFC, RN, Chief Naval Test Pilot and Commanding Officer for the captured aircraft.

Brown test flew the Me 262 at Farnborough after the war, and Jorg Czypionka was his primary transition pilot instructor. Brown reported: "This was a *Blitzkrieg* aircraft. You whack in at your bomber. It was never meant to be a dogfighter, it was meant to be a destroyer of bombers. . . . The great problem with it was it did not have dive brakes. For example, if you want to fight and destroy a B-17, you come in on a dive. The thirty millimeter cannons were not so accurate above six hundred fifty yards. So you normally came in at six hundred yards and would open fire on your B-17. And your closing speed was still high and since you had to break away at two hunderd yards to avoid a collision, you only had two seconds firing time. Now, in two seconds, you cannot sight. You can fire randomly and hope for the best. If you want to sight and fire, you need to double that time to four seconds. And with dive brakes, you could have done that."[4]

Although this flank attack tactic was effective, it came too late to have a real effect on the war. This method of attacking bombers became the standard until the invention and mass deployment of guided missiles. Some nicknamed this tactic the "*Luftwaffe's* Wolf Pack," as the fighters would often make runs in groups of two or three, fire their rockets, then return to base.

Yet, just as the Germans were learning how to exploit their new weapon, so were their opponents. RAF and USAAF fighter pilots, amazed at first and stunned at their new threat, began to study the jet. Intelligence reports, gun camera footage, and a captured jet that had been recovered after being shot down divulged a lot of information.

According to the tactic used by most Allied pilots, due to the great speed of the Me 262, the two best methods of shooting down the jets at high altitude were the dive in on the tail—preferably out of the sun—and ambushing the jet. If more than one Allied pilot was involved, one would take the lead, closing in for the kill. His wingman or others in his company would secure the flanks in case the jet went into a banking turn, while one would remain high in case the jet pulled up into a climb to escape.

One encounter occurred when P-47s of the 365th Fighter Group, the Hell Hawks, bounced a jet on March 13, 1945, from the account by Charles Johnson: "2nd Lt. Frederick W. Marling, flying Blue Three, with 2nd Lt. Henry Dahlen, his wingman, joined in a chase of Me 262s by the entire [388th] squadron. Soon they were outdistanced. [Archie F.] Maltbie then called the squadron to reform. Marling and Dahlen broke right and climbed back to seventeen thousand feet to rejoin the squadron. They came in from the rear and it was then that Marling saw an Me 262 fleeing eastward at seven thousand feet.

"Marling and Dahlen did a partial split-S coming in out of the sun right on the tail of the Me 262. The enemy pilot was unaware of their approach until Marling began firing from three hundred to four hundred yards. He continued to close rapidly until he was within six hundred feet, firing all the time. He was getting strikes all over the enemy plane. Marling kept shooting until he saw an explosion from the 262's fuselage; the jet, trailing smoke, dove steeply into the clouds and disappeared. Marling, arguing that the pilot had too little height to pull out of the dive, claimed a kill."[5]

One tactic that the Germans devised was the "two-cover method," where the covering fighters would take off just before the jets did, and then they would take off and fly top cover as the jets radioed in that they were returning. This was to fend off any Allied fighters that had the tendency to follow them home, hoping for an easy kill.

The second defensive tactic was to orchestrate the airfield defensive antiaircraft batteries. They would only fire when given the command, thus ensuring that they did not hit friendly aircraft. The combined tactic claimed many Allied pilots who took the bait, such as a young fighter pilot from the 357th Fighter Group, 364th Fighter Squadron, 1st Lt. (later Col.) Edward R. "Buddy" Haydon, just one of many pilots who fell victim to the "flak trap."

Haydon had two encounters with the Me 262 jets. One was at high altitude, when he went head to head with a jet and learned that the Me 262 was more maneuverable than he had been led to believe; he fell into the trap: "It was January 1945. On January 14, I shot up a couple of planes on the ground. On January 20, we ran into some 262s near Munich, and we got busted up pretty good trying to catch them. My flight included, I think, Dale Karger, who was in a *Lufberry* [circling formation] with a 262.*

"The jet had a higher speed, but the Mustang had a tighter turning radius. Each plane was trying to gain on the other without success. Well, I winged over and entered the chase, but from the opposite direction head on, I passed within inches of the 262, canopy to canopy, and this happened twice. I thought that it was crazy, but that I might hit him, bringing him down by guns or ramming him, and I might be able to bail out afterward. It was a stupid thought, and I woke up smartly after the second pass, but there was nothing I could do.

"I saw another 262 probably heading for home and decided he was not going to get away. I firewalled the throttle and dropped altitude, and there was no flak at all. I closed with him, using altitude for speed, and opened fire. I was getting good strikes as he went in for

*Karger was the youngest ace in U.S. Air Force history at age nineteen.

landing, with me screaming down on him at about five hundred knots. He was touching down, and I had to pull up or crash . . . and the best I could have claimed was a damaged or probable anyway.

"As I pulled up from the airfield, something shook my aircraft—like something had punched it. Instantly, I had fire in the cockpit, and smoke was pouring in, so I pulled straight up, using the high airspeed to gain altitude, and rolled the canopy back. I was still pulling good power even though the smoke was heavy and fire had broken out in the cockpit, so I lightly rolled the bird over and went out over the right side."[6] Another perspective on Haydon's last flight attacking Lechfeld, which was the most heavily defended Me 262 airfield, was chronicled in Merle Olmsted's To War with the Yoxford Boys:

"Lt. Col. Andrew Evans led the mission, escorting 3rd Division B-17s, again in marginal weather, which were bombing marshaling yards at Heilbronn. Two 262s were seen about noon in the Augsburg area, but neither was engaged. However, another was spotted in the target area at 18,000 feet, and Greenhouse White 1 and 2 (364th Sqn.) broke off the escort and gave chase. The section was led by Lt. Edward Haydon with Lt. Roland Wright as White 2. Wright's encounter report tells us:

'We were chasing an Me 262 about 1315 hours on the deck, and as it started an approach to land at Lechfeld airdrome, we turned across the edge of the field in order to fire on him. We were at an altitude of about 700 feet and Lt. Haydon was hit by flak before he could fire and pulled up and bailed out.

'I continued on in, getting close to the deck, and saw numerous strikes on the cockpit and wing area of the enemy aircraft. The 262 went off the runway. I stayed on the deck taking evasive action until I was away from the field, as the flak was thick all around me. After getting away from the field I looked back and saw black smoke coming from the field and believe the 262 burned.'"

Haydon spent the rest of the war as a POW, and over the years, it would appear that his encounter with the two Me 262s on January 20, 1945, were probably with Erich Rudorffer, who described a similar event during that time, flying the first jet, and Theodor Weissenberger, who managed to land his damaged jet on the airfield. Ironically, the airfield that Weissenberger and Rudorffer chose was their own base, and the Fw190D air cover was already engaged, hence the lack of piston engine fighters covering the approach.[7]

What Haydon did not mention, and perhaps did not know, was that if in fact he and Karger were actually in the midst of a half-dozen ace jet pilots of KG-54 and JG-7, most were damaged or low on fuel, touching down at the nearest base. Rudorffer's comments are of interest. Although he did not recall the exact date in January, his recollection of a similar event with Weissenberger in the same location is worth noting. He was *kommandeur* of I./JG-7, and Weissenberger had just been assigned to the unit as *kommodore*. Rudorffer described the event that he remembered:

"I had just been assigned to JG-7 after flying with JG-54. I had spoken to Walter Nowotny on occasion in Russia, as he was *kommandeur* of I./JG-54 and I was *kommandeur* of II./JG-54, but he was practically unknown to me.[8] When I joined the unit, they were relocating from Achmer to Lechfeld, which placed us further south. There was a lot of activity. I went head to head with this Mustang when I was on one of my orientation flights, but Weissenberger did this a couple of times with another one. It was very unreal, but no one was harmed and we landed, but he was damaged."[9]

If this was indeed Weissenberger's jet, it was the one hit by Haydon's 0.50-caliber fire, and he was extremely lucky on that occasion, as the air defenses had removed Haydon from the equation. There is no record of a damaged jet on this date from JG-7, so it may have been a KG-54 Me 262, as several were landing. It could have also been Weissenberger's, but due to such minimal damage, a report was not written, and the jet was repaired quickly that day. What was uncharacteristic was the lack of any significant piston-engined fighter cover protecting the jets. This may have meant that the airfield they landed on was not an officially operational jet field, but perhaps an emergency, training, or auxiliary strip nearby.

Galland had worked on devising the technique of protecting jets with flak and air cover, as he stated: "Operational survival was good as long as top cover was flown by conventional aircraft to protect the jets on takeoffs and landings. American fighters would hang around to try to catch them at those weak moments, which I was to learn firsthand in a few months. The big problem that was growing was that the Allies would target, bomb, and strafe the airfields, hoping to destroy the jets on the ground."[10]

Another pilot to experience the "flak trap" while doing a low-level airfield attack and pay a high price for the effort with captivity was Dudley M. Amoss of the 55th Fighter Group. Although his regular fighter was *Mah Ideel*, Amoss was flying a different P-51D, *Queenie*, on March 21, 1945, when his sixty-sixth mission became his last:

"We'd been assigned to go in and clear out airbases southwest of Münster ... My engine was acting up as we were heading home, but we took a strafing pass at an airfield and then my commanding officer told us to make another. I said, 'Let's not make another pass here, 'cause there's nothing down there but machine guns,' but we made another round. A fellow down there was shooting at me; I shot back at him and got a whole lot of lead. Just as I feared, a bullet hit my radiator. I kept going, but I knew I was hurt—there was smoke coming out as I was heading back, trying to reach Allied held territory in Belgium or at least get as far away from that German airfield as I could before my water-cooled engine seized up . . .

"I was puttin' along, driving real low on the ground . . . I didn't get a mile when my engine finally stopped. I had a complete loss of forward motion, but I could go down. I worked my way between the trees and had a lot of prayers answered when I saw an open field and bellied in near Lingen. There was a fire underneath. I stepped out, walked through what trees were left and saw a lot of people, 10 to 15 Krauts in an open field. I could see no choice—I just stepped out and walked toward them. They looked up and I said, 'Howdy . . . how ya doin'?'"[11]

Another pilot who was chasing a jet kill and was more fortunate was Capt. Robert P. Winks, also of the 357th Fighter Group, when he attacked and shot down an Me 262 on January 15, 1945, killing the pilot, nineteen-year-old Rhode. As soon as the jet went down, antiaircraft fire erupted from Schongau airbase:

"Boy . . . did they have flak coming at me! I went straight into the heavens and suddenly I realized that my engine had lost power, it was only wind milling. When I dropped my auxiliary fuel tanks, I had failed to turn the fuel selector switch on to the internal fuel tanks. I corrected the switch, and the speed gained in my dive on the Me 262 plus the speed of the wing milling prop sucked out any airlock in my fuel lines, and the engine roared back into full power and got me out of there, f-a-s-t!"[12]

Allied pilots would develop and often exploit the tactic of waiting near the jet airfields, either strafing jets on the ground or trying to catch them at takeoff or landing, when they were vulnerable. This was when the Me 262 was defenseless, and many German pilots lost their lives or, as Eder described, were lucky if they survived.

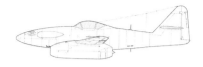

CHAPTER 13

Kommando Nowotny

I remember when we first sat in these jets.
We looked at each other and smiled.

Johannes Steinhoff

*K*ommando Nowotny was formed on the heels of the defunct *Kommando Thierfelder* on September 26, 1944, in Achmer and Hesepe with *Stab/ Kommando Nowotny* from Stab III./ ZG 26, 1./*Kommando Nowotny* from 9./ZG 26, 2./*Kommando Nowotny* from 8./ZG 26, and 3./*Kommando Nowotny*, giving the unit a strength of three *Staffeln* and a *Stab* flight. Galland was the man who was given the responsibility of organizing the unit and proving his point that the Me 262 could, if properly equipped and led, be able to achieve remarkable results. This was his chance to prove Göring and Hitler wrong, and he explained his decisions and method:

"After Thierfelder was killed in July, I was looking for the right type of pilot, someone daring and successful who could lead by example of his courage and determination, and Nowotny had all of these qualities. He was young, successful, energetic, intellectually gifted, and very brave.[1] According to his fellow pilots in his old unit, JG-54, and his former commanding officer *Oberst* Hannes Trautloft, he was absolutely fearless in battle. Thierfelder's death, despite the unit's initial successes, endangered the program.

"I had to find a replacement immediately, although Horst Geyer took over operational command for a while. However, in order to get Hitler interested in considering the fighter option, I needed a named hero, someone successful and highly decorated, liked by Hitler and one he recognized and hopefully admired.

"I received a telephone call from Hitler within a week of placing Nowotny in command of the test unit at Achmer, which was in September.[2] [The actual date was September 26, 1944, when "Nowi" took over operational command. Eder and Galland corroborated the date.] It seemed that Hitler was giving the jet fighter idea another lease on life, since his favorite Austrian fighter pilot next to [Hermann] Graf was in command. I knew that this situation had to be a success for Hitler to take his hands off the project, and I felt completely confident in my choice.

"I allowed Nowotny to choose his pilots and basically run the unit as he saw fit. He had requested his support fighters to come from his old unit, and Trautloft had my permission to send III./JG-54 to Achmer. It had transitioned from the Me 109 to the Fw 190D. This was a much better aircraft for engaging the enemy heavy bombers, and, in the hands of a good pilot, could tackle the Mustangs and Spitfires. [The Fw 190D unit transferred from III./JG-54 was commanded by *Hauptmann* Robert "Bazi" Weiss, and his *staffeln* leaders were *Hauptmann* Böttlander, and *Oberleutnants* Willi Heilmann, Peter Crump, and Hans Dortenmann.]

"With the Diamonds and over two hundred fifty victories, Nowotny was the right man for the job, and I liked him very much personally. [Nowotny had 255 confirmed, and thirty-two unconfirmed kills, which were listed as "probables" on the Eastern Front. Ironically, every single claim he made was verified. He scored his last three kills in the jet on November 8, 1944, the same day he was killed by Haydon at Achmer.] More important was the fact that Hitler liked him very much also. He reminded me very much of Hans-Joachim Marseille, only more mature. I saw to it that he was promoted to *major*, and he was only twenty-four years old, but more than qualified to be a *geschwaderkommodore*.

"Nowotny had been reassigned in February 1944 as a fighter instructor for JG-101 in France for a while following his being wounded, as Trautloft had ordered him into a rest period after his magnificent career in Russia. He had become perhaps too brave, or reckless, depending upon to whom you spoke. The one thing about Trautloft was that he really cared about his men, and Walter was one of his favorites.

"Being an Austrian, good-looking and well spoken, he was one of Hitler's favorite pilots. Perhaps only [Hans-Ulrich] Rudel, [Hermann] Graf and [Erich] Hartmann were held in equal esteem. In fact, although I was not there, I was informed that Hitler had initially ordered 'Nowi,' as we called him, off flight status. He and I discussed this briefly on the last day of his life."[3]

On October 3, 1944, *Kommando Nowotny* attained operational status with a complement of about forty Me 262-1As. Over the next month and a half, the unit operated against Allied aircraft, mostly the bomber formations raking the Reich from west to east, while at the same time trying to establish proper tactical doctrine for the unit. It also had to deal with many technical problems plaguing the unproven Me 262, which Galland explained:

"This was not a comforting thought for pilots expecting to go into battle outnumbered fifty to one on a very good day. The unit at Achmer had been doing great things since July 1944 under Werner Thierfelder, proving the value of the jet in combat. This success allowed us to push the issue to Hitler again, building upon that success once we began to get more 262s in the field."[4]

The unit was the first to realize that a dedicated protection squadron of single-piston-engine, single-seat fighters like the Me 109 and Fw 190 were a necessity for the jets, as the Me 262 could not maneuver or accelerate well at low speeds and thus was a sitting duck for any allied fighters nearby during takeoff and landing. Galland worked with Nowotny on tactics, standard operational procedures, staffing, and even maintenance issues. The powers in Berlin wanted results, and time was definitely not on Galland's side. Nowotny, having a great affinity for his old unit, had requested III./JG-54 to be assigned as his air cover, with all the aircraft, even his own Me 262 bearing the Green Heart on the fuselage, JG-54's emblem. Galland described the role they played:

"III./JG-54's mission was to engage enemy fighters and protect the jets from being ambushed on takeoff and landing, directly engaging the enemy fighters who made a habit of doing just that. Many times we would have American or British fighters flying around the air bases to ambush the jets returning from a mission, or strafe them on the ground."[5]

October 4, 1944, saw JG-7 engage American bombers and fighters, with *Hauptmann* Georg-Peter Eder shooting down a B-17G from the 97th Bomb Group (serial number 44-8586) and another from the 2nd Bomb Group (44-8043). The 2. *Staffelkapitän*, *Hauptmann* Alfred Teumer was killed upon trying to land a jet with engine damage, and he was replaced by *Oberleutnant* Franz Schall.

October 6 was another big day for the Germans and the Eighth Air Force. The 357th Fighter Group was out in force patrolling the known jet corridors along the Rheine airfields. Their mission was to ambush any jets they could locate, clearing the path for the forthcoming bombers pounding targets in northern Germany. The 1st Bomb

Division of B-17s from the 379th Bomb Group would hit Stargard, Stettin, Neubrandenburg, Stralsund, Kappeln, and Freienwalde. The 2nd Bomb Division of B-24s from the 489th Bomb Group was sent to Hamburg and other regions in that quadrant, while the 3rd Bomb Division B-17s from the 94th, 385th, 100th, 447th, and 490th Bomb Groups plotted their routes to Berlin, Spandau, and Tegel. Every unit in the Eighth Air Force provided fighter cover for the mission.[6]

III./JG-7 was the primary unit to engage, and the American force lost fourteen B-17s shot down and four written off upon their return to base. One B-24 was lost. During the mission eight F-5 reconnaissance P-38s and four Spitfires were also lost. I./KG-51 was also active and they lost *Feldwebel* Joachim Fingerloos while he tried to land, shot up by 1st Lt. C. W. Mueller of the 353rd Fighter Group. Mueller nosed down his P-47 after sighting two jets, confirmed as an Me 262 and He 280. Mueller reported that he saw two men parachute from the jet, which was high enough for a bailout even though the wheels were down for the landing. This was undoubtedly the two-seat trainer aircraft (work number 170117, 9K+XL) that KG-51 lost.[7]

The 7th Photo Recon group lost an F-5 Lightning, and the only claim made by a German against a P-38 was Georg-Peter Eder, who shot and then collided with the aircraft, scoring the kill, while losing his jet, becoming wounded in the process, as he explained:

"I was flying this mission to intercept the bombers, but I never quite made it. I saw several aircraft in the distance, and immediately recognized the P-38 for what it was. These were fast aircraft, but I had no trouble closing the range from astern, and they saw me. This one guy broke right, two broke left and one guy decided to climb. This was unwise, as I pulled up to get him, and I fired, but my speed was so great I smashed into him, cutting the fighter in half, and my left engine died. I started to go into spin and decided to leave the 262. I was OK except for a head wound from slamming into the control panel after my restraining harness broke and the glass shattered, cutting me. I got the kill, but lost the jet."[8]

October 7 saw JG-7 pilots intercept a B-24 formation over Magdeburg. Nowotny was unable to take off, but the JG-7 strike force was led by *Oberleutnant* Schall, *Feldwebel* Lennartz, and *Oberfähnrich* Heinz Russel, each pilot claiming a B-24 destroyed, and four Liberators did in fact fail to return from this mission. JG-7 lost two jets in the initial attack, when two P-47 pilots from the 479th Fighter Group, Col. Hubert Zemke and 1st Lt. N. Benoit, both shot down an Me 262.

These were *Oberleutnant* Bley and *Oberfähnrich* Russel, who both bailed out. [9]

The second part of this grand show is detailed by Foreman and Harvey, which is quite interesting when compared to the statements by 1st Lt. Urban L. Drew of the 361st Fighter Group, leader supporting a B-17 group hitting Czechoslovakia. Drew's contact occurred on the return leg near Osnabrück, when he saw two Me 262s taxiing and taking off, and his after-action report was as follows:

"I was leading decoy squadron when I went down to join a fight that was going on under the box of bombers behind our box. When I got there the fight had been dispersed, and I could not locate any E/A [enemy aircraft]. I had left my red section with the bombers, and I had just one flight with me due to a number of previous abortions. I couldn't locate our bombers so I joined up with some red tailed B-17s that were short on escort fighters. I stayed with them until I spotted two A/C [aircraft] on the A/F [airfield] at Achmer. I watched them for a while and saw one of them start to taxi. The lead ship was in takeoff position on the east-west runway, and the taxiing ship got into position for a formation takeoff.

"I waited until both airborne, then rolled over from 15,000 feet and headed for the attack with my flight following and caught up with the second Me 262 when he was about 1,000 feet off ground. I was indicating 450 mph. Me 262 couldn't have been going over 200 mph. I started firing from approximately 400 yards, 30 degrees deflection, and, as I closed, saw hits all over the wings and fuselage. Just as I passed him, I saw a sheet of flame come out near the right wing root and as I glanced back, I saw a gigantic explosion and a sheet of red flame over area of 1,000 feet.

"The other Me 262 was 500 yards ahead and had started a fast climbing turn to the left. I was still indicating 440 mph and had to haul back to stay with him. I started shooting from about 60 degrees deflection, and just hitting his tail section. I kept horsing back and hits crept up his fuselage to the cockpit. Just after that, I saw his canopy fly off in two sections, his plane roll over and go into a flat spin. He then hit the ground on his back at 60 degrees angle and exploded violently. I did not see the pilot bail out. Two huge columns of smoke came up from both Me 262s burning on the ground.[10]

"Immediately after shooting down the two Me 262s, the German antiaircraft opened up and it was a terrific barrage. I called to [1st Lt. Robert] McCandliss and ordered him to join up with me and take evasive action at treetop level. He admitted quite candidly in his report to me many years later, that since it was his sixteenth mission, and to that date, he had never had the opportunity to fire at the enemy, he disregarded my instructions and flew off to attack some antiaircraft batteries, destroying them. Unfortunately, he was not aware of the other batteries ringing Achmer, and they picked him off. The last time I saw his aircraft it was blazing from nose to tail and from wingtip to wingtip and I was calling over the RT 'Roll and bail out, Mac, roll and bail.' I did not see him bail out."[11]

McCandliss, who was the only American witness to "Drew's Two," managed to escape his burning Mustang and became a prisoner of war by bailing out at very low altitude. One of these kills by Drew was *Leutnant* Gerhard Kobert, and the most likely candidate for the second kill was *Hauptmann* Heinz Arnold. (Eder's postwar comments supported Drew, and through the efforts of German historian Hans Ring, Eder's statement saw Drew awarded those two belated kills and decorated with the Air Force Cross, albeit thirty-nine years later. This event created the great friendship that emerged between Drew and Eder, which lasted until Eder died of cancer in 1986.)

On October 10, *Kommando Nowotny* was up despite the lack of any major bombing effort. The only units active were 36th Bomb Squadron that sent six B-24s in conjunction with a few other aircraft dropping leaflets over Holland. The 25th Bomb Group sent four Mosquitoes on a weather reconnaissance mission, while four B-24s did the same over the Atlantic approaches to the United Kingdom.[12]

Oberleutnant Paul Bley, who had bailed out the day of "Drew's Two," claimed a Mustang kill on this date, although it may have been a Spitfire from the 341 Squadron over Holland.[13] The only other fighters operating that day were sixteen P-47s and eight P-51s on an anti-submarine reconnaissance, nowhere near Bley's operational area. Individual British units often flew lone weather or photographic reconnaissance missions, so this kill is not identified.[14]

On October 12, *Oberfeldwebel* Helmut Lennartz scored a kill over a RAF Mustang III from 129 Squadron, flown by a Warrant Officer Foster, who was reported missing in action. Later, Lennartz and Bley had to both dead stick land their jets at Bramsche and Steenwijk, respectively, due to fuel exhaustion.[15]

October 13 saw the RAF Tempest score its first kill over a 262 when Pilot Officer Bob Cole of 3 Squadron caught the Me 262 flown by *Unteroffizier* Edmund Delatowski short on fuel, blowing up the jet as the pilot bailed out slightly wounded. The four P-47s of the 356th Fighter Group also engaged chased-off jets going after four B-24s; no kills or claims were made by either side, although a 60th Squadron Mosquito flown by Lt. D. Sheldon and Flying Officer P. Snell was shot down, killing both men. The Me 262 that shot them down could only have been from *Ekdo* Lechfeld, since no other unit filed a claim against a Mosquito that day, and the pilot is still unknown to this day.[16]

The rest of the month was not as active, and during this period, the transition into JG-7 was started. Galland still had a special interest, and with Eder once again grounded for wounds, and with the loss of jets and pilots, orders were issued. A few jets had been damaged in sporadic encounters, until October 28, when Schall and Schreiber both claimed a single Mustang, with Schall's nose wheel collapsing upon landing. Bley was killed after his jet struck a flock of birds, blowing his engines on takeoff, causing him to impact nose first and explode. Eder described the event:

"I had been set aside by the medical officer, but I was still coordinating things from the ground. The jet was taking off, when a large flock of crows, I think, that had been feeding around the airfield were startled. The jet was almost ready to lift off when it happened. With gear down, off the ground, and then stalling, he never had a chance. That was a sad day indeed."[17]

Erich Hohagen also gave his report on that event, as he was taking off when this occurred: "He was right ahead of me to the right, and suddenly this large flying black mass emerged, I had a few strike my jet, hitting the nose and canopy, but I did not have any go into the engine. I was lucky. I saw him go into the ground, but given that taking off in the 262 was a very tense event during those days, I could not dwell upon it. It was so easy to forget that our enemies were not just flying fighters."[18]

On October 29, *Kommando Nowotny* was busy: Schreiber claimed a P-38 from the 7th Photo Recon Group, and then he collided with a Spitfire of 4 Squadron flown by a Flight Lieutenant Wilkins, with Schreiber bailing out uninjured. *Feldwebel* Büttner and *Oberfeldwebel* Göbel both claimed P-47s. The next few days saw the KG units engaged and losing jets and a couple of pilots, and even scoring kills.[19]

November 2, 1944 (ironically the date when British intelligence deciphered the Enigma code through Ultra and learned all about the unit) once again saw a maximum effort by *Kommando Nowotny* as the radar centers scrambled every unit due to the large numbers of enemy bombers crossing the border. This mission was to be unique, since it was the first time the underwing mortars were introduced to the jets, while they awaited the arrival of the R4M rockets. Conventional fighters attacked the main strike force of 638 B-17s at Merseberg, while the B-24 formation near Minden was hit by six Me 262s. The jets fired in unison, damaging aircraft, including a P-47 of the 56th

Fighter Group. The Americans lost forty bombers, thirty-eight B-17s, and two B-24s on this effort.[20]

Büttner claimed a P-51 and a P-47, while *Oberfeldwebel* Baudach claimed another P-47. Eder managed to escape being medically grounded and shot down a B-17. The only *Kommando Nowotny* loss was *Unteroffizier* Alloys Zöllner, who crashed on takeoff from Achmer. KG-51 lost a jet when *Hauptmann* Eberhard Winker was hit by flak and wounded.[21]

On November 3, the unit took another loss when *Oberfeldwebel* Banzhaff was shot down by Wing Commander (later Group Captain) J. B. Wray flying a Tempest of 122 Wing, as his after-action report details:[22]

"I was airborne in Tempest JBW carrying out an air test and also doing operational trials on a pair of anti-glare spectacles that had been sent to me for that purpose. I was flying at about 18,000 feet when two Me 262s flying in a south-westerly direction and camouflaged blue/gray. They saw me and turned in a wide arc to port, then set off in an easterly direction. I had already launched an attack, opening at full throttle and diving. My speed was in the region of 500 mph.

"I closed to about three hundred yards on the starboard aircraft and opened fire, firing about a four-second burst and hitting the tail plane. The Me 262 continued on course and started to pull away, but before he got out of range, I fired again. Suddenly a large piece flew off the aircraft and he flicked over onto his back and disappeared downwards into clouds in an inverted position. I followed, but the thickness of the cloud made it impossible for me to maintain contact." Wray claimed a damaged/probably destroyed, as he could not confirm a kill. However, he did in fact score the victory, as Banzhaff was killed when he crashed near Hittfeld.[23]

The following day *Kommando Nowotny* added to its laurels when *Oberfeldwebel* Göbel claimed a P-47 and Eder claimed a B-17. On the other side, the 356th Fighter Group claimed an Me 262 damaged, which was the one flown by *Oberfeldwebel* Zander, who landed due to the damage. That 262 claim was by Capt. R. A. Rann, and Flight Officer Willard W. Royer was shot down and killed by a jet over Dummer Lake, which was Göbel's victory. One claim for a ground destruction of a 262 on *Kommando Nowotny*'s airfield at Rheine was made by Pilot Officer H. F. Ross of the RAF 80 Squadron.[24]

Piecing together the remnants of their unit, which was threadbare due to a multitude of problems, *Kommando Nowotny* managed to have eight jets operational on November 5, as Eder stated: "We had about twenty-two jets, but due to battle damage, landing accidents, and just normal usage, as well as the lack of spare parts, we were lucky to put ten into the air on any given day. On this day I jumped into one jet, it would not start. I then climbed into another, and it started, and then the left engine died.

"I climbed into a third, and saw that my rpm and pressure gauges did not work, but that was not a great concern. My concern was the fact that the crew chief waved me off, and I found out that I had a flat right tire, and we had no spares. I ordered all unusable jets cannibalized for the parts to keep the rest working, and then I jumped into a fourth jet. It was fine, and I scored a Mustang victory that day."[25]

November 6 was a big day, with 1,131 B-17s and B-24s from the Eighth Air Force—with escort provided by the 357th and 361st Fighter Groups—hitting multiple targets, with the primary objective being Hamburg. *Kommando Nowotny* was active and ready. Five Me 262s from *Kommando Nowotny* intercepted a large formation near Osnabrück, and they were immediately sighted by the Mustangs of the 357th.[26]

American fighter ace Capt. Charles E. "Chuck" Yeager of the 357th Fighter Group shot down an Me 262 near an airfield six miles east of Essen, Germany:

"I spotted a lone 262 approaching from the south at five hundred feet. He was going very slow—around two hundred miles per hour. I split-S'd on it and was going around five hundred miles per hour at five hundred feet. Flak started coming up very thick and accurate. I fired a short burst from around four hundred yards and got hits on the wings. I had to break off at three hundred yards because the flak was getting too close. I broke straight up and looking back saw the jet enemy aircraft crash-land about four hundred yards short of the field in a wooded field. A wing flew off. I claim one Me 262 destroyed."[27]

Yeager's kill was confirmed, and it would appear that the pilot may have been *Oberfeldwebel* Freutzer, who managed to climb out of the wreckage and fly again. On this day, *Kommando Nowotny* lost the following Me 262s: work number 110402, when *Oberfeldwebel* Freutzer crash-landed near Ahlhorn; work number 110389, when *Leutnant* Spangenberg safely crash-landed low on fuel; work number 170045, when *Oberfeldwebel* Helmut Baudach safely crash-landed due to engine failure at Hesepe; and work number 110490, when *Oberfeldwebel* Helmut Lennartz safely crash-landed near Bremen after being damaged by Capt. Robert Foy of the 363rd Squadron, 357th Fighter Group.[28]

Robert Foy's after-action report describes the event: "Just north of Achmer airdrome, I received a call on R/T at 1100 hours stating that bandits were engaged in area north of Osnabrück. I retraced my course and returned to the area. Flying at 10,000 feet, I saw five Me 262s at 8,000 feet; two of these were about 100 feet lower than the others. I dispatched Cement White and Green flights after the high enemy aircraft and turned to engage the low two Me 262s. The enemy aircraft were closing on two P-51s who were apparently unaware that they were about to be attacked.

"I dove on to the 262s and was closing when the tail-end 262 apparently saw me. He started a gradual climbing turn to the left, and it appeared he climbed at a steeper angle as he gained altitude. During the climb at an altitude of 15,000 feet, I was closing in on him and always gaining during the climb. He continued turning to the left, leveling off as he did so, and pulled away from me gradually. He continued to pull away going into a shallow dive on a straight course. He dived into the clouds and I immediately dove under the under cast.

"The two 262s appeared beneath the clouds and just ahead of me. I took chase but in level flight, their speed was obviously greater than ours. I followed them for several minutes and saw them land on an airfield just southwest of Bremen and very close to town. I hit the deck and started a run to strafe the field. Immediately a wall of flak came between myself and the airfield. I turned off to the right and passed over a small town named Mahndorf.

"I observed as I passed over the town that the houses closest to the airfield were used as gun positions [for machine guns]. I hung to the deck and made 180-degree turn in toward the field. It was during this run that I strafed two flak emplacements and one machine gun emplacement. The flak emplacement personnel were eliminated but heavy accurate fire from the other emplacements made it impossible to hit the field."[29]

Foy saw two other 262s near Meppen ready for takeoff on the autobahn. These were definitely *Kommando Nowotny* jets. Also during this time, 1st Lt. J. R. Voss of the 361st Fighter Group claimed one jet destroyed: "One suddenly turned into me and I opened fire. I saw my bullets hitting his canopy and he immediately peeled off and went into the ground."[30] This account is perplexing when one looks at the actual loss records for all the Me 262 units. It is much more likely that Voss shot down an Ar 234, which would have been operating in that area.

The defining moment for *Kommando Nowotny* was to arrive and would forever change the dynamics of continued German jet operations. Foy's description of events was becoming all too familiar to Me 262 and other jet aircraft pilots. *Generaloberst* Alfred Keller (a World War I *Pour le Mérite* recipient, as well as a Knight's Cross holder, and who was already retired in 1943) and *Generalmajor* Adolf Galland had scheduled an inspection of the jets at Achmer for the afternoon of November 7, 1944.

Generaloberst Günther Korten (Keller's replacement) was already there to investigate the reports of possible sabotage of engines and fuel quality. Galland had already visited *Kommando Nowotny* several times and was deeply concerned over the high attrition rate and meager success achieved by the Me 262. Georg-Peter Eder recalled the event of the visit by the generals: "After inspecting the two airfields at Achmer and Hesepe, he [Galland] stayed in the Penterknapp barracks discussing the problems of the past few weeks. Several of the pilots had openly expressed their doubts as to the readiness of the Me 262 for combat operations, mainly due to the engines, replacement parts, fuel shortages, you name it.

"We were flying the most advanced aircraft in the world, but were on a short leash. We were outnumbered perhaps one hundred to one every time we went up, and that does not count the bombers. Sometimes we had five or six jets for a mission. There were that many American or British fighters hanging around our airfields during daylight and maybe four to five hundred enemy fighters passed by during the day, every day. It was incredible, and morale was still high among all of us."[31]

But fate was to play a cruel joke on Galland and almost jeopardize the Me 262 fighter concept.

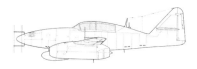

CHAPTER 14

The Death of Nowotny

When 'Nowi' died I just stood there.
It was as if at that very moment, the future of
Germany was clear to me.

Georg-Peter Eder

Galland was pleased that Hitler loved his choice of Nowotny to command the first operational jet fighter unit, and the dashing Austrian was a natural commander. Nowotny's career and command was to come to an abrupt end, as Galland explained:

"I arrived on that evening [November 7, 1944] to inspect the unit and write a report, plus I spoke with Nowotny that previous evening, and he was going to give me his pilots' reports concerning their actions for the previous three weeks. The next day [November 8] a flight of American bombers was reported heading our way, and the air raid warning went up. Nowotny smiled and ordered the jets warmed up, and so the unit took off, about six jets, if I remember correctly, in the first wave, then another."

The day started off with a bad omen, when four Me 262s were prepared for takeoff, *Oberfeldwebel* Erich Büttner and *Major* Franz Schall at Hesepe, and Nowotny and *Oberleutnant* Günther Wegmann at Achmer. At first only Schall and Wegmann managed to take off without any problems, because Büttner had punctured a tire during taxiing and Nowotny's engines refused to start. Galland recalled the event:

"Nowotny wanted to take off, and had to use a spare aircraft, if I recall, but I could be mistaken. The Fw 190Ds remaining on the ground were waiting on the runway to take off and cover their return, while an additional flight was already airborne, engaging the Allied fighters escorting the bombers, which were sure to follow the jets back to base. I was in the operations shack with [*Luftwaffe* chief of staff] *Generaloberst* [Günther] Korten and Eder, and we all stepped outside, where we monitored the radio transmissions over the loud speaker and could get an idea of what was happening." Also present was *Generaloberst* Alfred Keller.

Nowotny did take off in his White 8, work number 110400, for the first planned sortie, though that jet was down for an engine replacement. The engine replacement was eventually completed so he could finally take off. He engaged the enemy on his own, with Schall and Wegmann having since retired from the action after sustaining battle damage. Nowotny radioed that he had downed a bomber and a P-51 before he reported one engine failing and made one final garbled transmission containing the word "burning," as Galland again mentioned:

"Several bombers were called out as shot down. Schall called one, and Nowi called out one, then another, and finally a third kill. Then Nowotny radioed that he was approaching and had damage. The flight leader on the ground, [*Oberleutnant*] Hans Dortenmann, who had landed after engaging for rearmament, was ready to take off again, and requested permission to take off to assist, but Nowotny said no, to wait. The defensive antiaircraft battery opened fire on a few Mustangs that approached the field, but they were chased away, from what I could understand, and the jets were coming in."[1]

The Mustangs Galland mentioned were a combined escort force of P-51s from the 20th and 357th Fighter Groups. The attacking force of B-17s was in fact attacked in waves by the jets, after already running a gauntlet of flak, Fw 190s, and Me 109s on the way in. A major air battle had taken place, and the rattle of the guns could be heard on the ground far below.

The Mustangs had engaged the German fighters, as described by Haydon: "Well, we had just finished a bad skirmish with a lot of German fighters, up in the middle part of Germany, and it was time to go home. I was at around thirty thousand feet with the rest of the flight, watching for enemy fighters, which came up regularly. Since they were concentrating on the bombers, we were not expecting any trouble, and I was just daydreaming, thinking about what a bad day it had been."[2] Galland continued the commentary on the events:

"One Me 262 had been shot down [Schall's jet, and he bailed out], and Nowotny reported one bomber kill [which was believed at the time to be a B-24, but records show was a Boeing B-17], possibly a Mustang kill [which fits with the known losses for the day], and hits on another bomber over Dummer Lake, which was a B-17, that did not return to base. He was returning and he reported one of his engines was damaged. He was flying on the right engine alone, which he reported to be on fire, which made him vulnerable. I knew he was in trouble. Schall had already bailed out, but this was unknown to us at that time."[3]

Haydon continued recalling the events, which paralleled Galland's and Eder's interviews: "I was just glancing over the side when I saw this 262 jet below me at about ten thousand feet. Since there were a lot of German planes around, I broke the loose formation after calling him out. I dropped the nose and slipped a bit, and I watched the jet as I descended, never taking my eyes off of him. My aircraft was faster than that of my leader, Capt. Merle Allen, so I closed faster. I almost made no adjustments to get squarely on his tail, and he took no evasive action whatsoever, but stayed on that vector.

"I noticed that the 262 was not going as fast as it should have been, that there was a problem. I should not have been able to close on him so quickly. Well, the jet dropped to the deck on that same heading and leveled off, making no corrections, with me closing in with an altitude advantage. I was almost ready to fire, waiting to close in and shoot this sitting duck. Suddenly, off my right wing at great altitude I saw two Mustangs from the 20th Fighter Group that had arrived late but were diving, converting their altitude into speed.

"They were way out of range when the lead P-51 fired—I saw tracers fall short as much as sixty percent to the target—and there was no way he could have hit it. That pilot was Capt. Ernest Fiebelkorn, as I later discovered. Well, the Germans were alerted, and I knew what was coming. So I called to the flight to break hard right and away to avoid the flak while I went hard left to the deck, which was safe to some degree because the larger guns could not depress elevation to hit you. They could only shoot below the horizon with small arms, but I slipped in anyways. Suddenly I flew into everything they had. The jet pilot was good. He knew what he was doing. In case he had anyone on his tail, he would lure them into the flak zone, so he could drop to the flak free zone and land. No one would have voluntarily flown through that to get down to the jet. But see, I was already below this height at his level and made the turn."[4]

Galland then continued his description of the events: "I was outside with Eder, Korten, and other pilots, including Karl 'Quax' Schnörrer, Nowi's best friend and wingman for many years, and the ground crew personnel to watch his approach to the field, when an enemy fighter, clearly a Mustang, pulled away not far from us. I remember being surprised because rather than coming in from altitude, this Mustang was low [Haydon's fighter]."[5]

Haydon continued his statement: "I still had plenty of speed, and I thought for sure I would never see that jet again. I turned no more than twenty to fifty degrees, because I was receiving no fire, and rolled level. I was just trying to scoot across the field and either find a place to hide or rejoin the group. Directly in front of me appeared this 262 again, slowing down as if on a downwind leg, one hundred eighty degrees from his previous position, and he did not see me. I chopped the throttle, cutting power, sliding it back to the right a bit.

"Remember that when you cut power on a propeller driven plane, you lose speed quickly. I ended up in the perfect position, and let her drift right into him, just like shooting a student out of the traffic pattern. [I was] below two hundred yards and closing quickly, since he was slowing down. I was going faster, but I did not observe my airspeed, probably three hundred knots or less and falling . . . [at] about one hundred feet [altitude] or so—I was right on him . . . He may have lost the other engine, I don't know, but it was at this time he saw me. I was so close I could see right in the cockpit: I could see his face clearly.

"The moment he saw me he had a startled look on his face. He was totally animated, as if he thought, 'I have really screwed up.' He started thrashing around in the cockpit, as the jet appeared to stall. Then he suddenly snapped right in, falling no more than a half rotation to the left, and I was so enchanted with what was happening I never fired a shot, which would have given me the kill by myself. I thought about that a lot later, knowing that if I had fired, the gun camera would have recorded it, but Merle was watching from higher altitude. The jet snap rolled right in, with me following close behind, and I pulled up as he crashed into the ground."[6]

Galland, one of the two German eyewitnesses, continued his recollection: "Eder called out some Tempests as well, which I did not see. I heard the sound of a jet engine, and we saw this 262 coming down through the light clouds at low altitude, rolling slightly then inverted, and we could not see much as the forest obscured our view, but then came the sound of it hitting the ground.

"The Mustang I saw pulled up and away and around the tree line, so I lost sight of it, but I remember the markings on the nose. I later learned [after speaking with Jeffrey Ethell in 1982] that it was the same fighter unit that American ace Charles Yeager belonged to, which turned out to be the 357th Fighter Group. We had very good intelligence on enemy air force units, and the information gathered

Oberst Johannes Steinhoff flew with JG-26, JG-52, JG-77, JG-7, and JV-44 and scored 176 victories, 5 in the Me 262 with JG-7 and JV-44. He received the Knight's Cross with Oak Leaves and Swords after a stellar career on every front. He retired as a *generalleutnant* and NATO commander and became a prolific author on World War II. *Johannes Steinhoff*

Major Gerhard Barkhorn scored 301 kills with 2 possibly in the Me 262. He flew with JG-52, JG-6, and JV-44 until a landing accident nearly broke his neck. He was awarded the Knight's Cross with Oak Leaves and Swords, but the war ended before he could be approved for the Diamonds. *Ray Toliver*

Major Walter Nowotny, JG-54, JG-101, was the appointed leader of *Kommando Nowotny* (later JG-7). "Nowi" received the Knight's Cross with Oak Leaves, Swords, and Diamonds, scored 258 victories, with the last 3 scored in the Me 262 the day he was killed in close combat by Edward R. "Buddy" Haydon while trying to land at Achmer. Galland, Eder, and others, witnessed the event. *Ray Toliver*

Major Erich Rudorffer scored 222 victories, 12 in the Me 262, while flying with JG-4, JG-54, and JG-7. He also had a British submarine kill. Rudorffer was shot down over a dozen times, making nine parachute jumps. *Ray Toliver*

Oberstleutnant Heinrich Bär shot down 223 aircraft with 16 confirmed in the Me 262. He flew with JG-51, JG-77, JG-1, JG-7, and JG-3 before joining JV-44. He assumed command after Galland was shot down and wounded on April 26, 1945, receiving the Knight's Cross, Oak Leaves and Swords. *Ray Toliver*

Major Heinrich Ehrler scored 208 victories, 8 in the Me 262, and received the Knight's Cross with Oak Leaves. He flew with JG-5 and JG-7, flying jets following the *Tirpitz* disaster and resulting in a court-martial. *Ray Toliver*

Major Theo Weissenberger scored 208 victories flying with JG-5 and later JG-7, with his last 8 kills in the Me 262. He received the Knight's Cross with Oak Leaves and was *kommodore* of JG-7 following Steinhoff's departure. *Ray Toliver*

Oberleutnant Walter Schuck scored 206 victories with JG-5 and later JG-7, with 8 kills in the Me 262. Leading a somewhat charmed life, he survived two bailouts from crippled jets, one being the victim of Joe Peterburs, who became his friend after the war. *Ray Toliver*

Hauptmann Walter Krupinski received the Knight's Cross with Oak Leaves for shooting down 197 aircraft. His career saw him fly with JG-52, JG-26, JG-4, JV-44, and JG-11. He scored two kills confirmed in the Me 262, and he retired as a *generalleutnant* in the West German Air Force as a qualified F-15 pilot. *Walter Krupinski*

Hauptmann Franz Shall scored 16 kills in the Me 262 for a wartime total of 133. He flew with JG-52, *Kommando Nowotny*, and JG-7, receiving the Knight's Cross. He was shot down in the jet twice, once the day that Nowotny was killed over Achmer. *Ray Toliver*

Oberst Günther Lützow flew in the Spanish Civil War, and by the time of his death had scored 110 victories with JG-3 and JV-44, with 2 kills in the jet (perhaps more), receiving the Knight's Cross with Oak Leaves and Swords. He was the leader of the Fighter's Revolt that almost ended his career and the careers (if not lives) of Galland, Steinhoff, and others. *Ray Toliver*

Generalleutnant Adolf Galland flew in the Spanish Civil War and commanded JG-26 before becoming General of the Fighters. He scored 104 victories, the last 7 scored in the Me 262. Galland finished the war with the Knight's Cross, Oak Leaves, Swords, and Diamonds, and he has the distinction of being the highest-ranking combat squadron leader in history, as a three-star general by the age of thirty-three. *Ray Toliver*

Hauptmann (later *Major*) Georg-Peter Eder (second from left, facing right) and *Major* Erich Rudorffer (far right) in discussion on Rudorffer's transfer to the Western Front. After Nowotny's death, Eder temporarily became *kommodore* until Johannes Steinhoff took over; Steinhoff was replaced by Weissenberger. Rudorffer would later become *kommandeur* of I/JG-7 on January 14, 1945. *Ray Toliver*

Adolf Galland at Lechfeld during the time of his test flight. He was accompanied by all of the engineers, senior military officers, and even Adolf Hitler and Prof. Willi Messerschmitt in July 1943. *Ray Toliver*

The vaunted Me 262 in full profile as a clean straight fighter version. *Ray Toliver.*

The Me 262 in the bomb-carrying configuration. Every pilot dreaded the idea of carrying external ordinance, as the increased drag made the jet more vulnerable to air attack. *Ray Toliver*

Oberleutnant Rudolf Rademacher shot down ninety-seven aircraft with JG-54 and JG-7, with his last sixteen kills in the Me 262. He received the Knight's Cross and survived the war. *Ray Toliver*

Major Wolfgang "Bombo" Schenck received the Knight's Cross with Oak Leaves as a fighter-bomber and ground attack pilot, the most dangerous duty. He led *Kommando Schenck* to prove the Me 262 bomber concept and even admitted that the Arado Ar 234 was a better aircraft for bombing. *Wolfgang Schenck*

Heinz Bär (left of center, seated) apparently dressing down Eduard Schallmoser for ramming another enemy and losing the fighter. This may have been the day after he returned following his landing in his mother's garden. The pilot standing to the far left is more than likely Johannes Steinhoff. *Ray Toliver*

Steinhoff's Me 262. The heat was so intense it melted the fuselage, and due to explosions of the fuel, rockets, and 30mm ammunition, parts of the jet were found a half mile away. *Ray Toliver*

This second photo of the Steinhoff crash shows one of the Jumo 004 engines, dismounted due to the explosion that ripped the wing off. *Ray Toliver*

Late February 1945 during the forming stage of JV-44, the first ten pilots have a meal. Steinhoff is fourth from right, wearing a cap. JV-44, like most jet units, was even looser with regard to regulations and military formality. Junior enlisted men and officers ate together, without much distinction. "Saluting even became a rarity," according to Steinhoff. *Ray Toliver*

Major Wolfgang Späte scored ninety-nine confirmed victories with JG-54, JG-400, JG-7, and JV-44, with five kills in the jet. He was also the founding commander of JG-400 using the Me-163B Komet rocket fighter. He later flew with JG-7 and JV-44 with the Knight Cross and Oak Leaves for distinguished service. *Wolfgang Späte*

Prof. Ing. Willi Messerschmitt, the genius behind some of history's finest aircraft. *Ray Toliver*

Perhaps the greatest test pilot on either side of the war, Fritz Wendel standing next to the Me 262 "tail dragger" that started the entire jet revolution. *Jeffrey L. Ethell*

The radar-guided two-seater version of the Me 262 operated by NJG-11 and *Kommando Welter*. *Ray Toliver*

Oberfeldwebel Hermann Buchner started the war as a fighter and later was a ground attack pilot with JG-2 and SG-2, flying into history scoring fifty-eight kills, of which twelve were scored flying the Me 262. He finished the war wearing the Knight's Cross. *Hermann Buchner*

Oberleutnant Kurt Welter, perhaps the highest-scoring jet pilot of the war (and in history), with most of his kills flying single-seat day fighters, including the Me 262. He flew with JG-300, the *Wilde Sau*, and later formed his unit of night fighters. Welter scored sixty-three kills, with at least twenty in the Me 262 single seater. He was the lowest-ranking officer ever authorized to form and command a fighter unit. *Ray Toliver*

Major Wilhelm Herget was an old-timer ZG-76, NJG-3, JG-7, and JV-44, scoring seventy-three victories, fifty-eight as a night fighter, finishing the war flying jets. He received the Knight's Cross with Oak Leaves. *Ray Toliver*

Oberst Hajo Herrmann was already a legend as a Spanish Civil War and World War II bomber pilot when he became a night fighter, creating the *Wilde Sau* in July 1944. He spent a decade in the Soviet gulags and became a successful attorney following his repatriation. He was awarded the Knight's Cross, Oak Leaves and Swords. *Hajo Herrmann*

Captain Urban L. "Ben" Drew following his two Me 262 kills. He received the Air Force Cross and ace status four decades later, thanks to Georg-Peter Eder. The two became close friends until Eder's death from cancer in 1986. *Ray Toliver*

Group Capt. J. B. Wray, who was an established killer of Me 262s flying the Hawker Tempest. *Ray Toliver*

General Benjamin O. Davis, the founding commander of the 99th Pursuit Squadron and later the 332nd Fighter Group, better known as the Tuskegee Airmen. *Benjamin O. Davis*

Major Donald Bochkay, commanding officer of the 363rd Fighter Squadron, 357th Fighter Group, during the period of his jet encounters and two jet kills on February 9 and April 18, 1945. *Ray Toliver*

Joe Peterburs as a P-51 fighter pilot. His greatest day was when he shot down one of Germany's premier aces and jet pilots, Walter Schuck. Peterburs and Schuck became friends following a meeting organized by Kurt Schulze. *Joe Peterburs*

First Lieutenant (later Colonel) Edward R. "Buddy" Haydon of the 357th Fighter Group, who shared the kill of Walter Nowotny on November 8, 1944, with Capt. Ernest Fiebelkorn of the 20th Fighter Group. *Edward R. Haydon*

Hauptmann (later *Major*) Walter Nowotny receiving the Diamonds to his Knight's Cross, Oak Leaves and Swords from Adolf Hitler in 1943. *Rudolf Nowotny*

Me 262 in the Air Museum in Chino, California. *Norman Melton*

Adolf Galland welcoming the new recruits into JV-44 while shaking Krupinski's hand. *Oberst* Hannes Trautloft is behind Galland's left. *Adolf Galland*

Galland during one of his meetings with Hitler following his receiving the Diamonds in 1942. *Adolf Galland*

Major Erich Hartmann, a recipient of the Diamonds, was the world's highest-scoring fighter ace. By the end of the war he had shot down 352 aircraft. He test flew and qualified in the Me 262, but decided not to join JG-7. His return to his unit JG-52 was a decision that would see him spend ten and a half years in Soviet captivity. *Erich Hartmann*

Oberst Hajo Herrmann was a bomber pilot in the Spanish Civil War and in World War II until June 1943. He created JG-300, the Wild Boar night fighters, and ended the war with the Knight's Cross, Oak Leaves and Swords. He would join Hartmann and many thousands of others in the gulag system. *Hajo Herrmann*

Leutnant Jorg Czypionka spent most of the war as an instructor pilot before joining Kurt Welter in *Kommando Welter*/10./NJG-11. He was one of the few Me 262 night fighter pilots to shoot down an RAF Mosquito bomber, which was the most elusive aircraft in the Allied inventory. *Jorg Czypionka*

Unteroffizier Eduard Schallmoser with his mother after he parachuted out of his damaged Me 262 and landed in her garden, becoming tangled in the clothesline behind them. Although recruited into JV-44 by Steinhoff due to his natural abilities as a fighter pilot, he lost more jets than any other member of the unit by ramming enemy aircraft, earning him the nickname "Rammer." *Ray Toliver*

Major Erich Hohagen flew with JG-51, JG-2, and JG-7 and finished flying jets with JV-44. He earned the Knight's Cross and scored fifty-six victories, of which thirteen were four-engine bombers. After Steinhoff's crash he took over as the unit's operations chief. Hohagen returned to the military and became a *Brigadegeneral* in the postwar air force. *Erich Hohagen*

Oberfeldwebel Helmut Baudach flew jets with *Kommando Nowotny* and later JG-7, and scored twenty-one victories, including four four-engine bombers and five victories scored in the jet. He bailed out of his Me 262 (WNr. 110 781), striking his head against the vertical tail section, and died of the injury later the same day on February 22, 1945, while flying. *Ray Toliver*

from crashed aircraft and captured pilots also gave us great informa-tion. There were two other Mustangs that approached from altitude, perhaps a kilometer or so further away. The explosion of the jet rocked the air, and only a column of black smoke rose from behind the trees."[7]

Georg-Peter Eder recalled what he saw that day: "Galland, Korten, Keller, and I watched, we could hear everything, mostly drowning out the speakers that allowed us to hear what our pilots were saying. There was so much chatter you could hardly tell which pilot was saying what to whom. I saw this Mustang come out of nowhere from above the trees, maybe a hundred meters, no more, and then I heard the crash, and the smoke rise. That was Nowotny, I learned shortly afterward."[8]

Galland explained what happened next: "We all jumped in a car and took off and reached the wreckage, and it was Nowotny's plane. After sifting through the wreckage, the only salvageable things found were his left hand and pieces of his Knight's Cross, Oak Leaves, Swords and Diamonds decoration. He had simply disintegrated. The hole in the ground was about four meters deep, and the area for about one hundred meters all around was on fire and smoking. I remember the smell of the jet fuel being quite heavy in the air. We heard by radio that Schall was alive. Eder was standing next to me as we looked through the wreckage, and I promoted him on the spot to take over command of the unit. He just looked at me and said: 'Yes, sir,' and then turned away.

"Losing Nowotny was a great blow, but we had suffered so many by that time, it was almost expected. Hitler, from what I understand, was upset about his loss, but I don't think he really said anything about it to me. I was mostly concerned that Hitler might have perceived this as a failure, and killed the entire fighter program.

"Well, that did not happen, and the remains of that unit went to form JG-7, commanded by our friend Johannes Steinhoff who replaced Eder as *kommodore* for a while.[9] Later, Steinhoff recruited other great aces to command the various groups, and then he joined me in JV-44 and was my recruiting officer for that unit, going to the hospitals, training units, wherever he knew a pilot may be who perhaps might need a job."[10]

Nowotny was given a formal state funeral in Vienna, and the honor guard consisted of his best friend *Leutnant* Karl "Quax" Schnörrer, *Oberst* Gordon Gollob, *Major* Rudolf Schönert, *Hauptmann* Heinz Strüning, *Major* Josef Fözö, and *Major* Georg Christl. The eulogy was delivered by *General der Jagdflieger* Adolf Galland and *Generaloberst* Otto Dessloch. Nowotny was buried at the Zentralfriedhof in Vienna.

Nowotny's death, while tragic for the *Luftwaffe*, had been preceded by his technical and tactical innovations, which, though too little and too late to save Germany from losing the war, provided much valuable data. The successors to *Kommando Nowotny* would use that knowledge to great effect. Galland knew he had chosen wisely in Nowotny, who was a daring leader and a very brave pilot. The men whom he chose were like him: free spirits and aggressive hunters, willing to try anything new.

Galland said, "There were several other men who flew in the jet unit, which after Nowotny's death was re-designated JG-7. Men such as Erich Rudorffer, Theodor Weissenberger, Franz Schall, Walter Schuck, Johannes Steinhoff, Georg-Peter Eder, Heinrich Ehrler, and many others, all of them great aces, rapidly adapted. Eder already had a few bomber kills adding to his impressive score. I also think he was shot down more than any other pilot. I also think he was the most wounded pilot in the *Luftwaffe*."[11]

These men were the first unit to write the book that detailed all of the positive and negative qualities of the jet fighter by the crucible of hard combat. Their experiences would define the method by which the doctrine would be written, but as Johannes Steinhoff stated: "Every day presented a new challenge, a new event that made us re-think what we were doing and how to do it better. This was totally new, revolutionary in fact, and men's lives depended upon each of us doing the right thing, and then doing it better each time."[12]

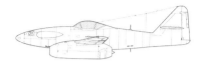

CHAPTER 15

Kommando Nowotny Carries On

I know it sounds crazy, but despite our losses, we still wanted to fly more missions, and almost everyone wanted to avenge Nowi.

Hermann Buchner

Nowotny's body was not yet cold when *Kommando Nowotny* was involved in a vicious three-day running skirmish November 9–11, as Eder claimed two P-51s. The next day, III./JG-7 was formed and relocated to Lechfeld on November 14 with *Major* Erich Hohagen in command. November 14 saw one Me 262 damaged when engaged by 1st Lt. Robert Berry in his 82nd Fighter Group P-38. Berry scored the hits and disappeared. There was no loss to a jet recorded for this date or any other until November 20, 1944.[1]

New parts and three replacement jets arrived at Achmer and two more at Lechfeld on November 20, 1944. The next day, Eder shot down a B-17, which was one of the Hell's Angels of the 303rd Bomb Group (42-102484) flown by 1st Lt. A. F. Chance, which had already been damaged by flak when Eder administered the *coup de grace*.[2] Eder recalled the event in question:

"We had been following this bomber formation, looking to see if there were any fighters around, as there usually were. I did not see any, and being low on fuel anyway, I saw this one B-17 smoking, and went in. I only had cannons, so it was a quick pass, nothing spectacular, except the explosion"[3]

On November 23, *Leutnant* Weber claimed a P-51, with November 24 showing a claim for a P-51 by *Oberfeldwebel* Göbel and two P-38s claimed by *Feldwebel* Büttner and *Oberfeldwebel* Baudach, respectively. Eighth Air Force records confirmed the two Lightnings being lost. On November 25, Eder claimed a P-51 destroyed and a B-17 as a "probable," which was, in fact, a kill.[4]

The following day, on November 26, *Major* Rudi Sinner shot down an escort P-38J flown by 1st Lt. Julius Thomas, who bailed out and became a prisoner at Kitzbühl. *Leutnant* Fritz Müller shot up a 60 Squadron Mosquito with Lt. P. J. Stoffberg and Flight Officer Andrews. Their left engine was smoking and they lost altitude, but managed to land back in Italy from where they had originated. Müller made the claim believing the Mosquito had spiraled in. *Oberfeldwebel* Hermann Buchner did in fact shoot down an F-5 reconnaissance version of the P-38 flown by 2nd Lt. Irvin J. Rickey, and he bailed out of his recon fighter named Rut (work number 43-28619) over Speehardt and was taken prisoner.[5]

KG-51 lost *Oberleutnant* Heinz Lehmann in a crash, probably as a result of being shot up by Flight Sergeant Cole, Flying Officer R. Dryland, or Squadron Leader Sweetman flying Tempests from the 2nd Tactical Air Force; all claimed damaged jets. First Lieutenant L. E. Willis of the 50th Fighter Group also claimed a "probable," and it may have been Lehmann. *Kommando Nowotny* lost *Leutnant* Schreiber, who was ironically the first German pilot to score five victories in the Me 262, when he went down during a test flight. Schreiber was killed in a crash while landing at Lechfeld flying Me 262 A-1a (work number 130 017). As he came in "hot," his wheels had caught the edge of a slit trench created for ground crews to dive into during air attacks, causing his Me 262 to cartwheel, break apart, and burn. Given that he called in damage, it is very likely that he was a victim of the American fighters as well.[6]

The last days of November gave *Kommando Nowotny* more claims, when Lennartz shot down a Spitfire from 683 Squadron, with the pilot, Pilot Officer Courtney being taken prisoner. KG-51 also suffered losses. November 1944 had been a hard month for all concerned. *Kommando Nowotny* had been proving itself slowly but certainly, and the results would hopefully pay off. Galland was quite pleased with the unit, and despite these setbacks, the knowledge gained was worth the effort. From the time Nowotny took command of the former *Kommando Thierfelder*, he began to make certain changes that reflected his personality and personal experience. The results up until his death are worth noting.

The unit had claimed twenty-two enemy aircraft with a loss of twenty-six of their Me 262s, of which eight jets were lost due to accidents and mechanical failures. Like a Phoenix rising from the ashes, following the death of their young *kommodore*, *Kommando Nowotny* was re-designated JG-7 under the command of soon-to-be-promoted *Major* Georg-Peter Eder, and soon afterward *Oberstleutnant* Johannes Steinhoff, until he was banished to Italy, and then later joined Galland in JV-44 (which is discussed in the next chapter).

As a result of Nowotny's efforts and Galland's influence, the unit's successor, JG-7, was to become the strongest jet unit in terms of number of planes and pilots. By November 19, 1944, III.JG-7 had formed as the first *gruppe* of the new *geschwader*. Initially based out of Lechfeld once leaving Achmer and commanded by *Major* Erich Hohagen, III.JG-7 suffered from an inadequate supply of new aircraft and replacement parts. Another problem was that the headquarters in Berlin was staffed by non-pilots for the most part, so new pilots just out of flight school were being assigned to jet units, which Galland called "a criminal act."

The first weeks were a period of frantic organization and activity as new jets arrived and pilots were trained in flying them. They also had their share of training accidents, with ten Me 262s being lost in the first six weeks due to mechanical failure or pilot error. Many of these were engine fires due to both faulty parts and student pilots ramming the throttles forward too rapidly in takeoff.

Later, JG-7 was expanded with the addition of I and II *gruppe* located at Brandenburg-Briest, when *Oberstleutnant* Johannes Steinhoff was assigned as the new *kommodore*. For the next six weeks, he worked to mold them into an effective fighting force, as he explained:

"Eder had been wounded again, and Galland called me. This was just before the Fighter's Revolt, and my being banished to Italy, where I commanded JG-77. When I was asked if I would like to fly jets, I did not hesitate. I caught the next transport to Munich, met with Galland, who was not in the best of moods. The 'Fat One' had really been getting under his skin since he had been fired as General of the Fighters. Ironically, he had just been promoted another rank in November [1944] to *generalleutnant*, but he had no command.

"The unit was named JG-7 from the former *Kommando Nowotny*, and when I took over command we were receiving a lot of jets. Hohagen had done a marvelous job given what he had to work with. The problem was that many were not combat ready. I had about a dozen or so that did not have engines; they came later. Quite a few did not have the avionics packages, since those were made at a different location, and the train bringing parts had been bombed. Then there was the fuel situation. This was supposed to be delivered by rail also, but since the tracks were out, they decided to bring the drums of fuel by road in trucks, which were strafed.

"I finally had what I needed to place about thirty jets in the air, and I had almost sixty pilots, most not yet qualified in the jet. I also had to get qualified, so I began my transition training, which was an easy thing to do for an experienced pilot. Once I was comfortable, I then began my version of the training model. By the time I was replaced by [*Major*] Rudi [Rudolf] Sinner and went to Galland's JV-44, the unit was quite formidable."[7]

Erich Hohagen described his problems as the first *kommandeur* of III./JG-7 following the creation of the unit:

"I was in command for a brief time, and when the *gruppe* was to be expanded as a *geschwader*, Steinhoff came in. I was very happy, as I hated the idea of being in command, with all of the paperwork, political problems, and operational issues that erupted. I think that any real fighter pilot hates a desk, and I was no exception. Steinhoff felt the same way. When he arrived with Galland, I said to him: '*Oberstleutnant*, I present you your new command,' and Galland laughed. Steinhoff looked at me, and asked where the operations room was. I pointed to it, and we walked inside. He looked at the small desk, one telephone, and the radio array sitting against the wall to the left.

"He looked around and said, 'Take the desk outside, I will work from there.' I had the desk moved, and as the men moved it, I asked him why he wanted the desk outside. He said: 'Because I want the men to see that I am omnipresent, watching everything, without walls to hide behind.' I thought that was quite a telling comment, as few leaders worked and walked around the men, so to speak. Steinhoff always wanted to be visible, asking questions, addressing concerns. I would also say that we in the jet units were more relaxed when it came to our military bearing. We still saluted, but the ramrod stiff days of the war were gone; every man chosen to fly was pretty much a veteran of a long war, and we all felt that we had more important things to worry about than clicking our heels together.

"Galland pulled me aside and asked for the reports and paperwork on the jets, fuel, munitions, pilot rosters, everything. I handed him three folders. We all three sat down, all three of us, and went through everything. I think that when Steinhoff saw all of the problems that were beyond our control, he was a little overwhelmed. His quick mind immediately began working out solutions, as he wrote notes to himself.

"We did not even have a flight training manual for the jets. An already qualified pilot gave pilots hands-on instruction. This Steinhoff liked, and I agreed with him that manuals tended to be a waste of time. I worked him, got him checked out along with Franz Schall, and he was qualified within a few hours, a really quick study. He then placed me as the executive officer handling requisitions, and he personally joined Schall in the training program. Within two weeks we had an operational unit on paper. We still had to have working jets."[8]

The pilots' straining was apparently the easiest part of the program, as demonstrated by the interviews that were conducted with the jet pilots by this author. A clear example is the following excerpt, as stated in Dr. Alfred Price's outstanding book *The Last Year of the Luftwaffe: May 1944–May 1945*:

Training to Fly the Me 262

In March 1945 *Leutnant* Walther Hagenah, an experienced fighter pilot who earlier had flown with *Sturmgruppe* JG-3, was posted to III./JG-7 at Lärz. He described the cursory training he received before flying the Me 262:

"Our 'ground school' lasted one afternoon. We were told of the peculiarities of the jet engine, the dangers of flaming out at high altitude, and their poor acceleration at low speeds. The vital importance of handling the throttles was impressed upon us, lest the engines catch fire. But we were not permitted to look inside the cowling of the jet engine, we were told it was very secret and we did not need to know about it!

"By the time I reached III./JG-7 there were insufficient spare parts and insufficient spare engines; there were even occasional shortages of J-2 [jet] fuel. I am sure all of these things existed and that production was sufficient, but by that stage of the war the transport system was so chaotic that things often failed to arrive at the front-line units.

"In our unit, flying the Me 262, we had some pilots with only about a hundred hours' total flying time. They were able to take off and land the aircraft, but I had the definite impression that they were of little use in combat. It was almost a crime to send them into action with so little training. Those young men did their best, but they had to pay a heavy price for their lack of experience."[9]

December 1944 opened with a bang. On December 2, 1944, *Leutnant* Weber shot down an F-5 Lightning of the 5th Photo Recon Group, killing 1st Lt. K. Skeetz, making this his fifth victory in the jet. The same day, II./KG-51's *Oberfeldwebel* Lübking shot down a B-17. During this week, KG-51 took heavy losses, losing four jets in three days, while JG-7 managed to remain fairly intact. The rest of the month was just as unkind to the bomber units.[10] Lübking was himself shot down and killed on December 17, 1944, when Wray caught him while flying his Tempest, as he chronicled:

"On this day the Germans unwisely attempted a fighter sweep through our forward area, which was something that they had not done for some time. Unfortunately, for them, my five Tempest squadrons, Dale Russell's Canadian Spitfire Wing and No. 125 Spitfire Mk XIV Wing had all just got airborne to carry out various missions. An air battle immediately ensued in which No. 122 Wing destroyed eleven aircraft, while the other wings also claimed their share as well.

"I had just taken off, and was scarcely airborne, when our ops center, Kenway, called me to say that there were two jets in the vicinity of Weert. I set off and immediately saw two Me 262s travelling west to east about five hundred feet below me at about two thousand feet. I latched onto the leader and told my wingman to go for the other aircraft.

"The one I was chasing went into a gentle dive, and as we approached the River Maas the German AA opened up. I was going flat out at about four hundred fifty miles per hour, but losing speed. He was about two hundred yards ahead, but drawing away. The visibility was not too good at the time, and I realized that I might lose him. I opened fire, and shot off about a four second burst, but with no apparent effect. I had hoped at least to get him weaving.

"Having thought that I had lost him, I was about to give up the chase, then he started to turn slowly, so I set off again. By this time he was right on the deck, and I was slightly above him, and I found that I was catching him up. I opened fire again, and there appeared to be strikes on the wings. He started to weave violently, which was not too clever at that altitude, but this allowed me to close to about three hundred yards. I was about to fire again when his port wing hit a building on the edge of the Rhine, and he pitched into the river. Heavy AA fire opened up, so I withdrew quickly."[11]

On December 23, III./JG-7 again displayed its dangerous attributes when *Feldwebel* Büttner shot down a 7th Photo Recon Group F-5, and he also claimed a P-51 along with *Feldwebel* Böckel, although U.S. records show that only one P-51 failed to return. Lost was *Feldwebel* Wilhelm Wilkenloh, who was shot down by Tempest pilots Flying Officers R. D. Bremmer and J. R. Stafford from the 2nd TAF. Although he successfully bailed out, his parachute failed to open.[12]

The end of December was still quite active, with KG-51 and KG-54 losing more aircraft and pilots, further proving Galland's assertion that bombing with the Me 262 was not such a great idea, while JG-7 also had mixed success. On December 29, *Feldwebel* Büttner shot down a Mosquito of 544 Squadron flown by Flight Lieutenant Olson, DFC, while the next day there was no great activity.[13]

On December 31, New Year's Eve, *Feldwebel* Baudach claimed a Mosquito, which turned out to be a 464 Squadron aircraft flown by Warrant Officer Bradley. Baudach also attacked a B-17, which was already damaged by flak, and then he turned his attention to a P-51 that came after him. The B-17 escaped Baudach's attack, but not the Mustang flown by 1st Lt. James A. Mankie of the 339th Fighter Group, who went down under Baudach's cannon fire.[14]

Witnessing the event was Capt. A. J. Hawkins, also of the 339th Fighter Group, who turned to get on Baudach's tail as he flamed Mankie, chasing the German ace's jet through the clouds. Baudach received damage but nothing critical. Hawkins never returned to base, and he may have fallen victim to one of Baudach's wing mates or to the German flak. Also, while unclear as to the exact date (30 or 31), Georg-Peter Eder scored his last confirmed kill in the jet, bringing down a B-17. He would be badly wounded again the following month, on January 22, 1945, being pinned by several aircraft, almost being killed, thus ending his war.[15]

The new year of 1945 was to bring more activity, and as the German forces began to fall back on all fronts, the jet units (as well as conventional fighter units) found themselves even more compressed. The adverse part was that the closer the airfields were to each other, the easier it was for Allied planes to bomb and strafe more easily and with greater effect. The positive side was that having such a short flight to the front to engage the enemy meant that pilots who were forced down were returned to their units more quickly, often flying more missions in new aircraft unless they were too severely wounded.

From this point forward, JG-7 was to operate as an authorized independent unit, rising from the ashes of *Kommando Nowotny* in the last five months of the war. The war of attrition would be their last great struggle.

CHAPTER 16

Victories in the Face of Defeat

When I saw the great numbers of American aircraft, and how few we had, I knew we could not win the war. I did hope that we could survive.

Georg-Peter Eder

Operation Bodenplatte—the New Year's Day German fighter-bomber offensive to attack the Allied airfields in Belgium, France, and the rest of the liberated territories—saw eight hundred aircraft thrown into a near suicide mission.

The creation of JG-7 also brought in fresh men from the fighting front. Galland had a lot of say when it came to staffing in JG-7, but once *Major* Theo Weissenberger took over from Steinhoff, Galland began to work on his own private consortium of specialized pilots. On January 15, 1945, *Major* Erich Rudorffer, a very successful ace who had flown on the Western Front with JG-2 until March 15, 1943, and then on the Eastern Front with JG-54 "*Grünhertz*" under Hannes Trautloft, was placed in command of I./JG 7.

Erich Rudorffer earned his nickname the "Fighter of Libau" on October 28, 1944, near the Latvian city of Libau. As he and his wingman, Kurt Tangermann, were preparing to land, he spotted a Soviet task force of sixty close air support aircraft (mostly IL-2 Sturmoviks) approaching the German airfields. He aborted the landing despite being low on fuel and engaged the enemy singlehandedly. Without any aerial support, he shot down nine enemy aircraft within ten minutes, and the Soviets aborted the bombing mission.

Among Rudorffer's other accolades, he was also credited with the destruction of a British submarine while assigned to JG-2, and he would finish the war with the Knight's Cross, Oak Leaves and Swords scoring 222 confirmed kills (perhaps 224) and become one of the first jet aces by scoring twelve victories in the Me 262, including ten four-engine bombers while with JG-7. His colorful career included being shot down sixteen times and bailing out of crippled fighters on nine occasions.

During this period, *Oberstleutnant* Johannes Steinhoff was asked to join Galland's JV-44 as his recruiting officer and was replaced by *Major* Theodor Weissenberger, who earned fame along with the Oak Leaves and Swords to his Knight's Cross with JG-5 *"Eismeer"* flying in the arctic of Norway and Finland, finishing the war with 208 confirmed victories. Later, *Major* Rudolf Sinner was put in charge from February 19, 1945, to March 3, 1945. Under Sinner's command, the war had heated up for III./JG-7 by 1945.

By late February 1945, III./JG-7 had launched a massive maximum effort in their concentrated attacks on the heavy bomber formations. *Kommando Nowotny* had been critical in establishing how the jet was to be implemented in the anti-bomber role, and the new JG-7 inherited this previous experience and the remaining pilots, and it successfully applied this process as doctrine. Several experienced JG-7 pilots were not in complete agreement regarding the appropriate tactics to employ against the heavy bombers. It was finally decided that the jets could not effectively employ the conventional head-on attack developed in 1943 by pilots such as Herbert Rollwage, Walther Dahl, Georg-Peter Eder, and Egon Meyer.

In this conventional tactic, the fighters would approach bombers from the front, at a higher altitude, and dive into or roll over inverted to dive and aim their heavy cannons at the bomber cockpit. This tactic was also proven most effective when using the Fw 190A series of fighters since they carried more heavy cannons than the Me 109s. The combined speed meant that the fighters had only a split second to fire, but this method was also safer for the German pilots as they were within the enemy's gun range for only a few seconds. The speed of the Me 262 and its lack of aerodynamic roll capability made this type of attack impossible to execute effectively.

The jet pilots decided to return to the standard rear attack method or even a five or seven o'clock stern-angled flank attack profile. With their superior speed, the jets could quickly close in on the bombers and fire their cannons and then quickly dive away or pull up from the bombers' protective defensive fire. As they approached, the jets would be exposed for approximately five to ten seconds to the defensive fire from the bombers' rear, ball turret, and waist gunners. Steinhoff himself was of the opinion that the jets should probably be launched against the escort fighters, allowing the bombers to be attacked by conventional prop fighters, such as the Fw 190s, which were more heavily armed than Me 109s. Steinhoff's opinions changed once the R4M rockets were introduced, which was a great force multiplier.

The first test for the new rocket system was on March 18, 1945, when III./JG-7 launched thirty-seven Me 262s to engage a force of 1,221 American bombers and 632 escorting fighters. The unit in question was the 100th Bomb Group of the Eighth Air Force, which had previously earned the nickname "Bloody Hundredth" after the fall raids in 1944. The first six jets from III./JG-7 came in from astern, led by *Oberleutnant* Günther Wegmann. All the jets fired their rockets, and two B-17s went down immediately, while a third struggled, suffering damage.

The second run finished off the third bomber already damaged and destroyed a fourth bomber. The jet pilots then nosed down to dive away from the pursuing Mustangs. Twenty-eight JG-7 pilots reported making direct contact with the formation, with a total claim of ten bombers (two others claimed by *Hauptmann* Steinmann of III./EJG-2) and one P-51.

The end result of the action saw twelve bombers and one fighter claimed, with the loss of three Me 262s. III./JG-7 losses were as follows: *Leutnant* Hans-Dieter ("Hadi") Weihs, who collided with his own wingman, and *Oberleutnant* Hans Waldmann, flying "Yellow 3" (work number 170097). Weihs bailed out safely, but Waldmann was killed. Walter Schuck described the event:

"But then he [*Major* Theo Weissenberger] grew serious, informing me that the *Staffelkapitän* of 3/JG-7, the Knight's Cross–wearer *Oberleutnant* Hans 'Waldi' Waldmann, had been killed in a crash shortly after takeoff from Kaltenkirchen airfield. The incident had occurred on 18 March when his Me 262 'Yellow 3' had been rammed by the machine of his wingman, *Leutnant* Hans-Dieter Weihs, while both were climbing away through low-lying cloud. And while 'Hadi' Weihs was able to land his crippled jet, Waldmann's body was found, parachute unopened, close to the scene of the accident near Schwarzenbek."[1]

Oberfähnrich Günther Schrey was killed flying "Yellow 2" (work number 500224), *Oberleutnant* Günther Wegmann bailed out wounded (work number 110808), and an unknown pilot in an unmarked jet was also shot down, but he returned safely. *Oberleutnant* Karl-Heinz Seeler was killed flying work number 110780, and his body was found in the crash. This was just the beginning of the most hectic and frenzied week of jet operations, and the rest of the week was proving the effectiveness of the rockets in conjunction with the 30mm cannon in carving Allied aircraft from the skies.

The Germans who claimed kills on March 18 were as follows: *Major* Theo Weissenberger of *Stab*/JG-7, three B-17s; from III./JG-7, *Oberfeldwebel* Lübking, one B-17; *Leutnant* Rudolf Rademacher, one B-17; *Leutnant* Gustav Sturm, one B-17; *Oberleutnant* Günther Wegmann, two B-17s; *Oberleutnant* Franz Schall, one P-51; *Leutnant* Karl Schnörrer, two B-17s; *Oberleutnant* Karl-Heinz Seeler, B-17; *Fähnrich* Ehrig, two B-17s; *Oberfähnrich* Ullrich, two B-17s; and *Fähnrich* Windisch, two B-17s. The actual losses due to the concerted Me 262 attacks from all units were twenty-four heavy bombers from the Eighth Air Force.[2]

The following day, March 19, 1945, was also a big day for JG-7, when eleven B-17s and one P-51 were shot down by the following pilots: *Gefreiter* Greim (I./JG-7), one B-17; *Unteroffizier* Koning (I./JG-7), one B-17; *Oberfeldwebel* Lennartz (III./JG-7), one B-17; *Oberleutnant* Franz Schall (III./JG-7), one B-17, one P-51; *Oberfeldwebel* Heinz Arnold (III./JG-7), one B-17; *Leutnant* Karl Schnörrer (III./JG-7), one B-17; *Oberfeldwebel* Reinhold (III./JG-7), one B-17; *Leutnant* Rudolf Rademacher, one B-17; and *Major* Erich Rudorffer (III./JG-7), two B-17s. Lost were *Leutnant* Harry Meier (work number 111545) from 11/JG-7, who was killed in action, and *Oberfeldwebel* Heinz Mattuschka, who was killed after being shot down flying work number 111005. Lost was another unknown Me 262, but the pilot was not killed.

March 20, 1945, was another maximum effort by both sides, with the following pilots from III./JG-7 scoring kills: *Feldwebel* Pritzl, two B-17s; *Fähnrich* Pfeiffer, one B-17; *Fähnrich* Ehrig, three B-17s; *Oberfeldwebel* Hermann Buchner, one B-17; *Fähnrich* (later *Oberfeldwebel*) Heiser, and one B-17; and *Oberleutnant* Gustav Sturm, one B-17. Lost were *Unteroffizier* Hans Mehn of I./JG-7 flying "White 7" (work number 111924), killed in action; *Obergefreiter* Fritz Gehlker of 10/JG-7 (work number 110598), killed in action; and *Oberfeldwebel* Erich Büttner of 10/JG-7 (work number 501196), wounded.

March 21 also saw a lot of action, as Stab/JG-7 pilots scored the following kills: Weissenberger, one B-17; *Major* Heinrich Ehrler, one B-17; I./JG-7 was represented by *Leutnant* Weihs, one B-17; and *Gefreiter* Heim, one B-17. Once again, III./JG-7 had the lion's share of victories with the following pilots claiming their kills: *Fähnrich* Pfeiffer, one B-17; Schnörrer, one B-17; Heinz Arnold, one B-17; *Leutnant* Weber, one B-17; *Leutnant* Ambs, three B-17s; *Unteroffizier* Giefing, two B-17s; *Leutnant* Müller, one B-17; Schall, P-51; and *Unteroffizier* König, one P-47.

JG-7 casualties during this engagement were *Leutnant* Hans-Dieter Weihs of III./JG-7, who landed his jet damaged; *Unteroffizier* Kurt Kolbe (work number 500462), killed in action; *Leutnant* Joachim Weber of 11/JG-7 (work number 110819), killed in action; and two additional unknown 262s, pilots wounded.

March 22 was also a harvest of victories, where JG-7 pilots again scored effectively against the bombers. From Stab/JG-7: Weissenberger, one B-17; and Ehrler, one B-17. From III./JG-7: Schnörrer, one B-17; *Oberfähnrich* Petermann, one B-17; Windisch, one B-17; Pfeiffer, one B-17, Lennartz, one B-17; Buchner, one B-17; Ambs, one B-17; Heinz Arnold, one B-17; *Unteroffizier* Köster, one B-17; Lübking, one B-17; *Leutnant* Schülter, one B-17; Schall, one P-51; and *Leutnant* Lehner of 10/JG-7, one P-51. Lost were three unknown Me 262s, with one unnamed pilot wounded and two unnamed pilots killed. Also lost was Lübking, when his B-17 victory exploded as he passed just above it, destroying his jet. He never bailed out.

Buchner described his B-17 kill during this mission: "During the return flight, at five thousand meters I saw a well-loaded B-17 that was clearing off eastwards. On the first attack I was able to make sustained hits to the right inside engine, starting a fire, which led to an explosion. After another go the crash followed, and moreover the gun camera had taken a picture of the aerial victory."[3]

March 24, 1945, saw JG-7 suffer additional losses. One unique American fighter pilot, 1st Lt. Roscoe Brown, of the 100th Fighter Squadron, one of the three squadrons of the famous Tuskegee Airmen, described the action that saw him score the first jet victory for the Fifteenth Air Force:

"On March 24, 1945, we were escorting a strike on Berlin, to attack the Daimler factory. We were leading a formation of B-17s—the 52nd Fighter Group had arrived at the rendezvous point too late. Then Ben Davis had engine trouble, and the next thing I know I'm leading the 100th Fighter Squadron. All of a sudden at nine o'clock I saw these streaks. I ordered, 'Drop your tanks and follow me.' I did a split-S, went under the bombers, did a hard right, pulled up, shot the jet, blew him up and that was the first jet victory for the Fifteenth Air Force. Two of my men got others. We got the Distinguished Union Citation for this mission."[4]

Two other pilots of the famous Tuskegee Airmen also scored a jet kill each; 1st Lts. Earl Lane and Charles Brantley. Lane scored his victory with a near-miraculous 2,000-yard long-range deflection shot while in a tight left-hand turn, leading far ahead of the jet perfectly. The 332nd had accomplished three jet kills, three probables, and two damaged. Their wartime commanding officer, Gen. Benjamin O. Davis, spoke about the significance of this mission:

"Not only had we destroyed the myths that blacks could not fly or compete in a white military world, we proved we could even exceed those expectations and rise above our white peers. That was important. The March 24, 1945, mission was also the longest fighter escort mission of the war, with a round trip of something like almost two thousand miles, including the return trip. It was also one of the best missions ever, because our group of fighters kept the German fighters away, and we did not lose a single bomber or a fighter that mission. Anytime you took off and came back with no losses was outstanding. Throwing in some kills was only icing on the cake, so to speak."[5]

The Fifteenth Air Force claimed a total of eleven Me 262s, three of which were by the 332nd Fighter Group. Three P-51s were lost and the 483rd Bomb Group lost two B-17s. JG-7 claimed a total of two P-51s, 12 B-17s, one P-38, and a Hawker Tempest that day. The actual losses for the *Luftwaffe* that day were 9/JG-7 *Leutnant* Alfred Ambs (killed by 1st Lt. Earl R. Lane); 11/JG-7 *Unteroffizier* Ernst Giefing, jet damaged in combat; 10/JG-7, *Oberleutnant* Franz Külp (shot down and wounded by 1st Lt. Roscoe Brown); and 10/JG-7, *Oberleutnant* Ernst Wörner (killed by 2nd Lt. Charles V. Brantley). Two jets from III./ KG-54 were bombed in an air raid on the ground.

The 100th Fighter Squadron's Me 262 claims were 1st Lt. Roscoe C. Brown Jr., shooting down Külp, wounding him for the duration of the war; 2nd Lt. Charles V. Brantley, who killed Wörner; 1st Lt. Earl R. Lane, who shot down Ambs, who was flying "Yellow 3." Ambs bailed out at 17,000 feet and landed in a tree.

Known 332nd Group Mustang losses were 2nd Lt. Leon Spears, 302nd Fighter Squadron, downed by a flak hit, taken POW in Poland; Flight Officer James T. Mitchell Jr., 302nd FS, shot down by *Leutnant* Walter Schuck of 3/JG-7 to become a prisoner of war; Flight Officer Arnett W. Starks Jr., 301st FS, also shot down by Schuck, becoming a prisoner. Schuck described the event of his two kills that day:

"As we closed in on them at top speed I recognized them as two American P-51 Mustangs and a P-38 Lightning. In a fluid diving curve I positioned myself behind the trailing Mustang of the trio and opened fire. The shells from the four thirty-millimeter cannons grouped in the nose of the Me 262 smashed with tremendous impact into the enemy machine, which was literally torn apart; the pilot of the Mustang was just able to bail out before it exploded in midair.

"I immediately maneuvered on to the tail of the second Mustang, which was continuing on its way, seemingly quite oblivious. Either the pilot had noticed nothing of his comrade's fate, or the suddenness of the attack had taken him by so much surprise that he was still sitting in his cockpit paralyzed with shock. The explosive rounds from my Mk 108 cannons chewed through the right wing of the Mustang. I must have hit its engine too, because it suddenly reared skywards, flipped on its back and went down trailing a long plume of smoke.

"In the meantime the Lightning had made good its escape by diving away at full throttle. Now I wasn't just enthusiastic about the Me 262's clean lines and amazing performance, I was also hugely impressed by its devastating firepower."[6]

The P-51 pilots Mitchell and Starks were probably escorting a Lockheed F-5 (photo recon version of the P-38) when they were jumped by Schuck. The F-5 escaped. Captain Armour G. McDaniel, 301st FS, suffered engine trouble, bailed out, becoming a prisoner of war.[7]

According to Galland: "JG-7's record was fairly good. It had around fifty jets, with perhaps thirty operational at any given time, despite a few always being grounded with technical problems, and they had shot down a few bombers, and losses had actually been minimal, with most of these losses being in July (as *Kommando Thierfelder*) as men learned to fly the jet."[8]

JG-7 continued the legacy of jet fighters, with some of its stellar members scoring most if not all of their jet kills in the Me 262. However, they also fell victim to their opponents. All pilots knew that altitude was life insurance, although nothing in war is perfect. The Germans also knew that they were most vulnerable during takeoff and landing, and the approach to an airfield was usually a white-knuckled approach for even the most seasoned *Luftwaffe* veteran, as demonstrated by Dorr and Jones, regarding an Me 262 strafing American troops near Duren on February 22, 1945. The classic "bounce" from higher altitude is chronicled, when pilots of the 388th Squadron of the Hell Hawks responded to the frantic calls from a ground controller:

"'Any P-47s in the air south of Aachen, we need some help!' Two Red Flight Thunderbolts were aggressively but vainly pursuing the Me 262 as it headed back into Germany. White Flight leader, 1st Lt. Oliven T. Cowan in *Touch Me Not*, angled to intercept, but the German pilot sighted the pursuit and fled east at high speed, just above the tree tops.

"Cowan and his wingman rolled in on the jet from eleven thousand feet. 'I pushed everything forward,' wrote Cowan. His howling Pratt & Whitney R-2800 using water injection soon had him indicating 530 miles per hour in the dive. The jet's pilot apparently never saw Cowan, coming in with the sun at his back. Cowan shallowed his dive, lined up the target, and fired.

"At his first burst, the 262 disappeared beneath Cowan's nose, just three feet off the deck. The pilot, from Lowell, North Carolina, instantly eased his stick forward for another shot. As the jet popped into view above the Thunderbolt's cowling, Cowan saw the Messerschmitt slam into the ground. A puff of black smoke—no flame—and scattered bits and pieces of wreckage were all that remained of the Messerschmitt. Cowan had used altitude and the Thunderbolt's superb diving ability to catch the speedy enemy. His downing of the enemy was the 175th aerial victory for the Hell Hawks, and it came exactly a year after the group had flown its first combat mission in the European Theater."[9]

During March 1945, Me 262 fighter units were thus able, for the first time, to deliver large-scale attacks on Allied bomber formations with some success. For example, on March 18, 1945, thirty-seven Me 262s of JG-7 intercepted a force of 1,221 bombers and 632 escorting fighters. They shot down twelve bombers and one fighter for the total loss of three Me 262s with three more damaged, but repaired.

March 31, 1945, was an interesting day for the pilots of JG-7, when I and II./JG-7 combined to claim eight Lancasters and three Halifaxes in one mission, another six kills scored later that day against another formation. In the words of Walter Schuck: "This was one of the most successful days in the history of *Jagdgeschwader* 7: even more welcome than almost twenty victories was the fact that they had not cost us a single casualty."[10]

The jet pilots from JG-7 and KG-54 had in fact, during the entire day, actually carved seventeen Lancasters out of the sky, for a loss of four JG-7 jets (one pilot killed, one safe, two missing) and one each from I and II./KG-54, with a pilot safely bailed out, and *Oberleutnant* Dr. Oberweg killed in action, respectively. When JG-7 finished the war it had the most impressive record of all jet units in air-to-air kills, but the unit paid a heavy price for that success.

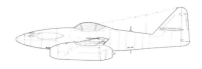

CHAPTER 17

Allied Forces Fight Back

*Once [the enemy] learned about our great weaknesses,
they were able to smash the hell out of us.*

Walter Krupinski

The standard approach against bomber formations, which were traveling at cruise speed, called for the Me 262 to approach the bombers from the rear at a higher altitude, diving in below the bomber's flight level to get additional speed before gaining altitude again and, on reaching the bomber's level, opening fire with its four 30 mm cannons at 600-meter (656-yard) range. Some of the jet pilots mastered the art as stated by Krupinski:

"However, this was only successful if you could do it very quickly, since the closing speed was fast, perhaps seven hundred miles per hour, giving perhaps a split second to fire into your target. The great benefit was that it greatly reduced the amount of defensive fire they received during the attack. Eder and Mayer were very good, and I knew Eder had shot down a few bombers in the jet, and even hitting some fighters."[1]

Allied bomber gunners, even when flying in their tight "box" formations, found that their electric gun turrets had problems tracking the jets, as they were too slow while revolving. Target acquisition was also quite difficult because the jets closed into firing range quickly and could fly into a good firing position only briefly. Bomber losses started to mount slightly since early 1944, when the first complete groups of P-51 Mustang fighters began long-range escorts of the bomber formations. This occurred for a variety of reasons, not just due to the new jets, but the jets were making an impact.

However, the gunners on the bombers did on occasion score some damage upon the jet fighters. One memorable event that Eder experienced was recounted during an interview when JG-7 attacked a B-17 formation late in 1944 before Christmas: "Unfortunately, the gunners hit my right engine, which just stopped, and the canopy shattered. The tail was shot up as I banked right and pulled up, and then I felt many strikes along the underside, just under my armor plated seat. Then I lost power, the left engine blew up internally, and I was flying nothing more than a heavy glider and out of control. I decided to try and roll the fighter upside right, stabilize it, and then roll slightly after dumping the canopy. This would then allow me to pull up, bleed off airspeed, and climb out to jump clear of the tail section, which was the preferred method, and I was used to it.

"As I did this and climbed out, a large bang shook the fighter, and instead of jumping clear I was blown free of the 262; the fuel cells had been ruptured, I guess. I do remember that as my body flew past the dead plane, I looked up and saw there was no tail section at all. I was later told by Franz Schall that when I pulled up I collided with a P-51, the one he shot down, in fact, with the American's propeller cutting my tail almost off. The P-51 had been shooting me up the whole time with Franz on his tail firing at him, with some of his thirty-millimeter rounds hitting me, which explained the heavy strikes I felt. He asked me if I wanted the victory. I told him no, he could keep it, but that he should claim two, as I was also one of his victims. He said, 'No, the gunners on that bomber got you first.'"[2]

Attacking bombers was the prime role of the jet fighters; with their collective armament of cannons and rockets, they could wreak havoc on formations, and then, if unscathed in the effort, return for additional passes and elude the enemy fighters protecting the formations. However, this did not always work. Allied pilots had learned to develop their own tactics and work as a team in attacking the jets. This method was to pay off many times. Merle Olmsted provided an example:

"Sometime in December or January, Colonel Irwin Dregne, commander of the 357th Fighter Group, analyzed the meager information on the 262 tactics and wrote the following: "It was found that a flight of four P-51s could box in an Me 262 and prevent it from evading. This tactic is being developed by the Group and will be used when possible. It is considered that if P-51s have initial advantage of altitude and position and a numerical superiority of 4 to 1, jet-propelled planes can be destroyed on every encounter."[3]

Major (later Brigadier General) Robin Olds, a P-38 and later a P-51 pilot, also commented on chasing the jets: "We called the damned things 'blow jobs,' and we began running into them pretty steady in March 1945; almost every mission someone was calling out a 'blow job.' My first encounter was over Magdeburg, when we saw six of them. We closed very fast, too fast for me to get off a shot head-on in the turn. This one pilot was only about fifty yards away, he had me, but did not fire. I still do not know why, but I probably would not be here if he had. At least we kept them off the bombers.

"The tactic we had devised was a tried and true one. If we could reach their base, especially if we followed them home, we knew they would be low on fuel, maybe even damaged. That was when you hoped for an easy kill, that is without getting nailed by flak. We also had the advantage of being able to out-turn them, and that is critical, especially if you could get a deflection shot within range. In combat I only managed to damage one Me 262, but never got a clean kill."[4]

While the fighter pilots had a method and inclination to engage the new jets, bomber pilots and crews began to dread the chance of an encounter, and for good reason. However, the crews of the Eighth Air Force bomber command were not the only people concerned with the losses to the bombers from all causes. There were those in the United States Congress and Senate who, although in the minority, were opposed to the funding of the bomber construction program.

The introduction of the Me 262 and the reports hitting Washington only bolstered their anti–heavy bomber campaigns, which had been well underway since Big Week of February 1944. The subsequent events, such as "Black Thursday," the massive losses in August 1944 during the Schweinfurt-Regensburg mission, and, in particular, the loss record of the Bloody Hundredth, the nickname for the badly mauled 100th Bomb Group, also compounded the problem. The Germans had introduced an effective weapon, but it was the potential psychological and political problems that were perhaps their greatest ally.

On September 1, 1944, USAAF Gen. Carl Spaatz had openly expressed his fear that if greater numbers of German jets were introduced, the losses to the heavy bombers would probably be enough to cause cancellation of the daylight bombing offensive. Congress held the purse strings, and the U.S. Senate had an oversight committee that was always looking to cut back funding on one project or another, in favor of their own personal political interests. Long-range bombing was not supported unanimously in Washington, DC, and bad results could have meant defunding, as stated by General Benjamin O. Davis:

"I think that perhaps the one greatest misunderstanding about the air war was the fact that it was not just a matter of combating the enemy in the air, and trying to survive. It was trying to make sure that we aviators, especially we black pilots, always performed better than expected. The introduction of the jets really created a problem, but not so much from a strategic standpoint. They did not have enough. However, from a politically tactical standpoint, they could have done our service far more harm in Washington than by shooting us down over Germany."[5]

The senior officers in England knew two things had to be accomplished if they were to save long-range bombing. First, in 1943, they knew that they had to employ a long-range fighter to escort bombers all the way to the targets and back, providing consistent air umbrellas, or losses would continue to exceed 10 percent, which was considered the unacceptable level.

The second was defeating the German fighters, where again long-range fighters would be necessary. The short-legged Thunderbolts, Lightnings and Spitfires were able to penetrate the Third Reich to varying degrees, but the Germans knew this, as stated by *Major* Kurt Bühligen, who finished the war with 112 victories (all against the British and Americans with JG-2 "*Richthofen*") and the Knight's Cross with Oak Leaves and Swords:

"We knew very well just how far by their range the Allied fighters could come. It was logical that we would take off, and the ground radar plotters would vector us into the bomber formations, and once the enemy fighters turned away, we went to work. This was dangerous enough, attacking four engine bombers, due to the high volume of fire. It was much more risky than dueling with enemy fighters. However, later when we had to attack the bombers and fight off fighters, this became madness, and our losses rose exponentially, mostly due to the introduction of the P-51. That plane and the quality of the pilots was really what killed us."[6]

It would not be until January 1944 before the P-51B Mustang, and later the C and even longer-range and faster D models, would be able to accomplish that task. Once the long-range fighters appeared, the losses tapered off to a degree (with notable exceptions as previously mentioned), depending upon the targets, how heavily defended they were by antiaircraft batteries and fighter bases and how many Mustangs were available at any given time.

The tactics devised against the Me 262 had to be developed quickly to counter the jet's great speed advantage. Escort fighters would fly normally very high above the bombers, allowing them the capability of diving from this height, giving them extra speed, thus reducing the speed advantage of the Me 262. Due to the Me 262 being less maneuverable than the Allied fighters, Allied pilots would be able to turn inside the jets, closing the distance in a deflection shot, if the opportunity presented itself.

The only tried-and-true tested method of dealing with the jets was to catch them on the ground and during the takeoff and landing phases. Jet bases were frequently bombed by medium bombers as Allied fighters lurked around the fields to attack jets trying to land or take off. This method was also dangerous, as previously mentioned, due to the overlapping flak array that ringed the perimeters of the airfields along the approach lines in order to protect the jets while Fw 190s or Me 109s flew top cover to intercept any Allied fighters chasing them back to base. This tactic, despite Allied fighter aircraft losses over Me 262 airfields, eventually resulted in greatest loss of the jets and, even more critically, the trained pilots.

Allied fighters were also using nitrous oxide injection in conjunction with the water injection for what pilots called "war emergency power," much like the Germans' own GM-1 fuel injection system. When in pursuit of an Me 262, the pilot had the option of injecting the nitrous oxide into the engine to produce a quick burst of speed. This would allow the Allied fighters to have several seconds to accelerate rapidly to catch the jets, closing the distance.

The two units that would feel the brunt of the Allied fighter presence were KG-51 and *Kommando Nowotny* (and later when it was formed as JG-7). On September 26, 1944, the Eighth Air Force launched a massive raid using the U.S. 1st Bomb Division, which sent 422 B-17s; the 2nd Bomb Division sent 317 B-24s; and the 3rd Bomb Division sent 420 B-17s to hit Hamm and the surrounding primary and secondary targets.[7] Several American fighter escorts were to have their first contact with the Me 262, such as one American pilot, 1st Lt. Urban L. "Ben" Drew of the 361st Fighter Group. Drew's after action report described the event:

"I was leading cadet Blue Flight in Cadet Squadron. We had just sighted the bombers and the marking flares in the vicinity of the target Hamm. We were flying at about twenty thousand feet. I saw this unidentified aircraft cross me about ten thousand feet below. He was flying on a course ninety degrees to ours. I could see it was a twin-engine ship of some sort. I called the squadron leader and got permission to go down on a bounce.

"I started down in about a sixty-degree dive with my wing tanks still on. As I got lower, I could see I wasn't gaining any on the aircraft so I dropped my tanks. I was hitting about five hundred miles per hour and didn't seem to be closing on the aircraft at all. He actually was pulling further away from me. Just about that time, I saw the spurts of smoke that usually come out of a jet-propelled aircraft and wasn't too much luck. By this time we were right on the deck. I could see I wasn't gaining on the jet job and was about to give up the chase when he started a shallow turn to the left.

"I immediately started a sharper turn to cut him off. As I was cutting him off, he started tightening his turn. When we finally passed each other all I got was about a ninety-degree deflection shot, which didn't do me any good at all. I racked my ship around and started after him again, thinking that his speed would have been cut down in his turn. As we straightened out, I could see he wasn't pulling away from me but I couldn't gain on him either. I had everything wide open and was indicating about four hundred ten miles per hour straight and level on the deck.

"I chased him on this leg of the hunt about thirty seconds when I observed this airfield directly ahead of me. I could see that the jet pilot intended to drag me across the field behind him. I called my flight and told them to hug the deck as closely as they could and I started a sharp right turn to skirt the edge of the airdrome. The flak was terrific, and one of my wingmen was hit and had to bail out.

"There was a small marshalling yard directly ahead of me, and I was going too fast to miss it. They opened up with another heavy flak barrage from all over the marshalling yard. The jet job was still ahead of me and flying on a fairly straight course. I had been firing on the ship in his turns and every time I thought I was anywhere near being in range so I had used up quite a bit of my ammunition.

"Just then another jet-propelled aircraft dropped out of the lower cloud layer, which was about four thousand feet, and headed for my flight. My wingman started a sharp turn into him, but the jet pilot kept right on going and made no attempt to stay around and mix it up. The first jet job started another shallow turn and I started firing from about a thousand yards.

"I was too far out of range and couldn't get any hits on him at all. The jet-propelled ship then headed back for the airfield. I had fired up all my ammunition except a couple hundred rounds and my wingman had been separated when he turned into the other jet, so I decided it was just about time I left. I climbed, after pinpointing myself for the rest of the Group, and headed home."[8] This would not be Drew's last encounter with the jets, and the Germans would not be as lucky in the future.

Drew would later claim two jet kills in the same mission on October 7, 1944, with both being JG-7 units. In a twist of irony, more than forty years later, an Air Force clerk noticed Drew's claim for his two Me 262 victories on the same mission. She contacted a custodian of German war records, who knew former *Luftwaffe* pilots who may have been alive and able to provide eyewitness testimony regarding his claims, since his wingman had been shot down by flak and was not a witness. Georg-Peter Eder had been set to lead the mission, but due to his jet having technical problems, he remained on the ground. Eder stated in his affidavit that he saw a yellow-nosed P-51 dive on the Me 262s and shoot both of them down just over the runway. Eder's detailed account was sufficient to confirm Drew's two Me 262 victories.

The rest of 1944 was very similar to the previously mentioned event. JG-7 would be thrown against an avalanche of enemy aircraft, often barely able to get a full squadron airborne, and each mission meant damaged or lost aircraft and wounded or possibly killed pilots. All of these events through 1944 established the jet as a threat, but a manageable one. The establishment of JG-7 from the remnants of *Kommando Nowotny*, and later the creation of JV-44, meant that while few in number, the German jets were being flown by some of the best and most combat-experienced pilots on earth.

One was *Major* Rudi Sinner, commanding officer of III./JG-7 who had previously seen action with JGs-27 and 54. Sinner was jumped by Mustangs at 0915 hours by Capt. Robert C. Coker and Capt. Kirke B. Everson while taking off from Rechlin on April 4, 1945.[9] Hermann Buchner just barely missed the action that almost killed Rudi Sinner:

"I flew as leader of the second *Schwarm*. Sinner started first with the first *Schwarm*, and I followed a few minutes later with the second. Over the airfield the cloud base was down to about a hundred meters, and as I pulled up the wheels and flaps and began to climb, I heard Sinner over the radio reporting enemy contact; but when we emerged from the clouds no American fighters were in sight. I led my flight towards Hamburg."[10] Sinner had apparently drawn all the enemy attention, leaving Buchner' path clear. Sinner described the action:

"Climbing up through the cloud I saw four enemy aircraft in formation above me and against the sun [Thunderbolts]. I climbed steeply but could not catch them, then one of the Thunderbolts dived steeply at me. I learned later that these enemy aircraft were Mustangs. My rockets would not fire and the rest of the *gruppe* had no luck.

"I tried to outrun the Mustangs, but saw four Mustangs behind me in an attacking position. I dived and turned sharply but was hit from behind and damaged. Then I tried a series of evasive maneuvers, but I could not throw off the Mustangs, as I was now too low. I was now running from eight Mustangs, which were shooting at me. I tried to find some cloud cover in the hope of losing my attackers and attempted to fire my rockets, but two of the Mustangs followed me closely. I did not see my rockets fire.

"As I pressed the rocket firing switch my cockpit began to fill with dense smoke, and I saw that my left wing was on fire. The fire soon reached the cockpit, and I decided to bail out. The airspeed was seven hundred kilometers per hour when I bailed out, and I struck the tail in doing so. I realized that my parachute was not open and that my right leg had become entangled in the harness."[11] He barely got his chute open on time.

This was his last bailout and wounding. His war was over. Rudolf Sinner had finished with thirty-nine victories in 305 missions, with thirty-six kills over the Western Front (including three four-engine bombers), and three kills in the Me 262. Three of his victories were over the Eastern Front. He had been shot down a dozen times and bailed out three times. He was wounded on five occasions.

April 4 also saw the loss of one of Germany's most successful aces and tragic heroes, *Major* Heinrich Ehrler, formerly a leading ace with JG-5 "*Eismeer*" with a wartime tally of 208 kills, the last eight in the Me 262, who had joined JG-7 with his old friend Weissenberger, also later joined by his friend Walter Schuck, also from his Arctic unit. Schuck tells the tale of Ehrler's final mission:

"At the time I was with a number of other pilots in the ops room, and we followed the R/T exchanges over the loudspeaker. Weissenberger had just reported the destruction of a B-17 when we recognized Ehrler's voice on air: 'Theo, Heinrich here. Have just shot down two bombers. No more ammunition. I'm going to ram. *Auf Wiedersehen*, see you in Valhalla!'

"As Weissenberger told us after landing, he had immediately looked in the direction where he imagined Ehrler to be, but apart from an Me 262 going down pouring smoke, he saw no signs of any explosions or of a bomber displaying the kind of damage that would be inflicted by a midair collision. Whether Ehrler actually did ram, or whether his machine was shot down before he could do so by the tail gunner of the B-17 he was aiming at, will remain just one of the many unexplained mysteries of the war."[12]

Upon his injuries after this engagement, *Major* Wolfgang Späte took command in his absence, but he was not to be in command long: "I was informed that I would take over after Rudi Sinner was wounded, but I was at that time still working with JG-400 and the *Komet* program. I did manage to get to III./JG-7 and fly a few missions, but then I received a note from Galland, and a phone call from Steinhoff, or perhaps it was the other way around. Anyway, I was asked to join JV-44, with the main unit stationed at Munich-Riem, with another *gruppe* located at Rusin/Prague. This seemed to be a gathering point for jets. It was also the graveyard for the JG-7 jets when the war ended.

"I read his report, and I was very disturbed to know that the Mustang pilots tried to strafe him when he bailed out, and he was lucky that they missed when he laid on the ground. He was beaten up pretty good, since his parachute only opened up in the last few seconds, and he hit the ground very hard, and had been burned and dragged through a barbed wire fence. He was in pretty bad shape all the way around. Even after many years after the war, he was never at his full potential."[13]

JG-7 suffered other losses on April 4, such as *Major* Heinrich Ehrler and *Oberfeldwebel* Gerhard Heinhold of Stab/JG-7, Ehrler being claimed shot down and killed by a Mustang near Schaarlippe and Reinhold suffering the same fate at Neu-Chemnitz. *Oberleutnant* Franz Schall of 10/JG-7 was shot down and bailed out uninjured near Parchim. II./JG-7 suffered the following losses: *Leutnant* Alfred Lehner was shot down by a Mustang near Leipzig and killed, with the same fate befalling *Unteroffizier* Hubert Heckmann. JG-7 lost seven other jets, those pilots' names unknown for the record, but none of these pilots were reported to have any injuries, although the jets were lost.[14]

April 8 was not that eventful where enemy contact was concerned, although Hermann Buchner had a memorable mission. His small group of four jets made two attacks against a formation of B-17s, getting hits, but nothing great, as the bombers' defensive fire and large numbers of Mustangs did not allow them to linger. Upon landing his jet: "Then, just before I set down, something blazed from my right wing, and I could also make out hits on the ground in front of me. As I landed the enemy fighter made out hits on the ground in front of me. As I landed the enemy fighter made further shots at the engine mounts.

"My machine began to burn. The Mustang or the fighter had surprisingly appeared from nowhere. He was too fast, or he had only seen me at the last moment, so he had no more time to take good aim. In spite of the flames on both sides, I was able to bring the machine to a standstill at the end of the runway. Now it was time to leave the cockpit—the flames were already joining together above the cockpit canopy. In my haste, I forgot to undo the harness. I forced myself to be calm, then undid the harness and left the cockpit. I went over the wings onto the grass and away from the burning machine. In my haste I still had my parachute on and it hit the backs of my knees hard. After about fifty meters I came to the end of my strength and collapsed, unconscious."[15]

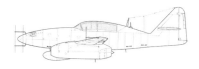

CHAPTER 18

The Last Death Throes of JG-7

*Flying with JG-7 was the highlight of my
career, but also the most painful.*

Georg-Peter Eder

April 10, 1945, was a busy day for I./JG-7: *Oberleutnant* Walter
Schuck confirmed four B-17s destroyed; *Oberleutnant* Grünberg
shot down two B-17s; *Oberleutnant* Stehle, *Oberleutnant* Bohatsch,
Flieger Reiher, and *Oberfähnrich* Neuhaus each shot down a B-17.
III./JG-7 also had a busy day when *Feldwebel* Pritzl shot down a
P-47, with one P-51 each falling to *Oberfeldwebel* Lennartz, *Leutnant*
Rademacher, and *Leutnant* Hagenah. *Fähnrich* Pfeiffer shot down a
B-17. I./KG-54 claimed nine destroyed and three "probables."

The only other kill within two days was a P-47 that Reiher shot
down on April 12. The greatest loss was Franz Schall, who had just
been invited by Galland to join JV-44 and was planning to arrive
within the week. Buchner wrote about the last flight of Schall: "On his
return *Oberleutnant* Schall could not land on the airfield and, having
too little fuel, was forced to land outside. He tried to do a belly landing
outside the airfield, but was killed when his machine rolled, crashed
and burned. . . . *Leutnant* Gustav Sturm took his Knight's Cross from
the gravediggers and, in spite of his imprisonment by Czechs and later
by the Poles, brought it back to *Oberleutnant* Schall's family."[1]

Schuck recalled the event: "As there were more than enough targets
to handle, I decided that I would 'surf-ride' along the length of the
bomber stream: dive on the enemy from a height of a thousand meters

above, select a bomber flying out on one of the flanks, put a short burst of fire into an inboard engine, pull up and away while still at least two hundred meters above the bomber in order to ensure safe recovery, climb back to a thousand meters and repeat the process. Even though a 'ride' of this kind above the bombers took up several kilometers, such was the length of the average stream that it was usually possible to achieve multiple successes in the course of the roller coaster pass."[2]

The B-17 crews had it rough; the jet pilots had found them, and they were in strength, with some of Germany's best pilots in the cockpits. Parachutes filled the sky as aircraft, often in large burning pieces fell to earth. One B-17 in particular was identified by Schuck:

"The thirty-millimeter shells gnawed greedily through the giant tail unit of a B-17. It broke away from the fuselage as if severed by a chainsaw and fell away earthwards. I pulled up the nose of my machine, gaining height before swooping back down on the bombers. I hit the next B-17 between the two starboard engines. As it tiredly lifted one wing prior to going down, I thought I caught a glimpse of a name written on the exposed nose section: *Henn's Revenge*. With the mortally wounded bomber already practically filling my windscreen, I had to break upwards to avoid colliding with it.

"Then I spotted a lone B-17 that had sheered out of formation and was heading north dragging a long banner of smoke behind it. At first I intended to give it the coup de grace, but as I drew closer I could see that a shell had ripped the starboard side of the fuselage open from the cockpit to behind the wing. As the bomber's fate was already sealed, I flew a wide circle around it, not wanting to shoot at defenseless crew-members: the co-pilot was slumped forward in his seat harness and the rest of the crew had gathered in the fuselage clearly preparing to bail out as none of the guns were manned. As I turned back toward the bomber stream I saw the crew leaving the stricken bomber—nine parachutes blossomed in the sky behind me."

This was Schuck's second kill. Schuck's third kill simply started burning and winged over toward earth. His fourth kill was a B-17 named *Moonlight Mission*, which lost a wing due to his accurate fire. Most of the crew had left the aircraft before it exploded at over 15,000 feet.[3] Schuck had scored four bomber kills in one mission, adding to JG-7's laurels, although Schuck would not escape unscathed:

"I was now out of ammunition and searched the sky in vain for any signs of my comrades. 'Right, let's get out of here,' I thought. 'That ride along the bomber stream had certainly paid off,' I was just thinking to myself, when suddenly a line of bullets stitched themselves across the surface of my port wing and into the front of the engine nacelle.

As I wrenched the Me 262 to the right to get out of the line of fire, a Mustang hurtled past me, all guns blazing. A hasty glance at the instruments told me I was at eight thousand two hundred meters, but the left hand engine was losing power'. . . . At least there was no sign of the Mustang, but the bad news was that smoke was pouring from my port engine. While I was still weighing up the chances of reaching Jüterborg, the panels of the engine cowling started to peel back as if somebody was opening a tin of sardines."[4]

Schuck was forced to bail out, only suffering two sprained ankles. JG-7 had suffered many losses, and this day was known as Black Tuesday. Schuck's victor was a P-51 pilot, 1st Lt. Joseph Anthony Peterburs, and in 2005 the two former adversaries, with the gracious assistance of Kurt Schulze, met for the first time at Kurt's house in 2005. They have been great friends since that day. Peterburs never knew that he had scored a "kill," as this extract from his report states:

"I saw one Me 262 hit at least two B-17s and I proceeded to attack it. I had about a five-thousand-foot altitude advantage, and with throttle wide open and fifty-caliber machine guns blazing I engaged the jet from the six o'clock position and was getting some hits and saw smoke. The jet headed for the deck with me in hot pursuit and Capt. Dick Tracy close behind me. We chased the jet to an airfield. As I approached I could see the airfield was loaded with all types of German aircraft. I called Dick and said, 'Do you see what I see?' He said, "Yes—let's go!' The Me 262 had entered a bank of low stratus clouds, and we broke off the chase and started to strafe the airfield."[5]

Peterburs and Tracy soon fell victim to the flak that had claimed so many Allied pilots, and both had to bail out. They were prisoners at the same POW camp, but soon escaped and joined a Russian tank unit until the end of the war. Schuck the pragmatist and true gentleman stated in his book: "The insanity of war had almost brought us to the point of killing each other. Today Joe and I, former adversaries in air combat, have become inseparable friends." This comment has long been shared by many pilots who fought each other, who after meeting, often gathering at the annual *Gemeinschaft der Jagdflieger* reunions, enjoy each other's company, far removed from the days of their dangerous work and remembering the adventures of their youth.

On April 17, 1945, every jet unit was involved in the action against the Eighth Air Force bombers and escort fighters. The U.S. 1st Air Division headed toward Berlin were attacked by seven jets from III./ JG-7, where one B-17 from the 305th Bomb Group, *The Towering Titan*, was confirmed as a kill, and was ironically the last B-17 lost by that unit during the war. The escort fighters were from the 357th

Fighter Group. One went down when it was shot up by 1st Lt. James A. Steiger, who snapped in behind a jet, fired, and ripped a wing off. The jet spiraled into the ground and there was no parachute.[6] Of interest, one of the 1st Bomb Division wing commanders, Brig. Gen. William Cross, was flying the mission to observe when his B-17 was hit by a fast-moving Me 262, and before the *coup de grace* could be administered, he managed to join the protection of the box formation.

This jet pilot was more than likely *Oberfeldwebel* Heinz Arnold, who at the time of his death was credited with forty-nine victories, with forty-two victories over the Eastern Front and seven on the Western Front (all in the jet), of which five were four-engine bombers. Heinz Arnold was not flying his normal jet that day, which was Me 262 (work number 500491) "Yellow 7" bearing his personal victory marks. This aircraft was captured by U.S. forces at the airfield in May 1945 and is now on display at the Smithsonian Institution.

The 20th Fighter Group was well represented when Lt. Col. Jack W. Hayes claimed a damaged Me 262, which was probably flown by *Leutnant* Grünberg of I./JG-7, who bailed out safely. Flying Officer Jerome Rosenblum and 1st Lt. Robert M. Scott claimed damaged jets, while Capt. Robert J. Frisch and Capt. John C. Campbell of the 339th Fighter Group each claimed a jet kill. Frisch's target bailed out of his jet, which was already visibly damaged (probably from bombers' defensive fire or the random fighter hits, which would explain one of the "damaged" claims).

Campbell finally caught his jet at Prague/Ruzyne as he tried to land (*Unteroffizier* Fick being killed), and the 357th claimed two destroyed on the ground. It is interesting to note that the identities of four of the five pilots shot down near Ruzyne are not known (only Grünberg and Fick being so identified); four were from I./JG-7 with one (Fick) belonging to III./JG-7. All of the jets led by Grünberg were shot down while trying to land under fighter attack.

The 4th Fighter Group Mustangs chased a jet that was not shot down, the aircraft was crash-landed by the pilot, while the 364th Fighter Group, also on escort duty had Capt. R. W. Orndorff claimed a 262 over Prague, with Capt. W. L. Goff claiming one over Pilsen. First Lieutenant W. F. Kissel claimed one destroyed on the ground. The 324th Fighter Group had Lt. Kenneth E. Dahlstrom and Lt. J. V. Jones claim a "probable" each; Lt. R. Pearlman claimed a "damaged"; Lt. D. L. Raymond and Lt. T. N. Theobald shared a damaged jet claim. First Lieutenant T. R. Atkins also claimed a "probable" while Lt. E. E. Heald and Lt. F. C. Bishop also shared a damaged claim. Major Hewitt of the 78th Fighter Group claimed an Me 262 destroyed while landing at Kalrupy, but the kill was not confirmed.[7]

Also on April 17, the scope of the Allied effort was amplified by the B-26 formations from the 17th and 320th Bomb Groups of the 1st Tactical Air Force. The 354th Fighter Group of the Ninth Air Force scored a kill when eight P-51s jumped a lone Me 262 near Karlsruhe, with Capt. Jack A. Warner claiming the kill. However, the records do not support the known jet losses, or even pilot casualties for this date, despite the confirmation.[8] It is more likely that Warner shot down an Ar 234, which was operating and recorded as lost during this timeline, although the unit designation is unknown.

The 371st Fighter Group, Ninth Air Force, encountered an Me 262, when 1st Lt. James A. Zweizig dropped his P-47 onto a jet at 6,000 feet, fired and had strikes, and claimed a kill. This again must have been an Ar 234, given the known loss records and reports of damaged aircraft.

The Americans did not have it all their way. *Major* Wolfgang Späte and *Oberleutnants* Bohatsch and Stehle each claimed a B-17 for I./ JG-7, while four more bombers were claimed by *Leutnant* Müller, *Oberfeldwebels* Pritzl and Göbel, and *Unteroffizier* Schöppler of III./ JG-7. April 17, 1945, was a big day for all concerned, yet the week was not over.[9]

Two days later on April 19, after a brief respite the day before, III./ JG-7 engaged a formation of B-17s of the 3rd Air Division as they targeted the marshaling yards at Aussig, Czechoslovakia, while B-17s of the 490th Bomb Group targeted Prague. As they turned into the bomb run, two Me 262s made a head-on pass and shot down the lead B-17. Three P-51s of the 357th Fighter Group flown by Capt. Ivan L. McGuire, Lt. James P. McMullen, and Lt. Gilman L. Weber gave pursuit. McMullen claimed a solo kill, while McGuire and Weber shared the second kill. Captain Robert Deloach of the 55th Fighter Group also claimed a kill, when he pursued two jets that flew through the formation, as one Me 262 shot down the B-17G flown by 1st Lt. Robert Glazner of the 444th Bomb Group. The crew bailed out and all were captured, but liberated a few days later.[10]

III./JG-7 had a bad start to their day when sixteen of their jets had just managed to get airborne over Prague when they were jumped by P-51s of the 357th Fighter Group, led by Lt. Col. Jack W. Hayes, who waited with his flight until the right moment. The Mustangs dropped rapidly and ambushed the flock of jets, with kills for one jet each confirmed for Hayes, Capt. Robert S. Fifield, Lt. Paul N. Bowles, and Lt. Carrol W. Othsun. Damaged claims were filed by Lt. W. J. Currie, Lt. G. A. Zarnke, Lt. F. A. Kyle, and Lt. D. C. Kocher. One of these kills was undoubtedly a jet flown by *Unteroffizier* Reischke of I./KG-54, which crashed at Slanem, Czechoslovakia, while the second was a III./ JG-7 aircraft, although the pilot was not identified. Reischke's victor was more than likely Fifield, whose account coincided with the German record of events. Reischke's left turbine caught fire and he rolled over into the ground.[11]

JG-7 had managed to claim the following victories: Schöppler, Grünberg, Göbel, Bohatsch, and Späte all scoring one B-17 each; while *Leutnant* Mai of I./KG-54 also claimed a heavy bomber.[12] Späte's account was quite vivid as he described this event in detail:

"We approached from the southwest, still climbing when we saw the formation. I was the leader technically, but Grünberg pulled ahead. We did not have rockets, and his jet pulled away from me faster. I saw him fire as we closed to about four hundred meters, and the bomber he hit immediately started burning on the outside right motor, smoke pouring out. I heard Bohatsch also call out 'Horrido!' for his bomber. I then fired at the one to the left and just behind, my cannon shells walking into the fuselage, then the tail section just seemed to break off. The bomber started floating down in two large sections, and I saw at least eight parachutes open several minutes later.

"Grünberg's bomber then began to burn even more and it dropped out of the formation. He came around and hit it again, and this time it was finished. I saw it drop beneath the cloud cover, but saw no parachutes. I then pulled around for another run, hit another bomber, but not much damage, and as I pulled up and to the right, I looked up and saw a B-17 falling down on top of me, so I pushed the stick hard forward and then hard back. I think the B-17 missed me by about twenty meters distance, and the men were bailing out. Then we saw the fighters, and I was out of ammunition, so I ordered the group to head back. I wanted to rearm, refuel, and catch them on the way out. When we arrived at the base, there were smoking wrecks all over, our jets that had been ambushed on takeoff. Very sad."[13]

This would prove to be the last engagement for III./JG-7 against the American bomber streams. Foreman and Harvey state: "This was the end for III./JG-7 in the west. Never again were its aircraft engaged by American fighters. A few jets were seen over Ruzyne in the last days of the war, but these avoided combat. Most British and American raids had ceased by 25th April and the Germans, in a desperate last-ditch effort to deny more of their territory to the Russians, threw their last reserves into actions on the eastern front. No information to this aspect of the war has ever been forthcoming from the Soviet Union however, but it must be assumed that III./JG-7 was from that time almost exclusively employed against the Red Air Force."[14]

During his interview, Wolfgang Späte confirmed the assessment by Foreman and Harvey: "At this time III./JG-7 was totally eliminated from being an effective combat unit. This was no secret, and I applied to Galland for a transfer to his JV-44. The rest of the surviving aircraft and pilots were then given orders to work as ground attack aircraft, once they were given more rockets, and they spent the rest of the war killing tanks, and even getting a few Soviet aircraft from what I understand. It was the end, really, and Galland had the only real active unit. It seemed ironic that once I landed back at the airfield, and saw the damage, my adjutant came to me and told me about Steinhoff. It was already spreading like the influenza around the jet fighter community."[15]

With III./JG-7 effectively out of the fighter versus bomber war in the west, only I and II./JG-7 remained to operate as under-strength units that would never again mount a great threat for the rest of the war. Despite their losses, they were not out of the war completely.

April 25, 1945, was a big effort by the Allies to hit not only German industry but also the jet airfields that were known to be active. The 4th Fighter Group flew their last mission of the war and their mission was to attack the airfield at Prague/Ruzyne, the former lair of elements of III./JG-7, which was then occupied by KG-51, also working against the Soviet tanks entering Czechoslovakia and Austria.

While having their attention diverted to the Soviet hoards in the east, III./JG-7 was ordered to attack the recently American-occupied airfield at Fürstenfeldbruck, which was the action that saw *Oberfähnrich* Hans-Guido Mütke land his fuel-starved jet at Dübendorf, Switzerland. Again the 17th Bomb Group would be engaged by a few jets although without any great effect, due to the successful fighter escorts keeping the predators at bay. The 344th BG B-26s were also saved from jet attacks by their P-51 escorts from the 370th Fighter Group, with Lt. Richard D. Stevenson and Lt. R. W. Hoyle sharing a jet kill, the last for the Ninth Air Force in the war.[16]

The 17th Bomb Group was lucky, but other American bomber units were less so. On this day, I./JG-7 had several pilots score kills against the enemy air armada: *Major* Späte claimed three B-17s; with one B-17 each claimed by *Unteroffiziers* Schöppler and Engler, *Oberfeldwebel* Göbel, and *Leutnant* Kelb (a former Me 163B *Komet* pilot with two kills), while former JG-7 luminary *Unteroffizier* Köster (who joined JV-44) claimed two P-51s. While I./JG-7 lost a jet at Ruzyne with the pilot killed in action, they also lost another flown by *Oberfeldwebel* Hermann Buchner, whose story regarding his last mission of the war was well chronicled by Foreman and Harvey:

"We flew an operation against four-engine bombers in the area of the Steinhuder Lake. We broke through the heavy fighter escorts and attacked the B-17s with our guns, saw hits, but then the Mustangs dived on us and we had to break away and try to escape. Our formation broke up and so I tried to find an airfield in the north. The flight time remaining for my return flight compelled me to fly to Bremen.

"I reached Achym, near Bremen, but as I flew over it I saw that the base had been overrun by British troops and armor. I then headed east, and reached Rotenburg airfield on my last drops of fuel. I could not see any Allied fighters in the area. In any case, I was fully occupied with my landing and was about to touch down when I was surprised to see gunfire hitting my right wing. As I landed, the fighter hit my engine nacelle. The fighter was going fast and flew over my aircraft. The engine began to burn as I tried to bring the aircraft to a halt.

"As it stopped, the flames reached above the canopy. I had difficulty in getting out of the right-hand side of the cockpit and, when I had reached a safe distance from the aircraft, my strength gave out and I collapsed and was taken to the hospital. It was not serious, just the initial shock. I was 'lucky' again; the Ami or Tommy pilot was either going so fast or had been surprised by my appearance that he had no chance to deliver a 100 percent decisive attack. I survived, and that was my last combat sortie in World War Two."[17]

Buchner was probably ambushed by either Warrant Officer Ockenden of 130 Squadron who claimed a "probable" or Flight Lieutenant Stowe of 403 Squadron who claimed a jet damaged on the ground. Regardless of who destroyed his jet, Buchner's war was over. Buchner was not alone, as most of the pilots still able to fly were either short of flyable aircraft or the fuel to fill them. Ammunition supplies had also become a problem, despite the fact that there were warehouses less than forty miles away with both products, driving on the roads was almost suicide by day, and the bombed-out roads were nearly impassable at night.[18]

The only base with an ample supply of materiel was the shared base at Ruzyne, which allowed both III./JG-7 and KG-51 to operate against the Soviets. They destroyed hundreds of aircraft and tanks with their rockets, but nothing could stop the Soviet advance, so on April 27 the unit moved north to Mühldorf in Bavaria. III./JG-7 no longer operated on assigned orders; every pilot who could (or wanted to fly) took off on his own to do what he could.

The last major action for JG-7 occurred on April 28 when the unit engaged Soviet forces in ground attack missions, with ten jets failing to return.[19] Another JG-7 pilot died when *Leutnant* Ernst-Rudolf

Geldmacher was shot down while taking off from Ruzyne. Due to the lack of claims for a jet either damaged or destroyed, Foreman and Harvey came to the logical conclusion that it must have been a Soviet aircraft that made the kill.[20]

April 29 was uneventful for JG-7, and this was also the last roll call for the unit. JG-7 was effectively out of the war, although a few pilots took to the sky on their own volition. JG-7 had no encounters, although KG-54 lost four jets in their fight against the Soviets during ground attacks. The following day, April 30 saw a *freie jagd* with *Leutnant* Fritz Kelb of I./JG-7 was killed after being shot up by two fighters of the 358th FG, which was according to Foreman and Harvey, the result of 1st Lt. Joseph Richlitzky and Capt. James H. Hall each claiming a shared damaged jet.

Oberfähnrich Wittbold scored two kills against IL-2s and *Oberleutnant* Schlüter shot down a Yak-9.[21] I./KG-54 lost another jet due to flak and the pilot was never recovered.[22] No confirmed kills were reported again until *Oberleutnant* Fritz Stehle, who shot down a Yak-9 over Czechoslovakia, recorded the last kill by an Me 262 on May 8, 1945, at 1600 hours. He had not heard that the war was over. Stehle had given the Parthian shot as JG-7 and the *Luftwaffe* faded into history, and its pilots and remaining jets fell into captivity and near obscurity.

JG-7 had been the premier jet unit scoring victories against the Allies, but it also became the primary target of Allied fighter pilots. Allied intelligence knew the locations of the airfields, which were relocated occasionally, although photo reconnaissance always provided these new locations in almost daily updates to Allied intelligence officers. By the end of the war most of its pilots were dead, captured, or lingering in hospitals, too badly wounded to fly anymore, thus suffering an ignominious end to a great promising future in aviation history.

As JG-7 died a slow death, a few of its pilots drifted over to a new and exciting, if somewhat belated, jet unit, a new *kommando* of stars led by their patron saint, a defrocked lieutenant general who was one of only twenty-seven men to wear Germany's highest decoration for heroism in combat. Their story is also unique and even more so when told in the words of a few of the surviving pilots themselves.

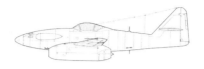

CHAPTER 19

Galland and the Squadron of Experts

Germany may not have won the war, but if they had the Me 262 even a year earlier, it would have been an even more tragic period for us.

Gen. James H. Doolittle

ORDER FOR FORMATION OF JAGDVERBAND 44

25 FEBRUARY 1945

JV 44 is established at Brandenburg-Briest with immediate effect. Ground personnel are to be drawn from 16./JG-54, Factory Protection Unit 1 and III./Erg JG-2. The commander of this unit receives the disciplinary powers of a Divisional Commander as laid down in Luftwaffe Order 3/9.17. It is subordinated to *Luftflotte Reich* and comes under *Luftgaukommando III* (Berlin). Verband 'Galland' is to have a provisional strength of sixteen operational Me 262s and fifteen pilots.

(signed) *Generalleutnant* Karl Koller
Chief of the General Staff of the *Luftwaffe*

Galland's JV-44, the legendary "Squadron of Experts," was established on February 5, 1945. The unit was commanded by its founder, the legendary *Generalleutnant* Adolf Galland. Hitler had himself given his permission for Galland to organize a small unit to demonstrate the superiority of the Me 262 as a fighter. Adolf Galland had long championed the jet fighter as being the only viable method of challenging the bomber streams pounding Germany and getting through the Allied fighter escorts that outnumbered sometimes fifty to one in the air. Ever since his test flight in 1943, he used every method and contact at his disposal to try to push his plan ahead, as he stated:

"In the previous August 1944 meeting, Speer and I had discussed the critical fuel shortages experienced by the military all over Europe. Speer had just met with Hitler and Göring the previous month, and he was also working on increasing fighter production, and I had previously given him the recommendation that the Me 109 be phased out, and only Fw 190D and the later models be produced as far as conventional aircraft. I also told him, following my first test flight in the Me 262 jet at Rechlin, that this was the fighter we needed to focus upon. This was also the subject of discussion in 1943.

"However, as the world knows, Hitler had other ideas. Göring knew the reality, and he was very excited by the 262, and told me personally that he would see to it we received the new fighter. He read the reports on how and why it was a better fighter. It was not just the faster speed and heavier armament, it was also able to operate on much cheaper and readily available fuel, and did not require the high-octane fuel that the conventional fighters did. Speer also mentioned that, in order to appease Hitler, he would increase construction on the Arado and Heinkel jet models as bombers, allowing us to have the 262 as a fighter.

"Speer and I again met with Hitler, and Speer tried to get him to rescind the order to have the two thousand new fighters just built sent to the Western Front. I agreed, and I explained to Hitler that, given the tactical situation, lack of fuel, few highly qualified and experienced pilots, that the best we could do would be to use these aircraft as a protective force at our critical industries, especially the petroleum and aircraft locations. Speer even gave him the data, which normally Hitler would examine in great detail.

"Speer and I did our best to persuade him. It was like talking to a deaf man. I explained the situation to Hitler, and also gave him proven statistics, but he went mad. He then stated that he would order the halt to all fighter aircraft production, the fighter arm was to be disbanded, and those industries were to be then focused upon building flak guns. He firmly believed that flak guns alone would keep Germany safe. I could not believe it.

"It was during this meeting that Göring brought up the possibility of strafing enemy pilots as they bailed out, and he asked me my thoughts on that subject. I told him in no uncertain terms that I would never issue that order, and I would court-martial any man who I could prove did such a thing. I also invoked the Geneva Convention, explaining that such a method was illegal.

"Göring seemed less interested in the laws of warfare, and as I learned much later after the war, I understood why. He was more concerned with the image of the chivalrous fighter pilot being tarnished, so he did not really push the issue further. He also told yet another story of his days in the Great War flying with Bölcke and Richthofen, and how chivalry was only seen in the air. Enemies respected each other. I agreed with him. The killing of parachuting airmen was then dropped.

"I knew from experience, after the Battle of Britain, and seeing the RAF ability, that if these fighter pilots had shorter distances to travel, they could concentrate on a smaller operational area, and focus upon attacking the enemy bombers over or near targets, that several things would happen. First, our men shot down would be able to be back in the air more quickly. Second, the larger numbers of German fighters in a more concentrated area would provide more opportunities to attack enemy bombers. Third, it would save on fuel. Hitler waved his hand and said he had heard enough. He had absolutely no interest in discussing anything that would have made him change his mind.

"Despite all of Göring's faults, I must say that he did support me in the position that the 262 should be specifically built as a fighter. I had his support by the time of my meeting with him in May 1944, after he had come to his senses regarding just how deep American fighters were entering German airspace.[1] [The actual date was May 29, 1944, and also present were *Generals* Korten and Bodenschanz and *Oberst* Petersen.]

"Speer reassured him that we had plenty of flak guns, but we did not have the munitions for them. He also told me that I should not worry about the fighter production, that he would work around Hitler. He actually managed to do this, as we still managed to get out jets, which allowed me to create my Jagdverband 44 in 1945."[2]

Galland already had the perfect man in mind when it came to staffing his new unit of elite pilots. Johannes Steinhoff, who wore the Knight's Cross with Oak Leaves and Swords and scored 176 victories during the war (six in the jet), was recruited by Galland to be the unit's training and recruitment officer, as Galland explained:

"I made Steinhoff my recruiting officer, and he traveled to all of the major bases, picking up pilots who wanted to once again feel a sense of adventure. Steinhoff managed to collect some of our best pilots, although not all of them. This was a direct result of my last meetings with Hitler in January 1945, and with Göring in December 1944, before the meeting that I was not invited to in January where I was fired by a telephone call; and those officers who supported me were likewise in a lot of trouble.

"We had most of the greats, like Gerd Barkhorn, Walter Krupinski, Johannes Steinhoff, Heinz Bär, Erich Hohagen, Günther Lützow, Wilhelm Herget, and others. I tried to get Erich Hartmann, but he wanted to stay with JG-52. That decision would prove very costly for him at the end of the war. We were finally stationed at Munich-Riem, and on March 31 flew the first of several missions, and later we were very successful using the R4M rockets, which we fired at bomber formations. The first confirmed victory over a fighter for JV-44 was on April 4, 1945, when Eduard Schallmoser miscalculated an attack, and crashed into the tail of a P-38. This was perhaps not the best of beginnings, but it at least showed we had determination.

"I was happy again, although I knew the war was lost. I was then able to choose all the pilots I could find who would join me, with Steinhoff's assistance, and almost all had the Knight's Cross or higher decorations. It was our badge. This was the beginning of March 1945, when I created *Jagdverband* 44."[3]

When Steinhoff soon found himself in the unique position of recruiting officer for *Jagdverband* (JV) 44, he was in his element. Steinhoff wrote many books about the war, and from his position as a fighter pilot and leader, his comments ring of experience. In his book *The Final Hours*, he mentioned the training program he conducted:

"I adopted a fairly informal approach to conversion training on the Me 262, feeling that time was running short and wanting to make it easy for the veterans. We had no instruction manuals or visual aids and the lessons were held in the open air with all of us squatting on the earthworks that had been thrown up around the jets. Or we sat on plain wooden benches near the telephone, on the alert, and I explained how one flew the Me 262.

"I told them what to do in order to fly it correctly, and what they absolutely must not do. I spoke of the aircraft's weaknesses, how it was very slow to gain momentum, jolting along the grass for an apparently endless length of time before one could risk pulling the stick back, and then only very, very carefully because an angle of incidence of one or two degrees sufficed to provide enough lift and because too steep an angle, caused by pulling too sharply on the stick, could kill one's speed, and with it oneself.

"I spoke of the phenomena of flight at speeds that none of them had flown before. How at high altitudes one should avoid touching the throttle at all if possible. How abrupt movements could cause explosions in the powerplant, heralded by a sudden increase in engine noise.

And I warned against over-steep gliding or diving at high altitudes since this could cause the ailerons to lose their effect without warning or even to have the reverse effect."[4]

The early missions for JV-44 were fraught with teething problems, as may have been expected, but problems or not, the war came to the unit. JV-44 was also suffering from the same malady of lack of supplies in all forms from the day it was created, which was not unusual for all fighter units in the *Luftwaffe*. For the jet units in the west, these problems were compounded by the fact that Allied tactical fighter-bombers destroyed anything moving in daylight, and roads, railways, and bridges had to be repaired around the clock to keep supplies moving. Also, Galland still had the problem of his superior, Hermann Göring, who had wanted his head for insubordination, if not treason. Galland related the issue:

"By the middle of April we were very hard pressed to receive fuel, and even ammunition was hard to come by. Our supplies were not coming, and there was a great bureaucracy strangling our operations. On April 10, I was again summoned to see Göring, this time at the Obersalzberg, and to my astonishment, he greeted me as if we were old friends. There was none of the arrogance and pompous, critical attitude I had known for almost five years."[5]

JV-44's missions and table of organization were rather unusual when compared with the conventional fighter units. Rarely did a unit at squadron strength operate under the command of lieutenant general, with the majority of the pilots holding the rank of lieutenant or higher, flying wingmen to lieutenant colonels. Also, there was no other unit in the *Luftwaffe* that had most of its members wearing the Knight's Cross—and half of those being the Oak Leaves or even higher.

One of the problems regarding their readiness for missions was explained by Erich Hohagen: "There was no local radar station, or even a main detection system that we had access to. There was a large station near Munich, which we used since we did not have one. We were like a gypsy band, moving here and there. We had a short-wave radio, which was mostly used for air to ground communications with our fighters, and a telephone, and when it rang, that was to usually inform us of an inbound enemy bomber formation. We rotated our pilots in and out of the cockpits, starting sun up and ending at sundown. During April through May, we kept the engines warmed up every two or three hours, making sure that the fuel lines were completely filled, no airlock, which would force a jet to be grounded until it could be cleared.

"We also had a ground crewman standing by, in case we had to take off. His job would be to remove the wheel chocks and intake covers, which we left on to keep debris from entering the engine. Since we usually operated from grass or dirt airfields, there was always the possibility of stones and large pieces of sod being thrown up into the engines, not good. Once I was taking off and I hit something on the runway, it threw my takeoff attitude out of line, and I momentarily lost control, but regained it and took off. The gear lifted fine, no problems. I had no idea what the hell had happened. When I landed later, my crew chief said that I had hit a large rabbit that ran across the field. Think of that, I almost lost an expensive jet, and maybe my life because of something that became that man's dinner that evening."[6]

However, JV-44 was also quite similar to most other units, in that the attrition rate among its pilots was high. Even the most experienced fighter pilots still felt themselves in a learning curve. The first missions were light duty compared to what most of the pilots had experienced during the war, especially the men who had flown on the Eastern Front, or in the West against the ever-growing American air armadas that never seemed to stop coming.

Klaus Neumann described what it was like flying in JV-44 after his experience of flying in Russia with JG-51 and later in the west against the bomber formations with JG-3: "The jet was a remarkable departure from flying the Me 109 or even the Fw 190. Do not get me wrong, as both of those were fine fighters. The 190 was a much better aircraft when it came to attacking bombers, and I did do rather well with that business. It could also take a lot more damage than a 109, especially since it had a more rugged airframe and air cooled engine in the A series of the fighter. It was fast and maneuverable.

"But the 262! It was like being a god in a way: fast, great firepower, and you had a lot of confidence in the plane. As long as you were not tangled up with enemy fighters or too heavily damaged after attacking the bombers to have reduced speed or maneuverability, then you always had a great chance of getting home. Once we had the R4M rockets, it gave us that extra punch; fire the rockets, do the damage, weaken the tight formation integrity of the bombers, then pick off the crippled stragglers.

"I scored five confirmed kills in the jet, although I know I must have damaged around twenty, many probably never made it back home, but who will ever know? I was at first assigned to JG-7, not long after it was created from the *Nowotny Kommando*, when Steinhoff was in command. Then he left and Weissenberger took command, and we just really did not hit it off that well. I know that he was a great fighter ace, and an excellent handler of the jet. I saw him in action, but I just do not think that he had the right temperament to be a good leader. He had a hot temper, and he became enraged when something did not go well. I asked for a transfer, and Steinhoff always liked me, and he convinced Galland to bring me over to JV-44. That was where I found happiness."[7] Neumann joined right as JV-44 was about to enter hard combat. Johannes Steinhoff commented on the strain that Weissenberger placed upon JG-7, which is an interesting sidebar:

"Once Weissenberger took command, we received a flurry of transfer requests, so many pilots just wanted to get away from him. I knew Theo, he was a great pilot and had fought a hard war in the Arctic, and he was also one of the bravest men in the *Luftwaffe*. But, he had his issues, alcohol being one of them, and his attitude was more like that of an overlord, very strict, and many of the men had grown comfortable under Nowotny's relaxed method of command, from what I was told—and Galland even told me that. I was also a professional, but a relaxed sort. I never had to raise my voice to get the job done. It was just done, but that was because I placed a lot of trust and responsibility in my subordinates, allowing them to show me what they could do.

"Weissenberger was a different animal. He was what you could call a micromanager. He had to oversee every small detail, and when you do that it erodes the confidence of your men. I will say this about Theo: he was a very intelligent man, but he was not of the caliber of Adolf Galland or Günther Lützow, but then again, neither was I."[8]

JV-44 flew its first full combat mission on April 5, 1945, and it started with a vengeance when five Me 262s lifted off from their new base at Munich-Riem, where they shot down a B-17 near Karlsruhe outright by Lützow, another B-17 claimed by Klaus Neumann, and two B-24s claimed (actually written off, damaged beyond being salvaged) also by Neumann and Heinz Bär, with another two claimed also by Bär and Fährmann. The records show that the 379th Bomb Group lost three B-24s, and the 388th and 453rd Bomb Groups also lost one bomber each.[9]

One eyewitness account of this mission, and confirmation of three B-24s going down in rapid succession, is the statement by 1st Lt. Charles M. Bachman, a B-24 pilot in the 379th Bomb Group: "I was not flying with my own crew on this mission to central Germany. I was an instructor with a new crew who had no previous combat experience. We called this the 'Dollar Mission' for the new crews. I was in charge of their B-24 Liberator as First Pilot. We flew bucket lead on this mission, and were well into German airspace when a fighter suddenly went past our aircraft from the rear, very fast. [Author's note: This must have been Klaus Neumann's jet, as he was the first to engage].

"'What the hell was that?' my co-pilot exclaimed. 'Messerschmitt 262,' I replied. 'Jet fighter.' Three B-24s went down in the first seconds of the attack and could never have known what hit them. Gunners reported another flight of jets coming in; where the hell were our escorts? I felt my aircraft shake as our gunners opened fire, and the stench of cordite filled the cockpit.

"One jet passed only feet above our heads as the guns rattled out [JG-7 fighters more than likely, as they engaged following the JV-44 attack]. The jet got smaller by the second to our front, leaving us as if we were standing still in the air. This jet suddenly exploded and disintegrated in front of the formation. Our upper gunner later reported that he had raked the jet's belly with his guns as it overshot us and was later given credit for destroying it. The formation lost two more B-24s from the second wave of jets. Almost fifty of our airmen lost their lives that day."[10] This fighter that exploded was definitely a JG-7 machine, one of the two they lost that day.

The 401st Bomb Group also lost a B-17 when a jet closed in fast, fired a burst, and then raced away, chased by Capt. John C. Fahringer. He closed, saw good strikes, and the jet slowed down. As they both emerged from the clouds, Fahringer scored the kill and the pilot bailed out. Who this pilot was is unknown, and he was reported as missing. However, the offending jet was also from JG-7, since the only two jets lost that day were from that unit, as JV-44 did not lose any planes or pilots.[11]

April 7 was also a busy day for the jet pilots, but in contrast to Foreman and Harvey, who state that "it is believed that aircraft of JV-44, equipped with R4M rockets, made an attack upon Fortresses over Thuringia, several being shot down."[12] The record according to the interviews conducted with German pilots and the *Luftwaffekriegstagebuch* show that no claims of destruction or damaged aircraft were made by JV-44 pilots. The only units making solid claims were JG-7 and KG-54 (see Appendix 14), for a total of nine aircraft claimed: five B-17s, one B-24, a P-38, and two P-51s. One of the P-38s (F-5 Recon) of the 30th Recon Squadron, Ninth Air Force, was shot down by *Oberleutnant* Walter Schuck of III./JG-7. The pilot, Capt. William T. Heily, bailed out and spent eight days as a prisoner of war until he was liberated by American forces.[13]

April 8 was to prove to be the litmus test for JV-44, as the RAF threw a formation of Lancasters against Hamburg. JG-7 was also heavily involved. JV-44 encountered P-38s, as Steinhoff, Krupinski, and Fährmann saw them pass by underneath. Steinhoff made his dive, chasing the fighters, until he decided better:

"I learned a long time ago that chasing the American fighters without having your own top cover was suicide, and I know that many of our pilots, becoming enthusiastic anticipating the easy kill, were jumped by high flying fighters. I radioed to my guys not to follow, and then I told them to follow me, as ground control had located a bomber formation. We were carrying rockets, and bombers were what we wanted. We did not have much flight time left, so a quick hit and run and we were gone. I think Krupinski had already turned back being low on fuel.

"We saw them below and closed in a diving pass as the escort fighters sort of broke all over the place. I lined up my aiming point and fired the rockets. Nothing happened! But I was going too fast to use the guns, so I blew right through the formation. I pulled up and banked and then was in a good firing position. I looked but did not see Fährmann. I learned later that he had been shot down. I saw a bomber trailing black smoke while another was drifting away, also smoking, so they must have been his victims. I then locked onto a B-17 and fired, and he was going down without question. I then headed back, and when I landed learned that Fährmann was safe, he had bailed out and was unhurt, just shaken up a bit."[14]

April 9 was uneventful while April 10 did not see much air combat, although JV-44 was strafed by the 353rd Fighter Group, losing three jets on the ground, while JG-7 lost twenty-seven jets in combat either destroyed or damaged. The only success for JV-44 on April 12 was a B-26 shot down by Heinz Bär, and the unit suffered no losses. April 13 was a down day, as were the next two days for Galland's group. April 16 was rather busy, as Galland took to the air in combat for the first time. Galland recalled his first enemy contact flying the Me 262, leading his group of heroes in a last-ditch effort to salvage their pride and honor when their world was crumbling around them: "During my first [successful] attack with rockets, Krupinski was on my left wing, and we witnessed the power in these rockets. I remember that I shot down two Martin B-26 Marauders."[15]

Krupinski recalled this mission: "Galland flew into the bombers, but nothing seemed to happen. Galland, who was leading our flight flew past the formation without firing, but he turned around and then fired his salvo of rockets at a group of B-26 bombers. In moments, one disintegrated and another was falling—the tail had been blown away, and both parts were fluttering down through the light clouds. I fired my rockets and had some near hits, and damaged a couple of the bombers, but the smoke from Galland's two kills obscured the sky in front of me. Seeing the result of those rockets hit was incredible, a fantastic sight really.

"After this attack we flew off a few hundred yards so as not to hit any debris or get jumped by enemy fighters, and then attacked again using our four thirty-millimeter cannons. I damaged a couple of bombers but scored no kills that day and Galland had the only confirmed victories. I had a rocket misfire myself, and only a few of my rockets fired and did not do their job well. Galland pulled around and fired again. Later he admitted that he had failed to take the safety off the rockets, and he did not even think about using his cannons.

"On the second approach was when he had fired, and during that mission he brought down two bombers. I lined one up, and then fired my cannons on the second pass. I heard some thumps and hits in my jet, but nothing major. I could not believe just how effective those rockets could be. It was like firing a shotgun into a flock of geese, really. Galland had some .50-caliber bullets that struck his fighter and it had to go in for repair after we landed."[16]

April 17 saw Galland again lead his band of nine jets on a mission to intercept heavy bombers in conjunction with I./KG-54, and the intercept was made just after the bombing run, as the B-17s were turning away from the flak zone. Steinhoff recalled the mission:

"I was with the boys two thousand meters above, just waiting for the bombers to exit the flak zone. I did not like flying through my own flak, because it was very accurate. Galland then gave the order to attack, so we dived in. It seemed that many of the B-17s were smoking, damaged, probably from the flak, and perhaps the other fighters. I fired my rockets, but again nothing happened, so I fired the guns into two bombers and saw some hits but nothing destroyed, and no one else had any success. Then I saw one of our jets shaking and then go into a skid and collide into a B-17. The jet's wing cut the bomber's tail section off, like a knife, and both planes fell to earth. I saw no parachutes from either aircraft. Krupinski said it was his wingman, Schallmoser. We all thought that he had been killed for certain. Well, I thought that we had really screwed up that mission. It just shows that we still had things to learn."[17]

The German tactic was to hit the bomber formations like wolves on a flock of sheep, like a prizefighter delivering a stunning blow before following up with the knockout punch. Some pilots came in too close when attacking, allowing the closing speed to get away from them. Galland gave his perspective regarding Schallmoser, who suffered from this problem during several air battles:

"I saw [Unteroffizier] Schallmoser, who was famous for ramming enemy fighters, fly past me, his 'White 5' too close for comfort, and I led the group head-on. As a result of my ignorance my rockets did not fire, but I poured thirty-millimeter cannon shells into one bomber, which blew up in spectacular fashion and then fell in flames, and I flew right through the formation, hitting another. I could not tell if that bomber was finished off, so I banked around for another run; all the while my jet was receiving numerous hits from the bombers' defensive fire."[18]

Klaus Neumann also recalled the mission: "Yes, I remember that day. Schallmoser actually flew right over me, and we were all firing at a bomber each, my rockets fired and I saw some hits but nothing really great. Then Schallmoser rolled just slightly left, and then he crashed into this bomber. I looked up and broke right hard to avoid being hit by either aircraft. I also broke the rule, I instinctively pushed the throttle as far as it would go, but it was already all the way forward. I just missed being hit by the tail section of this B-17. If that had hit me I would have been killed for sure. I thought for sure that Schallmoser was gone."[19]

Schallmoser had been hit with a solid stream of .50-caliber fire that shot out both engines and shattered his canopy. He lost control and hit the B-17. The gunner who shot him down was Technical Sergeant Murdock K. List of the 305th Bomb Group. He had shot Schallmoser up, and when he lost control he flew past List's bomber and crashed into the next one in the box formation. The crew and its pilot, 1st Lt. Brainard H. Harris, all perished. No one managed to bail out, as confirmed by Steinhoff.

Schallmoser was pinned in the wreckage, the force of the impact and g forces holding him in as it spun out of control, minus the right wing, and he kept pushing until he was sucked out into the subzero cold. As he left the aircraft his head struck the side of the fuselage, rendering him unconscious. Falling until he became conscious, he then pulled the ripcord, and landed in a field not far from a road, where he flagged down a car and was given a ride to a police station.

Hans "Specker" Grünberg, who ended the war with the Knight's Cross and eighty-two enemy aircraft in 550 missions, with five victories in the jet, was also on this mission, and provided his own perspective: "I saw Schallmoser streak toward the bombers. He always did that, we all did, but we always fired, pulled away and then considered another attack. The 'Rammer' was not of this mindset. I think that he simply became tunnel visioned, too focused, wanting the kill at all costs. He probably believed his own propaganda, where he used to say, 'I can't be killed; I am too pretty.'

"We would always laugh at him. But when I saw this plane break apart after the collision, I also, like everyone else, knew he was dead. How he survived that crash, and all the others, still puzzles me. They say that God protects drunks and fools. The Rammer was both, so I guess he had a good insurance policy."[20]

Neumann describes the reappearance of Schallmoser: "He showed up, with a bandage on his head, and his arm in a sling. He had dislocated his left shoulder. Someone said that his new nickname was 'The Ghost' because he came back from the dead. *Oberst* Lützow said, 'No, he is the Rammer,' and the name stuck with him. You know that he flew the next day? Incredible."[21]

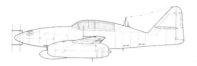

CHAPTER 20

The Loss of Steinhoff

There was not a dry eye in the entire
squadron when Steinhoff crashed.
We loved him like a brother.

Walter Krupinski

Some of Germany's greatest aces, who had finally fulfilled their wish to end the war on their own terms, flying the fastest and most heavily armed fighter in the world, would never survive the war. The war started to take a heavy toll on "Galland's Circus," and April 18, 1945, was the turning point that would lower morale and begin an attrition of the unit's best aces. Perhaps one of the luckiest to survive the war was Steinhoff himself, who was the first of the greats to be lost as a casualty, as related by Galland:

"We were taking off in a flight, with several of us trying to catch a B-17 formation on April 18. Steinhoff hit a hole in the stony airstrip, and his jet jumped into the air, then crashed and burst into flames. When he had crashed, Barkhorn, Schallmoser, Fährmann, Klaus Neumann, Krupinski, and I were taking off on a mission shortly after our base had been attacked, and Steinhoff's 262 hit a crater made from a bomb. His jet lifted into the air but without sufficient takeoff speed, then he nosed in and exploded. The fire exploded the rockets and ammunition, as the kerosene-based fuel engulfed him. He managed to stagger out, a human torch. I cried, because I knew he was a dead man, even though my gear was already up, I could look back and see the smoke.

"We returned to base after the mission to find him being carried to the hospital more dead than alive. The fact that he even survived is the most incredible thing, and I am glad he did, for he is one of my closest friends today. That crash was April 18, and soon after Lützow failed to return from a mission, which was April 24, if memory serves. For years after the war I hoped that he would turn up, perhaps long held by the Allies, or wounded, and recovering in anonymity. Very sad."[1]

Johannes Steinhoff gave his own personal account during his interview of the crash that should have killed him: "Many writers have covered that, but hardly anyone ever asked me about it, except for Raymond Toliver, so here is the true story. I was taking off in formation on April 18, 1945, for my nine-hundredth mission. Galland was leading the flight, which included Gerhard Barkhorn, [Klaus] Neumann, [Eduard] Schallmoser, [Ernst] Fährmann, and myself. The next flight to take off was to be Bär, Lützow, Barkhorn, Wübke, and some others.

"We were to fly formation and engage an American bomber formation. Our airfield had suffered some damage over the last several days due to Allied bombing and strafing attacks, and as my jet was picking up speed, the left undercarriage struck a poorly patched crater. I lost the wheel, and the plane jumped perhaps a meter into the air, so I tried to raise the remaining right wheel. I was too low to abort takeoff, and my speed had not increased enough to facilitate takeoff. I knew as I came toward the end of the runway that I was going to crash.

"The 262 hit with a great thump, then a fire broke out in the cockpit as it skidded to a stop. I tried to unfasten my belts when an explosion rocked the plane, and I felt an intense heat. My twenty-four R4M rockets had exploded, and the fuel was burning me alive. I remember popping the canopy and jumping out, flames all around me, and I fell down and began to roll. The explosions continued, and the concussion was deafening, knocking me down as I tried to get up and run away. I cannot describe the pain."[2]

Walter Krupinski was in the takeoff position just to the left and behind Steinhoff, and he gave his account of the crash as he witnessed it from his cockpit: "I had enough airspeed to pull back on the stick and I lifted up, just clearing his jet and avoiding the collision, even though his jet bounced up into the air, almost hitting me and again banged against the ground, ripping the undercarriage away, which I did not see. Once I was up and began raising my landing gear I looked back as I banked slightly, and I saw then the crunch of the impact and the explosion. The shock wave was felt even as I climbed away. I just knew Macky was dead. There was no way in my mind that he could have survived, and I was feeling very bad at that point.

"When Steinhoff's jet crashed and exploded, he was trapped inside the burning wreckage, with the burning fuel exploding the rockets and thirty-millimeter ammunition around him. There was Macky Steinhoff, trapped in this wreckage, but he managed to crawl out, on fire, rolling on the ground. They got him to the hospital and he somehow survived. I did not see that part after the crash as it happened, but everyone heard it. We were informed of his condition when we returned from the mission. He was the best friend any of us had, and a true patriot and leader."[3]

Klaus Neumann was behind and to the right of Steinhoff, at five o'clock, and he gave his perception of the crash, seeing it from a different angle: "I have to admit that I was not really paying much attention to him. I was always looking up and behind me, in case we were being jumped by enemy fighters while taking off, as that was a real concern. I started rolling about ten seconds after Steinhoff, parallel to Krupinski, as we took off in the *kette* formation, Steinhoff in the lead. Suddenly, out of nowhere, when I had reached about one hundred kilometers [per hour] I saw his jet in the air, and then hit the ground, and bounce again, then crash. I hit the right rudder with everything I had.

"I managed to go around him, and just as I did I saw the explosion. It rocked my fighter, and my left wheel came off the ground and I then moved the stick left and applied left rudder to correct the jet's attitude. I was still not fast enough to take off. I was thinking that perhaps he had been 'bounced' by a fighter. I then managed to lift off, and I retracted my landing gear. As I followed Galland, I looked over at Krupinski, who looked at me, and he simply shook his head. I knew that we were not to break radio silence until we saw the bombers, as Galland would tell us when to attack, after he confirmed the vector from the ground control. I knew Steinhoff was dead, because as I banked right to follow Galland, I looked over and saw this great pillar of fire and black smoke, and then an explosion, and then another. I felt sick."[4]

Hans Grünberg was also in the formation, having just arrived that morning for his first flight with JV-44 after having served in JG-7, and was technically still assigned to that unit. He was the last to take off and he also witnessed the event: "I was the last of eight jets to take off, I had only released the brakes when I saw this fireball. I never saw what caused it. I immediately thought that we were probably under enemy fighter attack, so I looked up and around, but saw nothing, so I kept on going, building up speed. Suddenly, I was almost running into this burning wreckage so I kicked the right rudder and moved to the right, but decided just to keep going until I could get off the ground.

"I looked over to my left and could not even tell whose aircraft it was. The explosions were buffeting me, the heat could be felt a hundred feet away—incredible. I then heard over the radio that it was *Oberst* Steinhoff. I did not know him well, but I liked him very much. Very sad for him."[5]

Franz Stigler did not see the crash, but he heard the explosion, as he related to Jeffrey Ethell: "I was in the operations shack, I was planning on taking one of the jets up for a test run as we had just mounted a new engine. I ran outside and I saw this figure trying to stand, engulfed in flames, and then he hit the ground, rolling, but he was rolling in the burning jet fuel, and then the cannon ammunition began to explode, throwing shrapnel all over the place. I ran towards him, as did all the ground crew. No one was thinking of themselves, and two of the mechanics received severe burns by grabbing him and dragging him away.

"It was horrible. We did not have an ambulance at our field, and we really did not even have much of a first aid station. We had no medical personnel, so I got on the phone and called the nearby hospital near Munich. It took them over an hour to get there. Steinhoff was moaning, his body still smoking, as he was obviously in great pain. We poured cold water on him, and his skin had just peeled off, and when his flight helmet was removed, all of his hair and scalp was melted to it. His hands were burnt claws. We tried to get his boots off, but we had to cut them off, and his feet peeled, the skin just rolled off exposing the muscles.

"I know that I was not the only one thinking this, but I thought, 'How much more merciful just to shoot him,' but then that thought went out of my head. Barkhorn and Lützow ran fast as hell to get there, and Lützow took over and issued immediate orders, never raising his voice, and ordered more cold water brought. He knelt down to speak with him, as did Barkhorn, and I could hear not a word. Then for the first time, I saw Lützow, this most stoic and disciplined man I had ever known, start to cry. No sound, just his eyes teared up. Same with Barkhorn. He held Macky's shoulder, staying with him.

"Barkhorn had flown as wingman to Macky in JG-52; in fact Krupinski, Gerd Barkhorn, Erich Hartmann, Pauli Rossmann, Günther Rall, and Macky Steinhoff were the most successful fighter pilots in the *Luftwaffe* and were the top scorers in JG-52, flying together for two or more years in some cases. Then I started to cry. In fact, there was not a dry eye in the whole damned group. The ambulance finally arrived, and they loaded him up. Barkhorn collected his medals, making sure that his wife, Ursula, could get them at some point.

"No sooner had they driven away then the jets came back from the mission, with Galland coming in to land first. He had called over the radio and asked about Macky, and I think it was Bär who told him in flight how bad he was, and then he took off on his own intercept mission with Barkhorn and the others. Galland landed and immediately jumped from the jet, followed by the others as they landed. The most frantic was Krupinski. He had flown with Steinhoff since the early days in Russia with JG-52, and they were the best of friends. Krupinski was devastated. I could see that all the energy was drained from him.

"That night no one celebrated Bär's two Thunderbolt kills scored on his sortie, not even Bär himself. That night he broke out a bottle of old cognac, bottled before the Great War, that he was saving for when the war was over. He opened it, and we all had a drink, to Macky Steinhoff. No one believed he would survive. Galland took off for the hospital to see him. Krupinski wanted to go, but Galland said no, he could go later."[6]

The loss of Steinhoff was much more than simply losing a highly qualified pilot and group commander. Losing Steinhoff was also a great blow to morale, as stated by Hohagen: "Steinhoff was like one of those charmed guys—the kind of fellow who you would follow anywhere, because you really felt that he would get you back home OK. I personally liked him very much, and I can say that without him as the unit recruiter, and also the chief transition instructor, from his experience with JG-7, our unit may have taken a lot longer to be readied than when it was. He was a good mentor to the younger pilots, and a real gentleman."[7]

The *Luftwaffe* had a bad day on April 18 for several reasons. The losses at Ruzyne had really affected JG-7 and Major Leonard "Kit" Carson of the 357th Yoxford Boys wrote about this mission from his viewpoint:

"I kept my squadron at Ruzyne on the southwest side. We circled the field at 13,000 feet and all hell broke loose. The flak batteries opened up and the sky looked as if it had measles. We fell back a couple of miles to size up the situation and cruised around waiting for the next move. It soon came. Under cover of the flak umbrella the Me 262 pilots cranked up and taxied one by one to the north end of the airdrome for takeoff. The moment of truth had arrived. They were going to try to punch their way through and get to the bombers anyhow. Our opposing strategy was now clear.

"My squadron would go down by flights of four, well spread to dilute the flak concentration on each of us as individual targets. As the first 262 started his takeoff roll we dropped our wing tanks and I started down with Red Flight from 13,000 with easy wingover and about 50 inches of mercury and 2,700 rpm. The Mustang would accelerate like a banshee going downhill. The 262 had his gear up and was going past the field boundary when we plowed through the intense light flak. As I came astern of him and leveled off at 400-plus, I firewalled it to hold my speed and centered the bull's-eye of the optical sight on the fuselage and hit him with a two-second burst. My timing had been off. If I'd split from 13,000 feet about five seconds earlier I could have had all six fifties up his tail pipes. Even though I scored only a few strikes, it's an even bet that he was too busy checking for leaks to make it to the bomber column. A solid hit can be just as good as a kill as a deterrent.

"We turned back to Ruzyne and found four jets over the field taking pot shots at some of our lads and baiting them into the flak-infested area over the field. I cut one off in a diving turn and gave him a long burst at about four hundred yards hoping that he would go into an evasive turn where I could cut him off and hit him again. He wouldn't have any of it. Even though I got a few strikes he leveled off and took off for other parts.

"Captain Chuck Weaver, my operations officer, did better. He nailed one that was attempting to land at Ruzyne and destroyed it. Don Bochkay, C.O. of the 363rd, shot one down that was taking off from an airdrome east of Prague where he was patrolling with the other two squadrons. He really didn't want to go to Budapest after all."[8]

Nearly every pilot flying in JV-44, with exception to those who had transferred from JG-7 after Steinhoff had been reassigned, owed their experience and possibly their lives to Steinhoff's often redundant and tenacious training program. The unique characteristics of the jet were so far removed from anything the men had flown before that they were both a blessing and a curse. Steinhoff explained:

"The jet was an entirely new way of flying; the basic aerodynamic principles remained, but there were many new factors that had to be learned to be successful. The most important thing was of course the throttles. The men had to learn what not to do even more important than what to do. The other major difference was the approaching speed for landing, as it required a lot more landing strip for a jet than for the prop fighter. When you cut power on a 109 or 190 you lost airspeed quickly, and dead stick landing was not a real problem. We were all trained in gliders, so powerless landings were no great problem. You also did not need much runway.

"The 262 changed all of that. There was also the problem of bailing out in the jet. Unlike the other aircraft, which were easy to roll over, or pull up, cutting the power to escape safely, the jet did not stop like this. If you lost power, you would drift for a while. Bailing out at nine hundred kilometers per hour was not considered a great idea, given the slipstream and the high vertical stabilizer and elevators that were waiting for you. Pulling up and then inverting was the best way, but then again, that supposes you had plenty of time to do all of that. You would not have that much time if an enemy was on your tail, shooting you up, or if you were on fire.

"But in the training, I hammered home about those damned throttles. 'Leave them alone!' I would say, once you reached operational speed. Only reduce power upon your glide path, the landing approach, and then shut down once you touched the ground if damaged. If undamaged, reduce the power and taxi off the apron. But wouldn't you know it; we still had some fools blow out an engine. Schallmoser was the greatest offender. There was a joke that he was a secret Allied agent, determined to destroy the *Luftwaffe* jet force from within, because he lost so many 262s. He was a great guy, but still a clown."[9]

These words regarding the throttles and other characteristics were supported by Walter Krupinski, who had himself learned the hard way about what not to do when taking off and flying the jet fighter:

"Steinhoff had told me about the jet a few months earlier, after he had taken over JG-7 for a short time. He loved the jet, and he explained the delicate nature of the engines, the problematic takeoff and landing characteristics, but also the great advantages of the 262. This was when Steinhoff and Galland stepped up to some of us on April 1, 1945. Steinhoff asked me: 'Graf . . . how would you like to fly the 262?' Well, he did not have to ask twice. I was well aware of the 'turbo,' as we called it. I had even seen photographs, but had not seen one in flight yet. I was very excited. I knew that I wanted to be a part of this program.

"The very next morning I jumped into the cockpit of a Messerschmitt 262 and flew my first test flight after a short familiarization period. I flamed out once when I was in transition training. I was used to pushing the throttle full open rapidly to increase takeoff power. This was a great error in the jet. I know that many of the pilots who were killed flying the jet probably died due to stalling out this way. The 262 was a very heavy aircraft when compared to the 109 and 190, and at low speed I would equate it to flying a brick.

"I joined *Jagdverband* 44, Galland's 'Squadron of Experts' at Munich-Riem, and then we moved to Salzburg in Austria, then Aibling-Heilbronn, and then back to Munich, and so on. What was interesting about the squadron was that, with only perhaps four or five exceptions, every pilot wore the Knight's Cross or a higher version of the Iron Cross. Also, we were the only squadron in history that was led into combat by the equivalent of an American two-star general. How many squadrons have a sergeant flying wingman to a full colonel, let alone a general? Almost every pilot in the unit was either an escapee from a hospital, pending some form of military reprimand or discipline, or had been in trouble in some fashion.

"There was no way we were going to dogfight with these Mustangs, Thunderbolts, and Lightnings. We had to just come in fast, hit them [bombers] very hard and then get away very quickly. Once we were at least four to five miles away we could turn back and line up another target. The one great advantage that we had in the 262 over the 109 or 190 was our approach and climbing speed. This was both a positive and a negative thing.

"Our speed allowed us, as I said before, to attack rapidly and then leave. That speed gave the enemy gunners on the bombers much less reaction time to sight in, lead us, and get a solid killing burst. Our speed also allowed us to approach from underneath, closing the gap quickly, and if you had the rockets that gave you a great advantage, as you could fire the R4Ms from outside the effective range of the fifty-caliber machine guns.

"The only great downside to having the jet was the loss of maneuverability; we could not turn as tight as the other fighters, so speed was our life insurance. The other problem with such a fast attacking and closing speed was that, just as the enemy gunners had little time to lead you for a kill, you had much less time to pick out a target. You had to be right the first time, and if you did not have rockets, you had to adjust your shooting to compensate for the much slower targets. In this case, there was very little deflection shooting. You closed in quickly, fired a quick burst, and then you left.

"The other problem you had was that, after you broke contact, and were usually out of ammunition and low on fuel, the enemy fighters would be following a few miles behind you. On a good day, you probably had about ten to fifteen minutes to approach, extend your gear hoping it would work, land, and get out of the cockpit. Many times we jumped out of our jets to have the shadows of enemy fighters pass overhead as they strafed us.

"My first couple of missions after joining JV-44 were uneventful, but on April 16, the squadron took off, armed with the R4M rockets mounted in racks under the wings. We were radio vectored by ground radar to the formation of [Martin B-26] Marauders, which were twin-engine American medium bombers. I damaged a couple of bombers but scored no kills that day and Galland had the only confirmed victories.

"We had many such missions, but we also ran into American fighters. Mustangs were a constant problem, and they would always follow us home, hoping for an easy kill. Taking off and landing, as I have said, were the most tense moments for a 262 pilot, as the plane built up speed slowly, and you could stall out easily if you pushed the throttles forward too quickly, which caused a flameout. This happened several times with pilots, and we finally learned how to throttle up slowly without killing ourselves."[10]

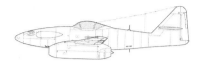

CHAPTER 21

Back in the Air

*I do not believe that any one of us could
strap in for takeoff, and not think that it
would be our last mission.*

Alfred Ambs

Following Steinhoff's near-fatal crash, Galland's absence was felt, but in his absence *Oberstleutnant* Heinz Bär knew, as did any good leader and executive officer, that the best way to get the men's minds off what had happened was to get them right back into combat, and he did. April 19, the day after the fiery crash, JV-44 joined JG-7 in an overlapping engagement against heavy bombers. JV-44 had three pilots score victories. Bär scored two B-17s, while Hans Grünberg, who had only just arrived at the unit, shot down a B-17, as he described:

"It was not really that exciting, unless you include bailing out of my burning jet over Prague. I shot down the bomber, and my jet took just a few hits too many. I lost complete control, one engine was dead and the other on fire, so I decided it was enough for one day. I rolled the jet left, sideways and pushed out. My parachute worked well, and that was pretty much the end of the war and flying for me."[1]

April 20 was uneventful from a scramble standpoint, but several pilots were going to fly reconnaissance missions once more fuel arrived. The first was Gerd Barkhorn, who was new to JV-44 and just recently transitioned into the jet. He had an uneventful day until he came in with an engine failure. Like many pilots with an engine fire, he opened his coffin lid canopy to jump out if necessary. Upon the hard impact, his canopy slammed shut as his body was thrown forward, the edge of the bezel slamming down on his neck. He was lucky that it was not broken, but, like his old friend Steinhoff, he was out of the war.

April 20, 1945, was Adolf Hitler's fifty-sixth birthday and was celebrated. It was also the official promotion day in the armed forces. On that day the 323rd , 397th, and 394th Bomb Groups of the Ninth Air Force were launched against Memmingen. In his memoir, Louis S. Rehr, who was the commanding officer of one of the squadrons that day, described the event: "Our initial point was a town called Kempten, south of Memmingen. Here we tightened up our individual groups of six for a four-minute bomb run. We opened the bomb bays and held steady. Arcs of light flak, probably from positions in the higher terrain, crossed our path. Fifteen more seconds until the drop.

"Suddenly, an aircraft ripped the skies directly overhead. Instantly, all hell broke loose. Within seconds, flames billowed from the left engine of a Marauder flying directly behind box leader Smith [probably Krupinski's kill]. Pieces of wing and fuselage blew past. The Marauder behind the damaged bomber barely avoided a midair collision. Then the ill-fated plane rolled over and dropped beneath the formation. Calls from other pilots to bail out went unheeded.

"Simultaneously, the Me 262 pulled straight up as it passed over the formation. Then he abruptly reversed direction and came at us head-on. What a hell of a mess. He dove underneath, preparing for another strike. For an instant, I wanted to break formation, chase him, knock him out of the sky with my forward firing guns. Somebody had to do something. Stick to the rules. Stay tight. Concentrate the firepower. Follow the leader. Now, bombs away!

"A couple of P-51s flew past with their guns blasting. Two more jets zoomed up from beneath, passing one hundred yards to my right. Gunners and P-51s diverted them from taking aim at Smith. Their sport did not end with the attack at the front of the formation. As the last six Marauders passed over the IP, a swarm of jets struck. Three jets following one another in ten-second intervals zoomed up from the six o'clock position, then dove on the formation. The first and second jets barely cleared the lead Marauder flown by 1st Lt. James Hansen. The third jet would have collided with Hansen's bomber, but at the last second, the German [Schallmoser] dove his jet under the Marauder's right propeller. Half the jet's rudder flew off [Schallmoser collided], and the aircraft fell away. Hansen was lucky. He managed to keep both engines running. However, every other Marauder that followed was in trouble.

"The last Marauder in his group of six took a hit and lost both engines. Then the right engine burst into flames, and the bomber dropped through the clouds. Fortunately, its crew managed to bail out over friendly territory. Guns from another jet [Steinhoff] sent an explosion into the cockpit of the number 5 Marauder. The B-26 pilot, 1st Lt. James Vining, flying *Ugly Duckling* in the 455th squadron, bled profusely from his lower right leg, where the blast had nearly severed his foot from his ankle.

"The jet's guns also knocked out his right engine. His copilot managed to crash land the plane, but it ran into a camouflaged tank trap. The aircraft broke into three pieces, killing the turret gunner and seriously injuring the others. The number 3 Marauder lost part of a propeller and continued flying on a single engine. Numbers 2 and 4 had damage, but kept going. P-51s arrived on the scene, but they were too little, too late.

"We ended the day with one of the highest casualty lists in the history of the 323rd. First Lieutenant Dale Sanders and his entire crew perished in the Marauder that blew up in front of me [Galland's spectacular kill]. In all, we lost seven men and three aircraft. Another seven men were wounded and seven aircraft damaged. From the waist of my bomber, Wolfe shot what may be the only photo of Marauders under attack by Me 262s. It is not easy to see the jets, which have dived well beneath us preparing for their treacherous climbs. Given the surprise and the speed of these attacks, it is a miracle there is any photo. Several of our gunners claimed hits on the jets, but at the end of the day, it was difficult to reconstruct those seconds of confusion and response.

"That day, however, the Germans lost no men. Eduard Schallmoser, the Me 262 pilot with the severed rudder, managed to parachute to safety. Several gunners fired on Schallmoser's jet, as did pilot Vining, who used his forward guns. Vining later admitted that as he took aim, he loosened his position in the formation. This made him an easy target for the German aces. Schallmoser claims that he dropped into his mother's garden with an injured knee. Before heading back to the base and then a hospital, he enjoyed a plateful of her pancakes."[2]

As incredible as it sounds, Schallmoser, despite hitting two of the bombers with cannons, did not score a victory that way, but he did clip the propeller of the B-26 flown by Hansen with his rudder, hence the aircraft disintegrating, forcing him to leave his doomed aircraft. Schallmoser did indeed land right in his mother's backyard, getting tangled in the clothesline under his parachute. He ignored the bleeding from his minor wound, where a .50-caliber round had pierced the fuselage, blown the armored plate section into his leg, and opened a superficial gash on his right knee, which his mother bandaged. Schallmoser wrote of the event:

"I turned too late and rammed the Marauder, which then fell away and crashed [actually Hansen managed to nurse his bomber back to base without further incident and no casualties, as stated accurately in Robert Forsyth, *JV-44: The Galland Circus*]. Meanwhile, my Me 262 "White 11" was a complete loss and I was able, with my last reserves of strength, to escape the aircraft by parachute and landed safely at my mother's home on the outskirts of Lenzfried-im-Allgäu."[3]

His mother made a telephone call to a local hospital, but due to the long period of time it would take to get there, she fed him a large meal, and they caught up on events. Schallmoser did score three confirmed kills and additional claims: a victory over a P-38 (which he rammed) on April 3, a B-26 on April 16 (shot and rammed), and a B-17 (which he shot up and also rammed) on April 17, and the B-26 which he'd clipped before landing at his mother's house. Schallmoser was taken to the hospital after the latter event and was released the next day.

Erich Hohagen recalled the news when they learned that "The Rammer" had survived. The pilots on the mission has seen him bail out, but leaving an aircraft during a heated battle did not ensure survival. "Fährmann received the call, as he answered the phone, and we learned that Schallmoser was alive. He called us himself after that call from the local *gauleiter*. He asked if anyone could confirm his kill. I told him, 'Not that I know of,' but we could confirm that he had cost us another jet. It was good that he was alive, and we could later confirm his victory."[4]

Schallmoser's Me 262 on this mission was work number 111745 and was a loss. Later, he would fly "White 14," which has been erroneously attributed to this mission. He had previously flown "White 5" and "White 11," which were lost. Galland's statement makes the actual aircraft he was flying that day quite clear. He should know, as he had just flown the same aircraft the previous day.

Galland's JV-44 had entered the war late, but they did so with a flurry of activity, such as on April 24, 1945, when the Hell Hawks escorted B-26 Marauders during their bombing of the oil storage facility at Schrobenhausen and encountered the jet fighters of JV-44.[5] On this day, JV-44, led by their intrepid fighter general, attacked a formation of B-26 Marauders of the 34th Bomb Squadron, 17th Bomb Group, whose primary target was the German ammunition supply depot at Schwabmünchen.

The first Marauder mission was terminated due to weather, while the second mission consisting of three bombers was uneventful. The third sortie flown with only three Marauders escorted by P-47s from the 356th Fighter Group in three staggered flights was a different story.

Of the escorts, Blue Flight led by Capt. Jerry G. Mast flew top cover at 20,000 feet, Green Flight led by 1st Lt. O. T. Cowan at 17,000, and White Flight was led by Major Hill poised below the bombers as an immediate interdiction force.

Four Me 262s emerged from the clouds for their favored attack approach, from the stern. The P-47 pilots saw them at six o'clock low, and the first to respond was a previous jet killer, 1st Lt. Oliven T. Cowan, who swooped in from 17,000 feet. He fired a few bursts into the jet on the far right of the formation. The rest scattered at being ambushed, forcing them to abandon the attack on the bombers.[6] Having altitude was indeed life insurance, but Allied pilots, especially those flying the heavy seven-ton P-47s, knew that if they had altitude, and the conditions were right, they could kill jets, as chronicled by Dorr and Jones:

"One of the jets turned for another pass at the tails of the B-26s. This time Capt. Jerry G. Mast spotted the Messerschmitt and executed a split-S from two thousand feet above, cutting off the enemy pilot, who dove sharply away. Picking up the chase was 2nd Lt. William H. Myers, who dove vertically at the jet at more than five hundred miles per hour. Myers, overtaking, waited for the jet to slow as it shallowed from its dive.

"When the *Luftwaffe* pilot began to level, he spotted both Mast and Myers closing from the rear, and pushed over again into a steep dive. It was a fatal mistake. Boxed in from above, the Messerschmitt slammed into the earth at terrific speed and exploded in a rain of flaming debris. Both Mast and Myers had to execute a punishing high-g pullout, Myers blacking out momentarily, to avoid the 262's fate. The rest of the squadron ran off the other three jets, which were unable to penetrate the 388th's fighter screen or hit a single Marauder."[7]

The action was also chronicled by Foreman and Harvey, as they described the event when White Flight saw the jets first, and called them out, and as they could not catch them in the climb, they radioed Green Flight to engage. As Green Flight went into the dive to engage, the jets streaked upward. Cowan had managed to get within range and get good strikes on the trailing Me 262, but could not follow it to confirm a kill as all the jets opened the distance between themselves and their pursuers.[8]

Captain Mast was able to catch one of the jets in a wide turn as he banked around for an attack on the bombers. At the last second, the jet pilot saw the danger and rolled into a dive through the cloud layer with Mast and Blue Flight close behind. The jet was headed into the covey of White Flight fighters, out of sight under the clouds. As the jet dropped under the cloud cover, he was picked up by 1st Lt. William H. Myers, Hill's wingman. He saw the jet drop within his line of sight with Mast right behind him.[9]

The jet pilot then tried to pull around to shake off Mast when he turned head-on into White straight ahead, with Myers coming head-on firing at him. The jet then dropped the nose and headed for the deck, Mast still behind him. The jet struck the ground and exploded. Mast managed to pull out of the dive, clipping some treetops in the process. Both Meyers and Mast shared the kill.

During all of this, another jet attacked the bombers. Blue Flight's 1st Lt. Byron Smith Jr. managed to get some strikes on the fins as the German pulled away into the clouds, out of sight. Smith shared the damaged claim with 1st Lt. Dale Seslar, and despite their efforts, two B-26 Marauders were shot down, flown by 1st Lt. Fred Harms (crashed at Oberoth) and 1st Lt. Leigh Slates (crashed at Untershönegg). Only Staff Sergeant Edward F. Truver survived out of both crews after bailing out to become a prisoner of war.[10]

Foreman and Harvey argue that it is most likely that the jet victory shared by Myers and Mast was flown by Oberst Günther Lützow, who failed to return from that mission. A detailed check of the German records and interviews of the German pilots by this author supports their conclusion. During the day's events, two P-47 pilots from the 27th Fighter Group, 1st Lt. R. E. Prater and 1st Lt. J. F. Lipiarz, both claimed one jet damaged each during their escort duty that day while working in the same area. 1st Lt. D. S. Renner of the 358th Fighter Group (Ninth Air Force) claimed two jets damaged near Odelzhausen.

April 24 was a long day for JV-44, and it was not finished, as they also engaged a group of straggling B-17s, with a flight led by Walter Krupinski, who scored a kill and a "probable" on this mission and actually collided with—or more accurately "bounced"—his victims. The P-47 was a claimed "probable" but not a confirmed kill accredited to him. His Me 262 survived the initial impact with the wreckage of the bomber, damaging the fighter, but then he took hits from another P-47.[11] Despite not having all of his records due to being captured at the end of the war, he recalled the event:

"Galland had shot a bomber earlier, but I did not see any hits, and then I fired on one, and then another fell, I saw this, but when I fired my bomber was smoking, only damaged. I had been hit by their gunfire, and my left engine was sputtering, the canopy had a large hole in both sides, the bullet had just passed behind my head, the armor seat under me felt as if a rabid dog was shaking it. It literally saved my ass. I then fired on a P-47 that was within range crossing in front of me, and he slowed to a stall, and we collided. It was a glancing blow, I bounced off. He fell away but I was fine. I did not know if he managed to get away, I did not see that, so I did not claim a kill."[12]

On April 25, 1945, JV-44 was vectored to intercept the B-26s of the 17th Bomb Group, their old nemesis, and both units were very familiar with each other by this time. Despite the three waves of JV-44 and I./JG-7 jets closing in on the bombers, the escort fighters proved effective in keeping them at bay. However, *Unteroffizier* Franz Köster just arrived from JG-7 (one of the men begging for a transfer from Weissenberger's command) just behind Neumann and Wolfgang Späte, another refugee. Köster had already scored two P-51s, and later would claim a P-38.

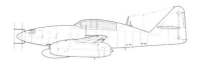

CHAPTER 22

Galland's Last Mission

Flying the 262 was the only thing that could lift my spirits after my experiences. I would have preferred death to having to hear Göring's voice again.

Adolf Galland

On April 26, 1945, the first five of twelve jets lifted off from Riem, followed within a few minutes by the last four jets, possibly led by Bär. The Munich radar control station directed them toward Ulm. Once again, the 17th Bomb Group had been dispatched to bomb an airfield, this time at Lechfeld, the home base for the remnants of JG-7. They were a French B-16 unit and sixty other B-26s from the 42nd Bomb Wing. Their escorts were sixty-three P-47s of the 27th and 50th Fighter Groups of the 64th Fighter Wing.

The first four Me 262s of JV-44 intercepted the B-26 formation containing twenty-four aircraft dead ahead from a twelve o'clock high approach, the closing speed so fast that neither side had time to fire. Galland led his flight into a wide arcing turn to attack from the eight o'clock stern position. Galland was the first to engage:

"I immediately had a bomber in my gun sight, I was closing fast. I fired right away, every round struck, and the bomber blew up in a great blinding flash, and then I fired the rockets, but I had forgotten to release the safety catch. I then fired on another bomber with my cannons. I saw some hits, and smoke, pieces flew away, but I did not have time to observe. I then felt many hits in my jet, like stones thrown against a metal wall. The aircraft shuddered. I had been hit by the fifties from the bombers. My jet still flew, no great problems, but I was losing fuel. I decided it was time to break off, and I radioed the flight of my situation."[1]

Robert Forsyth recorded the eyewitness account of Staff Sgt. Albert Linz, a gunner on the B-26 *My Gal Sal*, piloted by 1st Lt. Carl Johanson. Linz described his engaging the three jets, one in particular that failed to fire its rockets, which was undoubtedly Galland approaching at an altitude of 12,000 feet. Although Galland was unable to use rockets, his cannons blew up the neighboring B-26.[2] *My Gal Sal* did manage to return despite being damaged, landing on one engine at Luneville, France. The crew was uninjured.

Galland and his two wingmen, Schuhmacher and Kammerdiener, streaked under the bombers and attacked the formation. It is recorded by 1st Lt. Howard P. Husband, a navigator on the mission: "As we approached our target for the day in southern Germany, German jet fighters came at us from almost head-on at twelve o'clock. I was in the leading B-26 as they shot past without firing, two going right under our ship. A few seconds later I heard explosions and two Me 262s shot past our B-26 very close. One jet looped in front of us and our crews saw him shoot down one of our P-47 escort fighters. Also a total of three B-26 bombers were seen to go down from the formation. We were in bad weather at the time the jets appeared, about to turn back to base in France."[3] A fourth B-26 already damaged by Galland's second pass managed to return to base, but it was so badly shot up it crashed, killing all on board.

Once again Schallmoser was busy, this time flying "White 14" and blowing a Marauder out of the sky with his rockets. *Feldwebel* Otto Kammerdiener flew "White 10" and attacked a B-26, while *Oberfeldwebel* Leo Schuhmacher flew through the bombers unable to fire due to a weapons system failure. Kammerdiener had a victory with the B-26, but had to land his damaged jet on one engine. As this was happening, Galland had taken .50 fire from several gunners. The one gunner who probably was the most effective at slowing him down enough to be jumped later was Technical Sgt. Henry Dietz of the 34th Bombardment Squadron, whose account is chronicled in *JV-44*.[4]

Galland recalled: "I was shot down by a [Republic P-47D] Thunderbolt as we took off to intercept a bomber force. The fighter was flown by a man named James J. Finnegan, whom I met some years later and we became friends.[5] When large fifty-caliber bullets strike your fuselage, it makes a very interesting sound, unlike cannon fire or small-caliber .303-inch British bullets. It packs a heavy punch, and when several hit you, it shakes the aircraft. Once I felt I was out of range of the bombers' defensive fire, I tried to climb slightly and bank around for another pass, but my right engine began flickering and sputtering, then it caught again.

"Suddenly my instrument panel disintegrated, my canopy was shattered, and my right knee was struck by a bullet that grazed me. I had seen some P-51s in the area, and figured one caught me. I was losing power and in great pain. My right engine suddenly started losing thrust rapidly and then died. I thought about parachuting out but realized that might be dangerous, as some of our pilots had been strafed upon exiting their jets. [The practice had a quiet acceptance in the USAAF, since it was believed that jet pilots were premium, highly trained pilots and could not be allowed to return to the air.]

"I was also at a high rate of speed, perhaps five hundred miles per hour after I dropped the nose, then my airspeed bled off. What had happened, as I banked above and around for another attack, I was hit, apparently as I banked and bled off airspeed. I thought at the time, and for some years afterward, that it was one of the Mustangs that shot me, as I saw a few on escort duty. Later I learned it was Finnegan in a P-47. I had previously radioed for [Leutnant Heinz] Sachsenberg to get his fighters in the air. He was an outstanding and very reliable fighter pilot, and we trusted him with our lives. [Sachsenberg commanded the Fw 190D unit that protected the jets as they returned to the airfield.]

"I flew for the deck and headed for this field at the air base, which was also under attack. I cut the power to my good engine as I leveled out, and since I still had aileron and rudder control, stabilized my jet into a level attitude, and thumped across the field on the engines. My gear would not come down, and later I found that my nose wheel had been flattened, and smoke was pouring from my plane. The first thought I had was of Steinhoff and remembering what had happened to him. I also knew that it was not beyond reason and experience for pilots to strafe a downed jet, or the pilot, and I did not want to be sitting in it or even be anywhere around it. I opened the canopy, climbed out to get away, in case it should explode, only to find aircraft dropping bombs and firing rockets at me. Well, our mission netted five victories total, and none of the pilots were killed."[6]

Finnegan wrote to Galland after the war that he was pleased to have removed a great ace and German general from the war, but he also wrote to Galland: "However, as you are most aware, I also consider the experience one of a very lucky circumstance and realize that if the roles were reversed, I might not be writing to you today."[7]

Galland's response was interesting, and in the typical dry humor of the General of the Fighters: "Even today, I still have a little splinter in my right knee which is the property of the United States government . . ."[8] The state of JV-44 minus its commander was explained by Galland:

"From that point forward Bär took operational command, and before the month was out every unit in Germany with jets began bringing them to us at Riem airfield, near Munich. I was sent to the hospital, but I discharged myself, walking with a cane and relocated to Tegernsee, where I still had telephone contact with Bär. There was a rumor that we were the only unit to have jet fuel! For such a long time I had been begging for planes."[9] At the time Galland was fighting for his life, Capt. Robert W. Clark of the 50th Fighter Group shot down another Me 262, and the pilot bailed out.[10]

Galland landed his crippled jet near the autobahn just as a flight of P-51s flew overhead, strafing everything in sight. This would explain why he at first thought that a Mustang had shot him down. Jumping out of his jet, which had just become a target of strafing opportunity, he jumped into a bomb crater. This action probably saved his life.

In an article written by Mary Leydecker, a researcher located James Finnegan, and after comparing both the Galland and Finnegan reports and the after-action report from the 50th Fighter Squadron, 10th Fighter Group of the 9th Air Force, the two warriors were introduced in 1979 and became friends until Galland's death on February 9, 1996.[11]

Finnegan described his encounter in an interview: "I was leading the top-flight cover of P-47s that was escorting the B-26s to their target. As I gazed down, I saw two objects come zipping through the formation, and two bombers blew up immediately. I watched the two objects go through the bomber formation, and thought 'That can't be a prop job . . . it's got to be one of the 262 jets.' I was at about thirteen thousand feet and estimated them to be at about nine to ten thousand. They were climbing, and I pulled a split-S toward the one that turned left, and almost ended up right on top of him—about seventy-five yards away!

"I gave a three-second burst and saw strikes on the right-hand engine and wing root. I was going so fast, I went right through everything, and guessed my speed at about five hundred fifty miles per hour. I recorded it as a probable. I was flying a D model Thunderbolt with a bubble canopy, a natural metal finish, and a black nose. The 262 had a green and brown mottled camouflage with some specks of yellow. That turned out to be my last flight in a P-47. My total kills for the war were three, an FW 190 and an Me 109, in addition to the Me 262. Galland always impressed me as being a true warrior. He loved combat and the involvement, but was not out to kill. That was just part of it."[12] Finnegan passed away on April 26, 2008, and both were gallant men and heroes of their respective nations.

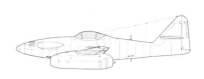

CHAPTER 23

The End of the War and JV-44

*Every man knew the war was over,
but we wanted to end it on our terms.*

Adolf Galland

Oberstleutnant Heinz Bär took command of the unit after Galland was wounded on April 27, 1945, and two days later the remnants of JV-44 made a hurried move to Salzburg-Maxglan to avoid the approaching U.S. Seventh Army. However, the war was not yet over for Galland's Circus even though their leader was out of the war.

On April 27, Galland was lying in a hospital bed while Heinz Bär led the remnants of JV-44 in sorties known as *freie jagd*, or "free hunting," where a fighter would attack targets of opportunity. Bär claimed two P-47s, but Foreman and Harvey believe that he may have actually mistaken a P-47 for a Soviet fighter, perhaps an LA-7, which was also a blunt-nosed radial engine fighter, since Soviet fighters were in the area.

It is hard to believe that he would make that kind of mistake, especially when JV-44 also claimed five of six IL-2 Sturmoviks destroyed, once a flight of twenty IL-2s were encountered. Bär was an experienced Eastern Front fighter leader, with 220 kills under his belt, of which sixteen kills were confirmed in the Me 262, and he was also an expert on aircraft identification. According to Foreman and Harvey, JV-44 lost two Me 262s that day. However, the *Luftwaffe* records do not reflect these losses for JV-44; JG-7 did in fact engage Soviet aircraft, and they lost two jets, so these two losses were probably from that unit. Bär scored his 220th and last confirmed kill of the war and his sixteenth in the jet, a P-47 over Bad Aibling.[1]

As the war came to an end, Galland had given Bär the order to send a negotiation team to handle the surrender of JV-44 to American forces. *Major* Wilhelm Herget volunteered and flew off with the letter in hand, but his Fieseler Storch was shot down; he never made it. Herget survived the crash and the war. Ironically, over seventy jets were flown to JV-44's airfield from every unit, including ground attack units, who had no more use for them. After years of begging, borrowing, and stealing jets, he now had more than he could ever use.

The Me 262s of JV-44 and the additional jets that were deposited were rolled out to the airfield, and having no response from the Americans, the order was given to put them all to the torch, as the remaining Me 262s were blown up by the JV-44 personnel placing grenades into the engine intakes. Some of the JV-44 Me 262s were flown out to Innsbruck, where they met personnel of JV-44 under the command of *Major* Hans-Ekkehard Bob, who was ordered to develop the Innsbruck airfield for operations. Other units either followed suit or just surrendered the jets, such as *Kommando Welter's* group. Bob's orders were rendered null and void due to the inadequate field length and lack of supplies.

Within a week the Seventh Army rolled within sight of their airfield and JV 44's remaining two dozen Me 262s of JV-44 (with others delivered) were destroyed before the advancing enemy troops could take possession of them. JV-44 was the most unique fighter unit in the world, its members being some of the most famous, successful, and highly decorated pilots of any nation in World War II. The method by which the unit was created and staffed was almost as unique as its list of members, as were the final hours of the Third Reich, the *Luftwaffe*, and JV-44.

Heinz Bär gave Bob his final orders on May 4, 1945: "The Americans were close to Salzburg airfield, which meant that we soldiers had to disappear. Firstly, the aircraft were made useless, again by removal of their regulators. I was ordered to go with the lorries and a detachment of sixteen men, well equipped with machine pistols and ammunition, and store the regulators safely somewhere in the mountains and then be available for the defense of the so-called *Festung Alpen* together with a detachment that was already there. . . . I established my head-quarters at a farm located at the highest point in the village. Again we waited for something to happen. But nothing did . . ."[2]

The pilots all ended their war in various ways. *Oberleutnant* Hans Grünberg flew "White 1" trying to get home near the old field at Kaltenkirchen, but had to land when he saw the British occupied the field, where he surrendered. *Major* Karl-Heinz Schnell and *Oberfeldwebel*

Herbert Kaiser surrendered in Salzburg. *Oberleutnant* Franz Stigler took off riding a *Kettenkraftrad*, used to tow aircraft, and ended up in British hands. Later he emigrated to Canada. *Leutnant* Klaus Neumann jumped on a motorcycle and went into the Alps. *Hauptmann* Walter Krupinski ended up in the POW camp at Bad Aibling until relocated. Galland surrendered at Tegernsee, where the general managed to get his American captors to look for Lützow, without success.

Hans-Ekkehard Bob and a few others escaped and heard the surrender on the radio. Bob made it home on foot following a journey of over a thousand miles that lasted six weeks. Schuhmacher was also captured and released after nine weeks. Galland, being a celebrity, was taken to England, while Bär, Krupisnki, Herget, Hohagen, Barkhorn, and Walther Dahl joined Galland later. Following their light interrogations, they were taken by ship to Cherbourg, France. This was where Krupinski was assaulted, receiving a near fatal head trauma, courtesy of a French rifle butt as two soldiers stole his Knight's Cross with Oak Leaves. His log book had already been stolen by an American soldier before he went to England.

Such was the end of JV-44, the most unique unit in history. All were brave men, most of them highly decorated and successful pilots. Some members of the unit always stood out as enigmatic figures, such as "The Rammer" Schallmoser, "Count Punski" Krupinski, and the nearly dead "Macky" Steinhoff, although perhaps none were as respected, controversial, and determined as Günther Lützow, as stated by its commanding officer, Adolf Galland:

"I was a mild and meek creature when it came to Lützow. This man was a fearless fighter and a great ace, and a demanding yet fair leader who never asked his men to do anything he had not already done. He would also be the first to fly a new aircraft, just in case there were any problems. Lützow was the spokesman as always; he was a great leader and a true knight, a gentleman. He was also a very serious person, and in all the years that I knew him I can probably count the number of times I ever saw him laugh on one hand.

"However, Lützow was a cold pilot, very unemotional, even on the radio in combat he was the calmest person I ever knew, even in a fight. It was as if he never exhibited any emotion except anger, and, ironically, this was usually directed at Göring, and never the enemy. He was never angry in combat, and he never hated his enemies."[3]

The final days of JV-44 and the leadership challenges faced by Galland were also chronicled. Galland did not want men to fly and die in a war that was irretrievably lost; he only wanted volunteers. He would not order men to die needlessly:

"On April 25, with no sign of Lützow, I called my men around, and told them the war was lost. I knew that I was not providing them with anything that they did not already know. What I did tell them, was that with the war lost, I would fly only with volunteers who wished to continue. I would not issue an order that may see them killed at this late day in the war. No one stepped aside, much to their credit.

"I ordered the remaining aircraft flown to Innsbruck, where Hans-Ekkehard Bob was located. I had sent Wilhelm Herget with Hugo Kessler in a [Fieseler Fi-156] Storch to get a message to General [Dwight D.] Eisenhower, for arranging a special surrender for JV-44. Herget was bringing back the message to Bär, but his plane was shot down. Herget was all right, just tossed around a bit, but the message never made it.

"Hearing nothing from Herget, I surrendered the unit, blew up the jets, and the Americans took me into custody. I was then sent to the RAF base at Tangmere, where I was interrogated and held until my release over a year later. Günther Rall was also there, along with [Hans-Ulrich] Rudel and others, all of those they thought could serve the American and British cause after the war. I guess that even at that time they were concerned about their Soviet ally."[4]

There has been great debate many decades after the war, as to what might have been had Germany had the jets much earlier. Gen. James Doolittle gave his impressions, believing the war would have still been won, but it would have been a much longer and more protracted, agonizing conflict. It could have also been the death knell of strategic bombing, had three thousand jets been made available in 1943 or perhaps even half that number. Had the loss percentages of heavy bombers exceeded twenty percent for even three months, it is highly likely that the U.S. Congress would have pulled funding for the expenditures for heavy bomber production, or at the very least focused upon the strategic bombing of Japan instead.

Another JV-44 pilot, retired *Generalleutnant* Johannes Steinhoff, had his own opinion as well: "I really think that had we had about a thousand jets or so in mid-1943, with a like production every month and with the trained pilots to fly them, I think that there could have been an even greater terrible toll inflicted upon the American bombers, as much as fifty percent in many cases, as long as we had enough fighter cover protecting our bases.

"I do not think that it would have won the war for us outright, but I really do think that the Allies would have had to re-think their unconditional surrender declaration. I also think that, as tragic as it would have been, the war would have dragged out long enough for the Western Allies to see the true intentions of Stalin and perhaps re-evaluated their alliance. But this is sheer speculation. It is better that things ended when they did. In fact, I would have been happier if Hitler had died much earlier and taken the Third Reich with him."[5]

Regarding flying with JV-44 and his experience in the Me 262, retired *Generalleutnant* Walter Krupinski ruminated upon his response during his interview and gave his thoughts on the unit, the jet, and the war in general:

"I served with JG-52 during most of my career in the east, but later served with JG-5, JG-11, JG-26, and *Jagdverband* 44, flying the Me 262 jet in the west from April 1, 1945, onward—not much combat time in jets. The fighting against the American fighter escorts and bombers was the worst, since they were excellent fliers and had so much top-rated equipment. I did manage to score kills in the jet, but I believe that only two were eventually confirmed, and I did damage a few other aircraft, all bombers. That was interesting. Galland once told us that if we did not have holes in our planes upon returning, then we must not have been doing our jobs. But that comes much later in the story.

"The B-17s and B-24 Liberators were difficult to engage due to their potent fifty-caliber defensive fire, and the American fighters made it even harder to get close, since they outnumbered us somewhere around ten to one on the average until later in 1944, when it often felt more like fifty to one. I found this all very frustrating and had to change the way I thought about things.

"I was only distraught over the fact that we did not have this plane sooner. Steinhoff had told me about the jet a few months earlier, after he had taken over JG-7 for a short time. He loved the jet, and he explained the delicate nature of the engines, the problematic takeoff and landing characteristics, but also the great advantages of the 262.

"Galland was using Steinhoff as his recruiting officer, and they had collected some of the best in the business. They also got Barkhorn and tried to get Hartmann, but Erich still had a soft spot for JG-52. His decision to remain with this unit would prove very costly. As you know, he spent over ten years in Soviet prison camps after the war, after the Americans handed them over to the Red Army in May 1945. I would not see him again until the late 1950s, and he was never the same man afterward.

"I still do not know how Galland and Steinhoff managed this, but I suppose when two officers enter wearing those high decorations, and who are both well-known heroes, very few low-ranking medical officers are going to rub them the wrong way. Galland had that way about him; cigar in his mouth, that smile and his very persuasive way of speaking. I can say that no matter how angry he was I never heard him raise his voice. He just stared into a person, made his point and never wavered. He even did this with his boss, the 'Fat One.'

[Regarding the R4M rockets] "We had some spectacular missions, especially when we received the R4M air-to-air rockets for our jets. My introduction to the unit was interesting. JV-44 had some success the previous day, when on April 8 Steinhoff shot down a Liberator and Ernst Fährmann shot down two B-17 Flying Fortresses.[6] Steinhoff had come over from JG-7, along with a few of the others, and they had already used the rockets with success even before we were a formed group. Having that experience in the unit was invaluable.[7]

"The first time I saw them work was I think on April 5, 1945, as the unit shot down five heavy bombers. I had recently been made adjutant of the unit, meaning paperwork, which I hated. There were quite a large number of enemy escort fighters around, so that tended to keep you busy in the cockpit. There was no way we were going to dogfight with these Mustangs, Thunderbolts, and Lightnings. We had to just come in fast, hit [the bombers] very hard and then get away very quickly. Once we were at least four to five miles away we could turn back and line up another target. The one great advantage that we had in the 262 over the 109 or 190 was our approach and climbing speed. This was both a positive and a negative thing.

"The other factor that supported our speed when flying 'clean jets' was that we were at least one hundred miles per hour faster than the Mustangs and other Allied fighters. They would have to drop from very high altitude, convert that into increased airspeed, and then hope to close in on one of us, and even get a good deflection shot. This was the most common way our jets were shot down, other than being shot up trying to take off or land, when we were very vulnerable and had no maneuverability or speed until about two to three minutes after takeoff. That is a lot of time when you have the enemy on your tail.

"The thirty-millimeter cannons were incredible weapons. It took only a half dozen or so to bring down a heavy bomber if you hit it in the wing root, which weakened the structural integrity of the aircraft, and also housed fuel cells. Just one explosive shell could bring down a fighter. When thinking back about those days, I never really had much fear in flying the jet even against such large numbers of enemies. Well, that was until I decided to land once after a mission. The one thing you had to be aware of was the fact that the Allied fighter pilots would use two methods of getting you once you broke off combat.[8]

"The next day [April 17] I took off with Galland, Steinhoff, Grünberg, and others, and I attacked a B-17 formation targeting

Munich. We scored hits, and one of our pilots collided with a B-17, which I think was Eduard Schallmoser, taking it down, and I managed to hit another B-17 myself, but it did not go down. I did not see this collision between Schallmoser and the bomber, but Steinhoff radioed this information to us.

"On the day Steinhoff crashed, his flight of six jets was commanded by Galland. Other pilots that day, including me, were Hein Wübke, Gerd Barkhorn, then with three hundred victories, 'the Rammer' Eduard Schallmoser [so named for his penchant for ramming his jet into enemy bombers once his ammunition ran out], Ernst Fährmann, Klaus Neumann, and Heinz Bär, who had sixteen kills in the jet, and myself were all either taking off for a bomber-intercept mission or preparing to go on the second mission on the morning of April 18, 1945.

"The reason Steinhoff crashed was that the previous day we had an American bombing raid on our field, and there were still a few potholes in the grass strip, bomb fragments scattered about, and although the men were trying to patch them up as well as possible, some remained filled with water and were sometimes hard to see. There had not been much damage inflicted upon the planes or the fuel depot, although one of the barracks took a hit and had some damage."[9]

The one thing that all the jet pilots faced was not just the enemy fighter streaking down to kill them landing or taking off or strafing their aircraft on the runway. The bombing raids that damaged and destroyed aircraft also damaged the runways, making them treacherous and just as dangerous as the enemy, as Krupinski stated:

"All of us felt that we were only a thread away from a similar fate [as Steinhoff] after that accident, as well as the later loss of Günther Lützow [who went missing on April 24], and others too numerous to list. Steinhoff suffered for many years with many surgeries after the war, but his strength of character and determination to survive pulled him through. I give his wife, Ursula, a lot of credit, as she was his strength during those tough years.

"Bär actually shot down two Thunderbolts on the mission that day, and he said that he would gladly give them back if he could trade them for Macky. Normally, we would celebrate victories, but no one felt like saying or celebrating anything. I would have to say that Steinhoff's crash dropped our morale, and Lützow's failure to return from a mission the following week plummeted our morale even further. Then Galland being wounded a few days later, and Barkhorn being injured and out of the war pretty much closed the door on JV-44.

"Although I scored one hundred ninety-seven victories in the war, I was only able to confirm two of them in the 262, with a third bomber claimed as a probable. This was on the April 16 mission with Galland, Steinhoff, Lützow, Bär, Barkhorn, Schallmoser, and I think Fährmann. There are probably many pilots who damaged enemy bombers that later crashed, but without verification on the ground or in the air these were not counted.

"I need to say something about some of the pilots in JV-44. [Gottfried] Fährmann [four kills in the jet] keeps coming to mind, along with Schallmoser, who was successful, but he was also a rammer, bringing his bombers down by crashing into them sometimes. These guys were just a different cut of the cloth. Günther Lützow was another great man. While not a great ace in the jet, he was an outstanding leader, and a very brave man for many reasons.

"At the end of the war the unit was disbanded. Galland had been badly wounded by a fighter and crashed his 262, but we did not have as near as many losses as, say, JG-7. However, we were also a smaller unit, and did not operate as a unit as long. Some of the JG-7 pilots were recruited by Steinhoff, such as Köster, Lützow, Grünberg, Fährmann, and a few others. These men brought great jet experience with them when Steinhoff brought them in. I still do not know how he and Galland managed to accomplish this, since both of them had fallen from grace with both Göring and Hitler. Steinhoff once said that if you looked a gift horse in the mouth, it was often missing teeth.

"As the war ended, and the fighters were being destroyed, I was captured when the unit surrendered after blowing up the last of our jets, when the Americans were practically rolling onto the airfield with tanks, infantry, everything. An American Intelligence officer found us and took us via Heidelberg to the U.S. Army Air Forces/Royal Air Force interrogation camp in England."[10]

Retired *Brigadegeneral* Erich Hohagen also recalled his introduction into JV-44, and gave his thoughts on the unit, the war, and the final days of the Third Reich: "I was in the hospital with Krupinski and some others, when I hear this voice. Then this head looked around the corner; 'Erich? Are you in there?' It was Steinhoff. I looked up and said, 'What in the hell are you doing here, Sir?' He said, 'Looking for you, you cripple. Get your things together, you are out of here.' I laughed and said, 'And who authorized this?' Then another voice, Galland, walked in, and I instinctively tried to jump to attention, forgetting that I was not in the best physical shape. They both laughed and came to help me get back up.

"Well, as I had already flown with JG-7 and had some victories and a lot of experience, I was asked if I would like to go back to flying. I told them that Weissenberger and Sinner had ruled me unfit to fly. Galland said, 'I have straightened all that out. I am forming my own unit, want to come along?' You know I said yes; it was better than flying a bed. I grabbed my cane, my uniform, and carry bag, and they helped me get into a car. That was how I joined. I never even saw paperwork. That's what having a general involved can do for you I guess.

"I became the technical officer, so it was my job to try and get everything we needed to keep the jets flying, from fuel, ammunition, tires, paint, even wiring. Most people do not know this, but the 262 had a problem electrically. For some reason, once we mounted the rockets on, and wired them into the cockpit, sometimes after the firing the wires would melt. It took a little time, but I finally had a *gefreiter*, who was an electrician by trade, who worked in the hospital, just happened to stop by and drop off some mail I had received.

"When asked what the problem was, I told him. He solved the problem; it was so simple I wanted to kick my own ass. He simply said double the gauge of the wire to handle the flow, and use solder mounts. That was it. We solved the problem. Steinhoff saw that he was promoted and Galland endorsed it. We had him assigned to our unit, and he became our master electrician. He actually had to wire a 262 from scratch, as there were no wiring diagrams, and he did a lovely job. [This was Krupinski's jet, as described previously.]

"Flying with JG-7 was a freedom I had never experienced when I was with JGs-51, 2, or EKG-2. But flying with JV-44 was almost like a paid holiday, minus the danger. Galland just wrote up the missions, and unless we had an alarm due to incoming aircraft, we flew freely; it was a great pleasure."

Franz Stigler also commented about how ending the war with JV-44 was unlike anything he had previously experienced during the war: "I would have to say that Galland ran a loose ship when it came to JV-44. This is not to say that discipline did not exist—just the contrary. But everyone in the unit was so seasoned, so experienced for the most part, that a direct order never had to be given. The respect we had for Galland and the senior officers made it unthinkable not to do everything within our power, and to the best of our ability, to accomplish every task.

"Working together, and accomplishing the near impossible was a standard event in all *Luftwaffe* units. But in Galland's outfit, there was never any tension. There was nothing but a relaxed atmosphere, which, given the dangers of the business at that stage in the war, was really what made it work so well. I think that our focus being upon just flying and nothing else was what gave us our success."[11]

Thus ended the operations of the last active jet fighter unit of World War II. The fighting and dying were over, but a new war, a scramble for technology, was just beginning, and the Me 262 was at the top of the list for Allied experts.

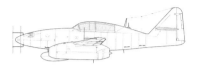

CHAPTER 24

Operations Lusty and Paperclip: The Postwar Scramble for Jets

What we collected from the Germans was incredible. I only wish the Soviets had not gathered as much as they did.

Group Captain John Cunningham, RAF

Before the war had ended, the British and Americans had already organized massive teams of technical experts to follow in the wake of the Allied ground advance. Knowing that their current ally, the Soviet Union, was not the most reliable friend in the future postwar arrangement, and also fearing that the Germans would destroy their technology before it could be captured, spurred these men on. Operations Lusty and Paperclip were separate yet also quite similar programs. Both programs will be briefly examined, with commentary from the participants as to the necessity and effectiveness of both programs.

Karl Baur, who was so involved with the Me 262 development, was truly a gifted man. He held a master's degree in aeronautical engineering from the University of Technology in Stuttgart and was a qualified glider and powered aircraft pilot, becoming instructor qualified as well as a test pilot. His knowledge, passion, and experience came not from the drawing board alone; he brought practical experience from the cockpit with him. He also knew that only the Western Allies should be the inheritors of German technology.

Baur, along with many other specialists, including Ludwig Hofmann, joined the entourage under the care of Col. Harold E. Watson. Their sole mission in life was to train American pilots on flying the captured jets, in particular the Me 262. German technology was the primary driving force in the Allied decision to push harder and further into German territory, with a few captured Me 262s and the overrunning of the V-buzz bomb sites following the invasion on June 6, 1944. Of particular interest, the first fully intact and operational Me 262 to fall into American hands came with a pilot, as stated in the following report as submitted by Merle Olmsted:

"Sometime during April, date unknown, the 357th Group pilots had the rare opportunity to meet and talk to an Me 262 pilot. The Monthly Intelligence Summary contained this item: The pilots and intelligence officers of the 357th Fighter Group were fortunate to receive a visit from Major Englander of the P/W & X Detachment during the month. The major stopped in on his way back to London from the 2nd Air Division. Accompanying Major Englander was one Hans Fay, one-time *Luftwaffe* pilot and until recently an acceptance pilot of the German Me 262s.

"An informal meeting of all pilots and I.O.s was called, Lt. Col. Evans presiding. The first part of the meeting was devoted to a discussion of tactics used against the Me 262s by our pilots who had encountered them. After the critique Major Englander took over the meeting and gave the background on Hans Fay.

"It seems that Fay, an anti-Nazi, had for some time considered joining the Allied fight against Hitler's gang, but naturally enough, decided to wait until his hometown in Germany had been liberated by the Allies, thereby protecting his family from S.S. and Gestapo reprisals. When he learned that his home had been freed, he selected an Me 262 fresh from the assembly line, took off, and a short time later landed safely in Allied territory surrendering his aircraft and himself to the American forces.

"After this summation, Major Englander acted as interpreter for the many questions asked of Fay. All facets of the subject were covered in the question bee. Fay was very cooperative to everyone's satisfaction. Colonel Dregne, on behalf of all attending, expressed appreciation to Major Englander for the visit. This was the only operational unit in the 8th AF that had the benefit of the session with the major and Hans Fay. Fay was not only a valuable source of information, but he had brought the Allies their first flyable Me 262, Werke number 111711, landing it at Frankfurt's Rhein-Maine airdrome, on 30 March, and surrendering to U.S. troops."[1]

The Operation Lusty personnel had already been selected, and teams were given known locations to investigate, but their interest was heightened when on February 24, 1945, an Ar 234B suffered a flameout in one of its engines when a P-47 forced it down into a hard landing near Segelsdorf. The jet was captured and was the first Ar 234 to fall into Allied hands still largely intact. This was perhaps the one circumstance that aided the American acquisition teams in getting a handle on just how critical keeping these machines out of Soviet hands was.

OPERATION LUSTY

During World War II, the USAAF Intelligence Service sent teams to Europe, initially based out of the United Kingdom to gain access to captured enemy aircraft, production, technical and scientific reports, research facilities, qualified personnel, and any and all weapons systems for study in the United States. The Air Technical Intelligence (ATI) teams from the Technical Intelligence School at Wright Field, Ohio, collected any and all enemy equipment to learn everything about Germany's technical developments.

These teams were also in direct competition with thirty-two other Allied technical intelligence groups all working to collect as much information and equipment recovered from crash sites, repair depots, airfields, and even spare parts warehouses as possible. These various intelligence teams found themselves changing from a purely tactical intelligence gathering unit to functioning as a postwar investigation and intelligence exploitation entity.

Watson's "Whizzers" was the nickname given to Col. Watson's Lusty teams in 1944 from the groups of intelligence experts located at Wright Field. These specialists had developed very detailed lists of advanced aviation equipment they wanted to examine, and the men assigned to Lusty were very qualified, as most were pilots, engineers, and maintenance men.

Watson worked with sheer autonomy, with having no one to answer to, and he had the freedom of movement to get anything he wanted by any means. Watson organized his Whizzers into two separate sections, with one team dispatched to collect all jet aircraft, while the other was given the mission of securing all new conventional piston engined aircraft and any jet and rocket equipment.

Perhaps the greatest bonus to Watson's efforts was the inclusion of the top *Luftwaffe* test pilots to their team. One example was *Hauptman* Heinz Braur, who on May 8, 1945, had flown seventy women, children, and wounded troops to Munich-Riem airport to escape the Soviets in the east. This field was in American hands, and they had captured nine Me 262s, intact, and they wanted to know how to fly them. Therefore, Braur was offered a choice: Go to a prison camp or fly and cooperate with the Whizzers team. Being a pragmatic man (as are all test pilots), Braur chose to fly, joining Karl Baur, Herman Kersting, Ludwig Hofmann, and engineer Gerhard Coulis.

The end of the war was really just the beginning of the hard work that lay ahead of the Whizzers, and time was not on their side. Following the Yalta Conference and subsequent agreements reached that previous February, time was a problem. The ink was not yet dry on the surrender documents when the four Allied powers began to secure their respective zones of military occupation. The Americans were much less concerned with the British and French occupation forces, as there were agreements on sharing captured technology. The great concern was the rapid, voracious, and quite unpredictable Soviet military incursions snapping up technology and the brilliant minds that created it, possibly leaving the Western Allies behind the curve.

Watson's units covered Europe by land and air to find the aircraft on their self-described "Black Lists." Once anything of value was found, it had to be broken down, inventoried, and packed up to be shipped back to the United States. Fortunately, for the effort, the British were willing to loan the small aircraft carrier HMS *Reaper*, where the captured aircraft would be loaded up at Cherbourg, France.

The Me 262s and other aircraft were flown from locations all over Germany and Austria to Lechfeld, where they were checked out further, and then flown to St. Dizier and Melun and then to Cherbourg. Upon arrival, all of the aircraft were disassembled, crated, and wrapped to protect them against the salt air and weather. Once they were prepared and manifested, they were loaded onto the carrier and brought to the United States, where various stateside teams of the U.S. Army and Navy evaluated them. The teams had collectively acquired 16,280 items (for about 6,200 tons), and of this collective, they selected 2,398 separate items for more detailed technical analysis.

Seeing the long-term value of the massive collection, Gen. Hap Arnold ordered the preservation of one of every type of aircraft used by the enemy forces once testing was completed. The Air Force brought their captured aircraft to Wright Field (later named Wright-Patterson Air Force Base), Ohio, with many of the surplus aircraft being sent to Freeman Field, Seymour, Indiana. Later, the larger aircraft were sent to Davis-Monthan Field, Arizona, and the fighter aircraft were sent to the Special Depot at Park Ridge, Illinois.

In 1953, some of the aircraft were moved to the National Air and Space Museum in Silver Hill, Maryland, and the remaining aircraft were scrapped.

The German aircraft technology was prioritized, with every known German design placed on a "wish list." Along with the Me 262 and Me 163, the AR 234 was on the "high priority" listing. The last Ar 234s were delivered early in March 1945, and on March 29, the order was given by Albert Speer for selective demolition teams to destroy the main Arado plant to deny it to the advancing Soviets. Speer resisted and, in fact, refused Hitler's directive to destroy everything, and the high-value assets in the west were, for the most part, left intact for the advancing Western Allies. This was not simply due to an altruistic moment; Speer knew that he had to have a bargaining chip when the war finally ended.

A total of 210 Ar 234Bs and fourteen Ar 234Cs were delivered to the *Luftwaffe*, yet due to the rapid deterioration of the German war machine, only a handful ever saw combat. A final inventory of existing Ar 234s on April 10, 1945, listed thirty-eight working units in service, of which twelve were bombers, twenty-four were reconnaissance aircraft, and two were built specifically as night fighters. These aircraft remained in active service until Germany surrendered on May 8, 1945. Most of these were shot down in air combat by enemy aircraft or destroyed by flak. Some were destroyed by their crews, especially in the east as the Soviets advanced. The surviving units were captured on their airfields, primarily due to a lack of parts or fuel to continue operations, as stated by Dietrich Pelz:

"The bomber units using both the Me 262 and the Ar 234 suffered from the same problems, primarily a lack of supplies, especially fuel. Ironically, it was not due to the fuel not being available, it was mostly due to the transportation network being so badly bombed and constantly strafed that nothing could move, and when it did, it did not move very far. Bridges would be blown, and they would have to be rebuilt. Rail was always destroyed, and that had to be repaired, and this was done almost on a daily basis. In the end, it was tactical Allied bombing of our transportation system that denied us the opportunity to fully exploit our jet aircraft potential, and much less Allied fighter superiority."[2]

The end of the war terminated a number of interesting and ongoing Ar 234 developments. A number of different variants of the Ar 234C were in the planning stage, including an advanced two-seat night fighter version with the newer version of *Neptun* and other detection devices, including an infrared targeting indicator, the first ever planned for use on an aircraft, although the Germans had a working model, which also made the Operation Lusty wish list.

There was also design work underway for the two-seat Ar 234D bomber and reconnaissance variant, which was planned to contain a powerplant of two Heinkel-Hirth He S011 turbojets, each with 2,850 lb of thrust, and for an additional version of the two-seat night fighter version, the Ar 234P. This version would have been complete with all of the above innovations, but with the addition of a pressurized cabin, a two-stage rocket-powered ejection seat for both the pilot and radar operator/navigator, and a radio-guided rocket attachment guided by a joystick, much like a modern cruise missile. According to Pelz, the speed of this aircraft would have exceeded 700 miles per hour.

One Ar 234 variant under construction that the Allies found particularly fascinating when they overran the factory building was the "crescent-wing" version. This model was composed of an Ar 234B fuselage mated to a concave-curved swept wing configuration. The powerplant powered was a pair of BMW 003R combined-turbojet rocket-assisted engines. The BMW 003R combined the turbojet with a liquid-fuel rocket ignition system that provided three minutes of enhanced power for takeoff, climb or "war emergency power" to escape enemy aircraft. Despite this prototype finally being scrapped, the crescent-wing idea was actually used by the British in the 1950s when they designed the Victor V jet bomber.

Interesting to note was that despite all the knowledge already gathered by Allied intelligence on the existing German aircraft designs, the Me 262 was still their main quarry during Lusty. This is perhaps best explained by Gen. James H. Doolittle:

"We definitely wanted all the rocket stuff, such as the V-2 and the guys working on that project. And for sure, any and all jet or rocket types were wanted. I have to say that, although I was not part of this program, I can understand why the 262 was the most wanted aircraft, even though it was in fact not even the most technically advanced of all the German aircraft types.

"I would also say that, because of the constant interaction between the 262s and our bombers and fighters, it was more of a case of wanting to know better the 'Devil you know' as opposed to the demons you only know about. Our fighter pilots all wanted to fly this thing. Hell, I was no exception. I did take a good look at those things when they brought them back home. I would have to say that the Germans really had their act together."[3]

Even before the shooting stopped, the race began to gather as many of the aircraft as possible. Me 262s and Ar 234s were scattered all over Europe, and the British had managed to capture about a dozen of the Arados, while the Soviets only captured one example. Four of the captured Ar 234s were packaged up and loaded onto the HMS *Reaper*, joining the V-2s, Me 262s, Me 163s, and other prizes.

Three Ar 234s were given to the U.S. teams, with two going to the U.S. Air Force and one being delivered to the U.S. Navy, although this aircraft proved to be non-airworthy and was never able to be adequately repaired. One of the three USAAF aircraft was tested at Wright-Patterson Air Force Base and upon completion was delivered to the Smithsonian Institution's Air & Space Museum, where it is now on permanent display. It is possible that this example in America is the only existing example of an Ar 234.

The knowledge collected by the Lusty teams advanced American technology at a great pace and saved a lot of time working out trial and error issues within the U.S. jet and rocket programs. However, having the machines in hand was only half the battle. Having the men behind the technology was also required, and another group of hunters were actively on that trail.

OPERATION PAPERCLIP

Operation Paperclip was just one of many Office of Strategic Services (OSS) programs led by World War I Medal of Honor recipient Gen. William "Wild Bill" Donovan. The OSS had many diverse missions during the war, from assassination to intelligence gathering, and working with various resistance units all over the world, becoming the genesis for future U.S. Special Forces. The OSS, through Paperclip, recruited German scientists from all areas of expertise for employment by the United States after World War II. The operations as a whole were overseen by the Joint Intelligence Objectives Agency (JIOA). Just as Operation Lusty was to deny German technology to the Soviets, Paperclip was the mission to prevent German scientists, engineers, and technicians from also falling into Soviet hands.

Although the JIOA's recruitment of German scientists only officially began after the war in Europe officially concluded, American agents from the counterintelligence corps were already combing the prisoner of war compounds, hospitals, and refugee camps, looking for anyone who may have been on the list. Ironically, most of the Germans who were able were already of the mindset that capture by the Americans or British was preferable to being in Soviet hands, and thousands tried to flee west. Included were many top jet and rocket engine designers, the very people the Americans wanted the most.

It is with some irony that U.S. President Harry Truman did not formally order the execution of Operation Paperclip until August 7, 1945, long after the vast majority of the most wanted were already in the hands of the OSS. Also, Truman's order expressly forbade the inclusion of anyone found "to have been a member of the Nazi Party, or an active supporter of Nazi militarism."

Truman's ill-conceived order would have had tragic results for the United States, since among the Germans were rocket scientists Dr. Wernher von Braun and Dr. Arthur Rudolph, and the physician Dr. Hubertus Strughold. The end result of following this order would have meant that the United States (and by proxy Great Britain and France) would have either been delayed by decades in developing supersonic aircraft, nuclear-powered submarines and surface ships, stealth aircraft design (such as it was then), rocket and missile technology, submarine and ground-launched intercontinental ballistic missiles, high-altitude pressure and g-force data, and the delay (if not failure) in creating the Redstone, Gemini, and Apollo space programs.

In essence, violating a presidential directive allowed the free west to compete with, and eventually destroy, the Soviet-dominated Communist bloc of Eastern Europe. Disobeying Truman's order probably prevented the Soviets from having such a technological advantage that a Third World War might have been unavoidable. Such is history.

To circumvent President Truman's anti-Nazi order, and the Allied Potsdam and Yalta agreements, the JIOA worked independently with master forgers, many of whom were Germans on the U.S. payroll, to create false employment and political biographies for the scientists. The JIOA also expunged from the public record the scientists' Nazi Party memberships and régime affiliations. After the paperwork was completed, the U.S. government granted the scientists their security clearances to work in the United States. Paperclip, the project's operational name, derived from the paperclips used to attach the scientists' new "clean" histories to their "U.S. Government Scientist" JIOA personnel files.

Throughout history, conquering nations occupied and appropriated everything within their dominion. Collecting German technology following the war was just a continuance of the age-old practice. The great difference was that the American and British methods were, for the most part, devoted to preventing future wars, healing fresh wounds, building strong alliances with a newly defeated enemy, and preventing the spread of Communism.

It seems ironic that the technological advances with which Hitler and the Third Reich sought to win a desperate war ended up being the genesis of a new world order that has, for the most part, preserved the world from another global catastrophe. It is in this regard that the Germans who flew the world's first combat jets were not just pioneers of aerial warfare, but also, in their own way, played a role in the future of world peace.

Appendix 1

My Last Mission

BY JOE PETERBURS

On 10 April 1945, airfields throughout England were launching some 1,300 B-17s and B-24s against targets in Germany. Targets included aircraft factories, ordinance depots, and Me 262 bases in the Oranienberg, Berlin, Brandenburg-Briest, and Magdeburg areas. The bombers were being escorted by 843 Mustangs (P-51s) and 62 Thunderbolts (P-47s). The 20th Fighter Groups assignment was to escort some 430 B-17s from the 1st Air Division whose targets were in the Oranienberg area. The 1st Air Division bombers were joined by 31 B-17s from the 398th Bomb Group led by Lt. Col. E. B. Daily. The bombers were all assembled and headed toward Germany and their targets at Oranienberg by 1205.

An hour and thirty-five minutes later at 1341, the fighters of the 20th Fighter Group rendezvoused with their bombers over Osnabruck. Through radio monitoring the Germans knew about this buildup even before the bombers took off. From Osnabrück, 1st Air Division's bomber stream turned slightly to the left. Heading 70 degrees the aircraft climbed higher and higher as they pushed into German-controlled territory. The two other bomber forces, the 2nd and 3rd Air Divisions with over 800 heavy bombers, would carry out their attacks slightly ahead of the 1st Air Division. These flew against Rechlin and Parchim in the north, against Burg and Zerbst in the south, and with a force of 372 heading for Brandenburg-Briest. The most advanced bombers were the 147 Flying Fortresses of the 3rd Air Division, which went straight against Burg in the south. Both *Oberleutnant* Stehle's Staffel and Me 262s of KG(J) 54 scrambled from this place. These fighters were first to intercept the Americans at around

1415 hours and shot down a couple of B-17s. But the Me 262s were too few.

Not many minutes later the bombers arrived over Burg, where they dropped 438 tons of bombs, which completely destroyed the airfield. Hangars and workshops were destroyed, the runway ploughed up by bombs, and sixty aircraft were destroyed on the ground—including ten Me 262s. Meanwhile, the alarm was sounding at the jet airfields at Rechlin-Lärz, Parchim, Brandenburg-Briest, and Oranienburg.

At 1415 hours, the Me 262s of IX./JG 7 and X/JG 7 scrambled from Parchim in the north. U.S. fighters attacked the jets as they were taking off, and two were shot down. Fifteen minutes later, Liberators of the 2nd Air Division bombed Parchim. Later, the damage inflicted on the runway caused a landing Me 262 to overturn and explode. The pilot was immediately killed. His name was Franz Schall, an *Oberleutnant* with 133 aerial victories on his account.

Some forty miles farther to the southeast, Liberators and Flying Fortresses completely destroyed Rechlin-Lärz aerodrome, with sixty-four aircraft put out of commission on the ground. III./JG 7 took into the air to meet them, but the Me 262s were forced to defend themselves against the large numbers of escort fighters. *Fähnrich* Pfeiffer claimed the only B-17 destroyed, while two Mustangs and a Thunderbolt were reported shot down. *Oberleutnant* Walter Wever, the Knight's Cross holder who commanded VII./JG 7, was killed when his Me 262 was shot down near Stendal.

The 372 B-17s from the 3rd Air Division that were tasked to attack Brandenburg-Briest—of which only 138 were able to complete the attack—were intercepted by Me 262s from Stab/JG 7 and I./JG 7, flying singly. *Oberleutnant* Hans Grünberg, a former JG 3 ace who ended the war with eighty-two victories, attacked a formation of B-17, which had just bombed Brandenburg-Briest, and shot down two. Taking part in the raid against Brandenburg-Briest, 486th BG lost two and 487th BG four B-17s, most of them due to the concentrated AAA fire. In return, I./JG 7's *Gefreiter* Heim and *Feldwebel* Schwarz were shot down and killed.

One of Germany's top aces with 202 confirmed aerial victories, *Oberleutnant* Walter Schuck, commanded the Me 262s of III./JG7 operating out of Oranienberg. At about the same time as the bombers left the English coast, Walter Schuck was instructed to put his seven Me 262 pilots on cockpit alert.

It was a beautiful, sunny, spring day with a clear blue sky. A perfect day for flying. The entire 1st Air Division was heading toward the airfield at Oranienberg along with about 290 P51s providing escort. The whole airspace over Germany was dominated by Allied air. The bulk of the *Luftwaffe* had been diverted to the Eastern Front to counteract the advancing Russians. About all that was left to defend Germany from the massive bombing attacks were a handful of Me 262s.

In contrast to most of the other fifty-five Me 262s that scrambled against the American bombers, Schuck managed to hold his seven jet fighters together as they shot higher and higher into the blue sky from Oranienburg. Ground control guided them against a large mass of heavy bombers that approached Oranienburg from the northwest at an altitude of 25,000 feet. Schuck managed to evade the Mustangs that crisscrossed the sky and made a wide turn that placed him and his compatriots behind the mass of bombers. Then he attacked!

Walter Schuck remembered the ruins in Hamburg when the nearest B-17 grew rapidly in size in front of his windscreen. He pressed the firing button. The 30mm cannons hammered, and in the next moment the whole giant tailfin of the bomber was dissolved by the exploding shells. Below, explosions and black billowing smoke showed that the bombs were falling over Oranienburg's aerodrome. Schuck had to pull up to avoid a collision as his Me 262 raced through the bomber formation. Bringing his compatriots along, Schuck aimed at the wing of a bomber in another formation. A quick burst of fire, and as Schuck pulled up to avoid a collision, he caught a glimpse of the B-17 going down in flames.

It was the 303rd Bomb Group's B-17G Serial No. 44-8427, call code VK-E. It had been baptized *Henn's Revenge* in honor of the tail gunner Sgt. Thomas Henn, who had been severely injured by AAA shrapnel in January 1945. The pilot, 1st Lt. Robert "Boss" Murray, was piloting the "ship" on its 22nd combat mission when 30mm shells slammed into the two right engines. The Mission Narrative noted:

> An unexpected attack by six to eight ME 262s was encountered just after departing the target. 303rd gunners claimed two destroyed. *Henn's Revenge* was hit by the attacking Me 262s coming in on the tail. It burst into flames between the #3 and #4 engines, held course for a few seconds, peeled up, slid over and down to the right, through the formation, apparently out of control. *Henn's Revenge* exploded at 2,000 feet and broke up into two main parts and crashed in the small Gross Glasaow Lake between Gross Schonebeck and Liebenwalde 20 km northeast of the target Oranienburg and about 28 km north-northwest of Berlin. A wing and engines fell in the upper part of the lake and the tail and part of the fuselage came down in the lower part of the lake. The wreckage could be seen 50 to 150 feet from the shore.

Seven of the crew members were immediately killed: Murray and his co-pilot 2nd Lt. Lawrence L. Fries, the navigator Flight Officer Harold S. Smith, the Spot Jammer Sgt. Gerald V. Atkinson, Technical Sgt. Theodore A. Bates, Sgt. Nicholas Rodock, and turret gunner Sgt. Robert P. Rennie. Staff Sergeant Vito J. Brunale and Technical Sgt. Carl O. Hammarlund managed to bail out, but only the former would survive. Hammarlund was shot to death by his German captors.

As Schuck pulled up to avoid a collision, his Me 262 raced through the bomber formation. Sergeant Alan Morton, in the top turret of another B-17, froze when he saw the Me 262. "Me 262 at five o'clock, closing fast!" Morton yelled through the intercom as he flipped on all gun switches. Precisely at that same instant, the entire Bomb Group formation was racked up hard left on its side turning off the target; desperately trying to slow down and slip behind them was this Me 262. Meanwhile, there was no way that Morton could react and turn his turret guns around on him. Finally, the Me 262 ended up sitting on the right wing tip of Morton's B-17. The German and the American made eye contact for a full second, just 50 feet apart. Then the Me 262 increased speed and attacked another section of the bomber stream.

Schuck and his group closed in on another formation of B-17s. Again he aimed at the engines when he opened fire at one of the bombers. The impact of the 30mm cannons was terrible. The giant bomber immediately slopped over and went down. On the next attack 30mm cannons immediately set the bomber burning and then one of the wings was torn off, making this his fourth kill in succession. Second Lieutenant James W. McAfee's B-17 of 398th Bomb Group was only seconds away from the drop point and already had the bomb bays open when the Me 262s attacked. The 30mm cannon shells hit from astern, blew the tail fin apart, shredded the waist gunner Sgt. Felix H. Tichenor and tore an arm off the ball turret gunner Sgt. Haskell Boyes.

Staff Sergeant Frank E. Lewis remembers that he got a sight of "the horrible scene" where the waist gunner had been massacred by the cannon shells, before he himself got out through the entrance hatch. Three other crew members managed to get out. The tail gunner Max W. Paxton came down safely in his parachute but was killed by German civilians on the ground. The pilot, 2nd Lt. McAfee, his co-pilot, 2nd Lt. Donald J. Jones, and Flight Engineer Technical Sgt. Arthur J. Roit went down with the plane and were killed on impact. Staff Sergeant Lewis and Technical Sgt. Paul Krup were luckier; after bailing out they were captured by German troops.

The impact of Schuck's ravaging among the heavy bombers was devastating. In a short while, four B-17s were blown out of the sky by Walter Schuck, and one of his pilots destroyed a fifth during the same pass. Schuck now had accumulated 206 aerial victories.

This was my 49th mission and, as it turned out, my last. I was in B Group led by Capt. Riemensnider, and I was filling number four position in Black Flight with Capt. "Dick" Tracy in the lead. Although there were originally four in the flight, numbers two and three aborted, so it was just Tracy and me. We took off at 1150 and rendezvoused with the bombers at 1341 over Osnabruck. All was going well to this point. The bombers visually bombed their targets at Oranienberg at 1438 with excellent results. Then all hell broke loose.

A swarm of Me 262s came barreling at us. I had visually locked onto an Me 262 slicing through the formation I was escorting. I saw Schuck's cannon fire blow up his third B-17, then on to his fourth B-17, starting it afire. By this time I had rolled over and started down at him. I had about a 5,000-foot altitude advantage and with throttle wide open I was closing on him fast. As he came off his fourth kill, I pulled into his 6 o'clock position and let my .50-caliber machine guns blaze away. I got some good hits on his left wing and engine and saw some smoke. He went into a rolling turn to the right with me in hot pursuit and with Tracy close behind me. The jet headed for the deck, and as I quickly lost my speed advantage, he pulled out of range, disappearing into a cloud bank. Walter Schuck tells of how this mission ended for him:

Just when I had shot down the fourth bomber, I was attacked from the astern by a Mustang which came in from above. I noticed some hits in the left wing and turned to the right in a shallow dive with the Mustang pursuing me. I passed Berlin and after a while the left engine started to emit smoke. I then entered a low cloud bank and as I turned my head, I could see that I had managed to get away from the Mustang. With the engine starting to disintegrate I decided to bail out. My first attempt to get out failed. The air current was too strong. I pulled the stick and climbed from 1,500 metres to 1,800 metres. Then I grabbed the handle with both hands and with one foot I kicked the stick to one corner of the cockpit. The result was that the Me 262 tipped its nose and I was flung out of the cabin. Floating in the airspace, I entered a flat spin. As I rotated, my right arm extended in 90 degrees from the body, and the G forces were too strong to permit me to pull it back. Only by grabbing the sleeve of my leather jacket with my left hand was I able to pull back my right arm, so that I could pull the handle which enveloped the parachute. In the meantime, I had descended to only around 500 metres altitude. The jerk when the parachute unfolded above my head came only a few metres above the ground. Looking down I could see a field with a barbed wire fence which came closer and closer. Desperately, I kicked in the air and pulled the strings of the parachute. The parachute tipped over and I barely dived over the barbed wire. I flung my feet forward and violently hit the ground, spraining both ankles. Although I was in a state of shock, I quickly pulled the parachute together. I had heard that the American fighter pilots would come down to strafe bailed out pilots, aiming at their white parachutes. Then I just lay down.

I lost sight of the Me 262 as it entered the clouds, and I then looked over my left wing and saw a German airfield loaded with all types of aircraft. I called to Dick, "Do you see what I see?"

Dick responded, "Yes, let's go!"

Tracy took over the lead; the airfield was several miles away so we descended to "cutting grass" level to gain some surprise. We did achieve surprise, and our first strafing pass was a breeze with each of us destroying two aircraft. By the time we came around for a second pass, airfield defenses were up and deadly. On the second strafing pass we each destroyed another aircraft. On the third pass, Tracy got hit just after destroying his fourth enemy aircraft while I went after a gun position. Tracy got a 20mm up the rear through the cockpit and into the engine. I saw a puff of smoke, engine fire, Tracy out, chute deployed and into a river.

This all occurred in a matter of a few seconds at about 300 feet as Dick was coming off target. At this time I decided to lower my seat and get as much armor behind me as possible and continued the attack. Being by myself, all the enemy guns were directed at me. On my fourth pass I destroyed a Ju 88 and set one of the three hangers afire. I also picked up a hit in the right wing, but it did not affect *Josephine*'s performance. With all those aircraft still left, I just couldn't pull myself away and decided to make one more pass.

As I came in low and fast I zeroed in on a four-engine Fw 200 Condor. My six .50 calibers raked the huge bird, and it burst into a mass of flames. As I was coming in for the kill on the Condor, I felt a thud, and as I pulled off the target I felt another thud and saw a flash in my engine. I continued my climb off target and was able to make it up to about 10,000 feet. By then the engine had overheated and was smoking. I started manipulating throttle, mixture, and prop controls to get the best I could out of the engine.

I knew that *Josephine* had it and that I needed to decide which way to go. East toward the Russians or west toward the Americans? While deciding, I called Colonel Montgomery, Group Leader, reported Tracy and my situation, and gave him directions to the German airfield. As I was leaving the target area, I could see a gaggle of P-51s headed toward the airfield to finish what Tracy and I had started.

I decided to head west. We had been briefed that American forces were fighting in the Magdeberg area and figured they were less than 100 miles away. When I was about 15 miles from Magdeberg I saw an Fw 190 coming into my three o'clock position. He was firing his guns and a volley of rockets and fortunately missed. By this time I was descending below 1,000 feet, the aircraft was burning, and I was unable to keep it flying. I was losing altitude fast, and I decided to bail out.

I unstrapped myself and ditched the canopy, looked at the altimeter, and saw I was passing 500 feet. I thought, "Crap, this is too low to bail out," and I started looking for a place to belly it in. Then I realized I was unstrapped and would kill myself bellying it, so I went over the side at about 300 feet. All this thought process took place in a matter of seconds and when I went over the side I thought again, "Crap! My mom is going to get a telegram about this," and I remembered how badly she took it when my brother Paul was killed.

I went out the left side of the cockpit (I think it was supposed to be the right side) and I hit my right knee on the horizontal stabilizer; I pulled the rip cord, chute opened, and I swung once and hit the ground—hard. After landing I noticed I had burns on my arms and legs and had hurt my ankles and back on impact. I knew I had to get up and survey the situation. I found myself in the middle of acres of farmland with nowhere to hide or take cover. I could immediately see the situation was hopeless and there was no way I was going to be able to avoid capture.

DAY'S END

In the distance, I saw a crowd of about ten people coming toward me and at the same time a flight of four P-51s flying at about 200 feet flew over checking out the situation. My reaction was get the hell out of here—you can't help me! As the civilians came closer I took out my .45-caliber automatic, removed the clip, and tossed each in opposite directions. I could see that the civilians were hellbent on doing me in, and I didn't want them using my own gun on me.

At the same time they reached me, a *Luftwaffe* sergeant stationed in the area came roaring up on his motorcycle, pulled out his gun, and protected me. Shortly thereafter, a group of town officials showed up, and the sergeant agreed to let them take me into town.

As we arrived in town a lot of people, including children, were crowding around to take a look. I was brought to an official-looking house and placed in a room with five or six older men. One was the

Bergermeister and another was in a police uniform. His left hand was artificial, made of black leather. He pulled out his Lugar and wanted to shoot me on the spot. They questioned me and emptied the many pockets of my flight suit. I always carried a rosary with me, and upon seeing it, they were astonished. How could this murderer of women and children be a Catholic? The questioning started to get rough, and an angry crowd was gathering outside, so the *Luftwaffe* sergeant said that was enough questioning. He took me out of the building, put me on his motorcycle, and headed toward the airfield he was stationed at. On the way he told me why the townspeople were so angry. Several days earlier some P-51s strafing in the area blew the head off a three-year-old girl. At the airfield, I was put in a very small cell and questioned by the Gestapo for about three days.

PRISONER OF WAR

Every night we had to go to the bomb shelter because of RAF night bombing raids. I felt very uncomfortable in the confined space of the bomb shelter with all the Germans staring at me. While at the airfield, my jailor, a *Luftwaffe* sergeant, could speak a little English and I could speak a little German, so we were able to communicate quite well. He told me about the testing that was being done there on new types of aircraft and how he thought the war was about over. His main concern was that I would give him a note saying he treated me fairly, and I did.

After about four days at the airfield, I was taken to the rail station where I was loaded in a boxcar that took me to Stalag 11. While waiting to be loaded, a German railroad employee gave me a shot of schnapps—wow! When I arrived at Stalag 11, the camp was practically empty. It had been going through evacuation because of advancing Allied Forces. I stayed there overnight and found out there were about 100 British enlisted troops still there.

The next morning, we were all rousted and started on a long march to the east. We were on a forced march for about ten days, during which we were constantly under attack by patrolling Allied fighter aircraft. Of course, they did not know we were POWs. Our German guards were really ticked off at the fact that we had Red Cross parcels to sustain us and they had black bread and water. They were usually able to get some substantial food when we spent the night at German farms sleeping in the barn. We, too, were able to scrounge an egg or two.

German army vehicles were almost at a standstill. They were unable to maneuver because the roads were completely clogged by thousands of refugees on bikes, walking, pulling wagons, etc.,

etc. It was complete pandemonium with thousands going east and thousands going west. German army personnel on motorcycles were scooting up and down the roads trying to establish some semblance of order, but it was completely hopeless. We ended up at a POW camp at Luckenwalde.

It was called Stalag 3 and was near Berlin. Most of the prisoners were Russian and Scandinavian but also included, to my great surprise, Captain Tracy and the B-17 crew members shot down on 10 April. They all arrived at the camp shortly after being shot down. Tracy told me he landed in a river, was OK, and remained there the entire time we were strafing the airfield. The Germans were taking pot shots at him while he was in the river, and he had to do a lot of maneuvering to avoid being hit. He said that on his last pass, he was hit from the rear with a 20mm cannon shell that passed through the cockpit, burning the seam of his flight suit, and continued into the engine. He was wearing the proof of the story.

After our group stopped strafing the airfield the Germans pulled him out and brought him to a building nearby. He was leaning on the building when, to his utter amazement, here comes Herman Göring mad as hell yelling and cursing, pulling out his Luger, which he pointed at Tracy several times while calling him all sorts of names. Finally, they took Dick away and brought him to Templehof Airport in Berlin. There he joined up with Sgt. Frank E. Lewis and Sgt. Paul Krup, both of whom were crew on 2nd Lt. James W. McAfee's B-17 of the 398th Bomb Group. They were only seconds away from the drop point, and already had the bomb bays open, when a Me 262 attacked.

Sergeant Lewis told me of his ordeal:

Our B-17 exploded only seconds after I came tumbling out of it. As I was approaching the ground at about 1,000 feet I could see I was being shot at by what appeared to be civilians on the ground. As I landed three German soldiers appeared and protected me from the civilians; then two of them took me to Berlin and Tempelhof airdrome. I was barefooted. My boots had slipped off when my chute opened and I was left with my felt-electric socks that were quickly tore up while I was running from the German civilians. I cut up my feet badly and had to hobble around like I was walking on hot coals. Walking like that on the streets and subways of Berlin must have looked insane. Two things struck me about Berlin. First the utter destruction we had wrote on the city with our bombings and second when I went into the subways that were brightly lit and spotlessly clean. The contrast was surreal.

In the subways, the Germans, mostly women, were hollering at me "swine" and other words that I finally figured out were "terror flier" and "Chicago gangster." At Tempelhof, I learned from the *Luftwaffe* people that the soldiers that saved me were SS troops and the *Luftwaffe* people hated the SS. I found it ironic that a *Luftwaffe* pilot tried to kill me in the air and civilians tried on the ground, but it was the SS soldiers that saved my life. The Germans at Tempelhof treated me well, and I ate in their mess hall with my guards. I was alone for several days before a P-51 pilot showed up—it was Capt. Richard "Dick" Tracy, and we were shipped off to Stalag 3 at Luckenwalde.

I often wonder if Göring was so pissed because I destroyed the Condor he was going to try to escape in. I found out later the Fw 200 was one of Hitler's Condors.

ESCAPE

Tracy, Lewis, and Krup (who could speak fluent Russian) had been planning an "escape" prior to my arrival. I went along with it. The plan was to go under the fence—security was practically nonexistent—and work our way toward the Russians. Within about 5 miles we were able to join a Russian tank unit that was fighting its way west and north.

The first town we arrived at after leaving Luckenwalde was Juterbug. It was a nice little town with some fine apartment complexes. I went with about ten Russian soldiers into one of the apartments. It was furnished real nice, and the Russians were making a big fuss about it. After a bit, one of them cleared us all from the room, went to its center, and let loose with his machine gun, destroying everything in sight while laughing his head off. I thought it weird but said nothing.

After leaving Juterbug we headed north toward Wittenberg on the Elbe. We were preceded by Stromovick fighter planes doing close air support for the advancing Russian force. There were some fierce battles and a couple minor skirmishes we were involved in. Hundreds of dead German soldiers were lying where they fell on both sides of our column. The death and destruction in ground warfare was a real revelation to this "flyboy."

The German civilians were terrified of the Russians, and as soon as they discovered there were Americans in the group, they sought us out. They wanted us to sleep with their daughters, stay in their homes, or let them stay with us. A middle-aged lady came up to me with her two beautiful daughters and begged me to stay with them. I said no, but I did stay at their house, and that protected them from rape and pillage for that night anyway. The Germans kept asking us why we were fighting with the Russians—didn't we know that we would be fighting them next?

At one point during the journey, we stopped at a German farm. The Russians had slaughtered a cow, some poultry, and a pig and were in the process of preparing a great feast. That evening we sat at a huge improvised banquet table seating a couple dozen people. We ate raw hamburger, steak, duck, pork, etc., with lots of wine and vodka. There were continuous toasts before, during, and after the meal. I had never consumed that much alcohol in my life, nor have I since. There were Russian dances and singing and a real rough-house affair that was enjoyed by all.

The next day one of the Russian officers talked me into "giving" him my watch as a token of friendship. I noted he had been admiring it for a couple of days. I noticed that most of their rolling stock was in ill repair. Gears stripped in the transmissions, and trucks only able to run in low was common. One day we came across a Russian soldier sitting alongside the road with his busted bike. We stopped and I took a look at it. I was an expert in bike repair as a youth. It was a simple problem with the sprocket, and I fixed it in about a half hour. He thanked me profusely with kisses and hugs, and we went on our way.

By the time we got to Wittenberg, the fighting was over. We were in open country by a bridge over the river Elbe when an American Infantry Patrol came across the river. They came over to make contact with the Russians, and when they saw me they insisted that the Russians let me return with them, which they were reluctant to do. Anyway, I returned with the patrol to their headquarters at Halle, Germany.

They were doing mop-up operations in the area, and I accompanied them on a couple of patrols. We would go into a village and have the people bring all their weapons to the town square where they would pile them up. It was at this time I picked up quite a few souvenirs, including a couple of Lugars, P-38 pistols, and a military honor sword. The army guys were able to swindle me out of my guns in short order while playing poker accompanied by a lot of booze. In a few days I took off on my own.

After walking about five miles I came across a C-47 parked in an open grass field. The crew was picking up some ex-prisoners of the Germans. The prisoners were in white and black striped uniform and were emaciated—barely able to stand. They were going to Paris, and I thought, "What's better than that?" The pilots said come on along. When we arrived in Paris I was stamped, deloused, and put under control. My few wandering days on my own were over. I was home by June 1945 and married my beloved Josephine;

however, I was not yet twenty-one years old, so I had to get my mother's permission.

OUT OF THE BLUE

In April 1998, fifty-three years after my last World War II combat mission, bailout, and capture, out of the blue I receive a letter from Burg, Germany. It was from a Werner Dietrich, who wrote that on 10 April 1945 he was a thirteen-year-old boy hiding in a ditch and watching the air battles going on above him. He saw a P-51 heading in a westerly direction and then saw an Fw 190 attack the P-51 firing its guns and rockets. Then he saw the pilot bail out and get captured, and he saw where the P-51 crashed.

Burg is in East Germany, and after reunification Werner had told the story to a local television network and asked them to help him locate and excavate the P-51 he saw go down. At first, the TV producer was a little reluctant; they had just reunified with the west and they were not certain as to how the authorities would take it. Eventually they agreed to do it as part of a documentary, and after considerable red tape they were able to start locating the aircraft with massive metal detectors. They brought in the backhoes and started excavating. At first the results were disappointing; however, they decided to go deeper and they hit pay dirt.

Parts started to appear, the prop, the guns, the engine, and many other bits and pieces. During the entire process, the TV cameras were rolling for a documentary. Using the serial number of the P-51, Werner started the long and arduous task of trying to learn who the pilot was. He wrote to the Air Force, the war archives, and every other place imaginable with no luck. He had been searching and corresponding for over nineteen months and was about to chuck it when he got one possible lead. He was told that the 20th Fighter Group lost several aircraft that day in that area and that he should contact the 20th Fighter Group Association's president Jack Ilfrey.

Upon receiving Werner's letter, Jack immediately wrote back: "Hell yes, I know the pilot. It's Joe Peterburs living in Colorado Springs, Colorado." With my name and address in hand, Werner wrote me the letter asking if I indeed was the pilot of the P-51 he saw when he was a boy. I responded yes, and nineteen months after Werner's project began, he was able to locate the pilot. The problem with the official records was that they had my name spelled wrong, Peterburg instead of Peterburs, and did not correlate the two.

After being able to identify me, he went back to the TV producer. The producer was overjoyed and wanted to arrange for me to come to Germany and visit the site and make a follow-up documentary. My wife, Josephine, had a stroke in 1997, and I could not and would not leave her side. The TV producer then made arrangements for Werner and the TV crew to visit me in Colorado Springs, bringing along parts of my aircraft and a beautiful bouquet of roses for Josephine. We had a nice visit, showed off all of my World War II memorabilia, and visited the Air Force Academy and Pikes Peak.

Of course, what Werner had seen as a boy was only part of my story. I told him of our raid on Oranienburg, my engagement with an Me 262, my strafing of the airfield, and the subsequent damage to my aircraft, trying to make it back to the lines and eventually bailing out—where Werner came into the picture.

After hearing these details, Werner became obsessed with the idea that he could find the Me 262 pilot that I engaged. When he returned home to Germany he relentlessly researched the records and eventually and miraculously found the Me 262 pilot that I had attacked. He is *Oberleutnant* Walter Schuck, one of Germany's top aces with 206 victories in the air. He is still alive and confirmed to Werner the events of that day.

Schuck told Werner that during my pursuit, he saw that he had pulled away from me. He then descended through a cloud bank at about 3,000 feet, but the damage was already done. His left engine started to disintegrate, it blew, and he bailed out. This was the first I knew that my guns did sufficient damage to his aircraft to cause it to go down. Even though Werner was positive it was Schuck I had engaged, I was a little skeptical. There were a lot of Me 262s in the air that day, and I figured the chance that it was Walter that I hit with my gunfire was between 25 and 50 percent. I was later proven wrong.

FURTHER SUBSTANTIATION

In March 2004, the Swedish author Christer Bergstrom contacted me and wanted me to furnish him an account of my 10 April 1945 mission. He was in the process of writing Walter Schuck's biography and wanted to compare it with Walter's account of events that day. After he read my account, he contacted me and said that both he and Walter are 100 percent sure that it was I who caused the damage to Walter's Me 262 resulting in his bailout. I asked how they could be so certain. Christer wrote:

> After the war, many attempts were made to identify the American fighter pilot who hit Schuck's Me 262 with machine gun fire. Several

suggestions are based on the erroneous assumption that Schuck engaged the B-17's near Magdeberg, over eighty miles southwest of Oranienberg. However, it is clear that on this day, Schuck and his 3/JG7 operated from Oranienberg and they engaged the 1st Air Division bombers that attacked Oranienberg. American fighter pilots claimed to have shot down no less than twenty Me 262s on this day—including three by pilots of the 20th FG. However, while none of these could apply to Schuck's aircraft, no other American fighter pilot than Peterburs appears to come into question for having shot down Schuck. Peterburs' account, which he wrote years before and without knowing anything about Walter Schuck, clearly describes the action of Walter Schuck. No other Me 262 pilot shot down several B-17s in a row over Oranienberg. The reason why no researcher previously has been able to identify Peterburs as the man who shot down Schuck is easily explained. Peterburs never reported that he shot down or even damaged a Me 262! In fact, it took almost sixty years before Peterburs even found out that he had shot down Walter Schuck.

I always thought that my actions after Tracy was shot down while we were strafing Schonwalde airport, as well as my activities and adventures that followed my eventual bailout and capture, were the highlights of my World War II experiences. It was nice to know that the Me 262 that I engaged was destroyed and that the pilot was a top German ace.

OBERLEUTNANT WALTER SCHUCK AND I MEET

In March 2005, I was contacted by Christer Bergstrom and several other friends of Walter Schuck. They told me of Walter Schuck's forthcoming visit to southern California. They asked me to contact Kurt Schulze, Walter's squadron mate during the war, for more details. In April I contacted Kurt and he said Walter would be there in mid-May for a visit. He also told me about Robert Bailey's "Escort Fury" poster depicting me shooting Walter down. I was really overwhelmed and surprised, since I had never been told that he was doing a print. Kurt then informed me that they wanted me there not only to meet Walter but to sign the print. I was very reluctant to leave Colorado Springs and was in a state of grief and deep depression having just recently lost my beloved wife, Josephine. After much more pressure from the friends of Walter and my grandson Rick and his wife, Sabrina, I decided to combine the visit to see Walter with a visit to my grandson's home in Roseville, California. I made the trip to Roseville in mid-May and spent several days there before Sabrina, Hannah, and I drove to Vista, California, where the meeting and signing was to take place. The meeting with Walter took place at the "Old, bold, pilots' Club" breakfast. After the breakfast, Walter and I were scheduled to sign the "Escort Fury" prints. On 18 May 2005, a historical meeting took place in Vista, California—Walter and I met, for the first time in person, since that fateful day over sixty years ago. The greatest thing about our meeting is that Walter and I took to each other immediately. We genuinely like each other. After the meeting and signing sessions, we went to the Chino Air Show where we were interviewed for the crowd and did a lot of signings. When Walter and I parted I can say we were good friends. Since then we have been together at least every year either here or in Germany and our relationship has grown into a truly great friendship.

Note: This narration of the last mission (number 49) flown on April 10, 1945, by 1st Lt. Joe Peterburs of the 20th Fighter Group, 55th Fighter Squadron, RAF Station Kings Cliff, England, is based on the recollections of Peterburs, Schuck, and various bomber crew members, the research of Christer Bergstrom, and the after-action intelligence reports of applicable units.

Appendix 2

German Ranks and Medals

CORRESPONDING GERMAN AND ALLIED AIR FORCE RANKS

German	American	British
Generalfeldmarschall	General of the Army/ Air Marshal of the Air Force (5 star)	Royal Air Force
Generaloberst	General (4 star)	Air Chief Marshal
General der Flieger	Lieutenant General (3 star)	Air Marshal
Generalleutnant	Major General (2 star)	Air Vice Marshal
Generalmajor	Brigadier General (1 star)	Air Commodore
Oberst	Colonel	Group Captain
Oberstleutnant	Lieutenant Colonel	Wing Commander
Major	Major	Squadron Leader
Hauptmann	Captain	Flight Lieutenant
Oberleutnant	First Lieutenant	Flying Officer
Leutnant	Second Lieutenant[1]	Pilot Officer
Sonderführer	Warrant Officer	Warrant Officer
Hauptfeldwebel	Sergeant Major	Flight Sergeant
Oberfeldwebel	First Sergeant	Chief Technician
Stabsfeldwebel	Sergeant First Class	Sergeant[2]
Feldwebel	Staff Sergeant	Junior Technician
Unterfeldwebel Technician	Sergeant[3]	Senior Aircraftman
Unteroffizier	Corporal	Senior Aircraftman
Privat	Private	Leading Aircraftman

1. This is usually the lowest rank for pilots in the U.S. military, although there were exceptions where enlisted pilots flew, but it was rare.
2. Usually the lowest rank for a pilot in the RAF. There were exceptions.
3. This was typically the lowest rank that a German pilot in training would normally hold. Given the one year of flight training and then advanced training, the average enlisted pilot would be a *feldwebel* or higher, although there were a few *gefreiters* and *obergefreiters* who flew. This also applies to the RAF pilots.

LUFTWAFFE TABLE OF ORGANIZATION

Office or Formation	Rank of Commander
Oberbefehlshaber der Luftwaffe	*Reichsmarschall* (Supreme Air Force Commander)
Chef des Generalstabes der Luftwaffe	*General der Flieger* or *Generaloberst* (Chief of Air Staff)
Fliegerkorps (Air Corps)	*General der Flieger* or *Generalleutnant*
Fliegerdivision (Air Division)	*General der Flieger, Generalleutnant* or *Generalmajor*
Geschwader (Wing)	*Generalmajor, Oberst, Oberstleutnant,* or *Major*, with title of *Kommandeur*
Gruppe (Group)	*Oberstleutnant, Major,* or *Hauptmann* (in rare cases) with title of *Kommandeur.*

This table is an operational matrix that was not engraved in stone. Many times, an officer with great ability but not holding the rank was placed in a command far above his pay grade. Also, combat attrition and the rapid redeployment of units and personnel issues factored into the equation as well.

This table remained more or less as stated above from 1939 to 1943, with few exceptions until 1942, when even more junior officers took higher levels of command responsibility. By 1944, this rank requirement was even lower in some cases.

Order of the Iron Cross and Knight's Cross

The Iron Cross and its subsequent higher levels was not just a medal awarded for valor on the battlefield. It was both a valor award and also based on an award scale, progressing from the lowest to this highest order, as listed below.

Iron Cross 2nd Class

Iron Cross 1st Class

Knight's Cross—Approximately 7,500 awarded.

Knight's Cross with Oak Leaves—Only 860 awarded.

Knight's Cross with Oak Leaves and Swords—Only 159 awarded.

Knight's Cross with Oak Leaves, Swords and Diamonds—Only 27 awarded, 10 to *Luftwaffe* pilots, 9 to fighter pilots. The one exception was Stuka pilot *Oberst* Hans-Ulrich Rudel.

Knight's Cross with Golden Oak Leaves, Swords and Diamonds—Only awarded to *Oberst* Hans-Ulrich Rudel.

Grand Cross of the Iron Cross—Only awarded to *Reichsmarschall* Hermann Wilhelm Göring.

Appendix 3

Additional Me 262 Data

GERMAN JET ACES

Name	Rank	Victories in Jet	Unit(s)	Total Victories	Notes
Kurt Welter	*Oberleutnant*	20+	KdoWelter 10/NJG 11	63	Possibly the all-time leading jet ace. Top Mosquito killer
Heinrich Bär	*Oberstleutnant*	16	EJG-2, JV-44	220	Started jet combat in 1945
Franz Schall	*Hauptmann*	14	Kdo Nowotny JG-7	137	Killed in flying accident April 10, 1945
Hermann Buchner	*Oberfeldwebel*	12	Kdo Nowotny JG-7	58	
Georg-Peter Eder	*Major*	12	Kdo Nowotny JG-7	78	Wounded for the 14th time on January 22, 1945
Erich Rudorffer	*Major*	12	JG-7	222 (Possibly 224)	10 B-17 kills
Karl Schnörrer	*Leutnant*	11	Kdo Nowotny Ekdo 262 March 30, 1945 JG-7	46	Wounded
Erich Büttner	*Oberfeldwebel*	8	Ekdo 262 Kdo Nowotny JG-7	8	Killed in action March 20, 1945
Helmut Lennartz	*Feldwebel*	8	Ekdo 262 Kdo Nowotny JG-7	13	First victory over a B-17 Flying Fortress by a jet fighter on August 15, 1944
Rudolf Rademacher	*Leutnant*	8	JG-7	126	
Walter Schuck	*Oberleutnant*	8	JG-7	206	
Günther Wegmann	*Oberleutnant*	8	JG-7 Ekdo 262	14	Wounded 18

Name	Rank		Unit		Notes
Hans-Dieter Weihs	Leutnant	8	JG-7	8	Midair collision with Hans Waldmann (Waldmann killed) on March 18, 1945
Theodor Weissenberger	Major	8	JG-7	208	Killed postwar
Alfred Ambs	Leutnant	7	JG-7	7	Shot down Mar. 24, 1945 by 1st Lt. Earl R. Lane in Me 262 "Yellow 3," bailed out at 17,000 feet, landed in tree
Heinz Arnold	Oberfeldwebel	7	JG-7	49	Killed in action on April 17, 1945. The actual Me 262 A-1a WNr.500491 Yellow 7 of II./JG-7 with his victory marks at the National Air and Space Museum Washington, D.C.
Karl-Heinz Becker	Feldwebel	7	10/NJG-11	7	
Adolf Galland	Generalleutnant	7	JV-44	104	Created JV-44 in March 1945. Wounded on April 26, 1945, shot down by Capt. James Finnegan, P-47 pilot.
Franz Köster	Unteroffizier	7	EJG-2 JG-7 JV-44	7	
Fritz Müller	Leutnant	6	JG 7	22	
Johannes Steinhoff	Oberst	6	JG-7 JV-44	176	Wounded on takeoff on April 18, 1945
Helmut Baudach	Oberfeldwebel	5	Kdo Nowotny JG 7	20	Killed in action on February 22, 1945
Heinrich Ehrler	Major	5	JG 7	206	Killed in action on April 4, 1945
Hans Grünberg	Oberleutnant	5	JG 7 JV 44	82	
Josef Heim	Gefreiter	5	JG 7	5	Killed in action April 10, 1945
Klaus Neumann	Leutnant	5	JG 7 JV 44	37	
Alfred Schreiber	Leutnant	5	Kdo Nowotny JG 7	5	First jet ace in history. Killed in flying accident November 26, 1944
Wolfgang Späte	Major	5	(JG-400) JV-44	99	

KOMMANDO NOWOTNY JET LOSSES

WNr.	Date	Fate	Pilot
170044	Oct. 4, 1944	Engine failure on landing at Hesepe with 75 percent damage killed in flying accident	*Oberleutnant* Alfred Teumer
170292	Oct. 5, 1944	Emergency landing on the autobahn near Braunschweig with 10 percent damage, repaired	*Oberfeldwebel* Helmut Baudach
110405	Oct. 7, 1944	Shot down during takeoff	*Leutnant* Gerhard Kobert
110395	Oct. 7, 1944		*Oberfähnrich* Heinz Russel
170307	Oct. 7, 1944	Shot down during takeoff	*Oberfeldwebel* Heinz Arnold
110402	Oct. 12, 1944	Emergency landing at Bramel with 10 percent damage, repaired	*Feldwebel* Helmut Lennartz
110399	Oct. 13, 1944		*Oberingenieur* Leithner
110401	Oct. 13, 1944		*Oberfähnrich* Heinz Russel
170041	Oct. 4, 1944	Undercarriage collapse while landing at Waggum with 20 percent damage, repaired	*Hauptmann* Franz Schall
110388	Oct. 12, 1944	Emergency landing at Steenwyk with 15 percent damage	*Oberleutnant* Paul Bley
110387	Oct. 29, 1944		*Leutnant* Alfred Schreiber
110481	Oct. 28, 1944	Crashed on takeoff at Achmer with 99 percent damage, killed in flying accident	*Oberleutnant* Paul Bley
110419	Oct. 28, 1944		*Hauptmann* Franz Schall
110386	Nov. 1, 1944		*Oberfähnrich* Willi Banzhaff
110368	Nov. 2, 1944		*Unteroffizier* Zöllner
170278	Nov. 2, 1944		*Oberfeldwebel* Siegfried Göbel
170310	Nov. 4, 1944		*Oberfeldwebel* Zander
110403	Nov. 4, 1944		*Oberfeldwebel* Siegfried Göbel
110483	Nov. 4, 1944		*Oberfähnrich* Willi Banzhaff killed in action
110389	Nov. 6, 1944	Cause unrecorded with 50 percent damage	*Leutnant* Spangenberg
170045	Nov. 6, 1944	Undercarriage failure upon landing at Hesepe with 25 percent damage, repaired	*Feldwebel* Erich Büttner
110402	Nov. 6, 1944	Emergency landing with gear up at Ahlhorn with 30 percent damage, repaired	*Oberfeldwebel* Freutzer
110490	Nov. 6, 1944	Emergency gear up landing near Bremen with 30 percent damage	*Feldwebel* Helmut Lennartz

110400 Nov. 8, 1944	Total loss in combat with 100 percent damage at Achmer.	*Major* Walter Nowotny, kill shared by Capt. Ernest Fiebelkorn of the 20th FG and 1st Lt. Edward Haydon of the 357th FG
110404 Nov. 8, 1944	Engine flameout 24,000 feet in aerial combat 100 percent damage, total loss	*Hauptmann* Franz Schall, bailed out
170293 Nov. 8, 1944	Blown tire on takeoff with 35 percent damage, repaired	*Feldwebel* Erich Büttner

JV-44 JET LOSSES

Date	Cause	Pilot
April 8, 1945	Shot down	*Leutnant* Klaus Fährmann
April 8, 1945	Collision	*Unteroffizier* Eduard Schallmoser
April 17, 1945	Collision	*Unteroffizier* Eduard Schallmoser
April 18, 1945	Crash on takeoff	*Oberstleutnant* Johannes Steinhoff
April 19, 1945	Shot down	*Oberfeldwebel* Hans Grünberg (still technically assigned to JG-7)
April 20, 1945	Collision	*Unteroffizier* Eduard Schallmoser
April 20, 1945	Crash landed	*Major* Gerhard Barkhorn
April 24, 1945	Shot down	*Oberst* Günther Lützow
April 26, 1945	Shot down	*Generalleutnant* Adolf Galland+

SURVIVING EXAMPLES OF THE ME 262

Me 262 A-1a WNr.501232 "Yellow 5," 3 Staffel/KG(J)-6
National Museum of the United States Air Force in Wright-Patterson Air Force Base, Dayton, Ohio.

Me 262 A-1a WNr.500491 "Yellow 7," II./JG-7
National Air and Space Museum, Smithsonian Institution, Washington, D.C.

Avia S-92 and Avia CS-92
Kbely Aviation Museum in Prague, Czech Republic.

Me 262 A-2a WNr.112372
RAF Museum RAF Hendon, United Kingdom.

Me 262 A-2a WNr.500200 "Black X 9K+XK," 2 Staffel./KG-51
Australian War Memorial in Canberra, Australia.

Me 262 A-1a
Luftwaffenmuseum der Bundeswehr, Germany. This is a generic reconstruction from parts of several crashed, damaged, and assorted Me 262s.

Me 262A, W.Nr. 500071 "White 3," III./JG-7
Deutsches Museum in Munich, Germany. Pilot was Hans-Guido Mutke of 9 Staffel/JG-7, was confiscated by the Swiss after an emergency landing there on April 25, 1945.

Me 262 B-1a/U1, WNr.110305 "Red 8," 10NJG-11
South African National Museum of Military History in Johannesburg, South Africa.

Me 262 B-1a, WNr.110639 "White 35"
NAS/JRB Willow Grove, Pennsylvania.

ME 262 PRODUCTION VARIANTS

Me 262 A-0
Prototype test aircraft fitted with two Jumo 004B turbojet engines with twenty-three built.

Me 262 A-1a
Production version, fighter and fighter-bomber.

Me 262 A-1a/R-1
Equipped with provisions for R4M air-to-air rockets.

Me 262 A-1a/U1
Single prototype with a total of six nose-mounted guns, two 20mm MG 151/20 cannons, two 30mm (1.18-inch) MK 103 cannons, and two 30mm (1.18-inch) MK 108 cannons.

Me 262 A-1a/U2
Single-seat night-fighter prototype with FuG 220 *Lichtenstein* SN2 90 MHz radar and *Hirschgeweih* antenna array.

Me 262 A-1a/U3
Reconnaissance version modified in small numbers, with *Reihenbilder* RB 20/30 cameras mounted in the nose, and occasionally one RB 20/20 and one RB 75/30.

Me 262 A-1a/U4
Bomber destroyer version with two prototypes fitted with the 50mm MK 214 or BK-5 antitank gun in the nose. Some pilots called it the "*einhorn*" (unicorn) or "*nashorn*" (rhinoceros). The extra weight made it easy prey for Allied escort fighters.

Me 262 A-1a/U5
Heavy jet fighter with six 30mm (1.18-inch) MK 108s in the nose.

Me 262 A-1b
Only difference from the A-1a was the BMW 003 engines, with two examples known to have been built.

Me 262 A-2a
Definitive bomber version retaining only the two lower 30mm (1.18-inch) MK 108s.

Me 262 A-2a/U1
Single prototype with advanced bombsight.

Me 262 A-2a/U2
Two prototypes with glazed nose for accommodating a bombardier.

Me 262 A-3a
Proposed ground-attack version.

Me 262 A-4a
Reconnaissance version.

Me 262 A-5a
Definitive reconnaissance version used in small numbers at end of the war.

Me 262 B-1a
Two-seat trainer.

Me 262 B-1a/U1
Me 262 B-1a trainers converted into provisional night fighters, FuG 218 Neptune radar, with Hirschgeweih antenna array.

Me 262 B-2
Proposed night fighter version with stretched fuselage, extra radar and armament. Never produced.

Me 262 C-1a
Single prototype configured from Me 262A WNr. 130 186 of rocket-boosted interceptor (Heimatschützer I) with the Walter HWK 109-509 rocket motor in the tail, first flown on February 27, 1945. Never mass produced.

Me 262 C-2b
Single prototype [made from Me 262A WNr. 170 074] of rocket-boosted interceptor (Heimatschützer II) with two BMW 003R dual powerplants with the early BMW 003 jet, with a single 1000-kilogram thrust BMW 718 rocket engine only flown on only one occasion on March 26, 1945. Never mass produced.

Me 262 C-3a
Design for the Heimatschützer III prototype of the rocket-boosted interceptor with Walter rocket, never produced.

Me 262 D-1
Proposed variant to carry heavy *Jagdfaust* under wing mortars, but not produced.

Me 262 E-1
Proposed heavy cannon-armed variant based upon the A-1a/U4 design.

Me 262 S
Zero-series test model for Me 262 A-1a airframe.

Me 262 V
Original test prototype for the Me 262 series.

Me 262 W
Design for Me 262 with pulse jet engines, never produced.

JG-7 PILOT COMMANDERS AND ACES
Geschwaderkommodore
Oberstleutnant Johannes Steinhoff, 1 January 1944
Major Theodor Weissenberger, 1 January 1945
Major Rudolf Sinner (acting), 19 February 1945

Gruppenkommandeure
I./JG 7
Hauptmann Gerhard Bäker, August 1944
Major Theodor Weissenberger, 25 November 1944
Major Erich Rudorffer, 14 January 1945
Oberleutnant Fritz Stehle (acting), April 1945
Major Wolfgang Späte, April 1945

II./JG 7
Major Hermann Staiger, 12 January 1945
Hauptmann Burkhard, February 1945
Major Hans Klemm, 15 April 1945–8 May 1945
III./JG 7
Major Erich Hohagen, 19 November 1944
Major Rudolf Sinner, 1 January 1945
Hauptmann Johannes Naumann, 5 April 1945
IV./JG 7
Oberstleutnant Heinrich Bär, 3 May 1945

JG-7 ACES

Rank	Name	Total Kills	Jet Kills
Major	Erich Rudorffer	222 (possibly 224)	12
Major	Heinrich Ehrler	208	8
Major	Theodor Weissenberger	208	8
Oberleutnant	Walter Schuck	206	8
Oberst	Johannes Steinhoff	176	6
Hauptmann	Ernst-Wilhelm Reinert	174	0
Oberleutnant	Fritz Tegtmeier	146	0
Oberleutnant	Hans Waldmann	134	3 claimed
Hauptmann	Franz Schall	133	17
Leutnant	Heinz Sachsenberg	104	0
Major	Siegfried Freytag	102	0
Major	Wolfgang Späte	99	5
Leutnant	Rudi Rademacher	97	16+
Oberfeldwebel	Helmut Ruffler	88	0

Oberleutnant	Hans Grünberg	82	5
Major	Georg-Peter Eder	78	12 (possibly 24)
Oberfeldwebel	Walter Ohlrogge	77	0
Oberleutnant	Adolf Glunz	72	0
Hauptmann	Lutz-Wilhelm Burkhardt	68	0
Leutnant	Viktor Petermann	64	0
Major	Hermann Staiger	63	0
Leutnant	Walter Jahnke	58	0
Leutnant	Hermann Buchner	58	12
Leutnant	Hermann Wolf	57	0
Major	Erich Hohagen	56	3
Leutnant	Karl Brill	52	0
Major	Ernst Dullberg	50	0
Oberfeldwebel	Heinz Arnold	49	7
Leutnant	Karl Schnörrer	46	11
Leutnant	Kurt Tangermann	46	0
Oberstleutnant	Walther Wever	44	0
Leutnant	Norbert Hannig	42	0
Oberfeldwebel	Gerhard Reinhold	41	1 (possibly 2)
Major	Rudolf Sinner	39	2 (possibly 3)
Oberfeldwebel	August Lübking	38	2 (possibly 3)
Leutnant	Alfred Lehner	37	2
Leutnant	Elias Kuhlein	35	0
Hauptmann	Johannes Neumann	34	0
Leutnant	Horst Schlick	34	0
Oberleutnant	Erwin Leykauf	33	0
Major	Klaus-H. Neumann	32	5
Leutnant	Karl-Heinz Schmüde	31	0
Oberleutnant	Alfred Seidl	31	0
Oberleutnant	Günther Stedtfeld	25	0
Oberfeldwebel	Erich Büttner	24	8
Feldwebel	Kurt Baten	24	0
Leutnant	Fritz R.G. Müller	23	6
Oberfeldwebel	Richard Raupach	23	0
Leutnant	Willi Unger	23	0
Leutnant	Erwin Müller	21	0
Oberstleutnant	Gustav Sturm	21	5
Oberfeldwebel	Helmut Baudach	20	8
Hauptmann	Rudolf Engleder	20	1

Leutnant	Günther Heckmann	20	1
Feldwebel	Otto Pritzl	19	8
Hauptmann	Werner Wenzel	18	0
Feldwebel	Hubert Drdla	18	0
Leutnant	Herbert Schlüter	17	0
Leutnant	Walter Hagenah	17	1
Leutnant	Siegfried Müller	17	0
Oberfeldwebel	Helmut Heiser	16	1
Oberfähnrich	Josef Neuhaus	15	1
Oberleutnant	Fritz Stehle	15	11
Feldwebel	Heinz Gomann	13	0
Oberfeldwebel	Albert Böckel	13	0
Oberfeldwebel	Rudolf Alf	12	0
Feldwebel	Karl Degener	12	0
Oberfeldwebel	Heinz Gossow	12	0
Feldwebel	Helmut Lennartz	11	8
Oberfeldwebel	Hans Todt	11	0
Feldwebel	Hans Heidenreich	11	0
Feldwebel	Ferdinand Loschenkohl	11	0
Oberstleutnant	Walter Bohatsch	10	3
Leutnant	Hubert Göbel	10	9
Oberfeldwebel	Albert Greiner	10	1
Feldwebel	Hans Langer	10	0
Feldwebel	Franz Holzinger	10	0
Oberleutnant	Franz Külp	10	1
Feldwebel	? Landsenbacher	10	0
Leutnant	Hermann Müller	10	0
Major	Wolfgang Rentsch	10	0
Feldwebel	Hans Theis	10	0
Fähnrich	Walter Windisch	10	6
Leutnant	Joachim Weber	9	9
Leutnant	Wilhelm Büschen	9	0
Leutnant	Erwin Stahlberg	9	0
Leutnant	Hans-Dieter Weihs	9	8
Leutnant	Rudolf Harbort	9	0
Oberfähnrich	Günther Engler	8	0
Oberleutnant	Karl-Heinz Seeler	8	1
Leutnant	Hein Führmann	8	0
Leutnant	Peter Köster	7	9
Oberfähnrich	Ernst Pfeiffer	7	7

Leutnant	Alfred Schreiber	7	7
Feldwebel	Fritz Taub	7	0
Feldwebel	Joachim Zeller	7	0
Leutnant	Alfred Ambs	7	7
Oberfeldwebel	Heinrich Humberg	7	0
Leutnant	Bruno Mischkot	7	0
Hauptmann	Hans Gottuck	7	0
Leutnant	Fritz Loose	7	0
?	Günther Bischoff	6	0
?	Fritz Wegner	6	0
?	Kurt Screiberer	6	0
Fähnrich	Friedrich Ehrig	5	7
Oberfähnrich	August Holscher	5	0
Oberfähnrich	Hubert Heckmann	5	1
?	Heim	5	5
Feldwebel	Rudolf Hener	14	5
Leutnant	Hans-Joachim Janke	5	0
Leutnant	Karl Kraft	5	0
Oberfähnrich	Herbert Müller	5	0
?	Rolf Prigge	5	0
Hauptmann	Gerhard Suwelack	5	0

PILOTS ASSIGNED TO JV-44 (NOT A COMPLETE ROSTER)

Rank and Name	Confirmed Jet Kills	Total Kills in All Units
Generalleutnant Adolf Galland	7	104
Oberst Günther Lützow	0	110
Oberstleutnant Johannes Steinhoff	6	176
Oberstleutnant Heinrich (Heinz) Bär	16	221
Major Gerhard Barkhorn	2	301
Hauptmann Walter Krupinski	2	196
Major Erich Hohagen	0	56
Leutnant Heinz Sachsenberg	0 Fw 190D commander	104
Hauptmann Waldemar Wübke	0 Fw 190D	15
Unteroffizier Klaus Faber	0 Fw 190D	0
Leutnant Karl-Heinz Hofmann	0 Fw 190D	0
Major Hans-Ekkehard Bob	0	60
Major Wilhelm Herget	1	73
Major Heinrich Brücker	0	0
Leutnant Heinz Arnold Döring	0	23

Major Diethelm von Eichel-Streiber	0	96
Leutnant Gottfried Fährmann	3	3
Leutnant Erich Fuhrmann	0	5
Leutnant Hans Grünberg	5	82
Oberleutnant Werner Gutowski (JV-44 Adjutant)	0	0
Leutnant Alfred Heckmann	2	71
Leutnant Erich Hondt	0	14
Leutnant Herbert Kaiser	0	68
Oberleutnant Georg Kiefner	0 Fw 190D	11
Leutnant Peter Köster	7 (2 probable)	9
Leutnant Klaus Neumann	5	37
Obergefreiter Eduard Schallmoser	3	3
Major Karl-Heinz Schnell	0 Fw 190D	72
? Karl-Hermann Schrader	0	2
Oberleutnant Franz Steiner	0	12
Oberleutnant Franz Stigler	0	28
Oberleutnant ? Richter	0	?
Oberleutnant ? Walter	0	?
Oberleutnant ? Blomert	0	0
Oberleutnant Wilhelm Roth	0	20

USAAF 357TH FIGHTER GROUP ME 262 VICTORY CREDITS
Confirmed Kills in Air Combat

1. Capt. Charles E. Yeager, November 6, 1944.
2. 1st Lt. Edward R. Haydon, November 8, 1944; 1/2 credit share with Capt. Ernest Fiebelkorn, 20th Group. Killed *Major* Walter Nowotny.
3. 1st Lt. James W. Kenney, November 8, 1944; Franz Schall pilot, bailed out.
4. Capt. Robert P. Winks, January 15, 1945.
5. 1st Lt. Dale Karger, January 20, 1945.
6. 1st Lt. Roland K. Wright, January 20, 1945.
7. Maj. Donald H. Bochkay, February 9, 1945.
8. 1st Lt. Johnnie L. Carter, February 9, 1945.
9. Maj. Robert W. Foy, March 19, 1945.
10. Capt. Robert S. Fifield, March 19, 1945.
11. Flight Officer James A. Steiger, April 17, 1945.
12. Capt. Charles E. Weaver, 18 April 1945.
13. Maj. Donald H. Bochkay, April 18, 1945.
14. Capt. Robert S. Fifield, April 19, 1945.
15. 1st Lt. Paul N. Bowles, April 19, 1945.
16. 1st Lt. Carroll Ofsthun, April 19, 1945.
17. 1st Lt. James P. McMullen, April 19, 1945.

18. 1st Lt. Gilman L. Weber, shared with Captain Ivan I. McGuire, April 19, 1945.

19. Lt. Col. Jack Hayes, April 19, 1945.

Credits for Me 262s Destroyed on the Ground

1. Col. Irwin H. Dregne, April 10, 1945, two destroyed.
2. 1st Lt. Anton Schoepke, April 17, 1945, one destroyed.
3. 1st Lt. Andy Duncan, April 17, 1945, one destroyed.

Probably Destroyed/Damaged in the Air

1. Major Robert W. Foy, February 9, 1945.

BRITISH RAF AND COMMONWEALTH JET CLAIMS/VICTORIES

Unit	Date	Pilot	Claim[1]
93 Sqn	Sept. 26, 1944	F/O. Francis Campbell	Me 262 Damaged
416 Sqn	Sept. 28, 1944	FLt. J. B. McColl	Me 262 Damaged
441 Sqn	Sept. 30, 1944	FLt. Ronald G. Lake	Me 262 Damaged
442 Sqn	Oct. 2, 1944	F/O F. B. Young	Me 262 Damaged
401 Sqn	Oct. 5,1944	SqLdr Roderick I. A. Smith	Me 262 ¼ Ground
401 Sqn	Oct. 5, 1944	FLt. Robert M. Davenport	Me 262 Shared Destroyed
401 Sqn	Oct. 5, 1944	FLt. H. J. Everhard	Me 262 Shared Destroyed
401 Sqn	Oct. 5, 1944	F/O A. L. Sinclair	Me 262 Shared Destroyed
401 Sqn	Oct. 5, 1944	FLt. John MacKay	Me 262 Shared Destroyed
3 Sqn	Oct. 13, 1944	P/O R. W. Cole	Me 262 Destroyed
3 Sqn	Oct. 21, 1944	FLt. A. E. Umbers	Me 262 Damaged
3 Sqn	Oct. 21, 1944	FLt. G. R. Duff	Me 262 Shared Damaged
3 Sqn	Oct. 21, 1944	F/O R. Dryland	Me 262 Shared Damaged
486 Sqn	Oct. 28, 1944	F/S R. J. Danzey	Me 262 Damaged
122 Wing	Nov. 3, 1933	W/C J. B. Wray	Me 262 Probable
486 Sqn	Nov. 19, 1944	SqLdr. Keith G. Taylor-Cannon	Me 262 ½ Probable
80 Sqn	Nov. 26, 1944	FLt. Price	Me 262 Shared Damaged
80 Sqn	Nov. 26, 1944	F/O Findlay	Me 262 Shared Damaged
80 Sqn	Dec. 3, 1944	FLt. J. W. Garland	Me 262 Destroyed
274 Sqn	Dec. 5, 1944	FLt. R. B. Cole	Me 262 Damaged
274 Sqn	Dec. 5, 1944	F/O G. N. Mann	Me 262 Damaged
56 Sqn	Dec. 10, 1944	F/S L. Jackson	Me 262 Damaged
122 Wing	Dec. 17, 1944	W/C J. B. Wray	Me 262 Destroyed
411 Sqn	Dec. 23, 1945	John Joseph Boyle	Me 262 Damaged
486 Sqn	Dec. 23, 1945	F/O R. D. Bremner	Me 262 Destroyed
486 Sqn	Dec. 23, 1945	F/O J. R. Stafford	Me 262 Destroyed

411 Sqn	Dec. 25, 1944	John Joseph Boyle	Me 262 Destroyed
486 Sqn	Dec. 25, 1944	FLt. John Henry Stafford	Me 262 ½ Destroyed
403 Sqn	Dec. 25, 1944	SqLdr. J. E. Collier	Me 262 Destroyed
411 Sqn	Dec. 26, 1944	FLt. E. G. Ireland	Me 262 Damaged
135 Wing	Dec. 26, 1944	WingCdr R. H. Harries	Me 262 Damaged
442 Sqn	Dec. 27, 1944	F/O M. A. Perkins	Me 262 Damaged
401 Sqn	Jan. 1, 1945	FLt. John MacKay	Me 162 ½ Damaged
401 Sqn	Jan. 1, 1945	F/S A. K. Woodill	Me 162 ½ Damaged
442 Sqn	Jan. 1, 1945	FLt. J. P. Lumsden	Me 262 Damaged
442 Sqn	Jan. 1, 1945	FLt. R. K. Trumley	Me 262 Shared Damaged
442 Sqn	Jan. 1, 1945	FLt. J. N. G. Dick	Me 262 Shared Damaged
442 Sqn	Jan. 1, 1945	F/O W. H. Dunne	Me 262 Shared Damaged
442 Sqn	Jan. 1, 1945	P/O E. C. Baker	Me 262 Shared Damaged
332 Sqn	Jan. 14, 1945	Capt. K. Bolsted	Me 262 Destroyed
411 Sqn	Jan. 23, 1945	Flt. Richard Joseph Audet	Me 262 Ground
56 Sqn	Jan. 23, 1945	FLt. F. L. McLeod	Me 262 Shared Destroyed
56 Sqn	Jan. 23, 1945	F/O R.V. Dennis	Me 262 Shared Destroyed
401 Sqn	Jan 23, 1945	SqLdr William T. Klersey	Ar 234 Damaged
401 Sqn	Jan. 23, 1945	FLt. Frederick T. Murray	Ar 234 ½ Damaged
118 Sqn	Jan. 23, 1945	FLt. J. L. Evans	Me 262 Damaged
118 Sqn	Jan. 23, 1945	FLt. K. M. Giddings	Me 262 Damaged
118 Sqn	Jan. 23, 1945	Flt. W. Harbison	Me 262 Damaged
401 Sqn	Jan. 23, 1945	F/O Church	Me 262 Destroyed
401 Sqn	Jan. 23, 1945	F/O G. A. Hardy	Me 262 Destroyed
401 Sqn	Jan. 23, 1945	F/O G. A. Hardy	Me 262 Shared Destroyed
401 Sqn	Jan. 23, 1945	FLt. W. C Connell	Me 262 Shared Destroyed
411 Sqn	Jan. 24, 1945	Flt. Richard Joseph Audet	Me 262 Damaged Ground
274 Sqn	Feb. 11, 1945	SqLdr. David C. Fairbanks	Ar 234B Destroyed
274 Sqn	Feb. 14, 1945	SqLdr. David C. Fairbanks	Me 262 Damaged
610 Sqn	Feb. 14, 1945	SqLdr. Frederick A. O. Gaze	Ar 234B Destroyed
184 Sqn	Feb. 14, 1945	Capt. A. F. Green DFC	Me 262 Damaged
439 Sqn	Feb. 14, 1945	FLt. L. C. Shaver	Me 262 Destroyed
439 Sqn	Feb. 14, 1945	F/O A. H. Fraser	Me 262 Destroyed
412 Sqn	Feb. 21, 1945	FLt. L. A. Stewart	Me 262 Damaged
309 Sqn	Feb. 23, 1945	W/O A. Pietrzak	Me 262 Damaged
274 Sqn	Feb. 24, 1945	FLt. R. C. Kennedy	Me 262 Damaged
402 Sqn	Feb. 25, 1945	FLt. K. S. Sleep	Me 262 Shared Damaged
402 Sqn	Feb. 25, 1945	FLt. B. E. Innes	Me 262 Shared Damaged
416 Sqn	Feb. 25, 1945	P/O L. E. Spurr	Me 262 Damaged
274 Sqn	Mar. 3, 1945	FLt. Pierre H. Clostermann	Me 262 Damaged

401 Sqn	Mar. 12, 1945	FLt. L. H. Watt	Me 262 Destroyed
402 Sqn	Mar. 13, 1945	F/O H. C. Nicholson	Me 262 Destroyed (This was possibly an Ar 234)
FE-F	Mar. 22, 1945	F/O Roy Emile Long	Me 262 ½ Ground Me 262 ½ Ground Me 262 ½ Damaged
126 Sqn	Mar. 23, 1945	F/O A. D. Yeardly	Me 262 Destroyed
129 Sqn	Mar. 23, 1945	FLt. G. H. Davis	Me 262 Damaged
309 Sqn	Mar. 23, 1945	W/O A. Pietrzak	Me 262 Damaged
126 Sqn	Mar. 31, 1945	F/O A. D. Yeardly	Me 262 Damaged
309 Sqn	April 9, 1945	FLt. M. Gorzula	Me 262 Destroyed
309 Sqn	April 9, 1945	FLt. J. Mancel	Me 262 Destroyed
309 Sqn	April 9, 1945	W/O A. Murkowski	Me 262 Destroyed Me 262 Damaged
306 Sqn	April 9, 1945	SqLdr. J. Zulikowski	Me 262 Destroyed
64 Sqn	April 9, 1945	F/O A. D. Woodcock	Me 262 Destroyed
41 Sqn	April 12, 1945	SqLdr. Frederick A. O. Gaze	Ar 234 ½ Destroyed
56 Sqn	April 15, 1945	FLt. J. A. McCairns	Me 262 Shared Destroyed
56 Sqn	April 15, 1945	FLt. N. D. Cox	Me 262 Shared Destroyed
41 Sqn	April 20, 1945	W/O V. J. Rossow	Me 262 Destroyed
29 Sqn	April 24, 1945	FLt. P. S. Compton	Me 262 Destroyed
421 Sqn	April 25, 1945	SqLdr Henry P.M. Zary	Me 262 Damaged
41 Sqn	April 25, 1945	FLt. P. Cowell	Me 262 Destroyed Me 262 Damaged
130 Sqn	April 25, 1945	FLt. W. N. Stowe	Me 262 Shared Probable
130 Sqn	April 25, 1945	W/O Ockenden	Me 262 Shared Probable
350 Sqn	April 25, 1945	FLt. Colwell	Me 262 Destroyed
486 Sqn	April 25, 1945	F/O K. A. Smith	Me 262 Destroyed
263 Sqn	April 26, 1945	FLt. W. J. Fowler	Me 262 Shared Destroyed
263 Sqn	April 26, 1945	P/O J. W. Shellard	Me 262 Shared Destroyed
263 Sqn	April 26, 1945	W/O H. Barrie	Me 262 Shared Destroyed
468 Sqn	May 2, 1945	P/O Desmond J. Watkins	Ar 234 1/3 Destroyed
402 Sqn	May 2, 1945	F/O G. N. Smith	Me 262 Damaged

ME 262 CLAIMS BY USAAF UNITS AND PILOTS
15th Air Force Claims in Order of Reporting

Unit	Date	Pilot	Claim
325th Fighter Group	Dec. 12, 1944	Lt. W. R. Hinton	1 Probable
82nd Fighter Group	Dec. 15, 1944	Lt. P. Kennedy	1 Damaged
82nd Fighter Group	Dec. 15, 1944	Lt. W. Armstrong	1 Damaged
31st Fighter Group	Dec. 22, 1944	Capt. E. P. McGlaufin	1 Shared

31st Fighter Group	Dec. 22, 1944	Lt. R. L. Scales	1 Shared
31st Fighter Group	Mar. 22, 1945	Capt. D. J. Willard	1 Destroyed
31st Fighter Group	Mar. 22, 1945	Capt. H. D. Naumann	1 Damage
31st Fighter Group	Mar. 22, 1945	Lt. B. J. Bush	1 Damaged
31st Fighter Group	Mar. 22, 1945	Lt. R. R. Blank	1 Damaged
31st Fighter Group	Mar. 22, 1945	Lt. C. E. Greene	1 Damaged
31st Fighter Group	Mar. 22, 1945	Lt. N. R. Hodkinson	1 Damaged
31st Fighter Group	Mar. 24, 1945	Col. W. A. Daniel	1 Destroyed
31st Fighter Group	Mar. 24, 1945	Lt. W. M. Wilder	1 Destroyed
31st Fighter Group	Mar. 24, 1945	Capt. K. T. Smith	1 Destroyed
31st Fighter Group	Mar. 24, 1945	Lt. R. D. Leonard	1 Destroyed
31st Fighter Group	Mar. 24, 1945	Lt. F. M. Keene	1 Destroyed
31st Fighter Group	Mar. 24, 1945	Lt. J. C. Wilson	1 Damaged
31st Fighter Group	Mar. 24, 1945	Lt. W. H. Bunn	1 Damaged
31st Fighter Group	Mar. 24, 1945	Lt. G. E. Erichson	1 Damaged
332nd Fighter Group	Mar. 24, 1945	Lt. R. C. Brown	1 Destroyed
332nd Fighter Group	Mar. 24, 1945	F/O C. V. Brantley	1 Destroyed
332nd Fighter Group	Mar. 24, 1945	Lt. E. R. Lane	1 Destroyed
332nd Fighter Group	Mar. 24, 1945	Lt. R. Harder	2 Damaged
332nd Fighter Group	Mar. 24, 1945	Lt. V. I. Mitchell	1 Shared damaged
332nd Fighter Group	Mar. 24, 1945	Capt. ? Thomas	1 Shared damaged
332nd Fighter Group	Mar. 24, 1945	Unknown	1 Probable
332nd Fighter Group	Mar. 24, 1945	Unknown	1 Probable
325th Fighter Group	April 4, 1945	Lt. W. K. Day	1 Damaged
86th Fighter Group	April 9, 1945	Unknown	1 Damaged
31st Fighter Group	April 11, 1945	Lt.Col. J. G. Thorsen	1 Damaged
325th Fighter Group	April 18, 1945	Maj. R. F. Johnson	1 Destroyed

9th Air Force Claims in Order of Reporting

Unit	Date	Pilot	Claim
365th Fighter Group	Oct. 2, 1944	Capt. V. J. Beaudrault	1 Destroyed
50th Fighter Group	Oct. 7, 1945	Capt. S. Mamalis	1 Damaged
50th Fighter Group	Oct. 26, 1944	Lt. L. E. Willis	1 Probable
10th Photo Recon Group	Jan. 14, 1945	Lt. C. G. Franklin	1 Shared Probable
10th Photo Recon Group	Jan. 14, 1945	Lt. M. V. Logothetis	1 Shared Probable
365th Fighter Group	Feb. 17, 1945	Lt. T. B. Westbrook	1 Damaged
365th Fighter Group	Feb. 17, 1945	Lt. C. E. Buchanan	1 Damaged
365th Fighter Group	Feb. 22, 1945	Lt. O. T. Cowan	1 Destroyed
366th Fighter Group	Feb. 22, 1945	Lt. D. B. Fox	1 Destroyed
361st Recon Squadron	Feb. 22, 1945	Lt. W. A. Grusy	1 Damaged

365th Fighter Group	Feb. 25, 1945	Lt. A. Longo	1 Damaged
365th Fighter Group	Feb. 25, 1945	Lt. J. L. McWhorter	2 Damaged
365th Fighter Group	Feb. 25, 1945	Lt. L. Freeman	1 Damaged
365th Fighter Group	Feb. 25, 1945	Capt. C. Ready	1 Damaged
366th Fighter Group	Feb. 25, 1945	Lt. M. R. Paisley	1 Damaged
366th Fighter Group	Feb. 25, 1945	Lt. J. T. Picton	1 Damaged
373rd Fighter Group	Feb. 25, 1945	Lt. E. P. Gardner	1 Damaged
373rd Fighter Group	Feb. 25, 1945	Lt. D. D. A. Duncan	2 Damaged
405th Fighter Group	Feb. 25, 1945	Capt. R. W. Yothers	1 Damaged (Possibly Ar 234)
354th Fighter Group	Mar. 2, 1945	Capt. B. Peters	1 Destroyed
354th Fighter Group	Mar. 2, 1945	Lt. T. W. Sedvert	1 Destroyed
354th Fighter Group	Mar. 2, 1945	F/O R. Delgado	1 Destroyed
107th Recon Squadron	Mar. 2, 1945	Lt. F. T. Dunmire	1 Probable
365th Fighter Group	Mar. 13, 1945	Lt. F. W. Marling	1 Destroyed
474th Fighter Group	Mar. 14, 1945	Lt. G. G. Clark	1 Damaged
474th Fighter Group	Mar. 14, 1945	Lt. J. J. Kozlik	1 Damaged
474th Fighter Group	Mar. 14, 1945	Lt. J. J. Kozlik	1 Shared Damaged
474th Fighter Group	Mar. 14, 1945	Lt. W. H. Barker	1 Shared Damaged
474th Fighter Group	Mar. 14, 1945	Lt. C. H. Darnell	1 Shared damaged
474th Fighter Group	Mar. 14, 1945	Lt. D. F. Lloyd	1 Shared damaged
354th Fighter Group	Mar. 17, 1945	Lt. ? Kuhn	1 Damaged
15th Recon Squadron	Mar. 19, 1945	Lt. N. A. Thomas	1 Damaged
354th Fighter Group	Mar. 21, 1945	Lt. T. W. Sedvert	1 Destroyed
12th Recon Squadron	Mar. 21, 1945	Capt. J. S. White	1 Damaged
358th Fighter Group	Mar. 31, 1945	Lt. P. M. Hughes	1 Damaged
162nd Recon Squadron	April 1, 1945	Lt. J. W. Waits	1 Damaged
162nd Recon Squadron	April 1, 1945	Lt. W. R. Yarborough	1 Damaged
474th Fighter Group	April 4, 1945	Lt. L. B. Alexander	1 Damaged
358th Fighter Group	April 8, 1945	Lt. J. J. Usiatynski	1 Destroyed
111th Recon Squadron	April 8, 1945	Lt. R. K. Wylie	1 Damaged
162nd Recon Squadron	April 8, 1945	Lt. P. Beavis	1 Damaged
162nd Recon Squadron	April 8, 1945	Lt. R. A. Rumbaugh	1 Damaged
162nd Recon Squadron	April 9, 1945	Lt. M. W. Geiger	1 Probable
354th Fighter Group	April 10, 1945	Capt. D. J. Pick	1 Shared Destroyed
354th Fighter Group	April 10, 1945	Lt. H. C. Schwartz	1 Shared Destroyed
358th Fighter Group	April 10, 1945	Lt. R. B. Manwaring	1 Damaged
107th Recon Squadron	April 11, 1945	Lt. C. W. Staatz	1 Damaged
354th Fighter Group	April 14, 1945	Capt. C. K. Gross	1 Destroyed
354th Fighter Group	April 14, 1945	Lt. A. J. Ritchey	1 Damaged

162nd Recon Squadron	April 14, 1945 Lt. R. M. Kollar	1 Shared Destroyed
162nd Recon Squadron	April 14, 1945 Lt. E. B. Scott	1 Shared Destroyed
162nd Recon Squadron	April 15, 1945 Lt. W. P. Simpson	2 Damaged
162nd Recon Squadron	April 15, 1945 Lt. G. B. Gremillion	2 Damaged
368th Fighter Group	April 16, 1945 Lt. H. A. Yandel	1 Destroyed
368th Fighter Group	April 16, 1945 Lt. V. O. Fein	1 Destroyed
354th Fighter Group	April 17, 1945 Capt. J. A. Warner	1 Destroyed
358th Fighter Group	April 17, 1945 Lt. E. E. Heald	1 Damaged
358th Fighter Group	April 17, 1945 Lt. F. C. Bishop	1 Probable
358th Fighter Group	April 17, 1945 Lt. T. R. Atkins	1 Probable
404th Fighter Group	April 19, 1945 Lt. B. F. Baylies	1 Damaged
354th Fighter Group	April 20, 1944 Lt. L. R. Blumenthal	1 Shared Damaged
354th Fighter Group	April 20, 1944 Lt. J. E. Carl	1 Shared Damaged
370th Fighter Group	April 20, 1944 Capt. M. P. Owens	1 Probable, 1 Damaged
370th Fighter Group	April 20, 1944 Lt. G. Caldwell	1 Probable, 1 Damaged
358th Fighter Group	April 24, 1945 Lt. D. S. Renner	2 Damaged
365th Fighter Group	April 24, 1945 Lt. O. T. Cowan	1 Damaged
365th Fighter Group	April 24, 1945 Capt. J. G. Mast	1 Shared Damaged
365th Fighter Group	April 24, 1945 Lt. W. H. Meyers	1 Shared Damaged
365th Fighter Group	April 24, 1945 Lt. B. Smith Jr.	1 Damaged
365th Fighter Group	April 24, 1945 Lt. L. D. Seslar	1 Damaged
358th Fighter Group	April 25, 1945 Lt. M. M. Esser	1 Shared Damaged
358th Fighter Group	April 25, 1945 Lt. C. G. Dickerson	1 Shared Damaged
358th Fighter Group	April 25, 1945 Lt. L. D. Volkmer	1 Probable
370th Fighter Group	April 25, 1945 Lt. R. D. Stevenson	1 Shared Destroyed
370th Fighter Group	April 25, 1945 Lt. R. W. Hoyle	1 Shared Destroyed
370th Fighter Group	April 25, 1945 Lt. C. L. Harman	1 Damaged
370th Fighter Group	April 25, 1945 Lt. I. B. McKenzie	1 Shared Damaged
370th Fighter Group	April 25, 1945 Lt. M. M. Deskin	1 Shared Damaged
370th Fighter Group	April 25, 1945 Lt. S. H. Banks	1 Damaged
358th Fighter Group	April 30, 1945 Capt. J. H. Hall	1 Shared Damaged
358th Fighter Group	April 30, 1945 Lt. J. Richlitsky	1 Shared Damaged
365th Fighter Group	May 4, 1945 Lt. A. G. Sarrow	1 Damaged
365th Fighter Group	May 4, 1945 Lt. A. T. Kalvastis	1 Damaged

1st Tactical Air Force Claims in Order of Reporting

Unit	Date	Pilot	Claim
27th Fighter Group	Mar. 22, 1945	Unknown	1 Damaged

371st Fighter Group	Mar. 31, 1945	Capt. W. T. Bails	1 Destroyed
324th Fighter Group	April 4, 1945	Lt. R. T. Dewey	1 Damaged
324th Fighter Group	April 4, 1945	Lt. J. W. Haun	1 Destroyed
324th Fighter Group	April 4, 1945	Lt. W. N. Clark	1 Probable
50th Fighter Group	April 8, 1945	Unknown	1 Destroyed
50th Fighter Group	April 8, 1945	Unknown	1 Damaged
324th Fighter Group	April 9, 1945	Lt. J. Q. Peeples	1 Damaged
324th Fighter Group	April 17, 1945	Lt. D. L. Raymond	1 Shared Damaged
324th Fighter Group	April 17, 1945	Lt. T. N. Theobald	1 Shared Damaged
324th Fighter Group	April 17, 1945	Lt. K. E. Dahlstrom	1 Probable
324th Fighter Group	April 17, 1945	Lt. R. Pearlman	1 Damaged
324th Fighter Group	April 17, 1945	Lt. J. V. Jones	1 Probable
371st Fighter Group	April 17, 1945	Lt. J. A. Zweizig	1 Destroyed
27th Fighter Group	April 23, 1945	Lt. B. V. Ackerman	1 Damaged
27th Fighter Group	April 24, 1945	Lt. R. E. Prater	1 Damaged
27th Fighter Group	April 24, 1945	Lt. J. F. Lipiarz	1 Damaged
27th Fighter Group	April 26, 1945	Capt. H. A. Philo	1 Destroyed
27th Fighter Group	April 26, 1945	Unknown	1 Damaged
50th Fighter Group	April 26, 1945	Capt. James Finnegan	1 Destroyed (originally claimed as damaged, this was Galland's Me 262, confirmed kill)
50th Fighter Group	April 26, 1945	Capt. R. W. Clark	1 Destroyed

8th Air Force Claims in Order of Reporting

Unit	Date	Pilot	Claim
78th Fighter Group	Aug. 28, 1944	Maj. J. Meyers	1 Shared Destroyed
78th Fighter Group	Aug. 28, 1944	Lt. M. O. Croy	1 Shared Destroyed
364th Fighter Group	Sept. 13, 1944	Lt. J. A. Walker	1 Damaged
78th Fighter Group	Oct. 7, 1944	Maj. R. E. Connor	1 Destroyed
361st Fighter Group	Oct. 7, 1944	Lt. Urban L. Drew	2 Destroyed
479th Fighter Group	Oct. 7, 1944	Col. Hubert Zemke	1 Shared Destroyed
479th Fighter Group	Oct. 7, 1944	Lt. N. Benoit	1 Shared Destroyed
78th Fighter Group	Oct. 15, 1944	Lt. H. H. Lamb	1 Destroyed
78th Fighter Group	Oct. 15, 1944	Lt. H. O. Foster	1 Damaged
56th Fighter Group	Nov. 1, 1944	Lt. W. L. Groce	1 Shared Destroyed
352nd Fighter Group	Nov. 1, 1944	Lt. W. T. Gerbe	1 Shared Destroyed
356th Fighter Group	Nov. 4, 1944	Capt. R. A. Rann	1 Damaged
4th Fighter Group	Nov. 6, 1944	Lt. W. J. Quinn	1 Destroyed

361st Fighter Group	Nov. 6, 1944	Lt. J. R. Voss	1 Destroyed
357th Fighter Group	Nov. 6, 1944	Maj. C. Yeager	1 Destroyed,* 2 Damaged
20th Fighter Group	Nov. 8, 1944	Capt. E. C. Fiebelkorn	1 Shared Destroyed
357th Fighter Group	Nov. 8, 1944	Lt. E. R. Haydon	1 Shared Destroyed (Haydon and Fibelkorn shared the victory over Maj. Walter Nowotny)
361st Fighter Group	Nov. 8, 1944	Lt. A. Maurice	1 Destroyed
362nd Fighter Group	Nov. 8, 1944	Lt. J. W. Kenney	1 Destroyed
364th Fighter Group	Nov. 8, 1944	Lt. R. W. Stevens	1 Destroyed
4th Fighter Group	Nov. 18, 1944	Lt. J. M. Creamer	1 Shared Destroyed
4th Fighter Group	Nov. 18, 1944	Capt. J. C. Fitch	1 Shared Destroyed
353rd Fighter Group	Nov. 18, 1944	Lt. G. E. Markham	1 Damaged
352nd Fighter Group	Dec. 5, 1944	Lt. B. Grabovski	1 Damaged
358th Fighter Group	Dec. 9, 1944	Lt. H. L. Edwards	1 Destroyed
353rd Fighter Group	Dec. 23, 1944	Capt. H. D. Stump	1 Damaged
353rd Fighter Group	Dec. 23, 1944	Lt. S. E. Stevenson	1 Damaged
339th Fighter Group	Dec. 31, 1944	Capt. A. G. Hawkins	1 Damaged
4th Fighter Group	Jan. 1, 1945	Lt. D. Pierine	1 Destroyed, 1 Probable
4th Fighter Group	Jan. 1, 1945	Lt. F. W. Young	1 Destroyed
20th Fighter Group	Jan. 1, 1945	Capt. W. M. Hurst	1 Damaged
55th Fighter Group	Jan. 13, 1945	Lt. W. J. Konantz	1 Destroyed
20th Fighter Group	Jan. 14, 1945	Lt. K. D. McNeel	1 Damaged
55th Fighter Group	Jan. 14, 1945	Maj. D. S. Cramer	1 Damaged
353rd Fighter Group	Jan. 14, 1945	Lt. B. J. Murray	1 Shared Detroyed, 1 Destroyed
353rd Fighter Group	Jan. 14, 1945	Lt. J. W. Rohrs	1 Shared Detroyed
353rd Fighter Group	Jan. 14, 1945	Lt. G. J. Rosen	1 Shared Detroyed
353rd Fighter Group	Jan. 14, 1945	Lt. M. A. Heinz Arnold	1 Shared Damaged
353rd Fighter Group	Jan. 14, 1945	Lt. G. E. Markham	1 Shared Detroyed
357th Fighter Group	Jan. 15, 1945	Lt. R. P. Winks	1 Destroyed
357th Fighter Group	Jan. 20, 1945	Lt. D. E. Karger	1 Destroyed
357th Fighter Group	Jan. 20, 1944	Lt. R. R. Wright	1 Destroyed
364th Fighter Group	Feb. 3, 1945	Lt. L. V. Andrew	1 Damaged
78th Fighter Group	Feb. 9, 1945	Lt. W. E. Hydorn	1 Probable
78th Fighter Group	Feb. 9, 1945	Capt. E. H. Miller	1 Probable
339th Fighter Group	Feb. 9, 1945	Lt. J. J. Sainlar	1 Damaged

*This loss was never recorded by the *Luftwaffe*, although it may have been a training aircraft, or an Ar 234, as several were lost.

339th Fighter Group	Feb. 9, 1945	Lt. S. C. Ananian	1 Destroyed
357th Fighter Group	Feb. 9, 1945	Capt. D. H. Bochkay	1 Destroyed
357th Fighter Group	Feb. 9, 1945	Lt. J. L. Carter	1 Destroyed
357th Fighter Group	Feb. 9, 1945	Maj. R. W. Foy	1 Damaged
20th Fighter Group	Feb. 14, 1945	Capt. J. K. Brown	1 Shared Damaged
20th Fighter Group	Feb. 14, 1945	Lt. K. D. McNeel	1 Shared Damaged
55th Fighter Group	Feb. 15, 1945	Lt. D. M. Amoss	1 Destroyed
356th Fighter Group	Feb. 21, 1945	Lt. H. E. Whitmore	1 Destroyed
20th Fighter Group	Feb. 22, 1945	Capt. R. M. Howard	1 Damaged
352nd Fighter Group	Feb. 22, 1945	Lt. C. D. Price	1 Destroyed
352nd Fighter Group	Feb. 22, 1945	Maj. E. D. Duncan	1 Damaged
353rd Fighter Group	Feb. 22, 1945	Lt. C. E. Goodman	1 Damaged
353rd Fighter Group	Feb. 22, 1945	Capt. G. B. Compton	1 Destroyed
363rd Fighter Group	Feb. 22, 1945	Maj. W. K. Blickenstaff	1 Destroyed
363rd Fighter Group	Feb. 22, 1945	Lt. R. L. Hunt	1 Damaged
363rd Fighter Group	Feb. 22, 1945	Lt. W. E. Randolph	1 Damaged
363rd Fighter Group	Feb. 22, 1945	Lt. L. H. Phipps	1 Damaged
363rd Fighter Group	Feb. 22, 1945	Lt. L. L. Lefforge	1 Damaged
353rd Fighter Group	Feb. 22, 1945	Lt. C. B. Kirby	1 Damaged 1 Shared Probable
353rd Fighter Group	Feb. 22, 1945	Capt. R. W. Stevens	1 Shared Probable
363rd Fighter Group	Feb. 22, 1945	Lt. G. O. Warner	2 Damaged
364th Fighter Group	Feb. 22, 1945	Lt. S. J. Price	1 Damaged
364th Fighter Group	Feb. 22, 1945	Capt. S. C. Phillip	1 Damaged
4th Fighter Group	Feb. 25, 1945	Lt. C. G. Payne	1 Destroyed
55th Fighter Group	Feb. 25, 1945	Capt. D. E. Penn	1 Destroyed
55th Fighter Group	Feb. 25, 1945	Capt. D.M. Cummings	2 Destroyed
55th Fighter Group	Feb. 25, 1945	Lt. J. F. O'Neil	1 Destroyed
55th Fighter Group	Feb. 25, 1945	Lt. M. O. Anderson	1 Destroyed
55th Fighter Group	Feb. 25, 1945	Lt. D. T. Menegay	1 Destroyed
55th Fighter Group	Feb. 25, 1945	Lt. B. Clemmons	1 Destroyed
78th Fighter Group	Feb. 28, 1945	Lt. W. F. Bechtelheimer	1 Shared Damaged
78th Fighter Group	Feb. 28, 1945	Lt. J. E. Parker	1 Shared Damaged
355th Fighter Group	Mar. 1, 1945	Lt. J. Wilkins	1 Destroyed
355th Fighter Group	Mar. 1, 1945	Lt. W. W. Beaty	1 Destroyed
355th Fighter Group	Mar. 1, 1945	Maj. H. H. Kirby	1 Damaged
364th Fighter Group	Mar. 2, 1945	Lt. F. T. O'Connor	1 Damaged
4th Fighter Group	Mar. 3, 1945	Col. E. W. Stewart	1 Damaged
339th Fighter Group	Mar. 3, 1945	Lt. R. G. Johnson	1 Damaged
353rd Fighter Group	Mar. 3, 1945	Lt. J. E. Frye	1 Damaged

355th Fighter Group	Mar. 3, 1945	Lt. W. S. Lyons	1 Damaged
357th Fighter Group	Mar. 3, 1945	Capt. J. L. Sublett	1 Damaged
357th Fighter Group	Mar. 3, 1945	Capt. I. L. Maguire	1 Damaged
55th Fighter Group	Mar. 9, 1945	Lt. J. F. O'Neill	1 Damaged
56th Fighter Group	Mar. 14, 1945	Lt. R. S. Keeler	1 Destroyed
2nd Fc Fce	Mar. 14, 1945	Lt. C. R. Rodebaugh	1 Destroyed
353rd Fighter Group	Mar. 18, 1945	F/O W. V. Totten	1 Damaged
355th Fighter Group	Mar.19, 1945	Capt. C. H. Spencer	1 Destroyed
357th Fighter Group	Mar.19, 1945	Maj. R. W. Foy	1 Destroyed
357th Fighter Group	Mar.19, 1945	Capt. R. S. Fifield	1 Destroyed
357th Fighter Group	Mar.19, 1945	Capt. J. L. Carter	2 Damaged
357th Fighter Group	Mar.19, 1945	Lt. J. W. Cannon	1 Damaged
357th Fighter Group	Mar.19, 1945	Capt. A. G. Manthos	1 Damaged
359th Fighter Group	Mar.19, 1945	Maj. N. K. Cranfill	1 Damaged, 1 Destroyed
20th Fighter Group	Mar. 20, 1945	Lt. J. C. Crowley	1 Damaged
20th Fighter Group	Mar. 20, 1945	Lt. C. Nicholson	1 Damaged
339th Fighter Group	Mar. 20, 1945	Lt. V. N. Barto	1 Destroyed
339th Fighter Group	Mar. 20, 1945	Lt. R. E. Irion	1 Destroyed
339th Fighter Group	Mar. 20, 1945	Lt. K. V. Berguson	1 Damaged
339th Fighter Group	Mar. 20, 1945	Lt. R. S. Hill	2 Damaged
356th Fighter Group	Mar. 20, 1945	Lt. E. G. Rudd	1 Damaged
78th Fighter Group	Mar. 21, 1945	Lt. W. E. Bourque	1 Destroyed
78th Fighter Group	Mar. 21, 1945	Lt. J. A. Kirk III	1 Destroyed
78th Fighter Group	Mar. 21, 1945	Lt. A. A. Rosenblum	1 Shared Destroyed
78th Fighter Group	Mar. 21, 1945	Lt. W. H. Brown	1 Shared Destroyed
78th Fighter Group	Mar. 21, 1945	Lt. R. D. Anderson	1 Destroyed
78th Fighter Group	Mar. 21, 1945	Capt. E. H. Miller	1 Destroyed
78th Fighter Group	Mar. 21, 1945	Lt. R. H. Anderson	1 Destroyed
339th Fighter Group	Mar. 21, 1945	Lt. B. E. Langohr	1 Shared Destroyed
339th Fighter Group	Mar. 21, 1945	Lt. N. C. Greer	1 Shared Destroyed
361st Fighter Group	Mar. 21, 1945	Lt. H. M. Chapman	1 Destroyed
55th Fighter Group	Mar. 22, 1945	Lt. J. W. Cunnick	1 Destroyed
55th Fighter Group	Mar. 22, 1945	Capt. F. E. Birtciel	1 Damaged
78th Fighter Group	Mar. 22, 1945	Lt. E. L. Peel	1 Shared Destroyed
78th Fighter Group	Mar. 22, 1945	Lt. M. B. Stutzman	1 Shared Destroyed
78th Fighter Group	Mar. 22, 1945	Capt. H. T. Barnaby	1 Destroyed
56th Fighter Group	Mar. 25, 1945	Capt. G. E. Bostwick	1 Damaged, 1 Destroyed
56th Fighter Group	Mar. 25, 1945	Lt. E. M. Crosthwait	1 Destroyed

339th Fighter Group	Mar. 25, 1945	Maj. Schaffer	1 Damaged
352nd Fighter Group	Mar. 25, 1945	Lt. R. H. Littge	1 Destroyed
479th Fighter Group	Mar. 25, 1945	Lt. E. H. Wendt	1 Destroyed
479th Fighter Group	Mar. 25, 1945	Lt. F. W. Salze	1 Damaged
55th Fighter Group	Mar. 30, 1945	Lt. P. L. Moore	1 Destroyed
55th Fighter Group	Mar. 30, 1945	Lt. P. A. Erby	1 Damaged
78th Fighter Group	Mar. 30, 1945	Col. J. D. Landers	1 Shared Destroyed
78th Fighter Group	Mar. 30, 1945	Lt. T. V. Thain	1 Shared Destroyed
339th Fighter Group	Mar. 30, 1945	Lt. R. F. Sargeant	1 Destroyed
339th Fighter Group	Mar. 30, 1945	Lt. C. W. Bennett	1 Damaged, 1 Destroyed
339th Fighter Group	Mar. 30, 1945	Lt. S. C. Ananian	1 Damaged
339th Fighter Group	Mar. 30, 1945	Capt. G. T. Rich	1 Damaged
352nd Fighter Group	Mar. 30, 1945	Lt. J. C. Hurley	1 Destroyed
361st Fighter Group	Mar. 30, 1945	Lt. K. J. Scott	1 Damaged, 1 Destroyed
364th Fighter Group	Mar. 30, 1945	Lt. J. B. Guy	1 Shared Destroyed
Unknown Unit	Mar. 30, 1945	Unknown	1 Shared Destroyed
364th Fighter Group	Mar. 30, 1945	Lt. R. L. Hunt	1 Damaged
56th Fighter Group	Mar. 31, 1945	Lt. F. H. Barrett	1 Damaged
78th Fighter Group	Mar. 31, 1945	Lt. W. L. Coleman	1 Damaged
353rd Fighter Group	Mar. 31, 1945	Lt. H. B. Tordorff	1 Destroyed
357th Fighter Group	Mar. 31, 1945	Maj. L. K. Carson	1 Damaged
357th Fighter Group	Mar. 31, 1945	Lt. M. A. Becraft	1 Damaged
368th Fighter Group	Mar. 31, 1945	Lt. P. M. Hughes	1 Damaged
361st Fighter Group	Mar. 31, 1945	Lt. G. R. Stockmeier	1 Damaged
361st Fighter Group	Mar. 31, 1945	Lt. Lt. E. E. Tinkham	1 Damaged
371st Fighter Group	Mar. 31, 1945	Capt. W. T. Bails	1 Destroyed
479th Fighter Group	Mar. 31, 1945	Lt. R. I. Bromschweig	1 Damaged
2nd Sc Fce	Mar. 1, 1945	Maj. F. B. Elliot	1 Damaged
2nd Sc Fce	Mar. 1, 1945	Capt. C. W. Getz III	1 Damaged
4th Fighter Group	April 4, 1945	Capt. R. H. Kanaga	1 Probable
4th Fighter Group	April 4, 1945	Lt. R. A. Dyer	1 Destroyed
4th Fighter Group	April 4, 1945	Lt. M. J. Kennedy	1 Shared Destroyed
4th Fighter Group	April 4, 1945	Lt. H. H. Frederick	1 Shared Destroyed
4th Fighter Group	April 4, 1945	Lt. C. W. Harre	1 Damaged
4th Fighter Group	April 4, 1945	Lt. H. H. Frederick	1 Damaged
56th Fighter Group	April 4, 1945	Capt. W. D. Clark Jr.	1 Damaged
56th Fighter Group	April 4, 1945	F/O J. W. Kassap	1 Damaged
339th Fighter Group	April 4, 1945	Lt. N. C. Greer	1 Destroyed

339th Fighter Group	April 4, 1945	Capt. K. B. Everson	1 Shared Destroyed
339th Fighter Group	April 4, 1945	Capt. R. C. Croker	1 Shared Destroyed
339th Fighter Group	April 4, 1945	Capt. H. R. Corey	1 Destroyed
355th Fighter Group	April 4, 1945	Lt. R. W. Cooper	1 Damaged
361st Fighter Group	April 4, 1945	Lt. L. F. Gendron	4 Damaged
361st Fighter Group	April 4, 1945	Lt. W. H. Street	2 Damaged
361st Fighter Group	April 4, 1945	Lt. E. Jungling	1 Damaged
361st Fighter Group	April 4, 1945	Lt. R. J. Farney	1 Damaged
361st Fighter Group	April 4, 1945	Lt. H. A. Euler	1 Damaged
361st Fighter Group	April 4, 1945	Lt. L. L. Jewell	1 Damaged
361st Fighter Group	April 4, 1945	Lt. H.S. Dixon	1 Damaged
364th Fighter Group	April 4, 1945	Maj. G. F. Ceulers	1 Destroyed
364th Fighter Group	April 4, 1945	Lt. J. S. Rogers	1 Damaged
479th Fighter Group	April 4, 1945	Lt. E. H. Sims	1 Damaged
2nd Sc Fce	April 4, 1945	Lt. W. H. Bancroft	1 Damaged
66th Fighter Wing	April 4, 1945	Lt.Col. W. C. Clark	1 Damaged
56th Fighter Group	April 7, 1945	Capt. G. E. Bostwick	1 Damaged
339th Fighter Group	April 7, 1945	Lt. O. K. Biggs	1 Damaged
339th Fighter Group	April 7, 1945	Lt. R. V. Blizzard	1 Damaged, I Probable
339th Fighter Group	April 7, 1945	Lt. P. E. Petitt	1 Damaged
339th Fighter Group	April 7, 1945	Lt. L. M. Carter	1 Damaged
339th Fighter Group	April 7, 1945	Lt. C. M. Mason	1 Damaged
339th Fighter Group	April 7, 1945	F/O J. J. Rice	1 Damaged
355th Fighter Group	April 7, 1945	Lt. Reiff	1 Shared Destroyed
355th Fighter Group	April 7, 1945	Lt. Griswold	1 Shared Destroyed
355th Fighter Group	April 7, 1945	Lt. Hartzog	1 Shared Destroyed
355th Fighter Group	April 7, 1945	Lt. R. V. Finnessey	1 Damaged
355th Fighter Group	April 7, 1945	Lt. Kouche	1 Damaged
356th Fighter Group	April 7, 1945	Lt. P. C. O'Quinn	1 Damaged
356th Fighter Group	April 7, 1945	Capt. S. P. M. Kinsey	1 Shared Damaged
356th Fighter Group	April 7, 1945	Lt. T. K. Epley	1 Shared Damaged
356th Fighter Group	April 7, 1945	Lt. E. L. Slanker	1 Shared Damaged
356th Fighter Group	April 7, 1945	Lt. J. S. Thorough	1 Shared Damaged
479th Fighter Group	April 7, 1945	Lt. R. G. Candelaria	1 Probable
479th Fighter Group	April 7, 1945	Lt. H. O. Thompson	1 Destroyed
479th Fighter Group	April 7, 1945	Capt. V. E. Hooker	1 Destroyed
479th Fighter Group	April 7, 1945	Maj. Robin Olds	1 Damaged
55th Fighter Group	April 9, 1945	Maj. E. B. Giller	1 Destroyed
55th Fighter Group	April 9, 1945	Lt. G. Moore	1 Destroyed

339th Fighter Group	April 9, 1945	Lt. H. F. Hunt	1 Damaged
339th Fighter Group	April 9, 1945	Lt. L. M. Orcutt, Jr.	1 Damaged
359th Fighter Group	April 9, 1945	Capt. M. F. Boussu	1 Damaged
359th Fighter Group	April 9, 1945	F/O R. C. Muzzy	1 Damaged
			1 Shared Damaged
359th Fighter Group	April 9, 1945	Lt. F. Rea Jr.	Shared Damaged
361st Fighter Group	April 9, 1945	Lt. J. T. Sloan	1 Destroyed,
			1 Destroyed
4th Fighter Group	April 10, 1945	Lt. W. W. Collins	1 Destroyed
20th Fighter Group	April 10, 1945	Lt. W. D. Drozd	1 Destroyed
20th Fighter Group	April 10, 1945	Lt. A. B. North	1 Destroyed
20th Fighter Group	April 10, 1945	F/O J. Rosenblum	1 Shared Destroyed
20th Fighter Group	April 10, 1945	Lt. J. W. Cudd	1 Shared Destroyed
20th Fighter Group	April 10, 1945	Capt. J. K. Hollins	1 Destroyed
20th Fighter Group	April 10, 1945	Capt. J. K. Brown	1 Destroyed
20th Fighter Group	April 10, 1945	Capt. D. Michel	1 Damaged
20th Fighter Group	April 10, 1945	Lt. R. W. Meinzen	1 Damaged
20th Fighter Group	April 10, 1945	Lt. G. R. Hall	1 Damaged
55th Fighter Group	April 10, 1945	Lt. K. R. McGinnis	1 Destroyed
55th Fighter Group	April 10, 1945	Lt. K. A. Lashbrook	1 Destroyed
55th Fighter Group	April 10, 1945	Lt. D. D. Bachman	1 Shared Damaged
55th Fighter Group	April 10, 1945	Lt. C. S. Chioles	1 Shared Damaged
56th Fighter Group	April 10, 1945	Capt. W. Wilkerson	1 Damaged
56th Fighter Group	April 10, 1945	Lt. W. J. Sharbo	1 Destroyed
56th Fighter Group	April 10, 1945	Lt. E. W. Andermatt	1 Damaged
352nd Fighter Group	April 10, 1945	Lt.Col. E. D. Duncan	1 Shared Destroyed
352nd Fighter Group	April 10, 1945	Maj. R. G. McAuliffe	1 Shared Destroyed
352nd Fighter Group	April 10, 1945	Lt. J. W. Pritchard	1 Shared Destroyed
352nd Fighter Group	April 10, 1945	Lt. C. A. Ricci	1 Shared Destroyed
352nd Fighter Group	April 10, 1945	Lt. C. C. Patillo	1 Destroyed
352nd Fighter Group	April 10, 1945	Lt. K. M. Waldron	1 Damaged
353rd Fighter Group	April 10, 1945	Capt. G. B. Compton	1 Destroyed
353rd Fighter Group	April 10, 1945	Capt. R. W. Abernathy	1 Destroyed
353rd Fighter Group	April 10, 1945	Lt. J. W. Clark	1 Shared Destroyed
353rd Fighter Group	April 10, 1945	Lt. B. D. McMahan	1 Shared Destroyed
356th Fighter Group	April 10, 1945	Lt. W. C. Gatlin	1 Destroyed
356th Fighter Group	April 10, 1945	Lt. T. N. Mauldin	1 Probable
359th Fighter Group	April 10, 1945	Lt. H. Tenenbaum	1 Destroyed
359th Fighter Group	April 10, 1945	Lt. R. J. Guggemos	1 Destroyed
359th Fighter Group	April 10, 1945	Lt. J. T. Marron	1 Damaged

359th Fighter Group	April 10, 1945	Capt. W. V. Gresham, Jr.	1 Damaged
359th Fighter Group	April 10, 1945	Lt. R. R. Klaver	1 Damaged
353rd Fighter Group	April 14, 1945	Lt. L. J. Overfield	1 Destroyed
55th Fighter Group	April 16, 1945	Maj. E. E. Ryan	1 Destroyed
20th Fighter Group	April 17, 1945	Lt. R. M. Scott	1 Damaged
20th Fighter Group	April 17, 1945	F/O J. Rosenblum	1 Damaged
339th Fighter Group	April 17, 1945	Capt. R. J. Frisch	1 Destroyed
339th Fighter Group	April 17, 1945	Capt. J. C. Campbell	1 Destroyed
357th Fighter Group	April 17, 1945	Lt. J. A. Steiger	1 Destroyed
357th Fighter Group	April 17, 1945	Lt.Col. J. W. Hayes	1 Damaged
364th Fighter Group	April 17, 1945	Lt. S. J. Price	1 Damaged
364th Fighter Group	April 17, 1945	Capt. R. W. Orndorff	1 Destroyed
364th Fighter Group	April 17, 1945	Lt. W. F. Kissell	1 Destroyed
364th Fighter Group	April 17, 1945	Capt. W. L. Goff	1 Destroyed
339th Fighter Group	April 18, 1945	Lt.Col. J. S. Thury	1 Damaged
356th Fighter Group	April 18, 1945	Lt. W. C. Gatlin	1 Shared Damaged
356th Fighter Group	April 18, 1945	Lt. G. W. Seanor	1 Shared Damaged
356th Fighter Group	April 18, 1945	Lt. L. B. Proctor	1 Shared Damaged
356th Fighter Group	April 18, 1945	Lt. O. L. Burwell	1 Damaged
357th Fighter Group	April 18, 1945	Maj. L. K. Carson	2 Damaged
357th Fighter Group	April 18, 1945	Lt. F. A. Dellorta	1 Shared Damaged
357th Fighter Group	April 18, 1945	Lt. R. H. Bradner	1 Shared Damaged
357th Fighter Group	April 18, 1945	Maj. D. H. Bochkay	1 Destroyed
357th Fighter Group	April 18, 1945	Capt. C. E. Weaver	1 Destroyed
55th Fighter Group	April 19, 1945	Capt. R. Deloach	Fighter Group
357th Fighter Group	April 19, 1945	Lt.Col. J. W. Hayes	1 Destroyed
357th Fighter Group	April 19, 1945	Capt. R. S. Fifield	1 Destroyed
357th Fighter Group	April 19, 1945	Capt. I. L. McGuire	1 Shared Destroyed
357th Fighter Group	April 19, 1945	Lt. G. L. Weber	1 Shared Destroyed
357th Fighter Group	April 19, 1945	Lt. J. P. McMullen	1 Destroyed
357th Fighter Group	April 19, 1945	Lt. P. N. Bowles	1 Destroyed
357th Fighter Group	April 19, 1945	Lt. W. J. Ofthsun	1 Destroyed
357th Fighter Group	April 19, 1945	Lt. W. J. Currie	1 Damaged
357th Fighter Group	April 19, 1945	Lt. G. A. Zarnke	1 Damaged
357th Fighter Group	April 19, 1945	Lt. F. A. Kyle	1 Damaged
357th Fighter Group	April 19, 1945	Lt. D. C. Kocher	1 Damaged
4th Fighter Group	April 25, 1945	unknown	

CLAIMED VICTORIES BY ME 262 PILOTS
IN CHRONOLOGICAL ORDER[2]

"Unknown" indicates that no individual pilot could claim the victory, therefore the kill was awarded to the unit, not to any individual pilot.

Due to a lack of accurate record keeping later in the war, this list is by no means complete. Several pilots scored kills with witnesses that never reached the OKL or OKW in Berlin.

For example, Georg-Peter Eder had 23 "claims" for aircraft, and had 12 confirmed, but he also had another 24 "probables," of which 17 were bombers.

Unit	Date	Pilot	Aircraft Type
Ekdo 262	July, 26, 2944	*Leutnant* Schreiber	Mosquito
Ekdo 262	Aug. 2, 1944	*Leutnant* Schreiber	Spitfire
Ekdo 262	Aug. 8, 1944	*Feldwebel* Weber	Mosquito
Ekdo 262	Aug. 24, 1944	*Oberfeldwebel* Baudach	Spitfire
Ekdo 262	Aug. 26, 1944	*Leutnant* Schreiber	Spitfire
Ekdo 262	Aug. 26, 1944	*Oberfeldwebel* Reckers	Mosquito
Ekdo 262	Sept. 5, 1944	*Leutnant* Schreiber	Spitfire
Ekdo 262	Sept. 6, 1944	*Oberfeldwebel* Göbel	Mosquito
Ekdo 262	Sept. 11, 1944	*Oberfeldwebel* Baudach	P-51
Ekdo 262	Sept. 12, 1944	*Hauptmann* Georg-Peter Eder	B-17
Ekdo 262	Sept. 12, 1944	*Hauptmann* Georg-Peter Eder	B-17
Ekdo 262	Sept. 12, 1944	*Hauptmann* Georg-Peter Eder	B-17 (probable)
Ekdo 262	Sept. 14, 1944	*Leutnant* Weber	Mosquito
Ekdo 262	Sept. 18, 1944	*Leutnant* Weber	Mosquito
Ekdo 262	Sept. 24, 1944	*Hauptmann* Georg-Peter Eder	B-17 (probable)
Ekdo 262	Sept. 24, 1944	*Hauptmann* Georg-Peter Eder	B-17 (probable)
Ekdo 262	Sept. 24, 1944	*Hauptmann* Georg-Peter Eder	B-17
Ekdo 262	Sept. 28, 1944	*Hauptmann* Georg-Peter Eder	B-17 (probable)
Ekdo 262	Oct. 4, 1945	*Hauptmann* Georg-Peter Eder	B-17
Ekdo 262	Oct. 4, 1944	*Hauptmann* Georg-Peter Eder	B-17
Kdo Nowotny	Oct. 6, 1944	*Hauptmann* Georg-Peter Eder	P-38
Kdo Nowotny	Oct. 7, 1944	*Oberleutnant* Franz Schall	B-24
Kdo Nowotny	Oct. 7, 1944	*Oberfeldwebel* Lennartz	B-24
Kdo Nowotny	Oct. 7, 1944	*Oberfähnrich* Russel	B-24
Kdo Nowotny	Oct. 10, 1944	*Oberleutnant* Bley	`P-51
Kdo Nowotny	Oct. 12, 1944	*Oberfeldwebel* Lennartz	P-51
Ekdo Lechfeld	Oct. 13, 1944	Pilot unknown	Mosquito
Kdo Nowotny	Oct. 28, 1944	*Oberleutnant* Franz Schall	P-51
Kdo Nowotny	Oct. 28, 1944	*Leutnant* Schreiber	P-38
Kdo Nowotny	Oct. 29, 1944	*Leutnant* Schreiber	Spitfire (collision)

Kdo Nowotny	Oct. 29, 1944	*Leutnant* Schreiber	P-38
Kdo Nowotny	Oct. 29, 1944	*Feldwebel* Erich Büttner	P-47
Kdo Nowotny	Oct. 29, 1944	*Oberfeldwebel* Hubert Göbel	P-47
Kdo Nowotny	Nov. 1, 1944	*Oberfeldwebel* Banzhaff	P-51
Kdo Nowotny	Nov. 2, 1944	*Feldwebel* Büttner	P-51
Kdo Nowotny	Nov.2, 1944	*Feldwebel* Büttner	P-47
Kdo Nowotny	Nov. 2, 1944	*Oberfeldwebel* Baudach	P-47
Kdo Nowotny	Nov. 2, 1944	*Hauptmann* Georg-Peter Eder	B-17
Kdo Nowotny	Nov. 4, 1944	*Oberfeldwebel* Hubert Göbel	P-47
Kdo Nowotny	Nov. 4, 1944	*Hauptmann* Georg-Peter Eder	B-17
Kdo Nowotny	Nov. 5, 1944	*Hauptmann* Georg-Peter Eder	P-51 (probable)
Kdo Nowotny	Nov. 6, 1944	*Oberleutnant* Franz Schall	P-47
Kdo Nowotny	Nov. 8, 1944	*Oberleutnant* Franz Schall	P-47
Kdo Nowotny	Nov. 8, 1944	*Oberleutnant* Günther Wegmann	P-47
Kdo Nowotny	Nov. 8, 1944	*Oberleutnant* Franz Schall	P-51
Kdo Nowotny	Nov. 8, 1944	*Oberleutnant* Franz Schall	P-51
Kdo Nowotny	Nov. 8, 1944	*Major* Walter Nowotny	B-24
Kdo Nowotny	Nov. 8, 1944	*Major* Walter Nowotny	P-51
Kdo Nowotny	Nov. 8, 1944	*Hauptmann* Georg-Peter Eder	P-51
Kdo Nowotny	Nov. 8, 1944	*Hauptmann* Georg-Peter Eder	P-51
Kdo Nowotny	Nov. 8, 1944	*Hauptmann* Georg-Peter Eder	P-51
Kdo Nowotny	Nov. 8, 1944	*Hauptmann* Georg-Peter Eder	P-38 (probable)
Kdo Nowotny	Nov. 8, 1944	*Major* Walter Nowotny	B-17
Kdo Nowotny	Nov. 9, 1944	*Hauptmann* Georg-Peter Eder	P-51
Kdo Nowotny	Nov. 9, 1944	*Hauptmann* Georg-Peter Eder	P-51
III./JG-7	Nov. 21, 1944	*Hauptmann* Georg-Peter Eder	B-17
III./JG-7	Nov. 23, 1944	*Leutnant* Joachim Weber	P-51
III./JG-7	Nov. 24, 1944	*Feldwebel* Büttner	P-38
III./JG-7	Nov. 24, 1944	*Oberfeldwebel* Göbel	P-51
III./JG-7	Nov. 24, 1944	*Oberfeldwebel* Baudach	P-38
III./JG-7	Nov. 25, 1944	*Hauptmann* Georg-Peter Eder	P-51
III./JG-7	Nov. 25, 1944	*Hauptmann* Georg-Peter Eder	B-17 (probable)
III./JG-7	Nov. 26, 1944	*Major* Rudolf Sinner	P-38
III./JG-7	Nov. 26, 1944	*Oberfeldwebel* Hermann Buchner	P-38
III./JG-7	Nov. 26, 1944	*Leutnant* Fritz Müller	Mosquito
III./JG-7	Nov. 27, 1944	*Oberfeldwebel* Lennartz	Spitfire
III./JG-7	Dec. 2, 1944	*Leutnant* Weber	P-38
III./JG-7	Dec. 2, 1944	*Oberfeldwebel* Lübking	B-17
10/NJG-11	Dec. 12, 1944	*Oberleutnant* Kurt Welter	Lancaster (night)
III./JG-7	Dec. 23, 1944	*Feldwebel* Büttner	P-38

III./JG-7	Dec. 23, 1944	*Feldwebel* Büttner	P-51
III./JG-7	Dec. 23, 1944	*Feldwebel* Böckel	P-51
III./JG-7	Dec. 29, 1944	*Oberfeldwebel* Büttner	Mosquito
III./JG-7	Dec. 31, 1944	*Oberfeldwebel* Baudach	Mosquito
III./JG-7	Dec. 31, 1944	*Oberfeldwebel* Baudach	P-51
III./JG-7	Dec. 31, 1944	*Hauptmann* Georg-Peter Eder	B-17
10/NJG-11	Jan. 2, 1945	*Oberleutnant* Kurt Welter	Mosquito (night)
10/NJG-11	Jan. 5, 1945	*Oberleutnant* Kurt Welter	Mosquito (night)
10/NJG-11	Jan. 10, 1945	*Oberleutnant* Kurt Welter	Mosquito (night)
III./JG-7	Feb. 1, 1945	*Leutnant* Rudolf Rademacher	Spitfire
III./JG-7	Feb. 3, 1945	*Leutnant* Weber	B-17
III./JG-7	Feb. 3, 1945	*Leutnant* Karl Schnörrer	B-17
III./JG-7	Feb. 3, 1945	*Oberleutnant* Günther Wegmann	B-17
III./JG-7	Feb. 3, 1945	*Unteroffizier* Schöppler	P-51
III./JG-7	Feb. 3, 1945	*Leutnant* Rudolf Rademacher	B-24
III./JG-7	Feb. 3, 1945	*Leutnant* Rudolf Rademacher	B-24
III./EJG-2	Feb. 5, 1944	*Leutnant* Harbort	P-38
10/NJG-11	Feb. 7, 1945	*Oberleutnant* Kurt Welter	Lancaster (night)
III./JG-7	Feb. 9, 1945	*Leutnant* Rudolf Rademacher	B-24
III./JG-7	Feb. 9, 1945	*Leutnant* Rudolf Rademacher	B-24
III./JG-7	Feb. 9, 1945	*Oberleutnant* Günther Wegmann	B-17
III./JG-7	Feb. 9, 1945	*Leutnant* Karl Schnörrer	P-51
I./KG-54	Feb. 9, 1945	*Major* Sehrt	B-17
I./KG-54	Feb. 9, 1945	*Major* Sehrt	B-17
I./KG-54	Feb. 9, 1945	Unknown	B-17
I./KG-54	Feb. 9, 1945	Unknown	B-17
III./JG-7	Feb. 14, 1944	*Leutnant* Rudolf Rademacher	B-17
III./JG-7	Feb. 14, 1944	*Unteroffizier* Schöppler	B-17
III./JG-7	Feb. 14, 1944	*Unteroffizier* Engler	B-17
10/NJG-11	Feb. 15, 1944	*Feldwebel* Becker	P-38
III./JG-7	Feb. 16, 1945	*Leutnant* Rudolf Rademacher	P-51
10/NJG-11	Feb. 20, 1945	*Oberleutnant* Kurt Welter	Mosquito (night)
10/NJG-11	Feb. 20, 1945	*Oberleutnant* Kurt Welter	Mosquito (night)
10/NJG-11	Feb. 20, 1945	*Oberleutnant* Kurt Welter	Mosquito (night)
III./JG-7	Feb. 22, 1945	*Oberfeldwebel* Hermann Buchner	P-51
III./JG-7	Feb. 22, 1945	*Oberleutnant* Günther Wegmann	P-51
III./JG-7	Feb. 22, 1945	*Unteroffizier* Nötter	B-17
III./JG-7	Feb. 22, 1945	*Unteroffizier* Nötter	B-17
III./JG-7	Feb. 22, 1945	*Leutnant* Waldmann	P-51
III./JG-7	Feb. 22, 1945	*Leutnant* Waldmann	P-51

JV-44	Feb. 23, 1945	*Oberstleutnant* Johannes Steinhoff	Il-2
III./EJG-2	Feb. 24, 1945	*Unteroffizier* Köster	Spitfire
III./JG-7	Feb. 24, 1945	*Leutnant* Rudolf Rademacher	B-17
III./JG-7	Feb. 24, 1945	*Leutnant* Weber	P-51
III./JG-7	Feb. 27, 1945	*Leutnant* Rudolf Rademacher	B-24
I./KG-54	Mar. 1, 1945	Unknown	P-51
I./KG-54	Mar. 1, 1945	*Feldwebel* Herbeck	B-17
III./JG-7	Mar. 3, 1945	*Hauptmann* Gutmann	B-17
III./JG-7	Mar. 3, 1945	*Oberfeldwebel* Lennartz	B-17
III./JG-7	Mar. 3, 1945	*Oberfähnrich* Russel	B-17
III./JG-7	Mar. 3, 1945	*Leutnant* Karl Schnörrer	B-17
III./JG-7	Mar. 3, 1945	*Oberleutnant* Wegmann	B-24
III./JG-7	Mar. 3, 1945	*Oberleutnant* Wegmann	P-51
III./JG-7	Mar. 3, 1945	*Major* Rudolf Sinner	B-24
III./JG-7	Mar. 3, 1945	*Major* Rudolf Sinner	B-24
III./JG-7	Mar. 3, 1945	*Oberfeldwebel* Heinz Arnold	B-17
III./JG-7	Mar. 3, 1945	*Oberfeldwebel* Heinz Arnold	P-47
III./JG-7	Mar. 7, 1945	*Oberfeldwebel* Heinz Arnold	P-51
III./JG-7	Mar. 7, 1945	*Major* Rudolf Sinner	P-51
III./JG-7	Mar. 9, 1945	*Oberfähnrich* Russel	Unknown Recon aircraft
III./EJG-2	Mar. 9, 1945	*Hauptmann* Engleder	B-26
III./EJG-2	Mar. 12, 1945	*Hauptmann* Steinmann	B-17
III./JG-7	Mar. 14, 1945	*Leutnant* Ambs	P-51
III./JG-7	Mar. 14, 1945	*Leutnant* Weber	P-51
III./JG-7	Mar. 15, 1945	*Leutnant* Weber	B-24
III./JG-7	Mar. 15, 1945	*Leutnant* Weber	B-24
III./JG-7	Mar. 15, 1945	*Oberfähnrich* Pfeiffer	B-17
III./JG-7	Mar. 15, 1945	*Fähnrich* Winisch	B-17
III./JG-7	Mar. 15, 1945	*Unteroffizier* Schöppler	B-24
III./EJG-2	Mar. 15, 1945	*Hauptmann* Steinmann	B-17
I./KG-51	Mar. 16, 1945	*Leutnant* Batel	P-47
Stab/JG-7	Mar. 16, 1945	*Major* Theo Weissenberger	P-51
III./JG-7	Mar. 17, 1945	*Oberleutnant* Wegmann	B-17
III./JG-7	Mar. 17, 1945	*Oberfeldwebel* Göbel	B-17
III./JG-7	Mar. 17, 1945	*Unteroffizier* Köster	B-17
III./JG-7	Mar. 17, 1945	*Unteroffizier* Köster	B-17
Stab/JG-7	Mar. 18, 1945	*Major* Theo Weissenberger	B-17
Stab/JG-7	Mar. 18, 1945	*Major* Theo Weissenberger	B-17
Stab/JG-7	Mar. 18, 1945	*Major* Theo Weissenberger	B-17

III./JG-7	Mar. 18, 1945	*Oberfeldwebel* Lübking	B-17
III./JG-7	Mar. 18, 1945	*Leutnant* Rudolf Rademacher	B-17
III./JG-7	Mar. 18, 1945	*Leutnant* Gustav Sturm	B-17
III./JG-7	Mar. 18, 1945	*Oberleutnant* Franz Schall	P-51
III./JG-7	Mar. 18, 1945	*Oberleutnant* Wegmann	B-17
III./JG-7	Mar. 18, 1945	*Oberleutnant* Wegmann	B-17
III./JG-7	Mar. 18, 1945	*Leutnant* Karl Schnörrer	B-17
III./JG-7	Mar. 18, 1945	*Leutnant* Karl Schnörrer	B-17
III./JG-7	Mar. 18, 1945	*Fähnrich* Friedrich Ehrig	B-17
III./JG-7	Mar. 18, 1945	*Fähnrich* Ehrig	B-17
III./JG-7	Mar. 18, 1945	*Oberfähnrich* Ullrich	B-17
III./JG-7	Mar. 18, 1945	*Oberfähnrich* Ullrich	B-17
III./JG-7	Mar. 18, 1945	*Fähnrich* Windisch	B-17
III./JG-7	Mar. 18, 1945	*Fähnrich* Windisch	B-17
III./JG-7	Mar. 18, 1945	*Oberleutnant* Karl-Heinz Seeler	B-17
III./EJG-2	Mar. 18, 1945	*Hauptmann* Steinmann	P-51
III./EJG-2	Mar. 18, 1945	*Hauptmann* Steinmann	P-51
I./JG-7	Mar. 19, 1945	*Gefreiter* Greim	B-17
I./JG-7	Mar. 19, 1945	*Unteroffizier* Koning	B-17
III./JG-7	Mar. 19, 1945	*Oberfeldwebel* Lennartz	B-17
III./JG-7	Mar. 19, 1945	*Oberleutnant* Franz Schall	B-17
III./JG-7	Mar. 19, 1945	*Oberfedlwebel* Heinz Arnold	B-17
III./JG-7	Mar. 19, 1945	*Leutnant* Karl Schnörrer	B-17
III./JG-7	Mar. 19, 1945	*Oberfedlwebel* Reinhold	B-17
III./JG-7	Mar. 19, 1945	*Leutnant* Rudolf Rademacher	P-51
III./JG-7	Mar. 19, 1945	Possibly *Major* Erich Rudorffer	B-17
III./JG-7	Mar. 19, 1945	Possibly *Major* Erich Rudorffer	B-17
III./EJG-2	Mar. 19, 1945	*Oberstleutnant* Heinrich Bär	P-51
I./JG-54	Mar. 19, 1945	Unknown	B-17
I./KG-54	Mar. 19, 1945	Unknown	B-17
III./JG-7	Mar. 20, 1945	*Feldwebel* Otto Pritzl	B-17
III./JG-7	Mar. 20, 1945	*Feldwebel* Pritzl	B-17
III./JG-7	Mar. 20, 1945	*Fähnrich* Pfeiffer	B-17
III./JG-7	Mar. 20, 1945	*Oberfeldwebel* Heiser	B-17
III./JG-7	Mar. 20, 1945	*Fähnrich* Christer	B-17
III./JG-7	Mar. 20, 1945	*Oberleutnant* Sturm	B-17
III./JG-7	Mar. 20, 1945	*Oberfeldwebel* Hermann Buchner	B-17
III./JG-7	Mar. 20, 1945	*Fähnrich* Ehrig	B-17
III./JG-7	Mar. 20, 1945	*Fähnrich* Ehrig	B-17
III./JG-7	Mar. 20, 1945	*Fähnrich* Ehrig	B-17

Stab/JG-7	Mar. 21, 1945	*Major* Theo Weissenberger	B-17
Stab/JG-7	Mar. 21, 1945	*Major* Heinrich Ehrler	B-17
I./JG-7	Mar. 21, 1945	*Leutnant* Weihs	B-17
I./JG-7	Mar. 21, 1945	*Gefreiter* Heim	B-17
III./JG-7	Mar. 21, 1945	*Fähnrich* Pfeiffer	B-17
III./JG-7	Mar. 21, 1945	*Leutnant* Karl Schnörrer	B-17
III./JG-7	Mar. 21, 1945	*Oberfedlwebel* Heinz Arnold	B-17
III./JG-7	Mar. 21, 1945	*Leutnant* Weber	B-17
III./JG-7	Mar. 21, 1945	*Leutnant* Alfred Ambs	B-17
III./JG-7	Mar. 21, 1945	*Leutnant* Ambs	B-17
III./JG-7	Mar. 21, 1945	*Leutnant* Ambs	B-17
III./JG-7	Mar. 21, 1945	*Unteroffizier* Giefing	B-17
III./JG-7	Mar. 21, 1945	*Unteroffizier* Giefing	B-17
III./JG-7	Mar. 21, 1945	*Leutnant* Müller	B-24
III./JG-7	Mar. 21, 1945	*Oberleutnant* Franz Schall	P-51
III./JG-7	Mar. 21, 1945	*Unteroffizier* König	P-47
III./EJG-2	Mar. 21, 1945	*Oberstleutnant* Heinrich Bär	B-24
III./EJG-2	Mar. 21, 1945	*Leutnant* Bell	P-38
10/NJG-11	Mar. 21, 1945	*Feldwebel* Becker	Mosquito (night)
Stab/JG-7	Mar. 22, 1945	*Major* Theo Weissenberger	B-17
Stab/JG-7	Mar. 22, 1945	*Major* Heinrich Ehrler	B-17
III./JG-7	Mar. 22, 1945	*Leutnant* Karl Schnörrer	B-17
III./JG-7	Mar. 22, 1945	*Oberfähnrich* Petermann	B-17
III./JG-7	Mar. 22, 1945	*Fähnrich* Windisch	B-17
III./JG-7	Mar. 22, 1945	*Fähnrich* Pfeiffer	B-17
III./JG-7	Mar. 22, 1945	*Oberfeldwebel* Lennartz	B-17
III./JG-7	Mar. 22, 1945	*Oberfeldwebel* Hermann Buchner	B-17
III./JG-7	Mar. 22, 1945	*Leutnant* Ambs	B-17
III./JG-7	Mar. 22, 1945	*Oberfedlwebel* Heinz Arnold	B-17
III./JG-7	Mar. 22, 1945	*Unteroffizier* Peter Köster	B-17
III./JG-7	Mar. 22, 1945	*Oberfeldwebel* Lübking	B-17
III./JG-7	Mar. 22, 1945	*Leutnant* Schlüter	B-17
III./JG-7	Mar. 22, 1945	*Oberleutnant* Franz Schall	P-51
III./JG-7	Mar. 22, 1945	*Leutnant* Lehner	P-51
Stab/JG-7	Mar. 23, 1945	*Major* Heinrich Ehrler	B-24
Stab/JG-7	Mar. 23, 1945	*Major* Heinrich Ehrler	B-24
Stab/JG-7	Mar. 23, 1945	*Oberfeldwebel* Reinhold	B-17 (probable)
10/NJG-11	Mar. 23, 1945	*Feldwebel* Becker	Mosquito (night)
Stab/JG-7	Mar. 24, 1945	*Major* Heinrich Ehrler	B-17
I./JG-7	Mar. 24, 1945	*Major* Erich Rudorffer	Tempest

I./JG-7	Mar. 24, 1945	*Oberleutnant* Walter Schuck	P-51
I./JG-7	Mar. 24, 1945	*Oberleutnant* Walter Schuck	P-51
I./JG-7	Mar. 24, 1945	*Leutnant* Weihs	P-38
III./JG-7	Mar. 24, 1945	*Oberfedlwebel* Heinz Arnold	B-17
III./JG-7	Mar. 24, 1945	*Leutnant* Rudolf Rademacher	B-17
III./JG-7	Mar. 24, 1945	*Leutnant* Lehner	B-17
III./JG-7	Mar. 24, 1945	*Oberleutnant* Külp	Unidentified heavy bomber
III./JG-7	Mar. 24, 1945	*Leutnant* Sturm	Unidentified heavy bomber
III./JG-7	Mar. 24, 1945	*Oberleutnant* Schall	Unidentified heavy bomber
III./JG-7	Mar. 24, 1945	*Oberfeldwebel* Pritzl	Unidentified heavy bomber
III./JG-7	Mar. 24, 1945	*Oberfeldwebel* Buchner	Unidentified heavy bomber
III./JG-7	Mar. 24, 1945	*Oberleutnant* Worner	Unidentified heavy bomber
III./JG-7	Mar. 24, 1945	*Oberstleutnant* Heinrich Bär	B-24
III./JG-7	Mar. 24, 1945	*Oberstleutnant* Heinrich Bär	P-51
10/NJG-11	Mar. 24, 1945	*Feldwebel* Becker	Mosquito (night)
10/NJG-11	Mar. 24, 1945	*Feldwebel* Becker	Mosquito (night)
III./JG-7	Mar. 25, 1945	*Leutnant* Rudolf Rademacher	B-24
III./JG-7	Mar. 25, 1945	*Leutnant* Müller	B-24
III./JG-7	Mar. 25, 1945	*Feldwebel* Taube	B-24
III./JG-7	Mar. 25, 1945	*Oberfeldwebel* Hermann Buchner	B-24
III./JG-7	Mar. 25, 1945	*Oberfähnrich* Windisch	B-24
III./JG-7	Mar. 25, 1945	*Oberfähnrich* Ullrich	B-24
III./JG-7	Mar. 25, 1945	*Oberleutnant* Franz Schall	P-51
III./JG-7	Mar. 25, 1945	*Leutnant* Karl Schnörrer	P-51
I./JG-7	Mar. 27, 1945	*Leutnant* Weihs	Unidentified heavy bomber
III./JG-7	Mar. 27, 1945	*Leutnant* Günther Heckmann	Lancaster
III./EJG-2	Mar. 27, 1945	*Oberst* Walther Dahl	P-47
III./EJG-2	Mar. 27, 1945	*Oberst* Walther Dahl	P-47
III./EJG-2	Mar. 27, 1945	*Oberstleutnant* Heinrich Bär	P-47
III./EJG-2	Mar. 27, 1945	*Oberstleutnant* Heinrich Bär	P-47
III./EJG-2	Mar. 27, 1945	*Feldwebel* Rauchensteiner	P-47
10/NJG-11	Mar. 27, 1945	*Feldwebel* Becker	Mosquito (night)
10/NJG-11	Mar. 27, 1945	*Oberleutnant* Lamm	Mosquito (night)
10/NJG-11	Mar. 27, 1945	*Oberleutnant* Kurt Welter	Mosquito (night)
10/NJG-11	Mar. 27, 1945	*Leutnant* Jorg Czypionka	Mosquito (night)

I./JG-7	Mar. 28, 1945	*Leutnant* Fritz Stehle	B-17
I./JG-7	Mar. 28, 1945	*Leutnant* Stehle	P-51
I./JG-7	Mar. 28, 1945	*Oberleutnant* Walter Schuck	P-51
I./JG-7	Mar. 30, 1945	*Flieger* Reiher	B-17
I./JG-7	Mar. 30, 1945	*Major* Erich Rudorffer	Unknown Fighter
I./JG-7	Mar. 30, 1945	*Major* Erich Rudorffer	Unknown Fighter
I./JG-7	Mar. 30, 1945	*Feldwebel* Geithovel	Mosquito
I./JG-7	Mar. 30, 1945	*Gefreiter* Heim	P-51
III./JG-7	Mar. 30, 1945	*Leutnant* Karl Schnörrer	B-17
III./JG-7	Mar. 30, 1945	*Leutnant* Karl Schnörrer	B-17
III./JG-7	Mar. 30, 1945	*Oberfähnrich* Petermann	B-17
10/NJG-11	Mar. 30, 1945	*Oberleutnant* Kurt Welter	Mosquito (night)
10/NJG-11	Mar. 30, 1945	*Oberleutnant* Kurt Welter	Mosquito (night)
10/NJG-11	Mar. 30, 1945	*Oberleutnant* Kurt Welter	Mosquito (night)
10/NJG-11	Mar. 30, 1945	*Oberleutnant* Kurt Welter	Mosquito (night)
Stab/JG-7	Mar. 31, 1945	*Major* Theo Weissenberger	B-17
Stab/JG-7	Mar. 31, 1945	*Major* Heinrich Ehrler	P-51
I./JG-7	Mar. 31, 1945	*Leutnant* Weihs	Catalina PBY on water
I./JG-7	Mar. 31, 1945	*Oberleutnant* Stehle	Lancaster
I./JG-7	Mar. 31, 1945	*Oberleutnant* Stehle	Lancaster
I./JG-7	Mar. 31, 1945	*Oberleutnant* Stehle	Lancaster
I./JG-7	Mar. 31, 1945	*Oberleutnant* Stehle	Lancaster
I./JG-7	Mar. 31, 1945	*Oberleutnant* Sturm	Lancaster
I./JG-7	Mar. 31, 1945	*Oberleutnant* Sturm	Halifax
I./JG-7	Mar. 31, 1945	*Oberleutnant* Grünberg	Lancaster
I./JG-7	Mar. 31, 1945	*Oberleutnant* Grünberg	Lancaster
I./JG-7	Mar. 31, 1945	*Leutnant* Todt	Lancaster
I./JG-7	Mar. 31, 1945	*Leutnant* Todt	Lancaster
I./JG-7	Mar. 31, 1945	*Flieger* Reiher	Lancaster
I./JG-7	Mar. 31, 1945	*Leutnant* Weihs	Lancaster
III./JG-7	Mar. 31, 1945	*Leutnant* Schenck	Lancaster
III./JG-7	Mar. 31, 1945	*Leutnant* Schenck	Lancaster
III./JG-7	Mar. 31, 1945	*Oberleutnant* Franz Schall	Lancaster
III./JG-7	Mar. 31, 1945	*Oberleutnant* Franz Schall	Lancaster
III./JG-7	Mar. 31, 1945	*Oberfeldwebel* Hermann Buchner	Lancaster
III./JG-7	Mar. 31, 1945	*Fähnrich* Ehrig	Lancaster
III./JG-7	Mar. 31, 1945	*Oberfähnrich* Windisch	B-17
III./JG-7	Mar. 31, 1945	*Oberfeldwebel* Pritzl	B-17
III./JG-7	Mar. 31, 1945	*Leutnant* Rudolf Rademacher	P-51

I./KG-54	Mar. 31, 1945	Unknown	B-24
I./KG-54	Mar. 31, 1945	Unknown	B-24
10/NJG-11	Mar. 31, 1945	*Feldwebel* Becker	Mosquito (night)
I./JG-7	April 1, 1945	*Oberleutnant* Stehle	B-17
III./JG-7	April 1, 1945	*Unteroffizier* Köster	Spitfire
10/NJG-11	April 3, 1945	*Oberleutnant* Kurt Welter	Mosquito (night)
Stab/JG-7	April 4, 1945	*Major* Heinrich Ehrler	B-17
Stab/JG-7	April 4, 1945	*Major* Heinrich Ehrler	B-17
I./JG-7	April 4, 1945	*Oberleutnant* Stehle	B-17
I./JG-7	April 4, 1945	*Gefreiter* Heim	B-17
I./JG-7	April 4, 1945	*Leutnant* Weihs	P-47
I./JG-7	April 4, 1945	*Leutnant* Weihs	P-51
III./JG-7	April 4, 1945	*Oberleutnant* Franz Schall	P-51
III./JG-7	April 4, 1945	*Leutnant* Rudolf Rademacher	B-24
III./JG-7	April 4, 1945	*Leutnant* Müller	B-24
III./JG-7	April 4, 1945	*Leutnant* Schenck	B-17
III./JG-7	April 4, 1945	*Oberfeldwebel* Pritzl	B-17
III./JG-7	April 4, 1945	*Fähnrich* Pfeiffer	B-17
III./EJG-2	April 4, 1945	*Oberstleutnant* Heinrich Bär	P-51
I./KG-54	April 4, 1945	*Leutnant* Becker	B-17
I./KG-54	April 4, 1945	Unknown	B-17
JV-44	April 5, 1945	*Oberstleutnant* Johannes Steinhoff	B-17
JV-44	April 5, 1945	*Oberfähnrich* Klaus Neumann	B-17
JV-44	April 5, 1945	*Oberfähnrich* Klaus Neumann	B-17
JV-44	April 5, 1945	*Oberfähnrich* Klaus Neumann	B-17
JV-44	April 5, 1945	*Oberst* Günther Lützow	B-17
I./JG-7	April 7, 1945	*Oberleutnant* Walter Schuck	P-38
III./JG-7	April 7, 1945	*Oberfeldwebel* Göbel	B-17
III./JG-7	April 7, 1945	*Unteroffizier* Schöppler	B-24
III./JG-7	April 7, 1945	*Oberfähnrich* Klaus Neumann	P-51
III./JG-7	April 7, 1945	*Fähnrich* Pfeiffer	P-51
I./KG-54	April 7, 1945	*Hauptmann* Tronicke	B-17
I./KG-54	April 7, 1945	*Hauptmann* Tronicke	B-17
I./KG-54	April 7, 1945	Unknown	B-17
I./KG-54	April 7, 1945	Unknown	B-17
I./JG-7	April 8, 1945	*Oberleutnant* Stehle	Lancaster
I./JG-7	April 8, 1945	*Leutnant* Weihs	P-38
III./JG-7	April 8, 1945	*Feldwebel* Geithovel	P-51
III./JG-7	April 8, 1945	*Feldwebel* Geithovel	P-51
JV-44	April 8, 1945	*Oberstleutnant* Johannes Steinhoff	B-24

JV-44	April 8, 1945	*Leutnant* Gottfried Fährmann	B-17*
JV-44	April 8, 1945	*Leutnant* Gottfired Fährmann	B-17†
I./KG-54	April 8, 1945	Unknown	Unidentified heavy bomber
I./KG-54	April 8, 1945	Unknown	Unidentified heavy bomber
I./KG-54	April 8, 1945	Unknown	Unidentified heavy bomber
I./KG-54	April 8, 1945	Unknown	Unidentified heavy bomber
I./JG-7	April 9, 1945	*Unteroffizier* Engler	Lancaster
I./JG-7	April 9, 1945	*Leutnant* Zingler	Lancaster
I./JG-7	April 9, 1945	*Gefreiter* Müller	Lancaster
III./JG-7	April 9, 1945	*Leutnant* Müller	Lancaster
III./JG-7	April 9, 1945	*Oberleutnant* Franz Schall	Lancaster
III./EJG-2	April 9, 1945	*Oberstleutnant* Heinrich Bär	B-26
III./EJG-2	April 9, 1945	*Oberstleutnant* Heinrich Bär	B-26
I./JG-7	April 10, 1945	*Oberleutnant* Walter Schuck	B-17
I./JG-7	April 10, 1945	*Oberleutnant* Walter Schuck	B-17
I./JG-7	April 10, 1945	*Oberleutnant* Walter Schuck	B-17
I./JG-7	April 10, 1945	*Oberleutnant* Walter Schuck	B-17
I./JG-7	April 10, 1945	*Oberleutnant* Grünberg	B-17
I./JG-7	April 10, 1945	*Oberleutnant* Grünberg	B-17
I./JG-7	April 10, 1945	*Oberleutnant* Stehle	B-17
I./JG-7	April 10, 1945	*Oberleutnant* Walter Bohatsch	B-17
I./JG-7	April 10, 1945	*Oberfähnrich* Neuhaus	B-17
I./JG-7	April 10, 1945	*Flieger* Reiher	B-17
III./JG-7	April 10, 1945	*Leutnant* Walter Hagenah	P-51
III./JG-7	April 10, 1945	*Fähnrich* Pfeiffer	B-17
III./JG-7	April 10, 1945	*Oberfeldwebel* Lennartz	P-51
III./JG-7	April 10, 1945	*Leutnant* Rudolf Rademacher	P-51
III./JG-7	April 10, 1945	*Oberfeldwebel* Greiner	P-51
III./JG-7	April 10, 1945	*Feldwebel* Pritzl	P-47
I./KG-54	April 10, 1945	*Leutnant* Palenda	B-17*
I./KG-54	April 10, 1945	*Leutnant* Palenda	B-17
I./KG-54	April 10, 1945	*Leutnant* Rossow	B-17
I./KG-54	April 10, 1945	*Leutnant* Rossow	B-17
I./KG-54	April 10, 1945	*Leutnant* Becker	B-17
I./KG-54	April 10, 1945	Unknown	B-17

*Actually a B-25.
†Actually a B-24.

I./KG-54	April 10, 1945	Unknown	B-17
I./KG-54	April 10, 1945	Unknown	B-17
I./KG-54	April 10, 1945	Unknown	B-17
I./KG-54	April 10, 1945	Unknown	B-17 (probable)
I./KG-54	April 10, 1945	Unknown	B-17 (probable)
I./KG-54	April 10, 1945	Unknown	B-17 (probable)
JV-44	April 12, 1945	*Oberstleutnant* Heinrich Bär	B-26
I./JG-7	April 12, 1945	*Flieger* Reiher	P-47
10/NJG-11	April 14, 1945	*Oberleutnant* Kurt Welter	Mosquito (night)
JV-44	April 16, 1945	*Generalleutnmant* Adolf Galland	B-26
JV-44	April 16, 1945	*Generalleutnmant* Adolf Galland	B-26
JV-44	April 17, 1945	*Unteroffizier* Eduard Schallmoser	B-17 (collision)
I./JG-7	April 17, 1945	*Hauptmann* Wolfgang Späte	B-17
I./JG-7	April 17, 1945	*Oberleutnant* Bohatsch	B-17
I./JG-7	April 17, 1945	*Oberleutnant* Stehle	B-17
III./JG-7	April 17, 1945	*Oberleutnant* Müller	B-17
III./JG-7	April 17, 1945	*Oberfeldwebel* Pritzl	B-17
III./JG-7	April 17, 1945	*Oberfeldwebel* Göbel	B-17
III./JG-7	April 17, 1945	*Unteroffizier* Schöppler	B-17
I./KG-54	April 17, 1945	Unknown	B-17
I./KG-54	April 17, 1945	Unknown	B-17
I./KG-54	April 17, 1945	Unknown	B-17
I./KG-54	April 17, 1945	Unknown	B-17
I./KG-54	April 17, 1945	Unknown	B-17
I./KG-54	April 17, 1945	Unknown	B-17
I./KG-54	April 17, 1945	Unknown	B-17
I./KG-54	April 17, 1945	Unknown	B-17
JV-44	April 18, 1945	*Oberstleutnant* Heinrich Bär	P-47
JV-44	April 18, 1945	*Oberstleutnant* Heinrich Bär	P-47
I./JG-7	April 19, 1945	*Hauptmann* Wolfgang Späte	B-17
I./JG-7	April 19, 1945	*Unteroffizier* Schöppler	B-17
I./JG-7	April 19, 1945	*Oberleutnant* Bohatsch	B-17
I./JG-7	April 19, 1945	*Oberleutnant* Grünberg	B-17
III./JG-7	April 19, 1945	*Oberfeldwebel* Göbel	B-17
JV-44	April 19, 1945	*Oberstleutnant* Heinrich Bär	P-51
JV-44	April 19, 1945	*Oberstleutnant* Heinrich Bär	P-51
I./KG-54	April 19, 1945	*Leutnant* Mai	B-17
JV-44	April 24, 1945	*Major* Gerhard Barkhorn	B-26
JV-44	April 24, 1945	*Major* Gerhard Barkhorn	B-26

JV-44	April 24, 1945	*Hauptmann* Walter Krupinski	P-47
I./JG-7	April 25, 1945	*Major* Wolfgang Späte	B-17
I./JG-7	April 25, 1945	*Major* Wolfgang Späte	B-17
I./JG-7	April 25, 1945	*Major* Wolfgang Späte	B-17
I./JG-7	April 25, 1945	*Unteroffizier* Schöppler	B-17
I./JG-7	April 25, 1945	*Oberfeldwebel* Göbel	B-17
I./JG-7	April 25, 1945	*Leutnant* Kelb	B-17
I./JG-7	April 25, 1945	*Unteroffizier* Engler	B-17
JV-44	April 25, 1945	*Unteroffizier* Köster	P-51
JV-44	April 25, 1945	*Unteroffizier* Köster	P-51
JV-44	April 26, 1945	*Generalleutnmant* Adolf Galland	B-26
JV-44	April 26, 1945	*Generalleutnmant* Adolf Galland	B-26
JV-44	April 26, 1945	Unknown	B-26
III./EJG-2	April 26, 1945	*Oberst* Walther Dahl	P-51
JV-44	April 27, 1945	*Oberstleutnant* Heinrich Bär	P-47
JV-44	April 27, 1945	*Oberstleutnant* Heinrich Bär	P-47
JV-44	April 27, 1945	*Major* Wilhelm Herget	P-47
JV-44	April 27, 1945	*Unteroffizier* Köster	P-47
JV-44	April 27, 1945	*Unteroffizier* Köster	P-47
JV-44	April 28, 1945	*Oberstleutnant* Heinrich Bär	P-47
I./KG-54	April 30, 1945	Unknown	IL-2
III./JG-7	April 30, 1945	*Oberleutnant* Schlüter	Yak-9
III./JG-7	April 30, 1945	*Oberfähnrich* Wittbold	Il-2
III./JG-7	April 30, 1945	*Oberfähnrich* Wittbold	Il-2
I./JG-7	May 8, 1945	*Oberleutnant* Stehle	Yak-9

RECORDED ME 262 LOSSES (THIS IS NOT A COMPLETE LIST.)

*Indicates Pilot Killed, #Pilot Missing
+Pilot Injured/Wounded ^Aircraft Repaired

Unit	Cause	Wk Nr	A/C ID	Pilot	Date
Ekdo 262	Training Lechfeld	130002	V1+AB	*Unteroffizier* Kurt Flachs*	May 19, 1944
Ekdo 262	Training Lechfeld	130008	VI+AG	*Feldwebel* Becker+	Jun. 16, 1944
I./KG-51	Crash[1]	130177	N/A	*Sfw* Mosbacher*	Jul. 14, 1944
Ekdo 262	Crash[2]	Unknown	N/A	*Hptm* Thierfelder*	Jul. 18, 1944
Leipheim	Bombing	130013	N/A	Static at Factory	Jul. 19, 1944
Leipheim	Bombing	170007	N/A	"	Jul. 19, 1944

[1]Damaged during bombing raid by ground fire, crashed near Amersee.
[2]Impacted at Landesberg, Werner Thierfelder killed, probably flak.

Leipheim	Bombing	170009	N/A	"	Jul. 19, 1944
Leipheim	Bombing	170012	N/A	"	Jul. 19, 1944
Leipheim	Bombing	170062	N/A	"	Jul. 19, 1944
Leipheim	Bombing	170065	N/A	"	Jul. 19, 1944
Leipheim	Bombing	170066	N/A	"	Jul. 19, 1944
Leipheim	Bombing	170050	N/A	"	Jul. 19, 1944
Leipheim	Bombing	170057	N/A	"	Jul. 19, 1944
Leipheim	Bombing	170064	N/A	"	Jul. 19, 1944
Leipheim	Engine fire[3]	170058	N/A	*Fhr* Kaiser bailed out	Jul. 30, 1944
I./KG-51	Forced down[4]	130189	SQ+XB	*Lt.* Eduard Rottmann*	Aug. 3, 1944
I./KG-51	Crash on takeoff^	Unk.	Unk.		Aug. 23, 1944
I./KG-51	Crash on takeoff^	Unk.	Unk.		Aug. 23, 1944
I./KG-51	Crash in France	Unk.	Unk.		Aug. 23, 1944
I./KG-51	Shot down	Unk.	Unk.	*Fw* Hieronymous Lauer	Aug. 28, 1944
I./KG-51	Shot down flak	170040	9K+DL	*Lt.* Rolf Weidemann*	Sept. 8, 1944
I./KG-51	Shot down flak	170013	9K+LL	*Oblt.* Werner Gartner*	Sept. 19, 1944
I./KG-51	Shot down flak	130126	9K+AL	*Uffz* Herbert Schauder*	Sept. 12, 1944
I./KG-51	Crash landing	170298	Unk.	*Fw* Bernhard Bertelsbeck*	Sept. 17, 1944
I./KG-51	Crashed	170046	KI+IZ	*Ufz* Lothar Luttin*	Sept. 27, 1944
I./KG-51	Shot down	170069	9K+NL	*Fw* Hieronymous Lauer+	Oct. 2, 1944
KdoNowotny	Crashed	170044	Unk.	*Oblt* Alfred Teumer*	Oct. 4, 1944
KdoNowotny	Crashed	170047	N/A	*Oblt* Franz Schall	Oct. 4, 1944
KdoNowotny	Fuel out^	170292	N/A	*Ofw* Helmut Baudach	Oct. 5, 1944
I./KG-51	Crashed	170082	9K+BL	*Uffz* Gerhard Franke*	Oct. 5, 1944
I./KG-51	Shot down[5]	170093	9K+BL	*Hptm* Hans-Christoph Büttmann	Oct. 5, 1944
I./KG-51	Shot down	170117	9K+XL	*Fw* Jachim Fingerloos	Oct. 6, 1944
KdoNowotny	Shot down[6]	110395	N/A	*Ofhr* Heinz Russel+	Oct. 7, 1944

[3]Crashed near Biberbach due to engine failure.
[4]Crashed at Lechfeld due to battle damage, cause unclear.
[5]Shot down by Spitfires over Nijmegen.
[6]P-51s shot him down over Achmer.

KdoNowotny	Shot down[7]	170307	N/A	*Oblt* Paul Bley	Oct. 7, 1944
KdoNowotny	Shot down[8]	110405	N/A	*Lt.* Gerhard Kobert*	Oct. 7, 1944
KdoNowotny	Shot down	Unk.	N/A	*Hptm* Heinz Arnold*	Oct. 7, 1944
I./KG-51	Shot down	Unk.	N/A	Unk.	Oct. 7, 1944
KdoNowotny	Fuel out^[9]	110402	N/A	*Fw* Helmut Lennartz	Oct. 12, 1944
KdoNowotny	Fuel out^	110388	N/A	*Oblt* Paul Bley	Oct. 12, 1944
KdoNowotny	Fuel out^	110401	N/A	*Ofhr* Heinz Russel	Oct. 13, 1944
KdoNowotny	Crashed	110399	N/A	*Obgr* Leuthner+	Oct. 13, 1944
I./KG-51	Combat damage	170064	9K+FL	*Uffz* Edmund Delatowski+	Oct. 13, 1944
10/EJG-2	Crash	Unk.	N/A	*Ofhr* Erich Haffke*	Oct. 14, 1944
I./KG-51	Shot down	170825	9K+UL	*Fw* Edgar Junghans+*	Oct. 15, 1944
I./KG-51	Crash landed	Unk.	N/A	Unk.	Oct. 15, 1944
KdoNowotny	Shot down	110388	N/A	*Oblt* Paul Bley*	Oct. 28, 1944
KdoNowotny	Landing^[10]	110479	N/A	*Oblt* Franz Schall	Oct. 28, 1944
KdoNowotny	Collision[11]	110387	N/A	*Lt.* Alfred Screiber+	Oct. 29, 1945
KdoNowotny	Shot down[12]	110386	N/A	*Ofhr* Willi Banzhaff+	Nov. 1, 1944
KdoNowotny	Take off^	110368	N/A	*Uffz* Allois Zöllner +	Nov. 2, 1944
KdoNowotny	Damaged^	170278	N/A	*Ofw* Hubert Göbel	Nov. 2, 1944
5/KG-51	Flak	170010	9K+CL	*Hptm* Eberhard Winkel	Nov. 2, 1944
KdoNowotny	Shot down	110483	N/A	*Ofhr* Willi Banzhaff*	Nov. 3, 1944
KdoNowotny	Fuel out^	110403	N/A	*Ofw* Hubert Göbel	Nov. 4, 1944
KdoNowotny	Force landed^	170310	N/A	*Ofw* Zander	Nov. 4, 1944
KdoNowotny	Fuel out^	110389	N/A	*Lt.* Spangenberg	Nov. 6, 1944
KdoNowotny	Damaged[13]	110490	N/A	*Fw* Helmut Lennartz	Nov. 6, 1944
KdoNowotny	Damaged^[14]	110402	N/A	*Ofw* Freutzer	Nov. 6, 1944
KdoNowotny	Engine failed^	170045	N/A	*Ofw* Helmut Baudach	Nov. 6, 1944
KdoNowotny	Shot down[15]	110404	N/A	*Oblt* Franz Schall	Nov. 8, 1944

[7]P-51s shot him down over Achmer.
[8]P-51s shot him down over Achmer.
[9]Landed out of fuel at Bramsche, no major damage.
[10]Nose wheel collapsed upon landing, flew again two days later.
[11]Collided with Spitfire over Nordhorn, Schreiber claimed kill, landed. Slightly wounded.
[12]P-51s jumped *Oberfähnrich* Willi Banzhaff over Zwolle during bomber intercept.
[13]Lennartz was shot up by fighters near Bremen during a mission to intercept a bomber formation.
[14]Damaged by fighters near Alhorn, possibly downed by Capt. Charles B. Yeager.
[15]Schall bailed out, two separate P-51s chased his empty jet, each thinking they had a kill, and each claiming a kill.

KdoNowotny	Shot down[16]	Unk.	N/A	*Ofw* Helmut Baudach	Nov. 8, 1944
KdoNowotny	Shot down[17]	110400	White 8	*Maj.* Walter Nowotny*	Nov. 8, 1944
KdoNowotny	Damaged^[18]	170293	N/A	*Fw.* Büttner	Nov. 8, 1944
2/KG-54	Crash takeoff	170107	B3+BK	*Ofhr* Richard Schöpe*	Nov. 20, 1944
I./KG-51	Shot down/ flak	170122	9K+KL	*Hptm* Rudolf Rosch*	Nov. 25, 1944
9/JG-7	Crash test flight	110373	N/A	*Ofw* Rudolf Alt*	Nov. 26, 1944
9/JG-7	Crash	110372	N/A	*Lt.* Alfred Schreiber*	Nov. 26, 1944
I./KG-51	Crash	110372	N/A	*Oblt* Heinz Lehmann*	Nov. 26, 1944
I./KG-54	Damaged	Unk.		Static/No pilot	Nov. 26, 1944
2/KG-51	Flak	170120	N/A	*Ufz* Horst Sanio*	Nov. 28, 1944
I./KG-54	Training crash	110551	B3+DH	*Ogfr* Hans-Joachim Mentzel*	Dec. 2, 1944
I./KG-51	Shot down	150335	9K+BH	*Oblt* Joachim Valet*	Dec. 3, 1944
I./KG-51	Crash[19]	170296	9K+EK	*Ofw* Karl-Heinz Petersen+*	Dec. 3, 1944
10/JG-7	Crashed	110369	N/A	*Uffz* Friedrich Renner*	Dec. 6, 1994
4/KG-51	Crashed	500010	9K+KM	*Hptm* Hellmut Brocke*	Dec. 7, 1944
4/KG-51	Shot down	500009	9K+IM	*Sfw* Hans Zander*	Dec. 9, 1944
I./KG-54	Wing stress[20]	Unk.	N/A	*Hptm* Kornagel	Dec. 9, 1944
I./KG-51	Shot down	170281	9K+FL	*Lt* Walter Roth+	Dec. 10, 1945
2/KG-54	Crash[21]	110504	B3+FK	*Oblt* Benno Weiss*	Dec. 10, 1945
I./KG-51	Flak[22]	170108	9K+WL	*Fw* Herbert Lenke*	Dec. 11, 1945
I./KG-51	Flak[23]	170080	9K+RL	*Ofw* Hans Kohler*	Dec. 12, 1944
I./KG-54	Flak[24]	Unk.	N/A	*Hptm* Kornagel	Dec. 12, 1944
I./JG-7	Crashed[25]	Unk.	N/A	*Uffz* Wilhelm Schneller*	Dec. 15, 1944
II./KG-51	Shot down[26]	110501	9K+BP	*Lt* Wolfgang Lübke*	Dec. 17, 1944
I./JG-7	Shot down[27]	Unk.	N/A	*Fw* Wilhelm Wilkenloh	Dec. 23, 1944
II./KG-51	Crashed	110591	9K+OP	*Uffz*	Dec. 24, 1944

[16]Baudach bailed out, unhurt, just as Schall did.

[17]Kill shared by 1st Lt. Edward R. Haydon of the 357th Fighter Group and Capt. Ernest Fiebelkorn of the 20th Fighter Group.

[18]Damaged on takeoff from strafing. Plane repaired.

[19]Pilot died two days later.

[20]*Hauptmann* Kornagel landed after combat, 30 percent damage, repaired.

[21]Jet probably damaged by defensive fire, pilot killed.

[22]Hit by friendly flak while engaging bombers, pilot killed.

[23]Hit by friendly flak while engaging bombers, pilot killed.

[24]Hit by friendly flak while engaging bombers, force landed at Obertraubling, pilot uninjured.

[25]At Schwabstadt.

[26]Killed by fighter at Hesepe.

[27]At Schwabstadt.

Axel von Zimmermann*

I./KG-51	Shot down[28]	170273	9K+MK	*Fw* Hans Meyer*	Dec. 25, 1944
II./KG-51	Flak[29]	110594	9K+MM	*Oblt*	Dec. 25, 1944
I./KG-54	Crashed	Unk.	N/A	Unk.	Dec. 25, 1944
II./KG-51	Missing	110624	9K+AM	*Fw* Walter Wehking#	Dec. 27, 1944
9/JG-7	Shot down[30]	500021	N/A	*Lt* Heinrich Lonnecker*	Jan. 1, 1945
9/JG-7	Damaged	500039	N/A	*Uffz* Detjens	Jan. 1, 1945
III./JG-7	Crashed	110407	N/A	Unk.	Jan. 1, 1945
2/KG-51	Unk. cause	Unk.	N/A	*Ofw* Erich Kaiser*	Jan. 3, 1945
10/EJG-2	Crashed	170306	White 4	*Uffz* Helmut Schmidt+	Jan. 7, 1945
I./KG-51	Crash landed	170098	9K+HL	*Ofw* Ernst Wiese*	Jan. 10, 1945
10/EJG-2	Crashed	110494	White 9	*Gfr* Ferdinand Sagmeister*	Jan. 12, 1945
I./KG-51	Shot down	110601	9K+FH	*Uffz* Alfred Farber*	Jan. 13, 1945
I./KG-54	Destroyed	Unk.	N/A	None/Static	Jan. 13, 1945
9/JG-7	Shot down[31]	110476	N/A	*Fw* Heinz Wurm*	Jan. 14, 1945
9/JG-7	Shot down[32]	500039	N/A	*Uffz* Detjens	Jan. 14, 1945
10/JG-7	Crashed[33]	110476	N/A	*Ofhr* Hans-Joachim Ast*	Jan. 14, 1945
III./JG-7	Shot down[34]	130180	Red 14	Unk.	Jan. 14, 1945
I./KG-51	Flak	110578	9K+MK	*Lt* Oswald von Ritter-Rittershain*	Jan. 14, 1945
6/KG-51	Shot down	110543	9K+LP	*Uffz* Friedrich Christoph	Jan. 14, 1945
I./KG-54	Destroyed	Unk.	N/A	None/Static	Jan. 14, 1945
I./KG-54	Destroyed	Unk.	N/A	None/Static	Jan. 16, 1945
III./JG-7	Crashed[35]	111564	N/A	*Uffz* Heinz Kuhn*	Jan. 19, 1945
III./JG-7	Landing gear failed	110755	N/A	Unk.	Jan. 19, 1945
I./KG-54	Engine fire	Unk.	N/A	Unk.	Jan. 19, 1945
I./KG-54	Landing gear failed	Unk.	N/A	Unk.	Jan. 19, 1945
I./KG-54	10 percent damaged	Unk.	N/A	None/Static	Jan. 19, 1945

[28]Jumped by a Spitfire near Liege, Belgium.
[29]Hit by enemy flak, pilot killed at Liege.
[30]Near Fassberg.
[31]Shot down by a fighter near Wittstock.
[32]Shot down by a fighter near Wittstock.
[33]Crashed near Krivits, cause unknown.
[34]Logow, Neuruppen, pilot unknown, no casualty reported.
[35]Cause unknown, pilot's parachute failed to open.

Unit	Fate	Werk Nr.	Marking	Pilot	Date
10/EJG-2	Crashed	110286	White 9	*Uffz* Karl Hartung*	Jan. 20, 1945
I./KG-54	Destroyed	Unk.	N/A	None/Static	Jan. 20, 1945
I./KG-54	Crashed	500054	N/A	Unk.	Jan. 21. 1945
10/NJG-11	Crashed	110610	N/A	*Oblt* Heinz Brückmann*	Jan. 21. 1945
9/JG-7	Shot down[36]	Unk.	N/A	*Hptm* Georg-Peter Eder+	Jan. 22, 1945
9/JG-7	Crashed	110564	N/A	*Ofhr* Karl Schnurr*	Jan. 23, 1945
12/KG-51	Shot down	170295	N/A	*Hptm* Hans Holzwarth	Jan. 23, 1945
I./KG-54	Crashed	110788	N/A	Unk.	Jan. 23, 1945
I./KG-51	Strafed	110361	N/A	None/Static	Jan. 29, 1945
I./KG-54	Crashed^	500049	N/A	Unk.	Jan. 29, 1945
III./EJG-2	Forced down	110529	N/A	Unk.	Jan. 30, 1945
III./EKG-1	Crash takeoff	110779	N/A	*Oblt* Hermann Knodler*	Jan. 30, 1945
I./KG-54	Technical failure^	500063	N/A	Unk.	Jan. 30, 1945
10/EJG-2	Force landing	110371	N/A	*Ofw* Helmut Klante+	Jan. 31, 1945
III./JG-7	Landing damage	170112	N/A	Unk.	Feb. 2, 1945
I./KG-51	Crash takeoff	110615	9K+NL	*Hptm* Karl-Heinz Buhring*	Feb. 2, 1945
III./KG-54	Tire burst landing^	110651	N/A	Unk.	Feb. 2, 1945
ISS.1	Damaged take off	111552	N/A	Unk.	Feb. 2, 1945
I./KG-54	Landing damage^	110560	N/A	Unk.	Feb. 3, 1945
III./JG-7	Engine failure	130163	N/A	Unk.	Feb. 4, 1945
III./KG-55	Crash takeoff	500013	N/A	Unk.	Feb. 4, 1945
10/NJG-11	Crashed	110932	N/A	*Ofw* Paul Brandl*	Feb. 4, 1945
10/NJG-11	Crashed	170051	N/A	*Oblt* Walter Eppelsheim*	Feb. 4, 1945
III./EJG-2	Engine fire crash	111053	N/A	Unk.	Feb. 6, 1945
II./KG-51	Damaged	110419	N/A	None/Static	Feb. 8, 1945

[36]Eder was coming in for a landing at Parchi, jumped by a fighter, shot through left leg and both legs were broken. Altogether, he flew 572 combat missions of which 150 were with the Me 262. On the Eastern Front he scored ten victories, and on the Western Front, sixty-eight, of which no less than thirty-six were four-engined bombers. With the Me 262 he scored at least twenty-four victories (most of them could not be officially confirmed). He was the leading scorer against the four-engined bombers, although Eder himself was shot down seventeen times, bailing out nine times. He was wounded fourteen times.

Unit	Fate	Werk Nr.	Code	Pilot	Date
II./KG-51	Damaged	110912	N/A	None/Static	Feb. 8, 1945
II./KG-51	Damaged	110337	N/A	None/Static	Feb. 8, 1945
9/KG-54	Training crash	110663	B3+ET	*Uffz* Heinz Maurer*	Feb. 8, 1945
Stab/KG-54	Shot down	500042	B3+AA	*Obslt* Volprecht Riedesel Freiherr zu Eisenbach	Feb. 9, 1945
I./KG-54	Combat damage^	110799	B3+AB	*Maj.* Ottfried Sehrt+	Feb. 9, 1945
I./KG-54	Shot down	110791	B3+BB	*Oblt* Walter Draht*	Feb. 9, 1945
I./KG-54	Shot down	110862	B3+GL	*Oblt* Günther Kahler*	Feb. 9, 1945
I./KG-54	Gear up landing	110561	N/A	Unk.	Feb. 9, 1945
I./KG-54	Crash landing	110609	N/A	Unk.	Feb. 9, 1945
10/EJG-2	Crashed	110415	White 18	*Uffz* Heinz Speck*	Feb. 9, 1945
III./JG-7	Forced landing	501200	N/A	Unk.	Feb. 10, 1945
II./KG-54	Forced landing^	500018	N/A	Unk.	Feb. 10, 1945
III./KG-54	Gear Damage	110651	N/A	Unk.	Feb. 10, 1945
II./JG-7	Shot down	Unk.	N/A	*Maj.* Hans Grözinger*	Feb. 11, 1945
III./EJG-2	Crashed	110499	N/A	Unk.	Feb. 11, 1945
I./KG-51	Crashed	111920	N/A	*Ofhr* Walter Kramer	Feb. 13, 1945
III./JG-7	Shot down	Unk.	N/A	Unk.	Feb. 14, 1945
I./KG-51	Taxiing	110498	N/A	Unk.	Feb. 14, 1945
I./KG-51	Missing	110615	9K+NL	*Fw* Rudolf Hoffman#	Feb. 14, 1945
I./KG-51	Shot down	110811	N/A	Unk.	Feb. 14, 1945
5/KG-51	Shot down	110571	9K+HN	*Fw* Werner Witzmann*	Feb. 14, 1945
II./KG-51	Crash landed	110538	N/A	Unk.	Feb. 14, 1945
II./KG-51	Crash Landed	500059	N/A	Unk.	Feb. 14, 1945
1/JG-7	Crashed	130171	N/A	*Uffz* Hans Werner*	Feb. 15, 1945
I./KG-54	Training crash	110803	B3+GH	*Uffz* Kurt Lange*	Feb. 15, 1945
I./KG-54	Forced landing	110601	N/A	Unk.	Feb. 15, 1945
I./KG-54	Shot down	110942	B3+LS	*Uffz* Litzinger	Feb. 15, 1945
III./KG-54	Crash landing^	111621	N/A	Unk.	Feb. 15, 1945
10/NJG-11	Damaged combat	500075	N/A	*Fw* Karl-Heinz Becker	Feb. 15, 1945
I./KG-54	Tire blow out^	110665	N/A	Unk.	Feb. 16, 1945

Unit	Fate	W.Nr.	Marking	Pilot	Date
III./KG-54	Destroyed strafed	110933	N/A	None/Static	Feb. 16, 1945
III./KG-54	Bombed	Unk.	N/A	None/Static	Feb. 16, 1945
III./KG-54	Bombed	Unk.	N/A	None/Static	Feb. 16, 1945
III./KG-54	Bombed	Unk.	N/A	None/Static	Feb. 16, 1945
I./JG-7	Engine failure^	111591	N/A	Unk.	Feb. 17, 1945
I./JG-7	Damaged	110971	N/A	Unk.	Feb. 17, 1945
III./JG-7	Crashed	111008	N/A	Ofw Hans Clausen*	Feb. 17, 1945
III./JG-7	Force landing^	501199	N/A	Unk.	Feb. 17, 1945
1/KG-54	Shot down	110922	B3+LH	Oblt Franz Theeg*	Feb. 17, 1945
10/NJG-10	Crashed	110603	Red 2	Ofw Walter Bockstiegel*	Feb. 17, 1945
Stab/JG-7	Force landed^	110608	N/A	Maj. Theodor Weissenberger+	Feb. 19, 1945
2/JG-7	Crash landed^	111539	N/A	Fw Alois Biermeier+	Feb. 19, 1945
I./KG-51	Force landed^	170091	N/A	Unk.	Feb. 19, 1945
I./KG-51	Taxi damage	170312	N/A	Unk.	Feb. 19, 1945
Stab/KG-54	Crash landed^	110581	N/A	Unk.	Feb. 19, 1945
I./KG-54	Technical failure^	110650	N/A	Unk.	Feb. 19, 1945
10/EJG-2	Crashed	111616	White 14	Fw Germar Nolte*	Feb. 20, 1945
I./KG-54	Strafed	170081	N/A	None/Static	Feb. 20, 1945
I./KG-54	Engine fire	110519	N/A	Unk. bailed out	Feb. 20, 1945
1/NAufrn-gruppe 6	Gear up^	500095	N/A	Unk.	Feb. 20, 1945
II./JG-7	Tire burst takeoff^	110810	N/A	Unk.	Feb. 21, 1945
III./JG-7	Technical failure	110964	N/A	Unk.	Feb. 21, 1945
II./KG-51	Tire burst^	170004	N/A	Unk.	Feb. 21, 1945
II./KG-51	Technical failure	500056	N/A	Unk.	Feb. 21, 1945
II./KG-51	Missing	170199	N/A	Ofhr Gerhard Rohde#	Feb. 21, 1945
II./KG-51	Crash landed fuel	170010	N/A	Unk.	Feb. 21, 1945
I./KG-54	Strafed	111600	N/A	None/Static	Feb. 21, 1945
III./KG-54	Technical failure^	111612	N/A	Unk.	Feb. 21, 1945
10/NJG-11	Damaged combat	110600	N/A	Unk.	Feb. 21, 1945

2. Naufk-gruppe 6	Crashed	110565	Red 2	*Oblt* Willi Knoll*	Feb. 21, 1945
Stab/JG-7	Shot down	111544	N/A	*Uffz* Nötter+	Feb. 22, 1945
Stab/JG-7	Shot down	110797	N/A	Unk.	Feb. 22, 1945
I./JG-7	Forced landing	110815	N/A	Unk.	Feb. 22, 1945
III./JG-7	Crash landing	110967	N/A	Unk.	Feb. 22, 1945
III./JG-7	Shot down	110466	N/A	Unk.	Feb. 22, 1945
III./JG-7	Crashed	110784	N/A	Unk.*	Feb. 22, 1945
III./JG-7	Damaged	110043	N/A	Unk.	Feb. 22, 1945
III./JG-7	Shot down	170778	N/A	*Ofw* Mattuschka	Feb. 22, 1945
10/JG-7	Shot down	110781	N/A	*Ofw* Helmut Baudach+*	Feb. 22, 1945
2/KG-51	Crashed pilot error	500026	N/A	*Lt.* Kurt Piehl*	Feb. 22, 1945
8/KG-54	Shot down	111613	B3+GS	*Ogfr* Jürgen Brink*	Feb. 22, 1945
I./KG-51	Damaged landing	110590	N/A	Unk.	Feb. 23, 1945
I./KG-54	Technical failure^	111633	N/A	Unk.	Feb. 23, 1945
III./KG-54	Bombed	120260	N/A	None/Static	Feb. 23, 1945
III./KG-54	Bombed	500016	N/A	None/Static	Feb. 23, 1945
III./KG-54	Bombed	110547	N/A	None/Static	Feb. 23, 1945
III./KG-54	Bombed	110920	N/A	None/Static	Feb. 23, 1945
III./KG-54	Bombed	110570	N/A	None/Static	Feb. 23, 1945
III./KG-54	Bombed	111571	N/A	None/Static	Feb. 23, 1945
I./KG-51	Crashed	500061	N/A	*Fw* Ernst Schulz*	Feb. 24, 1945
II./KG-51	Crash takeoff	110817	N/A	Unk.	Feb. 24, 1945
II./KG-51	Strafed landing	110588	N/A	Unk.	Feb. 24, 1945
II./KG-51	Technical failure	500050	N/A	Unk.	Feb. 24, 1945
I./KG-54	Forced landing	110737	N/A	*Fw* Hans Brömel*	Feb. 24, 1945
III./EKG-1	Technical failure	110827	N/A	*Lt.* Heinz Gratz+	Feb. 24, 1945
Stab/KG-54	Bomb damage	500012	N/A	None/Static	Feb. 25, 1945
Stab/KG-54	Strafed	same as above		Static	Feb. 25, 1945
Stab/KG-54	Strafed	110799	B3+AB	None/Static	Feb. 25, 1945
2/KG-54	Crashed combat	111887	B3+?L	*Lt* Wolf Zimmermann+	Feb. 25, 1945

2./KG-54	Crashed	110928	B3+LL	*Lt* Becker	Feb. 25, 1945
I./KG-54	Strafed	111633	N/A	None/Static	Feb. 25, 1945
I./KG 54	Crashed Combat	110569	N/A	*Fw* Felix Einhardt*	Feb. 25, 1945
I./KG-54	Strafed	110799	N/A	None/Static	Feb. 25, 1945
I./KG-54	Strafed	110787	N/A	None/Static	Feb. 25, 1945
I./KG-54	Strafed	120539	N/A	None/Static	Feb. 25, 1945
I./KG-54	Strafed	120549	N/A	None/Static	Feb. 25, 1945
5./KG-54	Shot down	110948	B3+AM	*Lt* Hans-Georg Knobel*	Feb. 25, 1945
5./KG-54	Shot down	111917	B3+BN	*Lt* Josef Lackner*	Feb. 25, 1945
5./KG-54	Shot down	110947	B3+DP	*Fw* Heinz Clausner*	Feb. 25, 1945
III./KG-54	Crash technical	110618	N/A	Unk.	Feb. 25, 1945
III./KG-54	Crash landed	110937	N/A	Unk.	Feb. 25, 1945
III./EJG-2	Shot down	110491	N/A	*Oblt* Josef Bohm*	Feb. 25, 1945
Stab/NAG-6	Force landing	111570	N/A	Unk.	Feb. 25, 1945
I./EKG-1	Crashed	170042	N/A	*Lt* Günther Elter*	Feb. 26, 1945
8./KG-54	Crashed	111602	N/A	*Oblt* Hermann Kleinfeldt*	Feb. 27, 1945
III./KG-54	Crash technical	111890	N/A	Unk.	Feb. 27, 1945
III./KG-54	Damage takeoff	110923	N/A	Unk.	Feb. 27, 1945
III./JG-7	Forced landing	110784	N/A	Unk.	Feb. 28, 1945
III./JG-7	Forced landing	110807	N/A	Unk.	Feb. 28, 1945
III./KG-54	Crash landed	500209	N/A	Unk.	Feb. 28, 1945
2.KG-54	Shot down	500218	B3+?K	*Lt* Hans-Peter Haberle*	Mar. 1, 1945
I./KG-54	Shot down	110562	N/A	*Fw* Josef Herbeck*	Mar. 1, 1945
5./KG-51	Shot down	110553	9K+EN	*Hptm* Fritz Abel*	Mar. 2, 1945
II./KG-51	Force landing	110941	N/A	Unk.	Mar. 2, 1945
II./KG-51	Force landing	110516	N/A	Unk.	Mar. 2, 1945
I./KG-54	Shot down	110913	N/A	*Fw* Günther Gorlitz+	Mar. 2, 1945
I./KG-54	Shot down	111899	N/A	*Fw* Heinrich Griems*	Mar. 2, 1945
I./EKG	Shot down	110655	N/A	*Ofhr* Horst Metzbrandt*	Mar. 2, 1945
9./JG-7	Shot down	110558	N/A	*Hptm* Heinz Gutmann*	Mar. 3, 1945
III./JG-7	Tech landing	500058	N/A	Unk.	Mar. 3, 1945
JG-7	Shot down	Unk.	N/A	Unk.	Mar. 3, 1945

JG-7	Shot down	Unk.	N/A	Unk.	Mar. 3, 1945
JG-7	Shot down	Unk.	N/A	Unk.	Mar. 3, 1945
JG-7	Shot down	Unk.	N/A	Unk.	Mar. 3, 1945
JG-7	Shot down	Unk.	N/A	Unk.	Mar. 3, 1945
10/NJG-11	Crashed	110610	N/A	*Ofw* August Weibl*	Mar. 3, 1945
III./EJG	Crashed pilot error	110472	N/A	Unk.	Mar. 4, 1945
II./KG-54	Crash tech failure^	110500	N/A	Unk.	Mar. 7, 1945
9/JG-7	Missing	Unk.	N/A	*Ofhr* Heinz Russel*	Mar. 9, 1945
II./KG-51	Crashed	170124	N/A	*Uffz* Günther Meckelburg*	Mar. 9, 1945
II./KG-54	Out of fuel crash	111925	N/A	Unk.	Mar. 9, 1945
II./KG-54	Crashed	110943	B3+HL	*Lt* Bernhard Becker	Mar. 9, 1945
I./KG-54	Tire burst takeoff^	110649	N/A	Unk.	Mar. 10, 1945
10/NJG-11	Damaged	111916	N/A	Unk.	Mar. 12, 1945
I./KG-51	Damaged^	111966	9K+AB	*Oblt* Harold Hovestadt+	Mar. 13, 1945
I./KG-51	Shot down	110915	9K+DL	*Ofhr* Jurgen Hohne*	Mar. 13, 1945
II./KG-51	Fuel fire	170284	N/A	Unk.	Mar. 13, 1945
III./KG-51	Crashed	111555	N/A	*Ofw* Georg Schabinski+	Mar. 13, 1945
III./KG-51	Crashed	110337	N/A	Unk.	Mar. 13, 1945
III./KG-54	Fire	110789	N/A	None	Mar. 14, 1945
8/KG-54	Crashed training	110938	B3+FS	*Ofw* Wilhelm Dirjus*	Mar. 17, 1945
3/JG-7	Collision wingman[37]	170097	Yellow 3	*Oblt* Hans Waldmann*	Mar. 18, 1945
3/JG-7	Collision wingman	Unk.	N/A	*Lt* Hans-Dieter Weihs	Mar. 18, 1945
3/JG-7	Shot down	500224	Yellow 2	*Ofhr* Günther Schrey*	Mar. 18, 1945
3/JG-7	Shot down	110808	N/A	*Oblt* Günther Wegmann+	Mar. 18, 1945
9/JG-7	Shot down	110780	N/A	*Oblt* Karl-Heinz Seeler*	Mar. 18, 1945
III./JG-7	Shot down	Unk.	N/A	Unk.	Mar. 18, 1945
10/JG-7	Shot down	111005	N/A	*Ofw* Heinz Mattuschka*	Mar. 19, 1945
11/JG-7	Shot down	111545	N/A	*Lt* Harry Meyer*	Mar. 19, 1945
I./KG-52	Strafed	Unk.	N/A	None/Static	Mar. 19, 1945
I./KG-52	Strafed	Unk.	N/A	None/Static	Mar. 19, 1945

[37]Weihs and Waldmann collided on takeoff at Schwarzenbeck.

I./KG-52	Strafed^	Unk.	N/A	None/Static	Mar. 19, 1945
III./KG-54	Strafed	Unk.	N/A	None/Static	Mar. 19, 1945
III./KG-54	Strafed	Unk.	N/A	None/Static	Mar. 19, 1945
III./KG-54	Strafed	Unk.	N/A	None/Static	Mar. 19, 1945
III./KG-54	Strafed	Unk.	N/A	None/Static	Mar. 19, 1945
III./KG-54	Strafed	Unk.	N/A	None/Static	Mar. 19, 1945
1/JG-7	Shot down	111924	White 7	*Uffz* Hans Mehn*	Mar. 20, 1945
10/JG-7	Shot down	110598	N/A	*Ogfr* Fritz Gehlker*	Mar. 20, 1945
10/JG-7	Shot down	501196	N/A	*Ofw* Erich Buttner+	Mar. 20, 1945
3/JG-7	Damaged	Unk.	N/A	*Lt* Hans-Dieter Weihs	Mar. 21, 1945
10/JG-7	Shot down	500462	N/A	*Uffz* Kurt Kolbe*	Mar. 21, 1945
11/JG-7	Shot down	110819	N/A	*Lt* Joachim Weber*	Mar. 21, 1945
JG-7	Shot down	Unk.	N/A	Unk.+	Mar. 21, 1945
JG-7	Shot down	Unk.	N/A	Unk.+	Mar. 21, 1945
3/KG-51	Shot down	111973	9K+AL	*Hptm* Eberhard Winkel*	Mar. 21, 1945
I./KG-51	Shot down	170118	9K+CK	*Lt* Erwin Dickmann*	Mar. 21, 1945
I./KG-51	Shot down	111605	9K+DL	*Uffz* Heinz Erben*	Mar. 21, 1945
I./KG-54	Shot down	500069	B3+CH	*Uffz* Willie Ehrecke*	Mar. 21, 1945
III./KG-54	Bombed	Unk.	N/A	None/Static	Mar. 21, 1945
III./KG-54	Bombed	Unk.	N/A	None/Static	Mar. 21, 1945
JG-7	Shot down	Unk.	N/A	Unk.*	Mar. 22, 1945
JG-7	Shot down	Unk.	N/A	Unk.*	Mar. 22, 1945
JG-7	Shot down	Unk.	N/A	Unk.+	Mar. 22, 1945
Stab/KG-54	Shot down	Unk.	N/A	*Oblt* König*	Mar. 22, 1945
Stab/KG-54	Bombed	Unk.	N/A	None/Static	Mar. 22, 1945
I./KG-54	Shot down	110602	B3+DK	*Uffz* Adalbert Egri+	Mar. 22, 1945
I./KG-54	Bombed	Unk.	N/A	None/Static	Mar. 22, 1945
I./KG-54	Bombed	Unk.	N/A	None/Static	Mar. 22, 1945
I./KG-54	Bombed^	Unk.	N/A	None/Static	Mar. 22, 1945
I./KG-54	Bombed^	Unk.	N/A	None/Static	Mar. 22, 1945
II./KG-54	Bombed	Unk.	N/A	None/Static	Mar. 22, 1945
II./KG-54	Bombed	Unk.	N/A	None/Static	Mar. 22, 1945
II./KG-54	Bombed	Unk.	N/A	None/Static	Mar. 22, 1945
10/EJG-2	Shot down	110485	NS+BM	*Ofw* Helmut Reckers*	Mar. 22, 1945
9/JG-7	Shot down[38]	110999	N/A	*Lt* Alfred Ambs+	Mar. 24, 1945

[38]Shot down 1st Lt. Earl R. Lane shot down in Me 262 "Yellow 3," bailed out at 17,000 feet, landed in tree.
[39]Shot down by 1st Lt. Roscoe Brown.
[40]Shot down by 2nd Lt. Charles V. Brantley.
[41]Ulrich was shot up by a fighter near Parchim, bailed out. Report was that he was strafed in his parachute.

11./JG-7	Damaged combat	110968	N/A	*Uffz* Ernst Giefing	Mar. 24, 1945
10./JG-7	Shot down[39]	Unk.	N/A	*Oblt* Franz Külp +	Mar. 24, 1945
10./JG-7	Shot down[40]	Unk.	N/A	*Oblt* Ernst Wörner*	Mar. 24, 1945
III./KG-54	Bombed	Unk.	N/A	None/Static	Mar. 24, 1945
III./KG-54	Bombed	Unk.	N/A	None/Static	Mar. 24, 1945
9./JG-7	Shot down	Unk.	N/A	*Oblt* Schatzle*	Mar. 25, 1945
9./JG-7	Shot down[41]	110796	N/A	*Fhr* Günther Ulrich*	Mar. 25, 1945
10./JG-7	Shot down[42]	110834	N/A	*Lt* Günther von Rettberg*	Mar. 25, 1945
10./JG-7	Shot down	111738	N/A	*Fw* Fritz Taube*	Mar. 25, 1945
3./JG-7	Damaged combat	Unk.	N/A	*Lt* Hans-Dieter Weihs	Mar. 27, 1945
11./JG-7	Damaged[43]	111541	N/A	*Ofw* August Lübking*	Mar. 28, 1945
2./JG-7	Shot down[44]	111593	N/A	*Lt* Erich Schulte*	Mar. 30, 1945
11./JG-7	Shot down[45]	Unk.	N/A	*Lt* Karl Schnörrer+	Mar. 30, 1945
JG-7	Shot down	Unk.	N/A	*Fw* Geisthovel	Mar. 30, 1945
Test Unit	Captured	111711	N/A	Hans Fay	Mar. 30, 1945
JG-7	Shot down	Unk.	N/A	Unk.*	Mar. 31, 1945
JG-7	Shot down	Unk.	N/A	Unk.#	Mar. 31, 1945
JG-7	Shot down	Unk.	N/A	Unk.#	Mar. 31, 1945
JG-7	Shot down	Unk.	N/A	Unk.	Mar. 31, 1945
I./KG-54	Shot down	Unk.	N/A	Unk.	Mar. 31, 1945
2/KG-54	Shot down	Unk.	N/A	*Oblt* Dr Oberweg*	Mar. 31, 1945
Stab/JG-7	Shot down	Unk.	N/A	*Maj.* Heinrich Ehrler*	Apr. 4, 1945
Stab/JG-7	Shot down	Unk.	N/A	*Ofw* Gerhard Reinhold*	Apr. 4, 1945
III./JG-7	Shot down[46]	Unk.	N/A	*Maj.* Rudolf Sinner+	Apr. 4, 1945
10./JG-7	Shot down	Unk.	N/A	*Oblt* Franz Schall	Apr. 4, 1945
11./JG-7	Shot down	Unk.	N/A	*Lt* Alfred Lehner*	Apr. 4, 1945

[42]Rettberg died in his fighter, Ulrich was his wingman. They were jumped by many fighters as they broke off the attack on a bomber formation.

[43]Pilot killed when his Me 262 fired rockets into a B-17. Bomber exploded, destroying the jet, sending it out of control.

[44]Body found in wreckage.

[45]Schnörrer and *Oberfähnrich* Viktor Petermann (sixty-four victories, Knight's Cross) intercepted USAAF four-engine bombers over Hamburg. Schnörrer claimed two B-17s shot down, but his Me 262 was hit by crossfire from the bombers. He was intercepted by P-51s. Damaged, he bailed out, striking the tail fin (leg amputation in hospital) and managed to open his parachute and land safely. This was his last mission, severely wounded and out for the rest of the war. "Quax" Schnörrer flew a total of 536 missions and recorded forty-six victories. He claimed thirty-five victories over the Eastern Front, including 10 IL-2 Sturmoviks. Of his eleven victories recorded over the Western Front, all were made flying the Me 262 and included nine four-engine bombers. Schnörrer, who was Nowotny's best friend and wingman for over 200 missions, died on September 25, 1979, at Nürnberg.

11/JG-7	Shot down	Unk.	N/A	*Uffz* Heckmann*	Apr. 4, 1945
JG-7	Shot down	Unk.	N/A	Unk.	Apr. 4, 1945
JG-7	Shot down	Unk.	N/A	Unk.	Apr. 4, 1945
JG-7	Damaged	Unk.	N/A	Unk.	Apr. 4, 1945
JG-7	Damaged	Unk.	N/A	Unk.	Apr. 4, 1945
JG-7	Damaged	Unk.	N/A	Unk.	Apr. 4, 1945
JG-7	Damaged	Unk.	N/A	Unk.	Apr. 4, 1945
JG-7	Damaged	Unk.	N/A	Unk.	Apr. 4, 1945
JV-44	Collision	Unk.	N/A	*Uffz* Eduard Schallmoser	Apr. 4, 1945
JG-7	Shot down	Unk.	N/A	Unk.#	Apr. 5, 1945
JG-7	Shot down	Unk.	N/A	Unk.#	Apr. 5, 1945
JG-7	Collision B-24	Unk.	N/A	Unk.*	Apr. 7, 1945
JG-7	Shot down	Unk.	N/A	Unk.#	Apr. 7, 1945
JG-7	Shot down	Unk.	N/A	Unk.#	Apr. 7, 1945
I./KG-54	Unk.	B3+	White 8	*Hptm* Tronicke*	Apr. 7, 1945
JV-44	Shot down	Unk.	N/A	*Lt* Fährmann	Apr. 8, 1945
3/JG-7	Damaged combat	Unk.	N/A	*Lt* Hans-Dieter Weihs	Apr. 9, 1945
2/JG-7	Bombed	Unk.	N/A	None/Static	Apr. 10, 1945
3/JG-7	Shot down	Unk.	N/A	*Uffz* Köhler*	Apr. 10, 1945
3/JG-7	Shot down	Unk.	N/A	*Gfr* Heim*	Apr. 10, 1945
3/JG-7	Shot down	Unk.	N/A	*Oblt* Walter Schuck	Apr. 10, 1945
3/JG-7	Shot down	Unk.	N/A	*Lt* Wagner*	Apr. 10, 1945
7/JG-7	Shot down	Unk.	N/A	*Oblt* Walther Wever*	Apr. 10, 1945
10/JG-7	Destroyed[47]	Unk.	N/A	*Oblt* Franz Schall*	Apr. 10, 1945
JG-7	Shot down	Unk.	N/A	*Fw* Schwartz*	Apr. 10, 1945
JG-7	Shot down	Unk.	N/A	Unk.#	Apr. 10, 1945

[46]While leading a flight of eight Me 262s, Sinner's group was attacked by P-51s of the 339th Fighter Group. Sinner was hit and had to bail out. Tangled in his harness, his parachute deployed late and did not completely open. He landed hard in a field and was dragged into a barbed wire fence. He played dead as the P-51s tried strafing him. After the P-51s left, he crawled into a furrow in the field for cover. His wounds kept him out the remainder of the war.

[47]Schall's jet landed at Parchim after engaging fighters, left wheel hit a bomb crater at high speed. His jet cartwheeled, exploded, killing him.

JG-7	Shot down	Unk.	N/A	Unk.#	Apr. 10, 1945
JG-7	Shot down	Unk.	N/A	Unk.#	Apr. 10, 1945
JG-7	Shot down	Unk.	N/A	Unk.#	Apr. 10, 1945
JG-7	Shot down	Unk.	N/A	Unk.#	Apr. 10, 1945
JG-7	Shot down	Unk.	N/A	Unk.#	Apr. 10, 1945
JG-7	Shot down	Unk.	N/A	Unk.#	Apr. 10, 1945
JG-7	Shot down	Unk.	N/A	Unk.#	Apr. 10, 1945
JG-7	Shot down	Unk.	N/A	Unk.#	Apr. 10, 1945
JG-7	Shot down	Unk.	N/A	Unk.#	Apr. 10, 1945
JG-7	Shot down	Unk.	N/A	Unk.#	Apr. 10, 1945
JG-7	Shot down	Unk.	N/A	Unk.#	Apr. 10, 1945
JG-7	Shot down	Unk.	N/A	Unk.#	Apr. 10, 1945
JG-7	Shot down	Unk.	N/A	Unk.#	Apr. 10, 1945
JG-7	Shot down	Unk.	N/A	Unk.+	Apr. 10, 1945
JG-7	Shot down	Unk.	N/A	Unk.+	Apr. 10, 1945
JG-7	Shot down	Unk.	N/A	Unk.+	Apr. 10, 1945
JG-7	Shot down	Unk.	N/A	Unk.+	Apr. 10, 1945
JG-7	Shot down	Unk.	N/A	Unk.+	Apr. 10, 1945
10/NJG-11	Bombed	Unk.	N/A	None/Static	Apr. 10, 1945
10/NJG-11	Bombed	Unk.	N/A	None/Static	Apr. 10, 1945
10/NJG-11	Bombed	Unk.	N/A	None/Static	Apr. 10, 1945
6/NAufk-gruppe-6	Bombed	Unk.	N/A	None/Static	Apr. 10, 1945
6/NAufk gruppe-6	Bombed	Unk.	N/A	None/Static	Apr. 10, 1945
6/NAufk gruppe-6	Bombed	Unk.	N/A	None/Static	Apr. 10, 1945
I./KG-54	Crashed combat	Unk.	N/A	*Lt* Paul Pallenda*	Apr. 10, 1945
I./KG-54	Crashed combat	Unk.	N/A	*Oblt* Beck*	Apr. 10, 1945
2/KG-54	Shot down	Unk. B3+Yellow 9		*Lt* Berhard Becker+	Apr. 10, 1945
3/KG-54	Shot down	Unk.	N/A	*Lt* Jürgen Rossow+	Apr. 10, 1945
I./JG-7	Shot down	Unk.	N/A	*Oblt* Hans Grünburg	Apr. 11, 1945
II./JG-7	Shot down	Unk.	N/A	*Lt* Arno Thimm+	Apr. 14, 1945
9/JG-7	Shot down	Unk.	N/A	*Oblt* Erich Stahlberg*	Apr. 14, 1945
9/KG-54	Shot down	Unk.	N/A	*Uffz* L. Ehrhardt+	Apr. 14, 1945
JG-7	Shot down	Unk.	N/A	Unk.+	Apr. 16, 1945
3/JG-7	Shot down	Unk.	N/A	Unk.+	Apr. 17, 1945
I./JG-7	Shot down	Unk.	N/A	Unk.+	Apr. 17, 1945
I./JG-7	Shot down	Unk.	N/A	Unk.+	Apr. 17, 1945

I./JG-7	Shot down	Unk.	N/A	Unk.+	Apr. 17, 1945
I./JG-7	Shot down	Unk.	N/A	*Oblt* Hans Grünburg	Apr. 17, 1945
II./JG-7	Missing	Unk.	N/A	*Ofw* Heinz Heinz Arnold#	Apr. 17, 1945
JV-44	Collision	Unk.	N/A	*Uffz* Eduard Schallmoser	Apr. 17, 1945
JV-44	Crash take off	Unk.	N/A	*Obslt* Johannes Steinhoff+	Apr. 18, 1945
III./JG-7	Shot down	Unk.	N/A	Unk.#	Apr. 19, 1945
III./JG-7	Shot down	Unk.	N/A	Unk.#	Apr. 19, 1945
III./JG-7	Shot down	Unk.	N/A	Unk.#	Apr. 19, 1945
III./JG-7	Shot down	Unk.	N/A	Unk.#	Apr. 19, 1945
JV-44	Shot down	Unk.	N/A	*Obfw* Hans Grünberg	Apr. 19, 1945
I./KG-54	Shot down	Unk.	N/A	*Uffz* Bruno Reischke*	Apr. 19, 1945
I./KG-54	Shot down	Unk.	N/A	*Lt* Mai*	Apr. 19, 1945
12/JG-7	Damaged by B-26	Unk.	N/A	Unk.+	Apr. 20, 1945
JV-44	Crash landed[48]	Unk.	N/A	*Maj.* Gerhard Barkhorn	Apr. 20, 1945
III./KG-54	Shot down	Unk.	N/A	Unk. *Unteroffizier**	Apr. 22, 1945
JV-44	Shot down	Unk.	N/A	*Obst* Günther Lützow	Apr. 24, 1945
I./JG-7	Crashed	Unk.	N/A	Unk.*	Apr. 25, 1945
9/JG-7	Force landing[49]	500071	N/A	*Fhr* Hans-Guido Mutke	Apr. 25, 1945
9/JG-7	Strafed while landing	Unk.	N/A	*Ofw* Hermann Buchner	Apr. 25, 1945
JV-44	Shot down[50]	Unk.	N/A	*Genlt* Adolf Galland+	Apr. 26, 1945
JV-44	Shot down	Unk.	N/A	*Maj.* Georg-Peter Eder	Apr. 26, 1945
JG-7	Shot down by Soviets	Unk.	N/A	Unk.#	Apr. 27, 1945
JG-7	Shot down by Soviets	Unk.	N/A	Unk.#	Apr. 27, 1945
JG-7	Shot down	Unk.	N/A	*Lt* Ernst-Rudolf Geldmacher*	Apr. 28, 1945
III./KG-54	Fire takeoff	Unk. B3+Red 1		*Hptm* Kornagel*	Apr. 29, 1945
III./KG-54	Missing	Unk. B3+Red 3		Unk.#	Apr. 29, 1945
III./KG-54	Shot down	Unk. B3+Red 2		*Hptm* Spadiut#	Apr. 29, 1945

[48]Barkhorn was nearly decapitated when his jet lurched and the canopy slammed down on his neck, ending his combat career.
[49]Forced down in Dübendorf, Switzerland, pilot interned.
[50]Galland was shot down by 22-year-old Capt. James Finnegan in his P-47.

III./KG-54	Shot down	Unk. B3+Red 2		Lt Paukner#	Apr. 29, 1945
1/JG-7	Missing	Unk.	N/A	Lt Fritz Kelb#	Apr. 30, 1945
I./KG-54	Soviet flak	Unk.	N/A	Unk.#	Apr. 30, 1945
KG-51	Shot down	Unk.	N/A	Lt Schimmel*	May 6, 1945
KG-51	Shot down	Unk.	N/A	Lt Strothman*	May 7, 1945
KG-51	Shot down	Unk.	N/A	Lt Poling*	May 7, 1945
1/JG-7	Surrendered	500210	Yellow 17	Lt Hans Dorn	May 8, 1945
1/JG-7	Surrendered	112372	Yellow 7	Uffz Günther Engle	May 8, 1945
1/JG-7	Surrendered	111690	White 5	Lt Friedrich-Wilhelm Schülter	May 8, 1945
1/JG-7	Surrendered	5000443	Yellow 5	Uffz Anton Schöppler	May 8, 1945
I./KG-54	Surrendered	Unk.	N/A	None	May 8, 1945
I./KG-51	Surrendered	Unk.	N/A	Hptm Rudolf Abrahamczik	May 8, 1945
I./KG-51	Surrendered	Unk.	N/A	Lt Anton Haeffner	May 8, 1945
I./KG-51	Surrendered	500200	X	Lt Fröhlich	May 8, 1945
I./KG-51	Crash landed	Unk.	N/A	Lt Wilhelm Batel	May 8, 1945
I./KG-54	Surrendered	Unk.	N/A	Unk.	May 8, 1945

JG-7 PERMANENT PERSONNEL

Geschwaderkommodore

Oberstleutnant Johannes Steinhoff, 4 December 1944
Major Theodor Weissenberger, 1 January 1945
Major Rudolf Sinner (acting), 19 February 1945

Gruppenkommandeure

I./JG 7

Hauptmann Gerhard Baeker, August 1944
Major Theodor Weissenberger, 25 November 1944
Major Erich Rudorffer, 14 January 1945
Oberleutnant Fritz Stehle (acting), April 1945
Major Wolfgang Späte, April 1945

II./JG 7

Major Hermann Staiger, 12 January 1945
Hauptmann Burkhard, February 1945
Major Hans Klemm, 15 April 1945 - 8 May 1945

III./JG 7

Major Erich Hohagen, 19 November 1944
Major Rudolf Sinner, 1 January 1945
Hauptmann Johannes Naumann, 5 April 1945

IV./JG 7

Oberstleutnant Heinrich Bär, 3 May 1945

Pilots Attached to JG 7
Major Heinrich Ehrler
Leutnant Karl Schnörrer
Oberleutnant Walter Schuck
Oberstleutnant Johannes Steinhoff
Oberleutnant Hans Waldmann
Major Theodor Weissenberger
Leutnant Rudolf "Rolf" Glogner (Me 163 B *Komet* pilot with JG-300)

BIBLIOGRAPHY

PRIMARY SOURCES

Bundesarchive/Militärarchiv (collectively at Koblenz, Freiburg and Berlin-Lichterfelde)

Doc. N 179-Literischer Nachwass vom Generfeldmarschall Erhard Milch.

Doc. RH 2/2196-Air Organization and Service Office (*Luftamt*)

Doc. RH 2/2197-Air Organization Office, Various Studies and Evaluations.

Doc. RH 2/2200-Weapons Office Rearmament Program and Development.

Doc. RH 2/2206-Weapons Office Report on Foreign Equipment.

Doc. RH 2/2273-Air Organization Office Reports.

Doc. RH 2/2291-Weapons Office, German Training Programs in the Soviet Union.

Doc. RH 2/2299-Air Organization Office, Various Studies and Reports.

Personal letters, data, information and documents from Hannes Trautloft, Erich Hartmann, Adolf Galland, Johannes Steinhoff, Eduard Neumann, Erich Hohagen, Wolfgang Falck, Georg-Peter Eder, Walter Krupinski, Dietrich A. Hrabak, Hermann Graf, Erich Rudorffer, Edward R. "Buddy" Haydon, Robert S. Johnson, Robin Olds, Franz Stigler, Raymond F. Toliver, Kurt Schulze, Ursula Steinhoff Bird, Günther Rall, Hajo Herrmann, Walther Dahl, Herbert Ihlefeld, Wolfgang Schenck, Dietrich Pelz, William F. Reid, John Cunningham, Hans-Joachim Jabs, James H. Doolittle, Rudolf Nowotny, Wolfgang Späte, Jorg Czypionka, Hans "Specker" Grünberg, Klaus Neumann.

SECONDARY SOURCES

17th Bomb Group. Paducah, KY: Turner Publishing Company, 1995.

Angelucci, Enzo, and Paolo Matricardi. *World Aircraft: World War II, Volume I* (Sampson Low Guides). Maidenhead, UK: Sampson Low, 1978.

Baker, David. *Adolf Galland: The Authorized Biography*. London: Windrow & Greene, Ltd, 1996.

Balous, Miroslav, Jir̃í Rajlich, and Martin Velek. *Messerschmitt Me 262* (in Czech/English). Prague: MBI, 1995.

Bekker, Cajus. *The Luftwaffe War Diaries: The German Air Force in World War II*. New York: Da Capo Press, 1994.

Boyne, Walter J. "Göring's Big Bungle," *Air Force Magazine*, November 2008, Vol. 91, No. 11.

_____. *Clash of Wings*. New York: Simon & Schuster, 1994.

Brown, Eric. *Wings on My Sleeve.* London: Weidenfeld & Nicolson, 2006.

Buchner, Hermann. *Stormbird: One of the Highest Scoring Me 262 Aces.* United Kingdom, Crecy, 2000.

Butler, Phil. *War Prizes: An Illustrated Survey of German, Italian and Japanese Aircraft brought to Allied Countries During and After the Second World War.* Leicestershire, UK: Midland, 1994.

Caldwell, Donald, and Richard Muller. *The Luftwaffe Over Germany: Defense of the Reich.* London: Greenhill Books, 2007.

Cooney, Patrick. "Dambusters Raid on the Ruhr," *World War II,* Vol. 14, No. 1. Leesburg, VA: Primedia Publications, May 1999, pp. 42–48.

Corum, James S. *Wolfram von Richthofen: Master of the German Air War.* Lawrence: University of Kansas Press, 2008.

_____. *The Luftwaffe: Creating the Operational Air War, 1918–1940.* Lawrence: University of Kansas Press, 1997.

_____. *The Roots of Blitzkrieg: Hans von Seeckt and German Military Reform.* Lawrence: University of Kansas Press, 1994.

Corum, James S., and Richard R. Muller. *The Luftwaffe's Way of War: German Air Force Doctrine, 1911–1945.* Nautical & Aviation Pub Co of America, 1998.

Daso, Dik Alan. "Operation LUSTY: The US Army Air Forces' Exploitation of the Luftwaffe's Secret Aeronautical Technology, 1944–45: Focus: The Shaft of the Spear," *Aerospace Power Journal,* Spring 2002. Located at the following website link: http://findarticles.com/p/articles/mi_m0ICK/is_1_16/ ai_90511915/

Donald, David (ed.) *Warplanes of the Luftwaffe.* Airtime Publications, 1994.

Dorr, Robert F. and Thomas D. Jones. *Hell Hawks: The Untold Story of the American Fliers Who Savaged Hitler's Wehrmacht.* Zenith Press, 2008.

Emde, Heimer, and Carlo Demand. *Conquerors of the Air.* New York: Viking, 1968.

Ethell, Jeffrey, and Alfred Price. *The German Jets in Combat.* London: Jane's Publishing Company, 1979.

_____. *World War II Fighting Jets.* St. Paul, MN: Motorbooks International, 1994.

Faber, Harold (ed). *Luftwaffe: A History.* New York: Times Books, 1977.

Foreman, John, and S. E. Harvey. *The Messerschmitt Me 262 Combat Diary.* Surrey, UK: Air Research Publications, 1990.

Forsythe, Robert. *JV-44: The Galland Circus.* UK: Classic Publications, 1996.

Forsythe, Robert, and Jerry Scutts. *Battle Over Bavaria: The B-26 Marauder versus the German Jets—April 1945.* UK: Classic Publications, 1999.

Galland, Adolf. *The First and the Last: The German Fighter Force in World War II.* London: Methuen, 1955.

Green, William. *The Warplanes of the Third Reich.* New York: Doubleday & Company, 1970.

_____. *War Planes of the Second World War, Vol. VIII: Bombers & Reconnaissance Aircraft.* New York: Doubleday, 1967.

Green, William, and Gordon Swanborough. *The Complete Book of Fighters.* 1994.

Gunston, Bill. *Aerei della seconda guerra mondiale.* Milano, Peruzzo editore, 1984.

_____. *The Illustrated Directory of Fighting Aircraft of World War II.* London, Salamander Book Limited, 1988.

_____. *World Encyclopaedia of Aircraft Manufacturers.* Annapolis, MD: Naval Institute Press, 1993.

Guttman, Jon. "Air War's Greatest Aces," *World War II.* Vol. 11, No. 6. Leesburg, VA: Primedia Publications, February 1997, pp. 22–36.

_____. "Another Jet for the Yoxford Boys," *American Fighter Aces Bulletin: Ace Profile.*

_____. "Dudley M. Amoss: Making Ace on Borrowed Time." *American Fighter Aces Bulletin: Ace Profile.*

Haunschmied, Rudolf A., Jan-Ruth Mills ,and Siegi Witzany-Durda. *St. Georgen-Gusen-Mauthausen: Concentration Camp Mauthausen Reconsidered.* Norderstedt, Germany: BoD, 2008.

Heaton, Colin D., and Anne-Marie Lewis. *Night Fighters: Luftwaffe and RAF Air Combat over Europe, 1939–1945.* Annapolis, MD: U.S. Naval Institute Press, 2008.

Heaton, Colin D. "Luftwaffe Wing Leader," Interview with Lt. General Dietrich Hrabak. *Military History,* Vol. 20, No. 6. Leesburg, VA: Primedia Publications, February 2004, pp. 42–48.

_____ "Interview: General Jimmy Doolittle. The Man Behind the Legend, Part 1," *World War II,* Vol. 13, No. 3. Leesburg, VA: Primedia Publications, March 2003, pp. 30–42.

_____. "Erich Hartmann's Last Interview," *World War II,* Vol. 17, No. 3. Leesburg, VA: Primedia Publications, September 2002, pp. 30–42, 85.

_____. "The Man Who Downed Nowotny, Interview with Col. Edward R. Haydon," *Aviation History,* Vol. 13, No. 1. Leesburg, VA: Primedia Publications, September 2002, pp. 22–28.

_____. "Colonel Hajo Herrmann: Master of the Wild Boars," Interview with *Luftwaffe* Colonel Hajo Herrmann. *World War II.* Vol. 15, No. 2. Leesburg, VA: Primedia Publications, July 2000, pp. 30–36, 78–80.

_____. "Interview: *Luftwaffe* Ace Günther Rall Remembers," *World War II.* Vol. 9, No. 6.

Leesburg, VA: Cowles History Group, March 1995, pp. 34–40, 77–78.

_____. "Jimmy Doolittle and the Emergence of American Air Power," Interview with General James H. Doolittle, Part 2. *World War II.* Vol. 18, No. 1. Leesburg, VA: Primedia Publications, May 2003, pp. 46–52, 78.

_____. "*Luftwaffe* Ace Adolf Galland's Last Interview," Interview with General of the Fighters Adolf Galland, *World War II.* Vol. 11, No. 5. Leesburg, VA: Cowles History Group, January 1997, pp. 46–52.

_____. "Interview: *Luftwaffe* Eagle Johannes Steinhoff," Interview with Major General Steinhoff, *World War II.* Vol. 13, No. 1. Leesburg, VA: Primedia Publications, May 1998, pp. 28–34, 74.

_____. "The Count: Luftwaffe Ace Walter Krupinski," Interview with *Luftwaffe* Ace Lieutenant General Walter Krupinski. *Military History.* Vol. 15, No. 2. Leesburg, VA: Primedia Publications, June 1998, pp. 62–68.

_____. "Interview: *Luftwaffe*'s Father of the Night Fighters," Interview with *Luftwaffe* ace Colonel Wolfgang Falck, *Military History*. Vol. 16. No. 6. Leesburg, VA: Primedia Publications, February 2000, pp. 42–48.

_____. "Interview: Wolfpack Ace Robert S. Johnson," *Military History*, Vol. 13, No. 3, August 1996, pp. 26–32.

Heiden, Konrad. *Der Fuehrer: Hitler's Rise to Power*. Trans. by Ralph Manheim. Boston: Houghton Mifflin Co., 1944.

Held, Werner. *German Fighter Ace Walter Nowotny: An Illustrated Biography*. Atglen, PA: Schiffer Publishing, 2006.

Heppenheimer, T. A. *Turbulent Skies: The History of Commercial Aviation*. New York: John Wiley, 1995.

Jablonski, Edward. *Terror from the Sky: Air War Vol.1*. New York: Doubleday & Co., 1971.

Jenkins, Dennis R. *Messerschmitt Me 262 Sturmvogel*. North Branch, MN: Specialty Press, 1996.

Kershaw, Ian. *Hitler 1936–1945: Nemesis*. New York and London: W. W. Norton & Co., 2000.

Killen, John. *A History of the Luftwaffe*. Garden City, NY: Doubleday, 1968 (reprint).

Leydecker, Mary. "Ace Finder," *Saga Magazine*, pp. 44–45, 64.

Linkowitz, Jerome. *Their Finest Hours: Narratives of the RAF and Luftwaffe in World War II*. Ames: Iowa State University Press, 1989.

Luftwaffe, The. Editors at Time-Life Books. Alexandria, VA: Time-Life Boos, 1982.

Macksey, Jenneth. *Kesselring: The Making of the Luftwaffe*. New York: D. McKay, 1978.

Mason, Jr., Herbert Malloy. *The Rise of the Luftwaffe: Forging the Secret German Air Weapon, 1918–1940*. New York: Dial Press, 1973.

_____. *Duel for the Sky*. New York: Grosset & Dunlap, Inc. Publishers, 1970.

Mayer, S. L., and Masami Tokoi. *Der Adler: The Official Nazi Luftwaffe Magazine*. New York: T. Y. Crowell, 1977.

Mitcham, Samuel W. Jr. *Eagles of the Third Reich: The Men Who Made the Luftwaffe*. Novato, CA: Presidio Press, 1997.

_____. *Men of the Luftwaffe*. Novato, CA: Presidio Press, 1988.

Mombeek, Eric. *Luftwaffe: A Pictorial History*. UK: Crowood Press, 1997.

Morgan, Hugh, and John Weal. *German Jet Aces of World War 2 (Osprey Aircraft of the Aces No. 17)*. London: Osprey, 1998.

Morgan, Hugh. *Me 262: Stormbird Rising*. Osceoloa, WI: Motorbooks International, 1994.

Murray, Williamson. *Strategy for Defeat: The Luftwaffe, 1933–1945*. Maxwell AFB, AL: Air University Press, 1983.

Obermeier, E. *Die Ritterkreuztraeger der Luftwaffe, 1939–1945, Band 2: Stuka und Schlachtflieger*. Mainz: Verlag Dieter Hoffmann, 1976.

Olmsted, Merle C. *The Yoxford Boys: The 357th Fighter Group on Escort over Europe and Russia*. Fallbrook, California: Aero Publishers Inc., 1971.

O'Connell, Dan. *Messerschmitt Me 262: The Production Log 1941–1945*. Leicestershire, UK: Classic Publications, 2006.

Price, Alfred. *The Last Year of the Luftwaffe: May 1944 to May 1945*. London: Greenhill Books, 1993.

_____. "Sleek and Deadly: The Messerschmitt Me 262." *Flight Journal*, February 2007.

_____. *German Air Force Bombers of World War I*. Garden City, NY: Doubleday, 1968.

Pritchard, Anthony. *Messerschmitt*. New York: G. P. Putnam's Sons, 1975.

Proctor, Raymond L. *Hitler's Luftwaffe in the Spanish Civil War*. Westport, CT: Greenwood Press, 1983.

Radinger, Willy, and Walter Schick. *Messerschmitt Me 262*. Berlin: Avantic Verlag GmbH, 1996.

Rigg, Bryan Mark. *Hitler's Jewish Soldiers: The Untold Story of Nazi Racial Laws and the Men of Jewish Descent in the German Military*. Lawrence, KS: University Press of Kansas, 2002.

Samuel, Wolfgang W. E. *American Raiders: The Race to Capture the Luftwaffe's Secrets*. University Press of Mississippi, 2004.

Schlaifer, Robert, and S. D. Heron. *Development of Aircraft Engines and Fuels*. Boston: Harvard University Press, 1950.

Shores, Christopher, and Clive Williams. *Aces High: A Tribute to Most Notable Fighter Pilots of the British and Commonwealth Forces in WW II*. London: Grub Street, 1994.

Schuck, Walter. *Luftwaffe Eagle: From the Me109 to the Me262*. UK: Crecy, 2010 (reprint).

Sims, Edward H. *The Greatest Aces: A Study of the Fighter Forces of the R.A.F, Luftwaffe and U.S.A.A.F in World War II*. New York: Ballantine Books, 1967.

Smith, J. Richard. *Messerschmitt: An Aircraft Album*. New York: Arco Publishing, 1971.

Smith, J. Richard, and Edward J. Creek. *Jet Planes of the Third Reich*. Boylston, Massachusetts: Monogram Aviation Publications, 1982.

Smith, Starr. *Jimmy Stewart: Bomber Pilot*. Minneapolis, MN: Zenith Press, 2005.

Speer, Albert. *Inside the Third Reich*. New York: Macmillan Publishing Co., Inc., 1970.

Spick, Mike. *Allied Fighter Aces of World War II*. London: Greenhill Books, 1997.

_____. *Fighter Pilot Tactics: The Techniques of Daylight Air Combat*. Cambridge, UK: Patrick Stephens, 1983.

Taylor, Telford. *Sword and Swastika*. New York: Simon and Schuster, 1952.

Thompson, J. Steve, with Peter C Smith. *Air Combat Manoeuvres*. Hersham, Surrey: Ian Allan Publishing, 2008.

Toliver, Raymond F., and Trevor J. Constable. *The Blonde Knight of Germany*. New York: McGraw-Hill Professional, 1986.

_____. *Fighter General: The Life of Adolf Galland*. Zephyr Cove, NV: AmPress Publishing, 1990.

van Ishoven, Armand. *Messerschmitt, Aircraft Designer*. Garden City, N.Y.: Doubleday, 1975.

_____. *Messerschmitt Bf 109 at War*. New York: Scribner's, 1977.

Warsitz, Lutz. English Edition. *The First Jet Pilot: The Story of German Test Pilot Erich Warsitz*. London: Pen and Sword Books Ltd., 2009.

NOTES

CHAPTER 1

1. See Colin D. Heaton and Anne-Marie Lewis, *Night Fighters: The RAF and Luftwaffe Air Combat over Europe, 1939–1945* (Annapolis, MD: Naval Institute Press, 2008).
2. Hermann Buchner interview.
3. Colin Heaton interviews with Hannes Trautloft 1984–92.
4. Colin D. Heaton, "Luftwaffe Ace Günther Rall Remembers," *World War II*, Vol. 9, No. 6, Leesburg, VA: Primedia Publications, p. 39.
5. Erich Hartmann interview. See abridged version by Colin D. Heaton, "Erich Hartmann's Last Interview," *World War II*, Vol. 17, No. 3, September 2002, Leesburg, VA: Primedia Publications, pp. 30–42, 85.

CHAPTER 2

1. See Hugh Morgan, *Me 262: Stormbird Rising*, Osceola, WI: MBI./Osprey Books, 1994, p. 12
2. Ibid., p. 10.
3. John Foreman and S. E. Harvey, *The Messerschmitt Me 262 Combat Diary*, Surrey, UK: Air Research Publications, 1990, p. 230.
4. Hermann Buchner interview.
5. Courtesy of Jeffrey L. Ethell.

CHAPTER 3

1. Morgan, p. 31.
2. Interview with Fritz Wendel by Jeffrey L. Ethell, 1976. Courtesy of Jeff Ethell.
3. Morgan, p. 32.
4. Ibid., p. 33.
5. See Ian Kershaw, *Hitler 1936–1945: Nemesis*, New York, London, 2000, p. 621.
6. Morgan, 37.
7. Ibid., p. 38; also Galland interview.
8. Ibid., pp. 23–24.
9. Hermann Buchner.

10. Morgan. p. 39.

11. Ibid.

CHAPTER 4

1. Buchner interview.

2. Schenck interview.

3. Steinhoff interview.

4. Morgan, p. 100.

5. Pelz interview.

6. Steinhoff interview.

7. Wolfgang Späte, *Top Secret Bird: The Luftwaffe's Me 163 Comet*, Missoula, MO: Pictorial Histories Publishing Company, 1989, p. 261.

8. Morgan, p. 96.

9. Galland interview extract from Jeffrey L. Ethell, 1978. Courtesy of Jeff Ethell.

10. Wendel interviews and data provided by Jeffrey L. Ethell.

CHAPTER 5

1. See Robert F. Dorr and Thomas D. Jones, *Hell Hawks: The Untold Story of the American Fliers Who Savaged Hitler's Wehrmacht*, Zenith Press, 2008, p. 244.

2. Ibid.

3. Colin Heaton interview with Dietrich Pelz in November 1990 (Jeffrey L. Ethell in attendance) and supplemental information obtained in 1993–1998 and 2000.

4. Ibid.

5. Ibid.

6. Morgan, p. 13.

7. Ibid., p. 14

8. Ibid., p. 28.

9. Ibid., p. 13.

10. Courtesy of Jeffrey L. Ethell.

CHAPTER 6

1. Courtesy of Arno Abendroth.

2. Interview with Galland 1993.

3. Morgan, p. 26.

4. Ibid. See the abbreviated interview at Colin D. Heaton, "*Luftwaffe* Ace Adolf Galland's Last Interview," interview with General of the Fighters Adolf Galland, *World War II*, January 1997, pp. 46–52, Cowles History Group, Leesburg, VA.

5. On Nowotny, see also Edward H. Simms, *The Greatest Aces*, New York: Ballantine Books, 1967, p. 183.

6. Walter Schuck, *Luftwaffe Eagle: From the Me 109 to the Me 262*, UK: Crecy, 2010, reprint, p. 201.

7. Rudolf Nowotny interview.

8. Eder interview. See also Edward H. Sims, *The Greatest Aces*, New York: Ballantine Books, 1967, p. 191

9. Colin D. Heaton and Anne-Marie Lewis, *The German Aces Speak*, Zenith Press, 2011., p. 68.

10. Interview with Georg-Peter Eder, 1984.

11. Schenck interview.

12. Starr Smith, *Jimmy Stewart: Bomber Pilot*, p. 252.

13. Eder interview.

14. Morgan, p. 96.

15. Steinhoff interview.

16. Wolfgang Späte interview.

17. Eder interview.

18. Steinhoff interview.

19. Buchner, p. 237.

20. Buchner interview.

21. Foreman and Harvey, p. 78.

22. Späte, p. 259.

23. Wolfgang Späte interviews, 1984–1986, 1992–1995.

24. Späte, p. 260.

25. Hajo Herrmann interviews.

26. Jorg Czypionka interview, 2011.

CHAPTER 7

1. Foreman and Harvey, pp. 30–32. See also Faber, pp. 178–179.

2. Hans Baur interview, 1985.

3. Interview with Traudl Junge, 1999.

4. Galland interviews.

5. Ibid.

6. Ray Toliver and Arno Abendroth.

7. Galland interviews.

8. Cunningham interview.

9. Interviews with Dietrich Pelz in November 1990 and supplemental information obtained in 1993–1998 and 2000.

10. Interview with Schenck.

11. Heaton and Lewis, *The German Aces Speak*, pp. 113–15.

12. Ibid, pp. 119–20.

13. Trautloft interview.

14. Starr Smith, *Jimmy Stewart: Bomber Pilot*, p. 251, Zenith Press, 2005, citing Major Gene Gurney, USAF, *The War in the Air: A Pictorial History of WW II Air Forces in Combat*.

15. Starr Smith, *Jimmy Stewart: Bomber Pilot*, p. 251.

16. Heaton and Lewis, *The German Aces Speak*, p. 120.

CHAPTER 8

1. Foreman and Harvey, p. 369.

2. Dorr and Jones, p. 245.

3. Doolittle interview. See the abbreviated two-part version, Colin D. Heaton, "Interview: General Jimmy Doolittle: The Man Behind the Legend," Part 1, pp. 30–42. *World War II*, March 2003, Vol. 17, No. 7, Primedia Publications, Leesburg, VA; and "Interview: Jimmy Doolittle and the Emergence of American Air Power," Part 2, pp. 46–53, 78. *World War II*, May 2003, Vol. 18, No. 1, Primedia Publications, Leesburg, VA.

4. Curtis Lemay interview, 1987.

5. Doolittle interview, 1986.

6. Galland interview, 1993.

7. Doolittle interview, 1986.

8. Gabreski interview, 2001.

9. Dorr and Jones, p. 243.

10. Pelz interview.

11. Dorr and Jones, pp. 296.

12. Ibid., p. 242.

13. Robert S. Johnson interview. See abridged version at Colin D. Heaton, "Interview: Wolfpack Ace Robert S. Johnson," *Military History*, Vol. 13, No. 3, August 1996, pp. 26–32.

14. Francis S. Gabreski interview, 1998.

15. Mahurin interview, 2001.

16. Doolittle interviews.

17. Galland interviews.

18. Pelz interview.

CHAPTER 9

1. Dorr and Jones, p. 247.

2. Eder interview.

3. Hermann Buchner interview. See also another version in Morgan, p. 95.

4. Buchner, p. 226.

5. Dorr and Jones, p. 249.

6. Hohagen interview.

7. Jon Guttman, "Another Jet for the Yoxford Boys," American Fighter Aces Association Bulletin Ace Profile: Robert P. Winks, 357th Fighter Group.

8. Dorr and Jones, p. 249.

9. Hermann Buchner, *Stormbird*, UK: Crecy, 2000, p. 220.

10. Schuck, pp. 190–191.

CHAPTER 10

1. Jorg Czypionka interview 2011.

2. Ibid.

3. Ibid.

4. Jon Guttman, "Dudley M. Amoss: Making Ace on Borrowed Time," *American Fighter Aces Association Bulletin Ace Profile.*

5. Eder interview.

6. Heaton and Lewis, *The German Aces Speak*, p. 64.

7. Ibid.

8. Franz Stigler interviews, 1987–1998.

9. Morgan, p. 96.

CHAPTER 11

1. Arno Abendroth.

2. Schuck, p. 203.

3. Steinhoff interview. See the abridged version, Colin D. Heaton, "Luftwaffe Eagle Johannes Steinhoff," interview with Lieutenant General Steinhoff, *World War II*, May 1998, pp. 28–34, 74, Primedia Publications, Leesburg, VA.

4. Eder interview.

5. Ibid.

6. Steinhoff interview.

CHAPTER 12

1. Steinhoff interview.

2. Späte, p. 260.

3. Eder interview.

4. Courtesy of Jeffery L. Ethell.

5. Dorr and Jones, p. 244.

6. See this extract from the abridged interview by Colin D. Heaton, "The Man Who Downed Nowotny," *Aviation History*, pp. 22–28, September 2002, Vol. 13, No. 1, Primedia Publications, Leesburg, VA. See USAAF mission log losses also at Freeman, *The Mighty Eighth*, pp. 426–427.

7. On Rudorffer see Sims, p. 184; on Weissenberger, p. 185.

8. Rudorffer letter to Colin D. Heaton dated November 11, 1991.

9. Rudorffer correspondence and interview.

10. Heaton and Lewis, *The German Aces Speak*, p. 122.

11. Guttman, "Dudley M. Amoss: Making Ace on Borrowed Time." See also Freeman, *The Mighty Eighth*, p. 469.

12. Guttman, *Another Jet for the Yoxford Boys*. See also Freeman, p. 424.

CHAPTER 13

1. See Werner Held, *German Fighter Ace Walter Nowotny: An Illustrated Biography*, Atglen, PA: Schiffer Publishing, Ltd, 2006, in total. Thierfelder died on July 7, 1944.

2. See Foreman and Harvey, p. 63, and Held, p. 143.

3. See Galland in Heaton and Lewis, *The German Aces Speak*, p. 121.

4. Ibid, p. 118.

5. Ibid, p. 122.

6. Freeman, p. 360.

7. Foreman and Harvey, pp. 72–73.

8. Eder interview.

9. Foreman and Harvey, p. 74.

10. Drew after-action report. Ibid., pp. 74–75. See also Morgan, pp. 78–79.

11. Drew letter to Harvey, p. 76.

12. Freeman, *The Mighty Eighth*, p. 363.

13. Foreman and Harvey, pp. 77–78.

14. Freeman, *The Mighty Eighth*, p. 363.

15. Ibid.

16. Foreman and Harvey, pp. 79–80. Freeman, *The Mighty Eighth*, p. 363.

17. Eder interview.

18. Hohagen interview.

19. Foreman and Harvey, pp. 82–84; Freeman, *The Mighty Eighth*, p. 372.

20. Ibid, p. 85; Ibid, p. 375.

21. Ibid, pp. 85–68; Ibid, p. 375.

22. Morgan, p. 74. Freeman, *The Mighty Eighth*, p. 376.

23. Foreman and Harvey, p. 87.

24. Ibid, p. 88; also Freeman, p. 376.

25. Eder interview; also Freeman, p. 377.

26. Freeman, *The Mighty Eighth*, p. 377–378.

27. Courtesy of Edward R. Haydon via Merle C. Olmsted, 1990.

28. Foreman and Harvey, p. 378.

29. Courtesy of Merle C. Olmsted via Edward R. Haydon, 1990.

30. Freeman, *The Mighty Eighth*, pp. 377–78.

31. Eder interview.

CHAPTER 14

1. See also Freeman, *The Mighty Eighth*, pp. 378–379.

2. Heaton, "The Man Who Downed Nowotny," p. 25. See also Freeman, *The Mighty Eighth*, pp. 378–379.

3. Heaton and Lewis, *The German Aces Speak*, p. 123.

4. Heaton, "The Man Who Downed Nowotny," p. 25. See also Freeman, *The Mighty Eighth*, pp. 378–379.

5. See also Freeman, *The Mighty Eighth*, pp. 378–379.

6. Heaton, "The Man Who Downed Nowotny," p. 25. See also Freeman, *The Mighty Eighth*, pp. 378–379.

7. Heaton and Lewis, *The German Aces Speak*, p. 124.

8. Eder interview, 1984.

9. See Held, p. 153; Steinhoff, p. 43, and his interview.

10. Heaton and Lewis, *The German Aces Speak*, p. 124.

11. See Sims, p. 185.

12. Interview with Johannes Steinhoff.

CHAPTER 15

1. Foreman and Harvey, p. 96.

2. Foreman and Harvey, p. 97; Freeman, *The Mighty Eighth*, p. 384.

3. Ibid.

4. Ibid.

5. Foreman and Harvey, p. 98; Freeman, *The Mighty Eighth*, p. 386. See also Buchner, pp. 224–225.

6. Foreman and Harvey, p. 100; Freeman, *The Mighty Eighth*, pp. 386–387.

7. Foreman and Harvey, pp. 77–78.

8. Hohagen interview.

9. Dr. Alfred Price, *The Last Year of the Luftwaffe: May 1944–May 1945*, Osceola, WI: MBI, 1992, p. 136.

10. Foreman and Harvey, pp. 108–109.

11. Morgan, p. 74.

12. Foreman and Harvey, pp. 108–109 .

13. Foreman and Harvey, pp. 114–115; Freeman, *The Mighty Eighth*, pp. 406–409.

14. Ibid.

15. Foreman and Harvey, p. 115.

CHAPTER 16

1. Schuck, p. 195.

2. Morgan, p. 76.

3. Buchner, p. 234.

4. Jon Guttman interview with Roscoe Brown.

5. Colin D. Heaton interview with Gen. Benjamin O. Davis.

6. Schuck, p. 195.

7. Courtesy of Jon Guttman.

8. Heaton and Lewis, *The German Aces Speak,* p. 122.

9. Dorr and Jones, p. 251.

10. Schuck, p. 198.

CHAPTER 17

1. Heaton and Lewis, *The German Aces Speak*, pp. 69–70.

2. Eder interview.

3. Merle Olmsted, "The Yoxford Boys."

4. Robin Olds interview.

5. Benjamin O. Davis interviews, 1986–1989.

6. Kurt Bühligen interview, 1984.

7. Forman and Harvey, p. 60; Freeman, *The Mighty Eighth War Diary*, p. 353.

8. Freeman, pp. 353–354.

9. Ibid, p. 479 (see mission claims); Forman and Harvey, p. 218.

10. Forman and Harvey, p. 218. See also Buchner, p. 238.

11. Ibid., p. 219.

12. Schuck, p. 201.

13. Wolfgang Späte interview.

14. Foreman and Harvey, p. 343.

15. Buchner, p. 240.

CHAPTER 18

1. Buchner, p. 241.

2. Schuck, p. 203.

3. Ibid, p. 204.

4. Ibid, pp. 205–206.

5. Ibid, pp. 214–215.

6. See Merle Olmsted, "The Yoxford Boys."

7. Foreman and Harvey, pp. 249-51.

8. Ibid, pp. 251–252; Freeman, *The Mighty Eighth*, pp. 490–491.

9. Ibid., p. 252; Ibid. 491.

10. Foreman and Harvey, p. 256.

11. Ibid., pp. 256–257.

12. Ibid., p. 256; Freeman, *The Mighty Eighth*, 494.

13. Späte interview.

14. Foreman and Harvey, pp. 257–258.

15. Späte interview.

16. Foreman and Harvey

17. Ibid., p. 266.

18. Ibid., p. 271.

19. Ibid.

20. Ibid.

21. Ibid., p. 272.

22. Ibid.

CHAPTER 19

1. Foreman and Harvey, p. 38.

2. Heaton and Lewis, *The German Aces Speak*, p. 115.

3. Ibid.

4. Johannes Steinhoff, *The Final Hours: The Luftwaffe Plot Against Göring*, Potomac Books, Washington D.C., 2005, pp. 142–143.

5. Galland interviews.

6. Erich Hohagen interview, 1984.

7. Klaus Neumann interview.

8. Steinhoff interview.

9. Foreman and Harvey, p. 226. Freeman, *The Mighty Eighth*, p. 480.

10. Foreman and Harvey, p. 226.

11. Ibid.
12. Foreman and Harvey, p. 227.
13. Ibid., pp. 229–30.
14. Steinhoff interview.
15. Galland interviews.
16. Krupinski interview.
17. Steinhoff interview.
18. Heaton and Lewis, *The German Aces Speak*, p. 136.
19. Neumann interview.
20. Grünberg interview.
21. Ibid.

CHAPTER 20

1. Galland interview.
2. Colin D. Heaton, "Interview: Luftwaffe Eagle Johannes Steinhoff," interview with Lieutenant General Steinhoff, *World War II*, Vol. 13, No., May 1998, Leesburg, VA: Primedia Publications, pp. 28–34, 74.
3. Krupinski interview in Heaton and Lewis, *The German Aces Speak*, p. 67. See the abridged interview in Colin D. Heaton, "The Count: Luftwaffe Ace Walter Krupinski," interview with *Luftwaffe* Ace Lieutenant General Walter Krupinski. *Military History*, Vol. 15, No. 2, June 1998, Leesburg, VA: Primedia Publications, pp. 62–68.
4. Neumann interview.
5. Grünberg interview.
6. Stigler interview.
7. Hohagen interview
8. Merle Olmsted, "The Yoxford Boys."
9. Steinhoff interview.
10. Heaton and Lewis, *The German Aces Speak*, pp. 62–66.

CHAPTER 21

1. Grünberg interview.
2. Louis S. Rehr and Carleton R. Rehr, *Marauder: Memoir of a B-26 Pilot in Europe in World War II*, Jefferson, NC: McFarland & Co., 2003.
3. Robert Forsyth, *JV-44: The Galland Circus*, UK: Classis Publications, 1996, pp. 216–217.
4. Hohagen interview.
5. Dorr and Jones, p. 288.
6. Ibid.
7. Ibid., pp. 288–289.
8. Foreman and Harvey, pp. 260–262.
9. Ibid.
10. Ibid.
11. Ibid., p. 262.

12. Krupinski interview.

CHAPTER 22

1. Galland interview with Jeffery L. Ethell.

2. Forsyth, *JV-44*, p. 247.

3. Galland interview.

4. Forsyth, *JV-44*, p. 249.

5. Foreman and Harvey, p. 268.

6. Galland interview.

7. Forsyth, *JV-44*, p. 255.

8. Ibid.

9. Galland interview; see also Heaton and Lewis, *The German Aces Speak*, p. 137.

10. Foreman and Harvey, p. 268.

11. Mary Leydecker, "Ace Finder," *Saga Magazine*, pp. 44–45, 64. Date unknown.

12. Finnegan interview, located at http://community-2.webtv.net/XY-MyOtherSel f/50thFGWarStories/

CHAPTER 23

1. Foreman and Harvey, p. 271.

2. Forsyth, *JV-44*, p. 317.

3. Heaton and Lewis, *The German Aces Speak*, pp. 107–127.

4. Ibid., pp. 135, 137–138.

5. Steinhoff interview.

6. Heaton, "*Luftwaffe* Ace Adolf Galland's Last Interview," *World War II*, January 1997, Leesburg, VA: Cowles History Group, pp. 46–52. See also Robert Forsythe, *JV-44: The Galland Circus*, UK: Classic Publications, 1996, in total; also John Foreman and S. E. Harvey, *The Messerschmitt Combat Diary Me.262*, UK: Air Research Publications, 1995, pp. 217–277.

7. John Foreman and S. E. Harvey, p. 85; see also Krupinski interview in Heaton and Lewis, *The German Aces Speak*, p. 63

8. Heaton and Lewis, *The German Aces Speak*, pp. 63–65

9. Ibid.

10. Heaton and Lewis, *The German Aces Speak*, p. 70.

11. Stigler interview.

CHAPTER 24

1. Merle Olmsted, "The Yoxford Boys."

2. Pelz interview.

3. Doolittle interview.

APPENDIX 3

1. Christopher Shores and Clive Williams, *Aces High: A Tribute to Most Notable Fighter Pilots of the British and Commonwealth Forces in WW II*, London: Grub Street, 1994, p. 102.

2. The sources used for this were Foreman and Harvey, pp. 369–378, and archive materials supplied by Arno Abendroth, Bundesarchiv Berlin-Lichterfelde, and documents supplied by the pilots themselves.

INDEX